ENCOUNTERING THE HISTORY OF MISSIONS

A. Scott Moreau, *series editor*

ALSO IN THE SERIES:

ENCOUNTERING THE HISTORY OF MISSIONS

From the Early Church to Today

JOHN MARK TERRY
AND ROBERT L. GALLAGHER

Baker Academic

a division of Baker Publishing Group
Grand Rapids, Michigan

2017

© 2017 by John Mark Terry and Robert L. Gallagher

Published by Baker Academic
a division of Baker Publishing Group
P.O. Box 6287, Grand Rapids, MI 49516-6287
www.bakeracademic.com

Printed in the United States of America

Library of Congress Cataloging-in-Publication Data
Names: Terry, John Mark, 1949– author. | Gallagher, Robert L., author.
Title: Encountering the history of missions : from the early church to today / John Mark Terry and Robert L. Gallagher.
Description: Grand Rapids : Baker Academic, 2017. | Series: Encountering mission | Includes bibliographical references and index.
Identifiers: LCCN 2017009972 | ISBN 9780801026966 (pbk.)
Subjects: LCSH: Missions—History.
Classification: LCC BV2100 .T44 2017 | DDC 266.009—dc23
LC record available at https://lccn.loc.gov/2017009972

17 18 19 20 21 22 23   7 6 5 4 3 2 1

Contents

Preface

My mother taught me (John Mark) to love history. She read me history books before I learned to read. Thus, researching and writing this book brought joy to me. I find the history of missions to be both instructive and inspiring. The history of missions instructs contemporary missionaries on what to do and what not to do. For example, the story of Adoniram Judson, pioneer missionary to Burma, instructs us on the importance of Bible translation. That same story should inspire modern missionaries to persevere amid hardship and tragedy. Yet, the problems that resulted from financial subsidy should inform decisions today.

Writing a book on the history of missions presents the writer with a great dilemma: what to include and what to omit. Kenneth Scott Latourette is recognized as the greatest missions historian. His massive *History of the Expansion of Christianity* is seven volumes, and it was published in 1938. A lot of history has happened since 1938. Robert Gallagher and I had to cover the entire history of missions in just one volume. Inevitably, students, professors, and reviewers will wonder why we did not include this or exclude that. I feel as the apostle John must have felt. At the end of his Gospel he wrote, "Jesus did many other things as well. If every one of them were written down, I suppose that even the whole world would not have room for the books that would be written" (John 21:25). There just was not space to include everything.

I am grateful to Scott Moreau, our editor, for his patience and helpful suggestions. I also thank Broadman & Holman Publishers for permission to use the material in chapter 1. That material appears in substantially the same form in *Missiology: An Introduction*. My career as a missionary has ended, and my years of teaching missions will end soon. I thank the Lord that he called me to serve as a missionary and allowed me to train many missionaries. Like the apostle Paul, I have sought to be faithful to my "heavenly vision" (Acts 26:19).

John Mark Terry

I (Robert) am thankful for the encouragement and affirmation of a number of people who have supported this project to its fruition. Particularly, I would like to thank:

- Paul E. Pierson, dean emeritus and senior professor of history of mission and Latin American studies at Fuller Theological Seminary, who first ignited my interest in the history of missions as I listened to his lectures in Travis Auditorium nearly thirty years ago.
- The late Gary B. McGee, distinguished professor emeritus of church history and Pentecostal studies at the Assemblies of God Theological Seminary, whose gentle guidance brought confirmation via my church history presentations at the American Society of Missiology, the Association of Professors of Missions, the Evangelical Missiological Society, and the Society for Pentecostal Studies.
- A. Scott Moreau, associate academic dean and professor of intercultural studies at Wheaton College Graduate School, who has been my colleague, coach, sponsor, editor, and friend for twenty years.
- The leadership at Wheaton College, who have generously provided resources for my research and professional development.
- Students in missions history and intercultural studies over the last ten years who gave valuable feedback on my manuscript, such as Will Abercrombie, Erika Anderson, Amanda Barnett, Kate and Phil Bookhamer, Taylor Burnham, Kathryn Crimm, Hannah Dagenhart, Sarah Kelly, Hannah Markley, Caprice Miller, Melody Scott, Harry Smith, Krissy Stuart, Luke Tseng, Joy Viguier, Sara Vroom, and Sarah Willing.
- Jim Kinney, Eric Salo, and the editorial team at Baker Academic, for the meticulous process of ensuring a high standard of quality for the textbook.

Most importantly, I am grateful for the love and support of my family:

- Luisa and Sarita Gallagher, who, as professors in the College of Christian Studies at George Fox University (Newberg, Oregon) were my conversation partners on this manuscript, giving me space and time to think out loud about the history of missions.
- Caprice, Landon, Sydney, Bobbie, Norlyn, and Otha, who provided inspiration and reinforcement.

- My wife, Jayna, was there when I initiated the book and walked with me through the years of writing. I admire the gracious wisdom and loving maturity she embodies as she joyfully lives her life while tirelessly providing moral and emotional support.

Robert L. Gallagher

Encountering the History of Missions Series

Encountering the History of Missions is the most recent addition to the award-winning Encountering Mission series. Each book focuses on mission from an evangelical perspective. For many years, J. Herbert Kane's textbooks, including *The Making of a Missionary* (1975), *Understanding Christian Missions* (1976), *Christian Missions in Biblical Perspective* (1976), *A Concise History of the Christian World Mission* (1978), *Life and Work on the Mission Field* (1980), and *The Christian World Mission: Today and Tomorrow* (1981), have been widely used in seminaries and Bible colleges as introductory texts. With the passing of time, however, his classic works have become dated, and Baker Publishing Group recognized that the time had come to develop a series of books to replace Kane's gifts to the mission community. The Encountering Mission series, then, builds on the best of Kane's work but also extends the discussion in significant ways to meet the needs of those who are preparing for effective missional engagement in today's world.

Missions in the Early Church

In AD 325 Emperor Constantine and Bishop Hosius welcomed 318 bishops to the Council of Nicaea. These bishops represented churches from Spain all the way to Persia. How did the church grow from the small group that met in the "upper room" in Jerusalem to the massive institution reflected at Nicaea? Answering this question is a worthwhile effort. As Martin Hengel said, "The history and the theology of early Christianity are mission-history and mission-theology" (Weinrich 1981, 61). He means that one cannot understand the history of the early church without considering the missionary activity of the church. Further, one can understand the development of the church today only by studying its past expansion. The successes and failures of Christianity's past should inform its future.

Therefore, in this chapter we will examine the ways in which the church expanded from AD 100 to AD 500. Historians usually discuss this period in two parts, divided by the Council of Nicaea in AD 325. The period before Nicaea is called the ante-Nicene, and the period after it is called the post-Nicene. The chapter will focus on the methods employed by the early church, not on geography. Hopefully, when you finish this chapter, you will understand how the church grew during this crucial period in its history.

Missions in the Ante-Nicene Church

The Church at the End of the Apostolic Age

The end of the apostolic age coincided with the death of John at Ephesus (AD 95–100). What was the state of the church at that time? The Acts and the

An earlier version of this chapter appears in John Mark Terry, "The History of Missions in the Early Church" in *Missiology: An Introduction to the Foundations, History, and Strategies of World Missions*, edited by John Mark Terry, Ebbie Smith, and Justice Anderson, 166–82. (Nashville: Broadman & Holman, 1998).

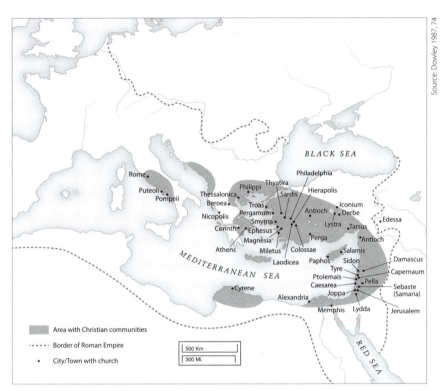

Source: Dowley 1987, 74

Map 1.1 The Extent of Christianity by AD 100

Epistles reveal clusters of churches in Palestine and Asia Minor, especially in western Asia Minor. Paul had planted other churches in Macedonia, Achaia, and Cyprus on his missionary journeys. Titus had ministered on the island of Crete, and unknown Christians founded the church at Rome. It seems there was a church at Puteoli near Naples, because Paul stayed with Christians there for seven days (Acts 28:13–14).

Traditions of the early church hold that Thaddeus preached in Edessa, Mark founded the church at Alexandria, and Peter preached in Bithynia and Cappadocia. There are also less likely traditions which assert that Paul went to Spain and Thomas went to India. Even if one accepts these traditions, it is clear that the number of churches was still quite small. Then, too, the size of the churches was limited. The churches at Jerusalem, Antioch, Ephesus, and Rome seem to have had large memberships, but probably most of the churches were rather small. For the most part, they were urban churches. This was because Paul preached primarily in the cities of the empire. It is not clear that this was a conscious strategy on his part, but it certainly was his pattern.

In the beginning the church reflected a strong Jewish influence. However, as the number of gentile churches increased, the churches became more Hellenistic.

This trend was greatly accelerated when Jerusalem was destroyed in AD 70, and the Christians of Jerusalem were scattered. Thus the New Testament was written in Greek, as were the majority of Christian documents during the second century.

Therefore, at the end of the apostolic age one can say that the church was limited in size, perhaps no more than one hundred congregations; mainly urban; and primarily Greek speaking.

General Factors Affecting the Church's Expansion

Most introductions to the New Testament list the factors that made 4 BC (or thereabouts) the right time for the incarnation. These same factors also positively affected the missionary activity of the early church. Perhaps the greatest general factor was the excellent Roman road system. Everywhere the Romans went they built fine roads. These roads improved commerce within the empire and also made it possible to dispatch Roman legions to trouble spots very quickly. During this period travel was safer than at any later time until the nineteenth century. The relative ease of travel was a great help to early missionaries.

Another reason for the safety of travel was the Pax Romana. The Romans brought and enforced peace in the Mediterranean world. Their legions and proconsuls ensured the stability of the region. The Roman navy cleared the sea of pirates so that sea travel was less risky than previously. All in all, the period under study was congenial to missionary travel.

The widespread use of the Greek language was also a tremendous advantage for the early missionaries. Whereas modern missionaries have to spend months or even years in language study, the evangelists of ante-Nicene times could go almost anywhere in the empire and communicate through the Greek language.

Greek philosophy was widely taught and admired all over the empire. This aided the Christian mission in two ways. First, it imbued the educated classes with a love for truth. Second, it caused people to become dissatisfied with the superstitions of their traditional religions.

The presence of Jews and synagogues in the cities of the empire was another significant factor. The Jews propagated a religion of strict monotheism. This was a novel concept to most citizens. The Jews also taught that God was personal and that people could have a personal relationship with him. The Jews proselyted actively, and in many cities there were a good number of "God-fearers" who attended the synagogue. These God-fearers proved to be a fertile ground for the early church planters. In fact, the opposition of the Jews to Christianity in Asia Minor and Greece was surely due in part to jealousy at the loss of their gentile adherents. Paul writes that "when the set time had fully come, God sent his Son" (Gal. 4:4). This was the "fullness of time" not only for the incarnation but also for church expansion.

3

Growth in the Second Century

It seems that Christianity spread naturally along the main roads and rivers of the empire. It spread eastward by way of Damascus and Edessa into Mesopotamia; southward through Bostra and Petra into Arabia; westward through Alexandria and Carthage into North Africa; and northward through Antioch into Armenia, Pontus, and Bithynia. Somewhat later it spread even farther, to Spain, Gaul, and Britain (Kane 1971, 10).

Egypt and North Africa became strongholds of Christianity during the second century. Tradition has it that Mark founded the church at Alexandria, but this is not certain. At any rate, the early church in Egypt was limited to those who spoke Greek. Probably Christians from Egypt carried the gospel into North Africa (Neill 1964, 36).

North Africa produced the first Latin-speaking churches. In the early years these churches seem to have appealed more to the upper classes, the Latin-speaking people. Then, too, the churches began primarily in the cities and towns. During this period the villages remained largely untouched (Neill 1964, 37).

Paul, Peter, and John had all evangelized in Asia Minor, and that region contained many churches, which grew steadily. Pliny, a Roman official, wrote to Emperor Trajan in AD 112 concerning the Christians in Bithynia. He complains, "There are so many people involved in the danger. . . . For the contagion of this superstition has spread not only through the free cities, but into the villages and rural districts"; Pliny goes on to say that "many persons of all ages and both sexes" were involved (Kidd 1920, 1:39). Obviously, the churches in Bithynia were growing and multiplying, and this seems to have been true in and around Ephesus as well.

Many scholars believe the church at Rome was founded by "Jews and converts to Judaism" who were converted on the day of Pentecost (Acts 2:10). While this is just a theory, it is a fact that the Roman church grew in size and prestige year by year. For the first one hundred years of its existence, church members used Greek in their services. This shows that the church drew its members from the poorer classes of society. There are no records of the size of the Roman congregation until the time of the Novatian controversy in AD 251. Eusebius quotes from a letter written by Bishop Cornelius of Rome in which he states that there were forty-six presbyters; seven deacons; seven subdeacons; forty-two clerks; fifty-two exorcists, readers, and janitors; and fifteen hundred widows and needy in the church. Some scholars have calculated the total church membership at that time at around thirty thousand. If that was true in AD 251, then the Roman church must have been large during the second century as well (Eusebius 1995, 265).

Kenneth Scott Latourette estimates that by the end of the second century Christians were active in all the provinces of the Roman Empire as well as in

Mesopotamia (1937, 1:85). This seems to be a fair estimation in light of a passage from Tertullian. Writing in about AD 200, he reports that many had become Christians, including "different races of the Gaetuli, many tribes of the Mauri, all the confines of Spain, and various tribes of Gaul, with places in Britain, which, though inaccessible to Rome, [had] yielded to Christ. Add the Sarmatae, the Daci, the Germans, the Scythians, and many remote peoples, provinces, and islands unknown to [them]" (Roberts and Donaldson 1951, 3:44).

In another book Tertullian boasts to the pagans: "We have filled every place belonging to you, cities, islands, castles, towns, assemblies, your very camp, your tribes, companies, palace, senate, forum! We leave you your temples only" (Kidd 1920, 1:143). Tertullian may have employed some hyperbole, but it does seem clear that the church had penetrated, at least to some extent, every part of Roman society by AD 200.

Growth in the Third Century

Christianity grew steadily but not dramatically from AD 200 until 260. Then, beginning about AD 260, the church grew very rapidly until Emperor Diocletian's edict of persecution in AD 303. Up until AD 260 the church had remained a mainly urban institution, but the mass movement in the latter third century was primarily a rural phenomenon. Several factors affected this remarkable growth. First, this was a period of civil strife in the empire. It was the era of the "barrack emperors," when the Roman Empire was threatened externally with invasion by Germanic tribes and internally with chaos in Rome itself. Second, there was great economic dislocation. Inflation made survival very difficult for rural folk, who found it challenging to market their produce. Even the shipment of produce became risky as peace and order began to break down.

As usually happens, the rural folk began to question their traditional cults as the hard times continued. In contrast, Christians presented a simple gospel that offered both social justice and assurance of power over demonic forces. Thousands, perhaps millions, rejected their old gods and accepted Christ. This was the greatest period of growth in the ante-Nicene era. The great growth was possible because the church was free of persecution during these forty years. The government was so preoccupied with other problems that it left the church alone. This respite from persecution continued during the early years of Diocletian's reign.

The era of peace and progress ended when Emperor Diocletian issued his edict of persecution in AD 303. This terrible period of persecution lasted until Constantine assumed control in AD 311. During the persecution fifteen hundred Christians died as martyrs, and many more suffered lesser persecutions. Many Christians recanted under torture or the threat of it, including

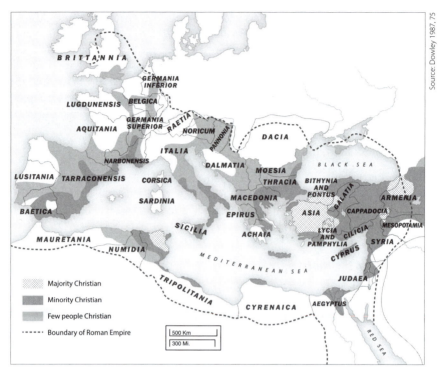

Map 1.2 The Extent of Christianity by AD 300

the bishop of Rome. Lasting peace came when Constantine issued his edict of toleration in AD 311 and his famous Edict of Milan in AD 313 (Kane 1971, 32).

The Expansion of the Church by AD 325

By AD 300 the gospel had been preached in every city and province of the empire; however, the distribution of the churches was very uneven. The church had grown more rapidly in Syria, Asia Minor, Egypt, and North Africa, including significant centers in Rome and Lyons. Growth in other areas—Gaul, for example—had been slow. German Lutheran theologian Adolf von Harnack believed that in one or two provinces at least half the people were Christians, and in several cities Christians were in the majority. He estimated the number of Christians in the empire at three or four million at the time of Constantine (1908, 2:325).

Under Constantine's rule the number of Christians increased rapidly. When Christianity became the state religion, church membership swelled, although the quality may have declined in proportion. Still, the ante-Nicene church had made remarkable progress and withstood tremendous onslaughts. The question remains: *How* did the church grow?

Missionaries in the Ante-Nicene Church

From its inception Christianity has been a missionary religion. The missionaries of the second and third centuries followed the example set by the apostles. Eusebius says of them: "The holy apostles and disciples of our Saviour, being scattered over the whole world, Thomas, according to tradition, received Parthia as his allotted region; Andrew received Sythia, and John, Asia, where . . . he died at Ephesus. Peter appears to have preached through Pontus, Galatia, Bithynia, Cappadocia, and Asia, to the Jews . . . finally coming to Rome" (1995, 82). According to Eusebius, the twelve apostles took deliberate steps to evangelize the world they knew.

It seems that there were itinerant missionaries in the second century who followed the Pauline model in their ministry. Eusebius tells of their work in his church history. The Didache from the second century also speaks of itinerant "apostles and prophets" in need of hospitality (Bettenson 1956, 71). So it seems there was a body of full-time missionaries in the second century. Origen testifies to their continuance in the third century: "Some of them have made it their business to itinerate, not only through cities, but even villages and country houses, that they might make converts to God" (Roberts and Donaldson 1951, 4:468). In fact, Pantaenus, the predecessor of Clement and Origen, left Alexandria and went into Asia as a missionary; Eusebius believed he traveled as far as India (1995, 190). This brief review of the source material indicates that the office of missionary continued in the church after the first century.

Missionary Bishops

During this period bishops continued the missionary activity of the apostles. The bishops of large urban centers led in the evangelization of the adjacent rural areas. Further, existing churches consecrated bishops and sent them into new areas to organize the Christians into churches. Also, a bishop or bishops living near a group of Christians would gather and instruct the believers until they could elect their own bishop (Conner 1971, 208).

Irenaeus and Gregory Thaumaturgos exemplify missionary bishops. Irenaeus (AD 130–200) was bishop of Lyons. In one of his books he speaks of preaching in the Celtic language to the tribes around Lyon (Neill 1964, 34). Gregory was won to Christ by Origen. About AD 240 he was chosen bishop of his hometown in Pontus. According to tradition, when he became bishop he had a congregation of seventeen, but when he died there were only seventeen

Portrait of Perpetua and Felicitas

"The ancient church rightly regarded Perpetua as a great hero of the church. Vibia Perpetua and her slave, Felicitas, became Christians at the same time. Roman authorities in Carthage arrested both of them during the persecution of Christians decreed by Emperor Septimus Severus. Though her family pleaded with her to consider their feelings and the welfare of her infant child, Perpetua remained true to her faith. Before she was led into the arena to die, Perpetua shared her faith with the crowd. As she entered the arena, Perpetua encouraged the weeping Christians: 'Give out the Word to the brothers and sisters; stand fast in the faith, love one another, and don't let our suffering become a stumbling block to you.'"

Ruth A. Tucker (2004, 33–34)

pagans left in the city. The numbers may be exaggerated, but clearly Gregory evangelized successfully. He exposed pagan miracles as frauds and performed so many wonders himself that he became known as Gregory Thaumaturgos (worker of wonders). He also substituted festivals in honor of the martyrs for pagan feasts. He thus sought to ease the transition from paganism to Christianity (Latourette 1937, 1:89–90).

Lay Missionaries

Though missionaries and bishops set an example in evangelism, no doubt laypeople spread the gospel for the most part. They shared the gospel while engaged in their daily activities. It is easy to imagine laypeople conversing with their acquaintances in their homes, at the market, and on the street corners (Green 1970, 173).

In addition, Christians shared the gospel as they moved about. Christian traders evangelized as they traveled throughout the empire, much as did the Christians dispersed from Jerusalem (Acts 8:4). Christians serving in the Roman army, though relatively few in the early years, carried the gospel as well. They witnessed wherever they were stationed. Some scholars believe Roman soldiers first brought the gospel to Britain. Further, the government pensioned retiring soldiers by giving them a plot of land in a new territory. These retired soldiers sometimes established churches in those remote places. This was definitely the case in southeastern Europe (Carver 1932, 51).

Women played a major part in the expansion of the church as well. Harnack writes:

No one who reads the New Testament attentively, as well as those writings which immediately succeeded it, can fail to notice that in the apostolic and sub-apostolic age women played an important role in the propaganda of Christianity and throughout the Christian communities. The equalizing of man and woman before God (Gal. 3:28) produced a religious independence among women, which aided the Christian mission. (1908, 2:64)

Because the early churches met in homes, many women were able to make their homes into house churches. Also, many women died bravely as martyrs and thus gave a testimony for Christ.

Missionary Methods

Paul and Peter often preached in public, and this practice continued in the second and third centuries when conditions permitted. Eusebius records that Thaddeus preached publicly at Edessa. Eusebius has Thaddeus saying, "Since I was sent to preach the word, summon for me, tomorrow an assembly of all your citizens, and I will preach before them and sow in them the word of life" (1995, 1:47). The early evangelists were fervent in their preaching. J. G. Davies says that they preached so as to "bring the hearers to repentance and belief . . . [and] to force upon them the crisis of decision" (1967, 19). The steady growth of the church testifies to their efforts.

W. O. Carver believed that teaching was another important method. The early catechetical schools developed into training schools for presbyters (pastors) in Antioch, Alexandria, Edessa, Caesarea, and other places (1932, 47–50). All these schools sent people into missions. Sometimes teachers, such as Pantaenus of Alexandria, set an example in this effort. These teachers worked as evangelists inside and outside their schools. Pagans as well as catechumens attended their schools and heard their teaching. Missionary bishop Gregory Thaumaturgos was won to Christ by Origen at the school in Alexandria (Harnack 1908, 2:362).

The early Christians often spread the gospel through the use of their homes. Because there were no church buildings until about AD 250, congregations met in one or several homes. The home setting provided a relaxed, nonthreatening atmosphere. The warm hospitality afforded by Christian homes no doubt influenced many. Whole households were sometimes converted, as was that of the Philippian jailer (Acts 16). The New Testament contains many references to house or home churches, and the early church followed this model (Green 1970, 207).

Oral witness through preaching and personal testimony was the main method of evangelism, but literature also became an increasingly effective means of propagating the gospel. Literature evangelism included apologies, letters, polemics, and the distribution of the Scriptures. Carver says that all the ante-Nicene fathers "were in varying degrees missionaries of the pen" (1932, 47–50).

9

The early church spread the gospel primarily through personal contact and example. This was much the same as in apostolic times. The church established no elaborate missionary societies or organizations; instead, Christians shared and demonstrated the gospel in their daily lives. Justin Martyr tells about this in his *Apology*: "He has urged us . . . to convert all . . . and this I can show to have taken place with many that have come in contact with us, who were overcome, and changed from violent and tyrannical characters, either from having watched the constancy of their neighbor's lives or from having observed the wonderful patience of fellow travelers under unjust exactions, or from the trial they made of those with whom they were concerned in business" (Kidd 1920, 1:74).

Christians also maintained a public testimony by their conduct at their trials and martyrdoms. Though some recanted under pressure or torture, many gave a wonderful testimony for Christ. When threatened with death if he did not recant, Polycarp of Smyrna said: "Eighty and six years have I served him, and he never did me wrong; and how can I now blaspheme my King that has saved me?" (Eusebius 1995, 146). Roman persecution did not destroy Christianity; rather, it strengthened it. The blood of the martyrs really did prove to be the seed of the church. Many pagans accepted Christ because of Christians' testimonies.

Early Christians won others through social service. Harnack lists ten different ministries performed by the Christians: alms in general, support of teachers and officials, support of widows and orphans, support of the sick and infirm, the care of prisoners and convicts in the mines, the burial of paupers, the care of slaves, providing disaster relief, furnishing employment, and extending hospitality (1908, 1:153).

It seems that these benevolent activities affected evangelism positively because the pagan emperor, Julian the Apostate (AD 332–363), complained about it: "Atheism [i.e., Christianity] has been especially advanced through the loving service rendered to strangers, and through their care for the burial of the dead. . . . The godless Galileans care not only for their own poor but for ours as well" (Neill 1964, 42). Thus in the early church there was no dichotomy between social service and evangelism. Both were natural activities integral to the church's mission.

Factors That Affected the Church's Expansion

So far this chapter has presented information about the geographical expansion of the early church and the methods used by the church to grow. This last section tries to answer the question, why did the church grow? Six factors are suggested.

1. *Divine blessing.* The church grew because of divine blessing. It was God's will for the church to grow, and God blessed the efforts of the early Christians. The early church was the instrument of the Holy Spirit in fulfilling the redemptive purpose of God. Origen said, "Christianity . . . in spite of the small number of its teachers was preached everywhere in the world. . . . We cannot hesitate to say that the result is beyond any human power" (Roberts and Donaldson 1951, 4:350).

2. *Christian zeal.* The church grew because of the zeal of the Christians. They gave of themselves sacrificially for the faith. The early Christians possessed a burning conviction that expressed itself in missionary activity.

3. *Appeal of the message.* The appealing message of the church was another important factor. Latourette says that the uniqueness of Jesus was the key. The love of God and the offer of forgiveness and eternal life through Christ appealed to the people of the Roman Empire (1937, 1:168).

4. *Organization and discipline.* The organization and discipline of the church aided its growth. Walter Hyde believes that the organization of the church on the imperial pattern was a positive factor (1946, 187). Certainly, the faithfulness of the bishops enabled the church to persevere in the face of persecution. Also, the strict discipline of the church presented a marked contrast to the pagan cults.

5. *Inclusiveness.* The church grew because of its inclusiveness. It attracted people of all classes and races. It became a universal religion. It burst the bonds of restrictive Judaism to become a religion for the world.

6. *High ethical standards.* Christianity prospered because of the ethical standards of the early church. This is not to say that the churches or believers were perfect, but their lives were so different from their pagan neighbors' that they attracted notice. Their morality and works of charity commended the faith to many.

Missions in the Post-Nicene Era

The story of the expansion of Christianity in the post-Nicene era differs in several respects from that of the ante-Nicene period. Until the Edict of Milan in AD 313, Christianity developed in an often hostile environment. With the favor bestowed by Constantine, the church enjoyed greatly improved prospects for growth. Because of the emperor's favor, new members inundated the churches. The transparent insincerity of many prompted the development of the monastic movement. Monastic communities thus played a major role in church expansion.

Though the emperor's favor was a mixed blessing, it did cause great church growth within the empire. Church leaders had to adjust to government involvement in ecclesiastical affairs. They also had to adjust to a situation in which the church expanded very rapidly.

The encroachment of pagan tribes also presented the church with a challenge. The migration of the barbarians caused the dislocation of many churches, but it also brought large groups of pagans within the effective reach of the church. The church rightly made great efforts to evangelize these tribes.

Though the church's situation changed in several ways, the church continued to employ many of the same missionary methods. Bishops continued to preach and reach out to pagans. Benevolent ministries also remained a public demonstration of Christian compassion. And, as always, individual Christians had a great impact through their speaking and manner of life. The story of the church's growth was also the story of great saints who ministered in often difficult circumstances. All in all, the expansion of Christianity from 313 to 500 was and is a remarkable era in the history of missions.

Constantine and Missions

Constantine and his sons encouraged the expansion of the church. Both Constantine and Constantius identified Christ's kingdom with the Roman Empire. Further, they saw Christianity as a way to maintain order within the empire and pacify warlike tribes outside its borders. Therefore, both emperors encouraged missionary activity. For example, Constantine wrote a letter to the king of Persia requesting protection for Christians in Persia: "And now, because your power is great, I commend these persons to your protection; because your piety is eminent, I commit them to your care" (Eusebius 1994, 544).

On another occasion Constantine told a group of bishops: "You are the bishops of those within the Church, but I would be a bishop established by God of those outside it" (Jones 1948, 169). The emperor truly believed he had a special responsibility to see to it that his pagan subjects were converted. Apparently, he did not promote missionary work outside the empire but rather concentrated on the pagans within it. His efforts certainly proved successful. Stephen Neill estimates that the number of Christians in the empire quadrupled in the century following the Edict of Milan (1964, 46).

Missionary Bishops

As in the ante-Nicene period, bishops played an important part in the expansion of the church. Outstanding examples of such bishops are Ulfilas, Martin of Tours, Ambrose of Milan, and John Chrysostom.

Ulfilas is remembered as the great missionary to the Goths (Visigoths). Ulfilas was the son of a Cappadocian father and a Gothic mother. He was consecrated in 341 to serve as bishop of the Christians already living in Gothic

Portrait of Ulfilas

Ulfilas may well have been the first missionary Bible translator. He served for almost forty years among the Goths in what is now southern Europe. This proved a great challenge because the Goths were nomadic people. Ulfilas translated from the Greek Bible in a very literal manner. His Bible omitted the books of 1 and 2 Samuel and 1 and 2 Kings. There are two reasons suggested for this. The more colorful is that Ulfilas did not want the warlike Goths to read about the wars and fighting in those books. The second possibility is that he died before he could complete his translation. His translation influenced both the Goths and the Vandals. He set an admirable example for a host of missionary translators to follow.

Ruth A. Tucker (2004, 36)

territory. These people were probably a mixed group of Romans and Goths. Ulfilas preached north of the Danube for seven years. During this time an intratribal war broke out. The two factions were led by Phritigernes and Athanaric. Ulfilas apparently allied himself with Phritigernes and supported his request for Roman assistance. Emperor Valens sent Roman troops, and Phritigernes triumphed eventually. Phritigernes received permission from Valens to move his faction south of the Danube. When this was accomplished, Phritigernes encouraged his people to adopt the religion of Emperor Valens, which was Arian Christianity. Ulfilas apparently accommodated himself to this and thereafter taught a modified Arianism (Frend 1976, 12).

After the transfer to Moesia south of the Danube, Ulfilas continued his ministry for thirty years. His devoted service and exemplary life commended him to the Goths. He also exercised a lasting influence by translating much of the Bible into the Gothic language. To do this he had to compose an alphabet and grammar for the Gothic language. This may have been the first Bible translation by a missionary (Neill 1964, 55).

It is difficult to judge the impact of Ulfilas on the conversion of the Goths. It seems clear that the majority became Christians because they moved into Roman territory. However, Ulfilas played an important role in consolidating the conversion of the tribe. His long ministry must have borne much fruit, and his translation of the Bible not only influenced the Goths but was also the basis for the translations into other tribal languages. Neill describes him as "one of the most notable missionaries" in the history of the church (1964, 55).

Martin of Tours (316–397) was an evangelistic and saintly bishop whose life was an example to many. Martin grew up in Italy and became a soldier like his father. He disliked military life and longed to become a monk. At the age of eighteen he was baptized, and two years later he was able to win his release from the army.

He studied for a time with Hilary of Poitiers and then joined a monastery near Milan. Later he rejoined Hilary at Poitiers and established a monastery nearby. He soon became famous as a miracle worker, and the people of Tours chose him as their bishop. He reluctantly agreed but insisted on living in a monk's cell in the monastery he established just outside the town.

As a bishop, Martin traveled widely throughout Gaul and won thousands of converts by his preaching and wonders. He destroyed pagan shrines and replaced them with churches or monasteries. Hundreds of churches were named after him. Historians remember Martin for his success in evangelizing the rural areas of Gaul and for introducing monasticism to that land (D. Schaff 1949, 26).

Ambrose of Milan is remembered for his outstanding preaching and influence on Augustine of Hippo. He won many pagans through his preaching in his own diocese, but he also encouraged missionary work in the Tyrol. On one occasion Frigitil, queen of the Marcomanni people in that area, met a Christian traveler who witnessed to her. She accepted Christ and asked the traveler for instruction in her new faith. The traveler advised her to consult Ambrose. When the queen wrote requesting instruction, Ambrose replied in a long letter written in the form of a catechism. He also urged her to persuade her husband to keep peace with the Romans. She convinced her husband, who federated his kingdom with Rome. Eventually all her people became Christians (Paulinus 1952, 39).

John Chrysostom, bishop of Constantinople and famous preacher, was concerned about missions. He wrote an apologetic with the aim of winning pagans and Jews. Chrysostom also sent missionaries into pagan areas, particularly the land of the Goths. While he was in exile in the Caucasus, he encouraged missionary work in Cilicia and Phoenicia (Latourette 1937, 1:186).

The bishops won many converts through direct missions, as described earlier, but they also influenced many converts through their benevolent ministries. These ministries had attracted many in the ante-Nicene period, and they continued to do so in the post-Nicene era. The favor of the government brought the church a prosperity that enabled the bishops to do much more than they had done previously. The church maintained hospitals, orphanages, and hospices for travelers, widows, and the indigent.

Monasticism and Missions

Monasticism began in the deserts of Egypt, where hermits such as Anthony of Thebes sought holiness through solitude. Before long the hermits began to develop the communities that eventually became monasteries. There was always a tension in the monastic movement. Some of the monks wanted to renounce the world completely and live in solitude, while others saw the need to preach to the pagans.

Many monks tried to resolve this tension by spending part of the year in the monastery and then going out on preaching missions for a period. When the monks were ordained, it was done primarily so that they could devote themselves to missionary work. Some of the most daring and effective missionaries were monks who went out boldly to spread the gospel (Yannoulatos 1969, 224).

Though the great age of monastic missions was still to come, the early monks accomplished remarkable things. During a time when Athanasius and his followers were being persecuted, the monasteries near Alexandria were disrupted by the army, and the leaders of the monasteries were sent into exile. Macarius and another monk were sent to an island in the Nile Delta where there were no Christians. All the people there worshiped in a pagan temple and believed that their priest was divine. When the monks arrived, the priest's daughter was suddenly possessed by a demon who berated the monks. The monks cast out the demon and presented the girl to her father, who promptly accepted Christ. The inhabitants followed his example and destroyed all their idols. They changed their temple into a church and accepted baptism (Socrates 1952, 24).

Hilarion of Gaza (291–371) was one of the great missionary monks of the East. He had studied in Alexandria and was influenced by Anthony of Thebes. Following Anthony's example, he lived for a time in the desert, but he later returned to Palestine to establish monasteries. He founded these monasteries to be centers of missionary activity. His monasteries had a wide impact. Many pagans came to Christ, including the family of Sozomen, who became a noted church historian. Whole villages became Christian as well as groups of nomadic Arabs in the desert of Kadesh (Yannoulatos 1969, 221).

Among notable missionary monks in the West was Ninian of Britain. Ninian was the son of an important local official in Britain. The Romans took him to Rome as a hostage. He remained there for many years and was trained as a presbyter. About 395 the church at Rome sent him to do missionary work among his own people. On this journey Ninian met Martin of Tours, who made a deep impression on the young missionary (Moorman 1973, 7).

After some months with Martin, Ninian completed his journey, arriving in Britain about 397. He immediately built a monastery at Whithorn in Galloway. He whitewashed the stones so that the monastery would be conspicuous. With the "white house" as their base, Ninian and his monks preached to the savage Picts along the Roman Wall, along the east coast of Scotland, and even as far as Wales. W. H. C. Frend says, "The conversion of Celtic Britain in the fifth century must in a large measure be attributed to the Celtic monks" (1976, 16).

Outstanding Missionaries

As in the ante-Nicene period, individual missionaries continued to itinerate after Nicaea. Philaster, who was called a "second Paul," traveled throughout

Portrait of Patrick

Patrick sought to win the local chiefs and kings to Christ and thus influence their subjects. He held the Scriptures in high regard and gave his converts thorough instruction in the Bible. He also encouraged them to participate in ministry. Though it is hard to separate fact from legend in regard to Patrick's work, Ruth Tucker estimates that Patrick planted two hundred churches and baptized one hundred thousand converts. He closes his *Confession* with these words:

But I pray those who believe and fear God, whosoever has deigned to scan or accept his document, composed in Ireland by Patrick the sinner, an unlearned man to be sure, that none should ever say that it was my ignorance that accomplished any small thing which I did or showed in accordance with God's will; but judge ye, and let it be most truly believed, that it was the gift of God. And this is my confession before I die.

Patrick (R. Tucker 2004, 40)

the empire preaching to pagans and Jews. He carried on notable evangelistic work in Rome itself and eventually became the bishop of Brixia (Latourette 1937, 1:186).

The most famous of the missionaries of this era must surely be Patrick of Ireland. Patrick (389–461) was born in Britain and raised in a Christian home. His father was a deacon, and his grandfather was a presbyter. When he was sixteen, he was captured by a band of marauders and taken to Ireland. Living as a slave, he tended cattle for six years. When he was allowed to leave, he boarded a ship that was blown to Gaul by a storm. Patrick was enslaved again in Gaul, but he managed to escape and return to his family in Britain. Not long after his homecoming, he experienced a vision in the night in which he saw an angel carrying a letter titled "The Voice of the Irish," which said, "We beseech thee, holy youth, to come and walk with us once more." Patrick interpreted this as a divine call and, against the wishes of his family, went back to Ireland to preach.

Patrick ministered in Ireland for over thirty years. In his *Confession* he speaks of baptizing thousands and ordaining presbyters to lead the new congregations. He faced much opposition from pagan priests and antagonistic rulers. He tried to win the local rulers and through them the masses, but this was not always successful. He faithfully taught Roman Christianity, though he was a man of little education.

Patrick was probably not the first Christian to preach in Ireland. Other Christians were taken prisoner, no doubt, and, most likely, Christian traders had some contact with the Irish. This does not negate Patrick's work but rather places it in its proper perspective. J. B. Bury writes that Patrick accomplished three significant things: (1) he organized the Christians who were already in Ireland; (2) he converted many districts that were still pagan, especially in the West; and (3) he brought Ireland into relationship with the Roman Church (1905, 212).

Lay Missionaries

Lay missionaries played an essential part in the expansion of Christianity after Nicaea, just as they did before that time. Captives, soldiers, and merchants were all active in evangelizing. Frend says, "The Christian merchant of this period was the propagator of his Faith as the Moslem merchant has been in more recent centuries" (1982, 240).

The kingdom of Axum (Abyssinia) was won to Christ through the witness of two young travelers, Aedessius and Frumentius. After being captured by the Abyssinians, they quickly impressed the king and became the stewards of his household. The king died, but his successor gave them even greater responsibility. The two young Christians held regular worship services and invited visiting traders as well as the Abyssinians to participate. After some time they received permission to return to their home country. Aedessius returned to Tyre, their hometown, but Frumentius went to Alexandria to report their activities to Bishop Athanasius.

When Athanasius heard the story, he said, "Who better than yourself can scatter the mists of ignorance and introduce among this people the light of divine preaching?" Immediately, Athanasius consecrated Frumentius as a bishop and sent him back to Abyssinia. There he worked diligently and founded the church that continues in Ethiopia to this day (Theodoret 1854, 1:22).

The Iberians, a warlike tribe that lived north of Armenia, were won to Christ by Nino, a Christian woman taken captive by them. Even in her captivity Nino worshiped the Lord faithfully, fasting and praying as she normally did. The Iberians, impressed with her piety, inquired about her religion but were not convinced by her testimony.

An Iberian child became sick, and after consulting many people the child's mother brought him to Nino. When Nino prayed for the boy, he was healed instantly though he was at the point of death. Some time later Nino prayed for the queen of the Iberians, who was also healed. The queen became a Christian and encouraged her husband to do so. Eventually he too became a Christian and urged all his people to accept Christ. The people agreed, built a church, and sent a delegation to Emperor Constantine to request priests (Sozomen 1952, 7).

The Growth of the Church at AD 500

By 500 the church's situation was much different from what it was in 300. Conversion had become a matter of norm and convenience rather than a bold act of faith. By 500 the vast majority of people within the empire called themselves Christians. Though the church had been shaken by doctrinal battles, by this time it had settled into Nicene orthodoxy.

The church expanded both inside and outside the boundaries of the empire. Many barbarian tribes settled within the empire during the fourth and fifth centuries. These tribes, including the Visigoths, the Burgundians, the Franks, and the Vandals, accepted Christianity. This pattern also held true in the eastern provinces. Several Arab tribes became Christian after they settled in Roman territory. Outside the empire the church spread into Ethiopia, Arabia, Mesopotamia, Persia, India, Germany, Georgia (Europe), and Ireland. The expansion to the east was inhibited by the opposition of the Persian authorities and by the strength of Zoroastrianism (Latourette 1937, 1:227–29).

Led by missionaries such as Saba (d. 487), who won an entire city to Christ, the church in Persia continued to grow. Throughout the East, however, Christians always remained a minority. The Eastern church never attained the dominance that the Western church did. Nevertheless, by 500 there were definitely Christian congregations in India and Ceylon, as well as Arabia and Persia (Latourette 1937, 1:231).

Factors Affecting Post-Nicene Expansion

Why did the church expand so rapidly during the fourth and fifth centuries? Basically, it grew after Nicaea for many of the same reasons that it grew earlier. First, the church provided an element of stability and security in a society that was disintegrating. Second, as Harnack insisted, monotheism met the religious needs of the day. Paganism was spiritually bankrupt, and the people of the empire were ready for a change. Third, the moral living of Christians demonstrated the superiority of Christianity day by day. Fourth, Christianity grew because of the zealous missionary activity of the bishops and individuals. And, fifth, it expanded because of the miraculous power its preachers demonstrated. Ramsay McMullen states that the missionary work of this period was characterized by power encounters. Early missionaries such as Martin of Tours demonstrated the power of Christ over that of pagan deities. One can hardly overestimate the influence of these power encounters on superstitious rural folk (1984, 112).

There were also new factors that affected the church's growth after 300. First, the official favor of the Roman government created a climate that encouraged church growth. Indeed, some emperors took an active role in enlarging the church. As noted above, though, this favor was a mixed blessing. Neill observes that with its newfound liberty the church was able to expand as never before, but at the same time, worldly vices came into the church as never before (1964, 47).

Second, monasticism became a force for church growth. Frend writes that monasticism brought about "the total eclipse of rural paganism throughout the Greco-Roman world" (1976, 15). The common people admired the monks

---

One of the most amazing and significant facts of history is that within five centuries of its birth Christianity won the professed allegiance of the overwhelming majority of the population of the Roman Empire and even the support of the Roman state.

Kenneth Scott Latourette (1953, 65)

---

greatly because they exorcised demons, healed the sick, helped the poor, and defended the oppressed against abusive public officials.

Third, Christianity enjoyed the momentum of success during this period. Success breeds success, and growth brings more growth.

Finally, Christianity grew because of the movement of tribes into Roman territory. E. A. Thompson holds that none of the Germanic tribes, with the exception of the Rugi, were converted while still living beyond the Roman frontier. He says, "It would seem to follow that the act of crossing the imperial frontiers and settling down on Roman soil necessarily and inevitably entailed the abandonment of paganism and conversion to the Roman religion" (1963, 77–78). Church growth experts teach that whenever a group migrates, it is open to assimilating new ideas. This was certainly true of the Germanic tribes.

Conclusion

By AD 325 the church existed in every part of the Roman Empire. The number of Christians was at least three million, and some have suggested figures as high as eight million. By 500 the vast majority of people in the empire called themselves Christians, and missionaries had carried the gospel to many lands outside the empire.

The church did not employ secret formulas to achieve growth. Rather, the church followed the example of the apostles in their preaching and teaching. The main innovation of the subapostolic church was literature evangelism, particularly the apologies. Still, the key remained, as it does today, the lives and witness of individual believers. The great missionary itinerants and bishops carried the banner of Christ, but it remained for rank-and-file Christians to make the most of the contacts and conversions.

Unity and Diversity in the Church

Paul G. Hiebert

*Adapted with permission
from Hiebert and
Hiebert (1987, 173–76)*

John Thompson argued wearily with himself as he looked out the tent at the hot road baked by the South India sun and at the dust swirling around an oxcart passing under the shade of a large banyan tree. In a few minutes the delegation of elders from the Farmer caste led by Venkat Reddy would come to hear his decision. Would he force them to take defiled Untouchables into their new church? Or would he ask the Untouchables (*harijans*) to start their own church near their hamlet outside town?

As he reflected, John thought back over the past few years. He and his wife, Shirley, had come to India six years earlier. Their mission board assigned them to pioneer work in the villages near Nellore. They managed to build a small bungalow and to hire three Indian evangelists to begin the work. For six to seven months each year—after the intense fieldwork following the monsoon rains let up—they toured the villages, with the evangelists camping in tents and preaching in the village squares at night. In the mornings they visited homes, and Shirley was often invited into the inner rooms reserved for women. In the afternoons John held Bible studies with the evangelists and curious inquirers from the villages. After preaching one or two nights in a village, they moved on to the next, as John was responsible for evangelizing more than three hundred villages.

The pace was grueling, particularly in the hot summer months, but there were rewards. At first, few were interested in the gospel, but prayer and faithful witness bore fruit. A number of families from the village of Konduru who belonged to the Farmer caste publicly became Christians. After their baptism, they wanted John to teach them more about their new religion. The Farmer caste was *suvarna* (clean) and ranked high in the village hierarchy of castes. John spent a week with them and taught them from the Bible, but he was concerned about their growth. Only two of them, an old man and a young boy who had been to the city, could read and write. However, there were other villages in which the people had never heard the gospel; there was no one else to go to them, so John moved on.

A year later, John returned to Konduru to hold meetings in the Untouchable hamlet just outside the village. He had come to realize that if he preached in a main village, only people from the clean castes would attend. The Untouchables, who made up more than 20 percent of the population, rarely showed up in such places in the main villages because they were considered ritually defiling. A person belonging to a clean caste who touched one of them had to take a ceremonial bath before he or she could eat or enter the temple. If John wanted to evangelize the Untouchables, he would have to go to their hamlets, which were located outside the main villages.

John's meeting in the hamlet near Konduru went well, even though the Farmer-caste Christians did not attend. They said they were too busy with fieldwork at the time. Their church had grown to fifteen families, and they had built a small church building at the edge of the village near their homes. There they met fairly regularly for worship services.

The second night, after the meeting in the hamlet, several elders of the Leatherworker caste (made up of Untouchables) led by Pappayya came to John and asked whether Untouchables, too, could become Christians. John joyfully told them that the gospel was for everyone. He pointed out that in Christ all persons are equal, that there are no distinctions of caste, class, or race. Over the next few days, six families from the Leatherworker caste publicly converted to Christianity and were baptized. John was very happy.

However, when John told this to Venkat Reddy and the elders of the Christian Farmers and asked them to accept the new converts into their church, they were shocked. How could they as clean caste people permit Untouchables to enter their church? They would be defiled, and their fellow castemen would put them out of the caste. They would be shunned by their friends and relatives. They would not be able to visit or witness to them, to eat with them, or to exchange brides and grooms with them. They would have no place to marry their children.

John told them that the gospel made all people one, but they said that if he forced them to take the Untouchables into their church, they would return to Hinduism. They said he did not understand their place in the caste system in the village. They would return the next day to hear his answer on the matter.

John knew that because of this caste system, millions of Untouchables lived in the most grinding poverty and oppression. They could not walk through the villages where the clean castes lived. They could not return goods they purchased or cook food for others, for they defiled everything they touched. Many were virtual slaves to their clean-caste masters.

John wondered what the gospel had to say to all of this. If he tried to break down the caste system in the church by requiring clean caste and Untouchable converts to worship together, would he not drive the clean castes away and leave a church that would itself be branded as Untouchable? Becoming a Christian would then be perceived by respectable-caste Hindus as becoming a member of an exceedingly low segment of society. Would this not close the door to the evangelization of high-caste people?

On the other hand, if he organized separate churches for the two groups, would he not be allowing Hinduism and its caste distinctions into the church and so undermine the gospel? Moreover, would the Untouchables be drawn to the gospel if the church offered them no deliverance from their bondage? Other churches in South India had found that where equality and a rejection of caste had been made a condition for entry into the church, many Untouchables entered. When the caste system was permitted inside the church, some high-caste people came, but the Untouchables stayed away.

John spent the afternoon and next morning in prayer and study of the Bible. Now the Farmer elders were coming for his answer. What should he say to them and what should he say to the elders of the Leatherworker Christians? Should he force them to form a single church? If he did, the Farmers would probably return to Hinduism. Or should he encourage them to form separate churches and then seek to build fellowship between them over time? But what would this say about the unity of the body of Christ to both groups? These arguments were rushing through his head as he saw the Farmer elders come down the road.

Reflection and Discussion

1. What would you advise John to say?

2. How might the experience of the early church inform his response?

Encountering Church of the East Missions

In 1998 Martin Palmer, secretary general of the Alliance of Religions and Conservation, discovered the ruins of the Da Qin Christian monastery—a seven-story octagonal pagoda built in AD 781 about thirty miles southwest of Xi'an, the capital of the ancient Tang dynasty. It was the second church built in China and is the oldest surviving Christian site in that country. The monastery and church erected within the sacred site of the Lou Guan Tai Taoist compound, the imperial temple of the Tang dynasty, suggest that the Christian faith had a special place in the empire and was not merely relegated to a marginal position as a strange Western religion.

Palmer validates the authenticity of the discovery in the following ways. The term *Da Qin* means "of the West," which implies something coming to China from the West. The site was oriented east to west instead of the traditional north-to-south direction of Chinese temples. In 1932 Peter Yoshiro Saeki, a Japanese religious scholar, visited the site and confirmed that it was the remains of a Nestorian building complex. In addition, several lines of Syriac graffiti were uncovered on the fourth floor of the structure in 2000, and the local people knew of the history of the five monks from the West and the church at the site. Last, archaeologists found Christian statues from about AD 800 on the second and third floors of the pagoda. The prominent statue was a ten-foot-high, five-foot-wide mountain sitting on the second floor depicting Mary in an Orthodox iconic nativity scene. Another statue was of Jonah under the gourd tree outside Nineveh, a symbol of Christ. How did Christianity come to China?

So much of Christian history focuses on the European and North American church, yet the expansion of the Christian faith is not the exclusive domain of the West. With information about the Western church so readily accessible, it is easy to slip into familiar patterns of Eurocentrism and miss the narrative of missions' development in the East. This chapter unveils the origins and growth of early Christianity in Asia by exploring the account of the Assyrian Church, which pushed toward unexplored territory. In particular, it surveys the beginning of this movement with focus on the legacy of Nestorius and the subsequent missional expansion through its training schools, monastic system, and lay ministry. A case study of Bishop Alopen of China supplements this examination, specifically his Christian theology, which oscillated between contextualization and syncretism. Finally, a brief history of the relationship between the Eastern church and Chinese authorities precedes the decline of Alopen's missionary initiative due to church corruption and the rise of Islam and its ensuing persecution.

Origins and Growth

The Church of the East has been described as "the most missionary church that the world has ever seen," providing the earliest missionary thrust to the east into Asia (Stewart 1928, 141). This movement spread beyond the borders of the Roman Empire from the third to the fourteenth centuries across Persia and Mesopotamia to Arabia, India, central Asia, Siberia, China, and Japan. In the eleventh century it was the largest group in Christendom, and, until

---

Hereupon our Tri-une (Eloah) divided His Godhead, and the Illustrious and Adorable Messiah, veiling His true Majesty, appeared in the world as a man. Angels proclaimed the glad tidings. A virgin brought forth the Holy one in Ta Ts'in. A bright star announced the felicitous event. Persians saw its splendor and came with tribute. He fulfilled the Old Law, as it was delivered by the twenty-four holy ones. He announced His great plans for the regulation of families and kingdoms. He appointed His new doctrines, operating without words by the cleansing influence of the Tri-une.

P. Y. Saeki (1916, 170)

---

after the thirteenth century its missionary expansion was unmatched (Philip 1996, 508; Phan 2011, 242). Herbert C. Jackson claims that "the Nestorians were the most thoroughly and extensively mission-minded of all Christian communities in history, yet the main streams of Christianity have relegated the Nestorians outside the fold as theological heretics" (1964, 2). Before we discover the reasons for the growth of this movement, it is important to consider the history surrounding the accusations of unorthodoxy that have remained such a controversial issue (see Gallagher 2005c, 102–5).

Legacy of Nestorius

The Church of the East, also known as the East Syrian Church or the Assyrian Church of the East, is usually called the Nestorian Church, named after Nestorius (archbishop of Constantinople [428–431]). This latter phrase, however, is a misnomer since the movement came into existence some three hundred years before Nestorius was born, and he never visited Syria. Yet theological conflicts and discussions of heresy surrounding Nestorius and the subsequent councils of the early church have stained the reputation of the Nestorian Church.

The resolution of the questions of Christ as fully divine and as fully human took place in the Councils of Nicaea (325) and Constantinople (381), respectively. The two natures of Christ were brought together at the Council of Chalcedon (451). Still, how did the two natures coexist in Christ? Nestorius, the patriarch of Constantinople, argued for the dual nature of Christ, that the divine and the human natures are completely separate—one being human and the other divine. This was in contrast to the popular view that stressed the unity of the two natures. The church leaders asked Nestorius to declare the suitability of *Theotokos* (God-bearer) as a title for the Virgin Mary. Unless connected with *anthropotokos* (man-bearer), he ruled that it would be wiser not to use the title. Nestorius's preferred title for the Virgin Mary was *Christotokos* (Christ-bearer), since God cannot be born of humanity. In other words, Jesus's humanity is different from his divinity because Mary gave birth to the person Jesus and not to "God." Nestorius did not deny the Godhead of Christ; nonetheless, he emphasized that Jesus was born with a body and soul as an authentic human being. Mark A. Noll reflects, "Sadly, the battle that followed soon became personal and episcopal as well as theological" (1997, 72).

Ecclesiastical rivalry between the patriarchs of Antioch (John I) and Alexandria (Cyril)—especially over the controlling influence of Constantinople—fueled the controversy, with Celestine I (bishop of Rome) siding with Cyril against Nestorius and Theodosius II (eastern Roman emperor). The result found Nestorius excommunicated from the church even though there was little proper defense of his doctrine. "As it turned out, Nestorius was condemned more for political than for doctrinal reasons" (Shelley 1982, 127). The Councils of Ephesus (431) and Chalcedon (451) condemned the beliefs of Nestorius, and his supporters fled to Persia. In 489 the bishops of the Eastern church refused to denounce the teachings of Nestorius as demanded by Rome and they separated from the Western church, functioning independently of the Roman Catholic and the Orthodox Churches. They remained faithful to the Nicene Creed even though they were condemned as heretics. Christianity in the East became one with Nestorianism, despite the fact that it "rarely held a doctrinal reference to the teachings of Nestorius" (England 1996, 4). Latourette affirms, "In their structure and customs the

Nestorians were very similar to the other Eastern Churches, and seem not to have stressed . . . their beliefs about the relations of the human and divine in Christ" ([1975] 2005, 323).

Theologians still do not agree in their assessment of Nestorius's doctrine. Some view him as guilty of the theological errors as charged by Cyril and Celestine, while for others he remains a dupe of political intrigue. "To this day it remains unclear to what extent Nestorius's teachings were actually heretical, and to what extent he suffered as a victim of misunderstanding and misrepresentations" (Shelley 1982, 127). Mar Aprem considers Nestorians as "Orthodox without *Theotokos*" and states that the theological rift with the Catholic and the Orthodox Churches was largely due to misunderstandings arising from linguistic, cultural, and philosophical differences (1976, 155). Ruth A. Tucker, lamenting the discounting of their "great evangelistic endeavors," concurs that "the charges of heresy were overstated and that the Nestorians were a vital part of the Christian missionary heritage" (2004, 47). This chapter will now consider the growth of the Nestorian missionary endeavor.

TABLE 2.1	
Timeline of the Origins of the Church of the East	
Date	**Events**
325	Council of Nicaea—Christ is viewed as fully divine.
381	Council of Constantinople—Christ is recognized as both fully divine and fully human.
428–431	Nestorius is archbishop of Constantinople.
431	Council of Ephesus—Nestorius's beliefs are condemned.
451	Council of Chalcedon—Nestorius's beliefs are condemned again.
489	Eastern church refuses to denounce the teachings of Nestorius and separates from the Western church.

Growth of Missions

During the time of the apostle Paul, Syrian Antioch became the epicenter of Christian missions. This continued with the advance of the gospel to the east, so that by the fourth century Antioch ranked alongside Rome, Constantinople, Alexandria, and Jerusalem as one of the five most influential Christian centers. The traditional view suggests that after the ascension of Christ the apostle Thomas sent his disciple Thaddeus (one of the seventy) from Antioch to the Syrian city of Edessa, located on the Silk Road—the four-thousand-mile trade route from the Mediterranean world to China. The gospel arrived at Edessa before the end of the first century, followed by the first translation of the New

Testament (Syriac-Aramaic) and the first Christian king (Abgar V) and state (Moffett 1975, 418; Winkler 2003, 12–13). This eastern city in the kingdom of Osrhoene in upper Mesopotamia became a theological and missiological training center for leaders and missionary monks of the Eastern church. From Edessa the gospel journeyed to Persia, where at Arbel another educational facility was started; and from these two cities, the Christian faith spread across Asia. By the end of the second century, Nestorian Christianity extended from Edessa to Afghanistan. In the fourth century, persecution further scattered Eastern Christianity into Arabia and the extremities of the Persian Empire.

Christianity came to India in the first century with the apostle Thomas. The East Syrian Church established connections with the Indian Christians, starting with Thomas of Cana in the fourth century, as a continuous band of missionaries, pilgrims, and traders journeyed from Persia. During this period the churches of India came under Persian authority until Patriarch Timothy I (c. 755) appointed a metropolitan bishop for the Thomas churches of India. The contemporary Mar Thomas churches still use Syriac for their liturgical language.

The Persian Empire had Seleucia-Ctesiphon on the Tigris as its capital and the center of the Church of the East (until c. 775, when it moved to Baghdad). From its strategic position at the western end of the Silk Road, this city was a "natural meeting place of mercantile caravans from Arabia, Central Asia, India, and China" (Atiya 1968, 257). Attracting laypeople and monks, this location became a staging area of Nestorian mission. The fifth century saw Eastern missionaries among the Turks and the Huns of central Asia, and by the sixth century they had ventured to India, Sri Lanka, Burma, Thailand, Vietnam, and Japan. In 544 Empress Komyo of Japan, for example, accepted Christianity through a Nestorian physician and ministered at a leper hospital (Philip 1996, 508, 510).

Timothy I sent over one hundred missionaries to unreached areas during the eighth century. Besides Persia, India, and China, during this time churches were planted in Tibet, Afghanistan, Sri Lanka, and Indonesia (Irvin and Sunquist 2001, 307; Jenkins 2008, 10). Samarquand, the king of the Turks, wrote to Patriarch Timothy requesting that he send a metropolitan to his people. Eighty monks, a metropolitan, and two bishops arrived in Turkestan in 781, and over the course of the next two centuries many of the Tartar people became followers of Christ (Atiya 1968, 260).

The Mongols of the twelfth and thirteenth centuries helped spread Nestorian Christianity into Mongolia, southern Siberia, and once again China. By the time of Marco Polo's expedition (1271–1290), the Church of the East was in Pegu, Burma, Turkestan, Quilon in southern India, and the island of Socotra off the coast of Somalia. Polo spoke of Nestorians along the Silk Road from Baghdad to Tibet and India to China. He reported, for example, that there were Christians at Yachi in Karajang Province, China (present-day Kunming

TABLE 2.2

Timeline of the Growth of Eastern Missions

Date	Events
First century	• The apostle Thomas sends Thaddeus to Edessa in Syria. • The New Testament is first translated in Syrian-Aramaic. • The kingdom of Osrhoene becomes the first Christian nation. • Edessa and Arbel in Persia become mission centers. • Christianity arrives in India with the apostle Thomas.
Second century	• Expansion from Edessa to Afghanistan occurs. • There are "Christians present on the Caspian Sea coast and in Kurdistan, Bactria (a province straddling present-day Afghanistan, Pakistan, and Tajikistan), and the Hindu Kush in the Kushan Empire" (Johnstone 2011, 25).
Third century	• Zoroastrianism becomes the state religion of Persia, and the 250,000 Persian Christians suffer severe persecution. • The Peshitta-Syriac Bible is important for the expansion into Asia. • Syriac (Aramaic) is the medium of Christian teaching and writing. • There are significant numbers of Christians in central Asia, despite persecution.
Fourth century	• Persecution in the Persian Empire scatters Christianity farther into Aden, Arabia, and central Asia. • The Eastern church establishes organizational connections with the churches of India. • The rise of cenobitic monasticism stressing community life becomes a principal means of spreading the gospel in the East.
Fifth century	• Missionaries are among the Turks and the Huns of central Asia. • "By 410, about 25% of the population of present-day Uzbekistan was Christian" (Johnstone 2011, 27).
Sixth century	• Missionaries travel to India, Sri Lanka, Burma, Thailand, Vietnam, and Japan.
Seventh century	• There is further expansion into Persia, India, and China.
Eighth century	• Timothy I sends over one hundred missionaries to unreached areas, including Tibet, Afghanistan, Sri Lanka, and Indonesia. • The center of the Church of the East moves from Seleucia-Ctesiphon to Baghdad (775).
Ninth century	• The Chinese emperor purges the kingdom of foreign religions, and the monks are forced to leave; nationals drift from the faith.
Tenth and eleventh centuries	• The Nestorian presence mostly vanishes from China. • The Kerait tribe in Mongolia is converted through the king's vision.
Twelfth and thirteenth centuries	• Monasteries suffer splits and declines. • The Mongols help spread Nestorian Christianity into Mongolia, southern Siberia, and China. • Marco Polo speaks of Nestorians along the Silk Road from Baghdad and Tibet to India and China.
Thirteenth and fourteenth centuries	• The Church of the East sends missionaries to the Keraits, the Uighurs, the Naimans, and the Merkites in central Asia.
Fifteenth and sixteenth centuries	• Nestorian missionaries travel as far as the Malayan Islands.

in Yunnan Province) (Polo [1958] 1987, 177). During the thirteenth and four-teenth centuries, the Church of the East sent missionaries to the Keraits, the Uighurs, the Naimans, and the Merkites in central Asia, with evidence that churches were also functioning in southern Siberia (Stewart 1961, 201–16). Finally, in the sixteenth century, Nestorian missionaries even traveled as far as the Malayan Islands (Stewart 1928, 51).

Training Schools

One of the key reasons for the growth of Nestorian Christianity was the utilization of training schools. After the Council of Ephesus (431), a number of Eastern bishops rejected the decision to anathematize Nestorius and formed a separate church movement. Its center was a school of theology previously developed in Edessa at the end of the second century under Ibas, a friend of Nestorius. Eventually, teachers at this school who believed in the teachings of Nestorius reluctantly moved to Nisibis under the supervision of Barsumas, a pupil of Ibas. For five hundred years the training institute at Edessa continued as a major center of theological education (Moffett 1982, 248; Winkler 2003, 26).

The Persian curriculum focused on instructing people in biblical under-standing. Guided by its most famous teacher, Narsai of Nisibis in the fifth century, the teaching institutes combined the doctrine of Christ's salvation with a universal mission modeled after Peter, Paul, and Jesus himself. Narsai was one of the most important Syriac poet-theologians, whose poetic approach revealed the deep mysteries of the Christian faith. At the school in Nisibis, Syrian theology emphasized sharing the gospel with all peoples, which made it as much a training ground for missions as one for the priesthood. A person needed to be a missionary to follow in the footsteps of Christ (Philip 1996, 513–14, 518). Followers submitted to austere rules of spiritual discipline and performed manual labor to support their educational outlay. A "son of cov-enant" was a student who took an oath regarding celibacy, monastic life, and community sharing, whereby taking on personal responsibility was considered as necessary as receiving God's grace (Jenkins 2008, 77).

A number of early writings in Edessa show the missional thinking of the training schools. As previously mentioned, tradition proposed that the apostle Thomas sent Thaddeus to share the gospel with the people of Syria. Con-sequently, the story of Thomas's journey to India, the Acts of Thomas, was widely read; it indicates that "Edessa's heroes were missionaries" (Moffett 1975, 419). Even though the work is full of exaggerated miracles, the gospel message is central. The book opens, "And when all the apostles had been for a time in Jerusalem . . . they divided the countries among them, in order that each one of them might preach . . . in the place to which the Lord sent him. And India fell by lot and division to Judas Thomas the apostle" (Klijn 1962, 65).

Another writing that shows the missional theology of the Eastern church is the Odes of Solomon. Written in Syriac at Edessa during the first century, this Christian hymn was influential in Syrian Christology. Portrayed as the Savior of the world, Christ gathered the nations. In Ode 10 Christ proclaims, "I took courage and became strong and captured the world, and it became mine for the glory of the Most High and of God my Father. And the Gentiles who had been dispersed were gathered together" (Charlesworth 1977, 48). Christ saves all people, and the knowledge of the Lord flows like a river. "For there went forth a stream and it became a river great and broad . . . for it spread over the surface of all the earth and it filled everything. Then all the thirsty upon the earth drank. . . . Blessed, therefore, are the ministers of that drink" (Ode 6, Charlesworth 1977, 30).

Methods of Eastern Mission

So far, we have established that the Church of the East provided the earliest missionary thrust beyond the borders of the Roman Empire. From the third to the fourteenth centuries the movement spread across Persia and Mesopotamia to India and central Asia, and then on to China and Japan. Central to this expansion of the gospel were its training schools, with their missional curriculum and passion to follow Christ to the remotest parts of the earth. This chapter will now examine two other important factors in understanding the missional growth of the Eastern church—namely, its monastic system and the missional involvement of laypeople such as traders, physicians, and scholars.

Monastic System

The training schools of Eastern Christianity provided biblical education not only for laity but also for leaders of their monastic tradition. After prescribed study, monks could become teachers in the monasteries or live as anchorites (hermits). Historians now consider monasticism to have first started in Syria and Persia, independent of any Egyptian stimulus. Although Nestorian monasteries were similar to those of Egypt and southern Europe, there were differences with respect to education and mission (Philip 1996, 505).

Nestorian asceticism did not necessarily incorporate seclusion. In the Gospel of Thomas, used in Edessa by AD 120, healing and travel are higher callings for monks than fasting, prayer, and giving money. The Gospel of Thomas quotes Jesus as saying, "The harvest is great, but the laborers are few; many are around the opening but nobody in the well" (Moffett 1987, 483–84). Interwoven with the call of Syrian literature to ascetic self-denial was a call to go, preach, and serve. Many monks, in desiring to imitate Christ and the apostles, became wandering missionaries, traveling from place to place healing the sick, feeding the poor, and preaching the gospel. They were "homeless followers of the homeless Jesus . . . on ceaseless pilgrimage throughout this world," following his example of bringing salvation to people (Moffett 1987, 483).

Beginning in the third century, the Eastern monastic structure grew throughout Persia and beyond, producing hundreds of celibate missionaries who proclaimed the good news of Christ, together with a love of Scripture, education, and mission. In the seventh century, at the height of Nestorian monasticism, self-supporting and self-propagating monasteries were operating near major cities along the trade routes from Persia to central Asia and from India to China. Thomas, bishop of Marga in the first half of the ninth century, wrote *The Book of Governors* about the monastic history of the first three hundred years of Beth Abhe, located northeast of Mosul (a city in present-day northern Iraq). He states that the monastery "sent out men [to] countries which were destitute of all knowledge of divine things and holy doctrines . . . that they might uproot the evil and sow the good, and drive out the darkness of error and make to shine upon them the glorious light of their doctrine" (Moffett 1998, 101).

These monasteries not only were centers of prayer, worship, copying Scripture, and missionary activity but also functioned as schools, inns, and medical facilities. John Stewart describes the monks as "men of great faith, mighty in scriptures, large portions of which they knew by heart, fervent in prayer, gentle and humble in manner, and full of love to God on the one hand, and love to their neighbor and all mankind on the other" (1928, 47).

Lay Participation

The monks of the East were certainly dominant contributors to Christian expansion, yet laypeople also played a significant role in the eastern spread of the gospel. Trained in the monastic schools, many laypeople were familiar with the basic doctrines of the Christian faith. Three prominent issues caused these men and women to leave their homes in Syria and Persia and become missionaries: sporadic persecution, entrepreneurial ventures, and opportunities of scholarship.

Intermittent persecution in the first two centuries forced numbers of believers in the Roman Empire to resettle in Persia, bringing the gospel with them and strengthening the existing churches. When Rome accepted Christianity, the populace of Persia associated Christians with the empire of the West, and many suffered for their beliefs. Others became refugees and traveled to Arabia and central Asia, sharing their faith as itinerant preachers (Aprem 1976, 18). Whether laity or professional, artisan or merchant, these immigrant tentmakers were dispensers of Christ's teaching, and monasteries established between Persia and India became shelters for those fleeing persecution (Moffett 1998, 353).

Business operations were another contributing factor that enabled the Nestorian laity to spread the good news. By 1300 friars and merchants from Persia and Mesopotamia had taken the gospel, without the protection of the military, across central Asia to the Pacific Ocean (Afghanistan, Tajikistan, Tibet, and China). Jerome described them as having "an innate love of commerce," which "makes them overrun the world" (Stewart 1928, 78). Traveling along the Silk Road and via the sea routes to India and Sri Lanka, these traders were the first to take the gospel to the eastern corners of the world. Sidebar 2.1 highlights several examples of this phenomenon.

Coupled with persecution and business enterprise, scholarship likewise played a significant role among laypeople in expanding the Eastern church. Medical knowledge was highly sought after in Asia, so the Nestorian school at Nisibis added medical training to its curriculum and built a hospital (Moffett 1987, 481; Phan 2011, 241). Consequently, Christian physicians served at the courts of the Sassanids in Baghdad and the Mongol Khans, as well as the Chinese and Japanese emperors (Couling 1925, 22; Emhardt and Lamsa 1926, 64–65). Eastern missionaries similarly made a noteworthy contribution to Bible translation. The Syrian Church was the first to have the Bible in its own language, and by the second century there were complete translations of the Bible available in the Akhmimic, Sahidic, and Boharic dialects. The translation of the Scriptures into indigenous languages became an integral contribution as missionaries traveled into the non-Syriac-speaking world.

In central Asia and Mongolia, where there was no written language, Nestorians developed local alphabets based on Syriac, although the spoken and written word was in the local tongue (Moffett 1975, 422–23). Among the Turkish and Mongol tribes, the Persian missionaries served as teachers and scribes; to the Chinese society, they were scholars and translators (Moffett 1982, 250). Fragments of manuscripts discovered in 1908 at a cave in Turfan, China, indicate that these cross-cultural workers translated at least thirty-five pieces of literature into Chinese, including hymns, the Apostles' Creed, and a catechism (Saeki 1916, 65–71). Much earlier, an archaeological discovery revealed additional missiological insights concerning the Church of the East.

Bishop Alopen: First Missionary to China

In 1623 at a building site in Hsi-an Fu, northern China (present-day Xi'an), workers found an eight-foot-high, three-foot-wide black stone tablet weighing nearly two tons. Erected in 781, this homage, titled "A Monument Commemorating the Propagation of the Ta-ch'in [Syrian] Luminous Religion in the Middle Kingdom [China]," listed in Syriac the names of 128 Christian

SIDEBAR 2.1

Examples of Nestorian Lay Missions

In 345 a Nestorian merchant, Thomas of Cana, led a group of four hundred immigrants, including deacons, priests, and a bishop, to Craganore in southwest India.

Two Nestorian laity accompanied a small group of ordained missionaries and an escaping Persian shah in 497, taking refuge with the Hephthalite Huns, a nomadic people in Turkestan, central Asia. The missionaries returned home seven years later, yet the laypeople, John of Resh-aina and Thomas the Tanner, continued their Christian witness, staying with the tribe for twenty-three more years, creating a written system of the indigenous language, teaching literacy, and introducing improved agricultural skills (England 1996, 43).

Kosmos Indikopleustes, a sixth-century Alexandrian trader, was one of the first travelers to south and west Asia. He went to Persia, Arabia, and India and was an early witness of the church in these regions. Between 520 and 525, he traded in India and was surprised to find Nestorian communities whose priests and bishops were ordained in Persia. He explained, "Even in [Sri Lanka], an island in Further India, where the Indian Sea is, there is a church of Christians, with clergy and a body of believers" (Kuriakose 1982, 8).

In 1009 Church of the East traders aided in the conversion of the Keraits in northern Mongolia. Tradition records that the king of the Keraits was lost in a snowstorm while hunting in the mountains and had a vision of a man telling him that he would be safe if he believed in Christ. On returning home, the king sent for Nestorian merchants, who shared the gospel. The ruler then requested the metropolitan to send presbyters and deacons to baptize his people, and some two hundred thousand Keraits converted to Christianity (Stewart 1961, 145–47).

When Marco Polo returned to Italy in 1295 after being at the courts of the Mongol leader Kublai Khan, founder of the Yuan dynasty, he told of Nestorian churches all along the Silk Road and the discovery of Christians in China (Polo [1958] 1987, 51, 57, 81, 91, 168, 274). Aiding in the expansion of Nestorian Christianity were women such as Alaghai Beki, one of the daughters of Genghis Khan, founder of the Mongol Empire, and Sorghaqtani Beki, the mother of Emperor Kublai Khan (Komroff 1930, 102, 119–20; Keevak 2008, 10).

Reflection and Discussion

1. How did Nestorian merchants and traders affect the East with the gospel message?
2. How might the gospel spread today in some areas of secular employment? What are some specific steps through which this could happen?

monks who were in China. In addition, the engraved monument told the story of Alopen, one of the first missionaries to that nation.

The Nestorian Stone, as it is often called, was inscribed with a brief history of the world written by the Persian priest Adam ("one purified by the Luminous religion") and the Chinese author Lu Hsiu-yen; this history covers the existence of God, creation, and the fall of humanity. In describing the incarnation of the Messiah, it speaks of his virgin birth and a life of holiness that ended with his provision of salvation for all humankind. The inscription speaks of the "Lord of the Universe," "One Person of our Trinity," "the Messiah," and a religion "which operates silently through the Holy Spirit." It also tells of how Alopen brought biblical truth (sutras) to the Chinese people, with the emperor ruling gloriously by accepting and promoting these Nestorian doctrines (Huc 1857, 47–49, 51–54).

Alopen, a seventh-century Nestorian bishop, was one of the first Christians to enter China. Commissioned by the Patriarch Yeshuyyab II of Damascus, he arrived in 635 at Chang'an, the eastern terminal of the Silk Road, at a most fortunate time. Ten years earlier the antiforeign rule of Kao-tsu (the first emperor of the T'ang dynasty, who died in 626) would have expelled Alopen from the country. His son, Emperor T'ai-tsung, who had an open policy toward religion, welcomed the Christian, since he believed that to develop a strong united empire he needed to allow the practice of Buddhism, Confucianism, and Taoism as well as Alopen's foreign religion.

In an environment of political uncertainty, the emperor emphasized the importance of education, and since the Nestorian religion was book based, he was interested. At the time, T'ai-tsung's library, of over two hundred thousand volumes, was the largest in the world. Three years after Alopen's arrival the emperor commissioned him, with the help of the palace's resident scholars, to translate the life and teachings of Christ. The adaptation took three years, and on receiving the finished work T'ai-tsung issued an edict of toleration, which gave approval for the propagation of the Christian faith throughout China. The following is an excerpt from the court records:

> In the ninth year of the period Chang-kwan [AD 635], he [Alopen] arrived at Chang'an. The emperor sent his minister, duke Fang Hsuanling, bearing the staff of office, to the western suburb, there to receive the visitor and to conduct him to the palace. The scriptures [Christian literature] were translated in the Library. [His Majesty] questioned him about his system in his own forbidden apartments, became deeply convinced of its correctness and truth, and gave him special orders for its propagation. In the twelfth Chang-kwan year [638], in autumn, in the seventh month, the following proclamation was issued . . . [which] let it have free course throughout the empire. (J. M. L. Young 1984, 214)

In addition, the emperor built a Nestorian monastery, staffed by twenty-one monks, and allowed Bishop Alopen to translate the Bible into the Chinese language. Christian believers remained a small minority, however, even though the emperor believed "the Way" and promoted the faith among his subjects (Baum 2003, 47). "In the north-east of the I-ning Ward there was the Persian temple. In the twelfth year of Chêng-kuan [638], the Emperor T'ai-tsung had it built for A-lo-ssŭ [Alopen], a foreign monk from Ta-Ch'in" (Couling 1925, 53).

Excerpts of the Inscription from the Nestorian Stone

Following are selected excerpts from an inscription on the Nestorian Stone:

> Behold! there is One who is true and firm, who being Uncreated, is the Origin of the origins; who is ever Incomprehensible and Invisible, yet ever mysteriously existing to the last of the lasts; who . . . created all things, and who . . . is the only unoriginated Lord of the Universe. . . .
>
> Dividing the Cross, He determined the 4 cardinal points. Setting in motion the primordial spirit (wind), He produced the two principles of Nature. The dark void was changed, and Heaven and Earth appeared. The sun and the moon revolved, and day and night began. Having designed and fashioned all things, He then created the first man and bestowed on him an excellent disposition, superior to all others, and gave him to have dominion over the Ocean of created things.
>
> The original nature of Man was pure, and void of all selfishness, unstained and unostentatious, his mind was free from inordinate lust and passion. When, however, Satan employed his evil devices on him, Man's pure and stainless (nature) deteriorated; the perfect attainment of goodness on the one hand, and the entire exemption from wickedness on the other became alike impossible for him.
>
> In consequence of this, three hundred and sixty-five different forms (of error) arose in quick succession and left deep furrows behind. They strove to weave nets of the laws wherewith to ensnare the innocent. Some pointing to natural objects pretended they were the right objects to worship; others denied the reality of existence; . . . some sought to call down blessings (happiness or success) by means of prayers and sacrifices; others again boasted of their own goodness, and held their fellows in contempt. (Thus) the intellect and the thoughts of Men fell into hopeless confusion; and their mind and affections began to toil incessantly; but all their travail was in vain. . . . They increased the darkness still more; and losing their path for a long while, they went astray and became unable to return home again.

P. Y. Saeki (1916, 170)

Reflection and Discussion

1. Compare this excerpt with the creation and fall stories in Genesis 1–11. What is missing? What is added?
2. How do you think a Chinese audience would react to this early attempt at contextualization?

Toward Contextualization

In Alopen's writings, the Syrian missionary endeavored to show that Christianity was not subversive to Chinese society and was worthy of serious examination. In particular, his teachings uphold fundamental Confucian ideals such as filial piety and submission to rulers. Alopen's *Jesus: Messiah Sutra* also expounds orthodox Christian theology. Alopen asserts that God is omnipresent and eternal, the creator of all things—a monotheistic description that leaves little room for any other deity. When Adam's original sin passed to all peoples, "the Lord of Heaven" came to earth to suffer for humanity's sin. Jesus was born of a virgin (lines 150–52), was baptized in water (line 167), had a healing ministry (lines 178–81), endured Pilate's unjust trial (lines 190–97), and suffered a Roman crucifixion (lines 198–204). In this work, Alopen claims that as followers of "the Way of Heaven" believers need to obey the Lord Jesus in their lives (lines 90–132).

On the other hand, the Nestorians contextualized the gospel in a way that gave meaning to the central Asian and Chinese people. The inscriptions of the Nestorian Stone, for instance, show that the missionaries used Buddhist, Confucian, and Taoist expressions to communicate their beliefs. The stone tablet had the Persian cross standing in a lotus blossom, a Buddhist symbol, with other images being Buddhist adaptations (Saeki 1916, 165; England 1997, 159, 161). Alopen's *Jesus: Messiah Sutra* speaks of God using the Chinese term for Buddha, while his other writings use Buddhist themes (D. Scott 1985, 92, 95–96). A description of Christian salvation speaks of "the Great Sanctifying transformation, which the Holy Wind of God brings to all, through the life, death, and resurrection of Jesus" (England 1996, 134). John C. England claims that the Nestorian writers employed indigenous imagery and language in addressing the people of central Asia while remaining true to Christian orthodoxy, and he rejects any accusation of syncretism (1997, 165).

Toward Syncretism

Chinese society in the T'ang dynasty saw Buddhism, Confucianism, and Taoism as three religions intertwined as one. Many of the temples had inscriptions on the gates that read "Temple of the Three Religions." This cultural tendency toward syncretism may have influenced Nestorian teachings. In Alopen's *Jesus: Messiah Sutra*, not only is God called "Buddha" but the emperor is elevated to a divine being (line 81), believers are encouraged to worship all devas (supernatural beings more powerful than human beings—line 96), and mention is made of "various Buddhas" (line 99). Furthermore, the *Messiah Sutra* teaches that a person's way of life governs his or her eternal destiny, and how a person lives results in punishment or reward (lines 133–41).

Engraved on the Nestorian Stone is the phrase "The Lord of the Universe," a description used of Buddha, "The Highly Honored of the Universe." It records that Jesus established the eight cardinal virtues, which parallel the eight precepts of Buddhism. As Savior, he paralleled the Buddhist Bodhisattva, who descended from God to save humans. Echoes of Buddhist teachings resound in Jesus's "purging away the dust from human nature and perfecting a character of truth" and "bringing life to light and abolishing death" by opening "three constant gates." Buddhism believes that the open gates to enlightenment come through the eyes, ears, and nose. These metaphors of the Nestorian Stone emphasize that God's light and life is available to believers. T. V. Philip argues that the result of this syncretic portrayal saw many Chinese equating Christianity with Buddhism (1998, 83).

Along these same lines, the Church of the East also clothed its gospel message in Taoist expressions. In the Nestorian writing *A Discourse on Monotheism*, God is referred to as "equal to Pure Emptiness itself" (line 58) and living in a world of nonaction (lines 62–69), both central doctrines of Taoism. This dialogue correspondingly describes one member of the Godhead creating another member of the Godhead (line 42). Further reinforcement of this syncretism came with the 1907 discovery by Mark Aurel Stein of sixth- and eighth-century manuscripts from caves at Turfan and Tun-huang in Kansu province, China. Nine Chinese manuscripts and a number of Syrian writings indicate that Buddhism and Taoism influenced the theology of the Chinese Nestorians. Two of the writings are "more Taoist than Christian," with a number of these texts written by Ching-Ching, a scholarly monk who helped compose the inscription of the Nestorian Stone (Moffett 1998, 301).

Politics and Religion

The previous section showed that the teachings of the Church of the East in China supported orthodox Christian theology together with Confucian ethics and Buddhist and Taoist images and themes. Why did these early Syriac missionaries accommodate these other beliefs to communicate the message of "the Lord of Heaven"? One possible reason involves politics. Expulsion of foreigners from the country occurred if the reigning emperor disapproved and vice versa. In the case of Bishop Alopen, Emperor T'ai-tsung in a milieu of political insecurity welcomed the Christian religion alongside other faiths to develop a strong united kingdom. The emperor gave the church "free course throughout the empire" (J. M. L. Young 1984, 214), yet to show that Christianity was not a dissident element in Chinese society, the Nestorians upheld the fundamental ideals of the competing religions by using their tenets as vehicles of propagation.

In ancient China, the survival of the Christian religion continued to depend on the acceptance or rejection of the supreme ruler. For example, during the reign of Kao-tsung in the latter half of the seventh century, Alopen became "the Spiritual Lord, Protector of the Empire." Following the death of the emperor in 683, the Buddhist empress dowager Wu-tse-t'ien usurped the throne and brought sporadic persecution to the Nestorian Church until her death in 705. Jui-tsung, her third son, the successor of the T'ang dynasty, however, initiated a policy of foreign assistance to build his empire. During his reign, the Uighurs of northwest China, who were Nestorian converts, supported government affairs. Their position and influence encouraged imperial favor toward Christianity and resulted in the growth of the Chinese church for over one hundred years (Moffett 1998, 294, 299).

Then, in 845 Taoist emperor Wu-tsung declared a purge of foreign religions in China, with Buddhism and Christianity specifically targeted. Compliance with this imperial edict resulted in the deportation or forced return to civilian life of some 3,000 Christian monks, nuns, and priests and approximately 260,000 Buddhist religious (Irvin and Sunquist 2001, 322; Baum 2003, 50). In addition, the authorities destroyed Buddhist monasteries and Christian churches and persecuted their religious leaders. The Taoist government viewed the monastic orders as unprofitable to humanity since the monks did not work or serve the people; instead, they lived from donations and accumulated wealth. By dissolving the religious communities, the Taoist government freed assets and land for the benefit of the social order and released the monastics so that they could contribute to the empire (Philip 1998, 84).

Decline of the Church of the East

With the expulsion of foreign Nestorians from China in 845, the indigenous Christians attempted to lead the church. Because they were inadequately trained for such a situation, however, the remaining believers were gradually absorbed into other religions. The Uighurs, for example, shifted their allegiance to Muhammad, believing that the Christian faith was a deviant form of Islam. Those who did not convert to the Muslim faith gradually aligned themselves with sects such as the "Religion of the Medicine of Immortality" (Kin Tan Kiao), whose doctrines were sprinkled with Christian notions (Saeki 1916, 51, 54).

Before the Taoist persecution of Wu-tsung, Buddhism was the national religion of China. After this persecution, it took over four hundred years for it to regain any influence in Chinese society. Chinese Christianity suffered a similar outcome, except that by the end of the tenth century it was extinct. In 987 six Nestorians from the east arrived in China and could not find a Christian remnant (Huc 1857, 90). It appears that history completely forgot the early Nestorian missionaries until nearly nine hundred years later when construction workers at Xi'an discovered the Nestorian Stone of 781. The seventeenth-century Jesuits used this finding to confirm the early presence of Christianity in China and thus silence the Chinese intellectuals who questioned Christian truth due to its lack of history in their country (Couling 1925, 19, 30).

Several other factors affected the vitality of the Church of the East, including church exploitation and the rise of Islam with its succeeding persecution. As early as the eighth century, Nestorian monasteries began to decline in mission effectiveness as indicated by reports of heresy, schisms, insubordination, immorality, and neglect of arable lands. In the next century, during a debate between a Christian and a Muslim before al Ma'mūn (786–833), the caliph of Baghdad, the Christian responded, "Now the monks are no longer really missionaries" (Moffett 1998, 361).

The reintroduction of Nestorian Christianity occurred after a gap of two hundred years. Christianity was extinct in China by the end of the tenth century, when the Mongols conquered northern China and established the Yuan dynasty (1271–1368). Then, in 1206, at the Baljuna Covenant, Genghis Khan, a shamanist, united nine tribal groups (representing Buddhists, Christians, and Muslims) and founded his Mongol Empire, which was tolerant of all religions. Church of the East missionaries of the seventh and eighth centuries had brought Nestorian Christianity to the tribes of central Asia, such as the Kerait, the Naimans, the Merkit, and the Öngüd, and now the new thrust of Christian mission came from within the empire through the wives of the royal court. The sons of Genghis Khan married Christian princesses of the Kerait clan who so influenced the Khan lineage that by the time of the Great Khan Möngke, Genghis's grandson, the main religion of the kingdom was that of the Christian East. One of the major Christian figures among the Mongols was the Kerait princess Sorghaghtani Beki, daughter-in-law of Genghis Khan by his son Tolui and mother of Möngke, Kublai Khan, Hulagu Khan, and Ariq Boke, all of whom married Christian wives. The missionary influence continued with Doquz Khatun, wife of Hulagu and mother of the Ilkhan Abaqa, who in 1265 married Maria Palaiologina, daughter of the Byzantine emperor Michael VIII Palaeologus (Runciman [1951] 1999, 246, 293, 296, 299).

The year 1235 saw a Nestorian church and theological school established in the Mongol capital, Khanbaliq (present-day Beijing), and Mar Yaballaha III, an Öngüd Mongol, became the patriarch of the Nestorian Church from 1281 to 1317 (Grousset 1970, 191). By 1330 the archbishop of Soltania, Iran, estimated that there were over thirty thousand Nestorians in China, while the *History of the Yuan* records that there were seventy-two Nestorian churches in China between 1289 and 1320 (Sunquist, Sing, and Chea 2001, 596–98). Nonetheless, when in 1254 William of Rubruck, a Franciscan monk from Flanders, reached Karakorum, China, he described the Nestorian ministers as drunkards, usurers, polygamists, and so uneducated that they could not read their Syrian texts (Stewart 1961, 200).

In 1271 Marco Polo reported that Kublai Khan requested that the Venetian trader's father, Niccolò, and uncle, Maffeo, ask Pope Gregory X to send one hundred missionaries to China. When the Europeans asked the Mongol emperor why he had not become a Christian, since he believed that it was the superior religion, he replied, "The Christians [Nestorians] who live in these parts are so ignorant that they accomplish nothing and are powerless." Polo

39

also claimed that the Nestorians practiced astrology and magic (Polo [1958] 1987, 119, 158, 298).

Internal corruption in conjunction with Islamic growth accelerated the decline of the Nestorian Church. Always a minority, the Church of the East depended on government favor to live peacefully with the local inhabitants. Following the rise of Islam in the seventh century, Persian Christians were a protected minority under Arabic rule and continued their missionary endeavors, yet they failed to produce indigenous leadership. In Persia, by the ninth century there was a ban on proselytizing Muslims, and followers of Christ suffered economic and social discrimination. Churches were destroyed, and the building of new ones was forbidden. Forced to wear distinguishing clothing, Christians were subject to double taxation and often tortured to force them to recant their faith.

With the Chinese revival of the mid-fourteenth century and the collapse of the Mongol Empire in 1368, the Nestorian Church had disappeared by the fifteenth century. The conquests of Tamerlane, the Mongol leader who from 1370 to his death in 1405 destroyed Christian communities and sacred buildings from western China to Asia Minor and southward into northern India, hastened the deterioration. His military forced involuntary conversions to Islam and propelled the remaining faithful to escape to the Kurdistan Mountains (Atiya 1968, 276). The Nestorian persecution by Tamerlane crippled the churches and stopped their missionary enterprise. By the end of the fourteenth century, the Islamic conquest that began in the seventh century had achieved control of the Middle East, North Africa, and much of central Asia.

Conclusion

In this chapter, we have addressed the theological controversy surrounding Nestorius and shown that the growth of the Church of the East occurred through its training schools, monastic system, and the missional involvement of laypeople such as physicians, scholars, and traders. A survey of the teaching of Alopen, a seventh-century Syrian missionary in China, found that he supported orthodox Christian theology alongside Buddhism, Confucianism, and Taoism. Such syncretism was a matter of political survival, and the reasons for the failure of the Eastern church, even after a Mongol resurgence, were internal corruption and the rise of Islam.

In spite of ethnic and religious persecution and a decline in membership since their height around the fourth century, the Assyrian Church of the East has survived into the twenty-first century. It is one of the churches that today claims continuity with the historical Patriarchate of Seleucia-Ctesiphon—the Church of the East. Due to the unstable political, religious, and economic situation in the church's historical homeland of the Middle East, many church members now reside in Western countries. Today over 323,000 descendants of this Semitic group are located in Armenia, Australia, Denmark, Germany, India, Iran, Lebanon, the Russian Federation, Sweden, and Syria, in addition to the United Kingdom and the United States. The largest expatriate concentration of church members is in the United States, mainly situated in Illinois and California.

In 1980 Mar Dinkha IV, the patriarchate of the Assyrian Church of the East, went into exile and transferred the patriarchal see to Chicago, Illinois. Much of his patriarchate focused on caring for the Assyrian diaspora community and ecumenical attempts to strengthen relations with other churches, since unlike most other churches that trace their origins to antiquity, the modern Assyrian Church of the East was not in communion with any other churches, either Eastern Orthodox, Oriental Orthodox, or Catholic. A major breakthrough came in relations between the Assyrian Church of the East and the Roman Catholic Church in November 1994, when Patriarch Mar Dinkha IV and Pope John Paul II signed a Common Christological Declaration at the Vatican. The statement affirmed that Catholics and Assyrians are "united today in the confession of the same faith in the Son of God" and envisaged broad pastoral cooperation between the two churches, especially in the areas of catechesis and the development of future priests (Powathil 2004, 8–10).

3

Encountering
Celtic Missions

Over the course of eight hundred years, thousands of Celtic women and men traveled across Scotland and throughout continental Europe. They sacrificed their families and homeland to bring the good news of Jesus to peoples ravaged by violence and paganism. With an intense love of God, compassion for the marginalized, and a dependence on the Holy Spirit accompanied by supernatural manifestations, Celtic believers propagated the first de-Romanized Christianity without the sociopolitical burdens of the Greco-Roman world. They helped people absorb the gospel into their social norms and developed a unique type of religion by allowing them to follow Christ without condemning their culture. They also transformed societies by establishing monastic centers of mission and education. By examining the lives of such notable Irish monastics as Patrick and Brigit of Ireland, Columba of Britain, Columban of southern Europe, and the English monk Boniface of Germany, we can unveil their motivation and methods of mission and glean lessons for cross-cultural workers in the twenty-first century.

Celtic Society in Ireland

The Celts were a restless people who probably began a migration around 1200 BC from northern India that ended in Ireland some 850 years later. They swept across Europe in two broad paths: one along northern Africa and up through Spain into Gaul, and the other through Asia Minor. The common linguistic roots of the words "Galatia" in Asia Minor and "Gaul" in France are clues to this migration. There are also similarities in food and music between Ireland and the northern province of Galicia in Spain, dating back to the Celtic migration. The Celts left an archaeological trail behind them showing that Ankara (in present-day Turkey) was once their capital and leaving evidence that they sacked Rome and built salt mines in Austria (Ellis 2003, 61–64; Koch 2005, 885).

After the collapse of the Roman Empire in the fifth century, western Europe was left fragmented and in a state of anarchy. The Celts of Ireland, geographically removed from the chaos, were a tribal people governed in small chiefdom states throughout the rich and fertile rural countryside. There were no cities, so the major political divisions of Ireland began with five kingdoms. By the fifth century, two additional kingdoms had emerged, and all seven centered on Tara, the home of the high king (*Ard Ri*). Within the seven sectors, each governed by a king, were small regions called *tuaths*. Daphne D. C. Pochin Mould claims that there were anywhere from eighty to one hundred of these smaller kingdoms, each ruled by its own king (1953, 18).

Ownership of land was the criterion for leadership in Ireland, and consequently fighting for power over various territories was common. At the beginning of the fifth century, 250,000 to 500,000 Celts shared a common language and culture. Although they had heard the Christian message from a weakened Catholic Church, they remained independent of the Roman Empire and still followed their traditional religions.

Celtic Religion in Ireland

The Celts were intrinsically religious, with a natural mysticism. They believed that the entire world was holy. Three orders of learned men dominated both religion and politics in ancient Irish society: the bairds, the brehons, and the druids. The bairds carried the poetic and historical tradition of the people; the brehons served as lawyers; and the druids provided the knowledge of religion through divination and magic. The druids were their priest figures, who led the clans in human sacrifice, communal decisions, prayers, marriages, and funerals. "Their theology was simple; nature and object or idol-worship, or rather respect for nature's great signposts to God: the sun, the moon, and the stars overhead. . . . The druids were . . . interpreters, prophets, teachers, magicians, lawyers, judges, bards, and poets" (Gallico 1958, 62). The druids acted as stewards to gods who controlled the concerns of human life—such as the god Dagda, whose name means "good for everything" and who aided in scores of daily needs.

As revealed by their cultural storytelling and high degree of spirituality, fifth-century Celtic society relied largely on the experience of the senses rather than intellect. There were, however, organized schools for training druids and bairds in the arts and beliefs of their ancient religion. Some schools demanded as many as twelve years of work. Transmittance of all information was through poetry, song, and story, using symbol and ceremony (McNeill 1974, 73).

Mission *to* Ireland

It is important that we begin our consideration of Celtic missions with a non-Celt. He was the first major figure in missions in Ireland, a man who worked within the worldview of Irish society and "wedded his world to theirs, his faith to their life" (Cahill 1995, 115). After thirty years of missionary activity among the Celtic people, he had not only converted one hundred thousand followers to Christ but also established seven hundred churches and ordained one thousand priests. In all, he converted 40 or more of Ireland's 150 tribes to Christianity. He was the first to move beyond the borders of the Roman Empire to plant churches where no church had ever been previously. Simply put, he was a catalyst for the religious and cultural transformation of the Irish people. His passion for Christ ended slavery, decreased violent crime and intertribal conflict, and introduced literacy to a people who, within a century, irreversibly influenced the shape of European history. His name was Magonus Sucatus Patricius, but we know him as Saint Patrick.

Patrick's Beginnings

Patrick was born into an upper-class British family around AD 385. Although his father, Calpornius, was a deacon, and his grandfather, Potitus, a priest, his family was only nominally Christian. At that time, the Roman Empire (including Britain) had adopted Christianity, which served to unite the

> Was it without God, or according to the flesh, that I came to Ireland? Who compelled me? I am bound in the Spirit not to see any one of my kinsfolk. Is it from me that springs that godly compassion which I exercise towards that nation who once took me captive and made havoc of the menservants and maidservants of my father's house? . . . I am a slave in Christ to a foreign nation for the unspeakable glory of the eternal life which is in Christ Jesus our Lord.
>
> Patrick of Ireland (White 1918, 6)

nations inside the empire. Its citizens, called "Holy Romans," saw outsiders such as the Irish as barbarians (Hamilton 1932, 16–18).

At sixteen years of age, Patrick was abducted from his father's farm in western Britain by Irish raiders, who sold him to the Irish druid Miliuc maccu Boin. Forced to work as a shepherd for the next six years, Patrick drew closer to the God of his childhood during this difficult time (Tobin 1999, 22). God responded to his faith through visions and dreams—forms of communication that became common for Patrick throughout his life. Once, while still enslaved as a shepherd, he received a dream from God to flee to a port (some two hundred miles away) where he could board a ship and escape. In response, he left for Gaul and stayed with the Augustinian monks of Auxerre until he could return to Britain, where he served as a parish priest for over a decade. Then, at forty-two years of age, Patrick received a vision in which God told him to return to Ireland (see Gallagher 2005c, 90–92, 99–101).

LOVE OF GOD

Patrick was a man of both intellectual and spiritual depth. In his autobiography, *Confession*, he describes how he coped with his enslavement—revealing the depth of his intimacy with God.

> After I came to Ireland—every day I had to tend the sheep, and many times a day I prayed—the love of God and his fear came to me more and more, and my faith was strengthened. And my spirit was moved, so that in a single day I would say as many as a hundred prayers, and almost as many in the night, and this even when I was staying in the woods and on the mountain; and I used to get up for prayer before daylight, through snow, through frost, through rain, and I felt no harm, and there was no sloth in me—as I now see, because the Spirit within me was then fervent. (Bieler 1953, 25)

After his escape from Ireland, Patrick traveled with the ship's crew through deserted country for twenty-eight days, desperately lacking food. In his *Confession*, he writes of the captain challenging him, "You say that your God is

SIDEBAR 3.1

Biblical Prayer

The Bible serves as the pattern for a number of Patrick's written prayers. There are more than two hundred references to the Scriptures in his *Confession* alone. When examining his writings, we find very little circular reasoning and relatively few allegorical references made to Scripture, in contrast to the works of his contemporaries, including Athanasius, Jerome, and Ambrose. Nor did he follow the normal theological writing style of his day. His works are completely devoid of rhetoric. Instead, his style is straightforward and his use of the Bible, plain. He did not employ the proper Latin phrases of his day but rather used the Bible to explain his own experiences. He described his life in such a way that his writings were a tapestry sewn with biblical verse (Hanson 1983, 36).

Reflection and Discussion

1. What events in Patrick's life drew him closer to God?
2. How did his faith and prayer manifest in the everyday?

great and all-powerful. Why, then, do you not pray for us?" So Patrick prayed, and God sent a herd of pigs that saved them from starvation.

LOVE OF THE IRISH

First sent by the church in Britain to work with some Catholic churches in southern Ireland, Patrick soon found that he was "exceedingly broken in heart" for the Irish people. For the next thirty years, he served them as a missionary. With an altogether different perspective from that of the educated of his time, Patrick spoke against the suffering of the least of the least, often slaves, and especially women. Many spoke of him as a loving man, "a good and brave man, one of humanity's natural noblemen" (Cahill 1995, 109). Accepted by the Irish, he displayed his love for them through a rebuke in *Letter to the Soldiers of Coroticus*:

> Not that I wished my mouth to utter anything so hard and harsh; but I am forced by the zeal for God; and the truth of Christ has wrung it from me, out of love for my neighbors and sons for whom I gave up my country and parents for my life to the point of death. . . . Is it of my own doing that I have holy mercy on the people who once took me captive and made away with the servants and maids of my father's house? . . . It is not my grace, but God who has given this solicitude into my heart. (Bieler 1953, 41, 43–44)

DEPENDENCE ON THE HOLY SPIRIT

Only the Holy Spirit can illumine one's life experiences by such love. In his *Confession* Patrick acknowledges, "It was because of his indwelling Holy Spirit who hath worked in me until this day." Again, he states, "The Spirit was merciful and guided Patrick back to Ireland," and "I am bound in the

---

And if I ever imitated anything good for the sake of my God whom I love, I pray him to grant to me that I may shed my blood with those strangers and captives for his name's sake, even though I should lack burial itself, or that in most wretched fashion my corpse be divided limb by limb to dogs and wild beasts, or that the fowls of the air eat it.

Patrick of Ireland (White 1918, 32)

Spirit not to see any one of my kinsfolk." It is clear throughout his writings that his spiritual sensitivity guided a number of his actions. Patrick even mentions the power of the Spirit protecting him from the elements, as well as having heard the Holy Spirit praying over him. He also records multiple different visions through which God's Spirit spoke to him (*Confession* 17, 24, 25, 29, in Bieler 1953).

SUPERNATURAL MANIFESTATIONS

Many stories about the supernatural abilities of Patrick are contained in the oldest biography available, *St. Patrick's Life*, written around AD 700 by Muirchu-maccu-Machtheni. The saint himself made no claims to such wonders, so it seems judicious to consider these stories with care since the Celts had a tendency toward exaggerated storytelling. One of the most repeated stories tells of a confrontation between Patrick and the chief druid, Lucat-Mael. In a series of contests between gods, a trial by fire was proposed. Locked in a greenwood hut that was then torched, the druid covered himself with Patrick's cloak. Placed in another greenwood hut that was also torched, Benignus, Patrick's disciple, wore the druid's cloak. Flames consumed the druid and his hut, yet Patrick's cloak remained unsinged. Benignus and his hut stayed unscathed, while Lucat-Mael's cloak burned to ashes (Ghezzi 1996, 164).

Regardless of the stories' veracity, one of the main reasons that Christianity spread and took root among the Celts was the people's belief in these narratives of power encounters and miracles (Smyth 2008). For instance, Gall, fishing on Lake Constance, overheard a conversation between the mountain demons and those of the lake, complaining about the servant of Christ who had come (McNeill 1974, 169). Celtic Christianity established itself in Ireland and Europe through this mixture of history and legend.

Patrick's Mission Strategy

Although Patrick did not introduce Christianity to Ireland, he established its prominence, shaped its direction, and empowered its influence. Traveling widely throughout the country, he founded numerous monasteries, ordained priests, and cared for the poor. He converted, baptized, and brought into church membership thousands of Irish. Before Patrick, the Celts were a warlike people. Yet Ireland was one of the few countries into which Christianity came without bloodshed—a testimony to the loving humility of God's missionary. His life was one of self-denial of family, physical security, and material wealth. He was a sincere and humble person, a man of integrity, not highly educated, penitential and ascetic, always in prayer, and passionate in his love of God, the Bible, and the Irish.

Furthermore, Patrick and his followers helped the Irish people incorporate the gospel into their social norms and develop a unique type of Christianity by absorbing their pre-Christian heritage. Here was the first de-Romanized Christianity in human history, a religion without the sociopolitical encumbrances of the Greco-Roman world, a Christianity that absolutely absorbed the Irish culture. The Irish became Christians without denouncing their culture. How did Patrick and his monks achieve this welding of a Christian worldview with that of Celtic society?

MONASTIC COMMUNITIES

Irish society in the Middle Ages consisted of small rural tribal groups, which were not conducive to the Roman ecclesiastical city model. Patrick adopted a new system and melded Catholic and Irish traditions by founding monastic communities throughout Ireland; they would later grow into centers of population. These Irish monasteries differed from Roman monasticism, in which the prime aim of the monk was to save his own soul through ascetic practices and isolation. The Irish monasteries, in contrast, were centers of community and missionary outreach.

Patrick and his followers would first ask permission of the local chieftain to form a monastic community. They would then evangelize the region by preaching and teaching. After conversion of the people came literacy teaching, followed by theological training. Thousands came to Christ and monasteries established to propagate the faith. The Celtic warrior culture was friendly to the ascetic, community lifestyle presented by the Irish monastic tradition. Invited into the fellowship of the monastery, the inhabitants experienced the life of faith, and then in time, as they discovered a belief in Christ, they committed themselves to the monastic life. This was in contrast to the Roman model of presenting the gospel message, giving people an opportunity to decide, and then asking them to join the community (Hunter 2000, 53).

In these communities, the Celts did not separate the sacred and the secular but were holistic in their ordered life of prayer, work, worship, and study. As men and women came and dedicated themselves to service, they would build a "church, refectory, kitchen, guesthouse, library, and workshops" (McNeill 1974, 75). Within these monastic seminaries, which brought in scholars from Britain and the rest of Europe, the students were educated in reading and writing Latin (McNeill 1974, 120). Some Irish monasteries, such as Clonard (begun in 520), were well known for their scholarship and attracted students from as far away as Asia (Zimmer 1969, 45–46). Many of the communities had extensive manuscript collections of classical literature, writings of the early church fathers, and the New Testament. The transcription of these works was of prime importance to the monasteries from the sixth century onward (Ryan 1972, 380).

IDENTIFICATION WITH THE DRUIDS

The early Celtic monks followed a leadership style that was more druid than Roman. They dressed and cut their hair after the manner of the local priests and, some say, so identified with the druidic culture that their magical beliefs "endured through Patrick's apparent compromise with paganism" (R. Tucker 2004, 39). Yet Patrick's writings record a strong renunciation of traditional religious practices. In the *Canons*, which describe the ecclesiastical orders given by Patrick and two of his bishops, Auxilius and Iserninus, we read, "A Christian who believes that there is such a thing as a vampire, that is to say, a witch, is to be anathematized" (Bieler 1953, 52). Again, in Patrick's *Confession* he states: "Hence, how did it come to pass in Ireland that those who never had a knowledge of God, but until now always worshipped idols and things impure, have now been made a people of the Lord, and are called sons of God, that the sons and daughters of the kings of the Irish are seen to be monks and virgins of Christ?" (Bieler 1953, 34). The social hierarchy and recognition of spiritual leadership already present facilitated a transition to Christianity. In Patrick's identification with the Irish culture, he used the role of the druids for the sake of the gospel.

Use of Triads

Patrick certainly used the Celtic fascination with triads to share Christ. Celtic art and poetry often reflected this threeness. Even their gods assembled in threes (Hunter 2000, 81). Patrick used this obsession as an opportunity to connect the gospel story. For example, in Patrick's poem "The Lorica," he enveloped the prayer with the phrase, "I arise today, through the mighty strength, the invocation of the Trinity, through the belief in the Threeness, through confession of the Oneness towards the Creator" (Bieler 1953, 69, 71) (see sidebar 3.2). This trinitarian emphasis is apparent in Patrick's *Confession* and endures to this day embedded in Celtic theology (Power 2006). "In light, therefore, of our faith in the Trinity I must make this choice, regardless of danger I must make known the gift of God and everlasting consolation, without fear and frankly I must spread everywhere the name of God so that after my decease I may leave a bequest to my brethren and sons whom I have baptized in the Lord—so many thousands of people" (Bieler 1953, 25).

Fear of the Spirit World

In contrast to the Celts' poetic fascination with triads was their fearsomeness in battle. Described as a tall, fair-haired people, they brought terror to their enemies by charging naked into battle, howling like demons as if they were being transformed into "killing machines." After they decapitated prisoners of war, the heads became footballs in victory celebrations (Cahill 1995, 82–85).

Yet for all this warlike fury, they feared their gods and the spirits that populated nature. To guard themselves from the demonic forces, the Celts used druid incantations. Each day included multiple acts that needed a magic spell for protection, and they lived in fear of breaking one of these taboos. One demonstration of this trepidation was in the appeasement of the spirit

"The Lorica" by Saint Patrick

I bind unto myself today
The strong Name of the Trinity,
By invocation of the same
The Three in One and One in Three.
I bind this today to me forever
By power of faith, Christ's incarnation;
His baptism in Jordan river,
His death on Cross for my salvation;
His bursting from the spiced tomb,
His riding up the heavenly way,
His coming at the day of doom
I bind unto myself today.
I bind unto myself the power
Of the great love of cherubim;
The sweet "Well done" in judgment
    hour,
The service of the seraphim,
Confessors' faith, Apostles' word,
The Patriarchs' prayers, the prophets'
    scrolls,
All good deeds done unto the Lord
And purity of virgin souls.
I bind unto myself today
The virtues of the star lit heaven,
The glorious sun's life giving ray,
The whiteness of the moon at even,
The flashing of the lightning free,
The whirling wind's tempestuous
    shocks,
The stable earth, the deep salt sea
Around the old eternal rocks.
I bind unto myself today
The power of God to hold and lead,
His eye to watch, His might to stay,
His ear to hearken to my need.
The wisdom of my God to teach,
His hand to guide, His shield to ward;
The word of God to give me speech,
His heavenly host to be my guard.
Against the demon snares of sin,
The vice that gives temptation force,
The natural lusts that war within,

The hostile men that mar my course;
Or few or many, far or nigh,
In every place and in all hours,
Against their fierce hostility
I bind to me these holy powers.
Against all Satan's spells and whiles,
Against false words of heresy,
Against the knowledge that defiles,
Against the heart's idolatry,
Against the wizard's evil craft,
Against the death wound and the
    burning,
The choking wave, the poisoned
    shaft,
Protect me, Christ, till Thy returning.
Christ be with me, Christ within me,
Christ behind me, Christ before me,
Christ beside me, Christ to win me,
Christ to comfort and restore me.
Christ beneath me, Christ above me,
Christ in quiet, Christ in danger,
Christ in hearts of all that love me,
Christ in mouth of friend and
    stranger.
I bind unto myself the Name,
The strong Name of the Trinity,
By invocation of the same,
The Three in One and One in Three.
By Whom all nature hath creation,
Eternal Father, Spirit, Word:
Praise to the Lord of my salvation,
Salvation is of Christ the Lord.

Joyce (1998, 71–72)

Reflection and Discussion

1. What do you learn from "The Lorica" about Patrick's theology of Christ?
2. How would you describe Patrick's understanding of the role of God in this world?
3. In what ways does this poem reflect your Christian life? How does this poem not represent your form of Christianity?

world through human sacrifices—such as prisoners of war to the gods of war and infants to the harvest gods.

Patrick emphasized that Jesus was the ultimate sacrifice once for all time, and that there was no longer any need for human sacrifice. In the "Hymn on Saint Patrick," written by his contemporary Secundinus, Patrick uses the ritual of communion to highlight this truth.

> Boldly he proclaims the name of the Lord to the heathens,
> And gives them eternal grace in the bath of salvation.
> He prays to God daily for their sins,
> For them he offers sacrifices, worthy in the eyes of God.
>   (Bieler 1953, 63)

However, in his ministry there was also an understanding of the wonder of nature. Patrick emphasized how God, the Creator and controller of all life, was loving and faithful. He defused the magical fear of nature and the spirit realm by focusing on the adventure and beauty of creation obtainable in Christ through prayer and contemplation.

FEAR OF END TIMES

Fear of the spirit world was only one terror within Celtic society. There was also a dread of the cataclysmic wrath to come. Hence, Patrick's writings emphasize the end times. This suggests that he saw his mission to Ireland, considered at that time as the extremity of the civilized world, as the fulfillment of Matthew 24:14, "And this gospel of the kingdom will be preached in the whole world as a testimony to all nations, and then the end will come." Patrick's message of salvation from the judgment to come brought hope to a people familiar with such druidic concerns and played an important role in his message of freedom in Christ (Carey 1996, 51).

Celtic Women in Missions

Another way the early Irish monks worked within the worldview of Celtic society was their use of women in missions. Many women entered the religious life in the early Celtic church. Kathleen Hughes and Ann Hamlin have observed that a calendar written around AD 800 had "scores of them to be remembered" (1977, 8). Despite this early growth, very few religious houses for women survived. There are two possible explanations for this phenomenon. First, ancient Irish laws restricted a woman's ownership of land to her lifetime. Upon death, a woman's land passed back to the family. Only land received as a gift or earned through service could remain for the woman to give to people outside the family. This resulted in small groups of religious women, endowed by inheritances, who disbanded upon the benefactress's death. Second, many families objected to the vow of chastity of the religious life. In Patrick's *Confession* we read:

> Among others, a blessed Irishwoman of noble birth, beautiful, full-grown, whom I had baptized, came to us after some days for a particular reason: she told us that she had received a message from a messenger of God, and he admonished her to be a virgin of Christ and draw near to God. Thanks be to God, on the sixth day after this she most laudable and eagerly chose what all virgins of Christ do. Not that their fathers agree with them; no—they often suffer persecution and undeserved reproaches from their parents; and yet their number is increasing. How many have been reborn there so as to be of our kind, I do not know. (*Confession* 41 and 42, in Bieler 1953)

Brigit of Kildare

Due to the coming of Christianity, Brigit was one of the first women allocated a more active role in the spiritual life of Ireland. This fifth-century Irish saint, also known as Mary of the Gael, was a woman of gentleness, generosity, and humor, her heart completely devoted to God. Her traditional prayer was, "We implore thee, by the memory of Thy Cross's hallowed and most bitter anguish, make us fear Thee, make us love Thee, O Christ." Numerous stories of miracles surround her, some of which speak of the resurrection of a stillborn baby, the healing of the blind and lepers, and the healing of a nurse by turning water from a well into ale. To this day, pilgrims still travel to wells blessed by her, in hopes of finding healing.

At eighteen (around 468), Brigit committed her life to God, took the vow of chastity before Bishop MacCaille, and joined seven other nuns to establish a community at Cill-Dara (Kildare). This was the first religious community for women in Ireland, governed by the leading Irish bishop, the abbess, and the abbot. The king of Leinster donated land that had belonged to an ancient pagan sanctuary to build the convent. Brigit founded the convent not only as a center of scholarship and hospitality but also as a school of art that produced metalwork and illumination. Eventually, the religious community grew to include men as well as women. Kildare became a symbol of hospitality, especially for the poor, and "though sometimes plundered by the Danes and others, [it] subsisted until the Reformation, having during many centuries been acknowledged head of numerous convents in every part of Ireland" (Kelly 1857, 66).

During this period, the slave women of Ireland had no rights. Scores of Christian women worked for pagan nobility and were consequently restricted in the practices of their faith. Brigit desired to provide opportunities for these women to live in Christian community together. Traveling by chariot extensively throughout Ireland, she preached the gospel, performed miracles of healing, and established monasteries for women who had taken vows. Those who joined the religious communities tended the garden, minded the cattle,

Reflection on Brigit

When Brigit was eighteen she began a consecrated life, settling with seven other like-minded young women near Croghan Hill to devote themselves to God's service. She had a generous and compassionate nature. With a deep love for the Irish people, and her devotion to prayer and doing the work of an evangelist, she bridged the gap between Christian and pagan cultures. In light of the material on Brigit, note the following short prayer:

We implore Thee, by the memory of Thy Cross's hallowed and most bitter anguish, make us fear Thee, make us love Thee, O Christ. Amen.

Prayer of St. Brigit (http://oodegr
.co/english/biographies/arxaioi
/Bridget_Kildare.htm)

Reflection and Discussion

1. What inspired Brigit to begin her work among the poor?
2. How did she demonstrate her dedication to serving the least?
3. How are the actions of modern-day Christian leaders used as examples of life and faith?

and did household duties, much like their tasks as slaves—only now they had human dignity and freedom in serving Christ (Blácam 1942, 58). This repressive situation provided the motivation for Brigit to found a number of nunneries within Ireland. At the time of Brigit's death, there were thirteen thousand nuns under her authority as the mother abbess (Curtayne 1954, 70).

As head abbess, Brigit led by example. Serving beggar and lord alike, she would wash their feet and give them all she could. She believed in ministering to the whole person by "being as Christ" to them. Her ministerial philosophy was shaped by her belief that Christ was present in the stranger, especially the poor, and that each act of charity offered to people was done to God (Curtayne 1954, 86). When she received word of someone's illness, she would sit with the person until his or her recovery or death. She cared for the destitute, providing them with food and clothing. Therefore, "she remained in her people's memory as a spiritual leader of great humility and power, a woman of joy and deep compassion, a friend to those with broken hearts and broken bodies" (Mulhern 2000, 31).

As an administrator, Brigit did much to continue the initial work of Patrick by organizing the Irish church. She was influential in a number of policy-making conferences with bishops and abbots and became the leader of a network of nunneries. Religious women, holding ecclesiastic authority, became valuable neutral negotiators between the kings of Ireland and the bishops. There was a need to bring Christianity to both titled and commoner; religious women were effective communicators of God's love through their practical service and preaching. Brigit was undeniably one such influential woman, and she received much veneration. Among the poor (former slaves and monks) in the central plains from Dublin to Galway, there was a large population of Brigit followers. Her message of compassion and hospitality to the powerless eventually spread from Ireland to Scotland, Wales, Britain, France, and Italy (J. E. C. Williams 1973, 39).

Mission *from* Ireland: Pilgrims of God

Patrick's motivation for mission became the foundation for future Irish monks and nuns, such as Brigit, not only to spread the gospel in Ireland but also to leave their homeland and travel to distant lands. Patrick's burning love for Christ required that no sacrifice be too great to endure. He yearned to win all peoples to the kingdom of God, and many Irish monks had this same passion to carry the gospel beyond Ireland to Europe. The Celtic monks wandered for God, sharing the good news of Christ wherever the Spirit guided them.

Thus Irish monasticism was responsible for not only Ireland following Christ but also England, Scotland, and parts of Europe such as Germany, Holland, and Italy. Separated from their family and country, these Irish missionaries gave themselves to God in ascetic discipline, bringing Christianity back to central Europe. Living an ascetic lifestyle to find fulfillment in self-mortification motivated many of them. Dying to self by leaving their country allowed them to achieve a greater degree of obedience to the divine call to accumulate treasure in heaven.

Ireland, this small nation that had only recently accepted Christianity, became the new mission center, flooding Europe with God's word. Monks left their Irish monastic schools and planted monasteries outside their homeland to propagate their faith and learning. Seeking favor with local rulers, they cooperated with secular authorities wherever possible, even while keeping their freedom of opinion. They spread not only the gospel but also the creative arts, languages, history, and the sciences, relaying the foundations of Western culture after it had been largely destroyed by the invasions of the northern tribes. These missionaries, called the *peregrini*, were pilgrims walking on God's journey. They frequently moved about in groups of twelve plus a leader, each wearing a white robe with his head shaved from ear to ear; many had parts of their bodies tattooed, including the eyelids. Most of them traveled only by walking and carried the essentials of a water bottle, a staff, and a gospel writing. Seeing physical toil as a spiritual discipline, they desired to connect with the people they were trying to evangelize (McCarthy 2002, 3).

Columba's Mission to Britain

Columba became one of the first notable Irish missionaries to preach outside his country. He had established forty monasteries in Ireland, including those at Derry, Durrow, and Kells, before he led a team of twelve monks (in 563) to the

SIDEBAR 3.4

"Song of Trust"

Columba, while hiding from pursuers who intended to kill him (Hale 1976, 62), wrote this "Song of Trust":

> God's elect are safe,
> Even on the battlefront.
> No man can kill me before my day
> Even in close combat;
> No one can save me,
> When the hour of death comes.
> No magic can tell my fate,
> No bird on twig or crooked oak.
> The voice of birds I do not
>   idolize,
> Nor luck, nor love of son or wife.
> My druid is Christ, the Son of
>   God.

> Inspire us with Thy charity, O Lord,
> That our loving quest for
>   Thee may occupy our inmost
>   thought;
> That Thy love may take complete
>   possession of our being,
> And divine charity so fashion our
>   senses,
> That we may know not how to
>   love anything else but Thee.
>   Columba (Dubois 1963, 48)

Reflection and Discussion

1. Whom do you think Columba's audience might have been?
2. In what ways does Columba's composition reflect the Psalms?

island of Iona off the west coast of Scotland. Iona became a major missionary training center, resulting in the establishment of twenty-three monasteries in Scotland and thirty-eight in England by the time of Columba's death in 597 (Zimmer 1969, 19–20).

At Iona, Columba established a monastery to evangelize non-Christians. Picts inhabited the northwest and north of Scotland, Scots the southwest, and Britons the southeast. Columba's focus was the Picts, the Celtic inhabitants of northern Scotland. According to Reginald B. Hale, Columba and his disciples spent the first few years on Iona in quiet witness to their faith, and then miracles began to occur. For example, he showed the chief druid, Broichan, God's power over the weather. As Columba was leaving one region by ship, the druid caused a storm that the saint passed through without harm. Soon after this demonstration of the superiority of the Christian faith, the druid became fatally ill, and the king asked for Columba's help. The monk gave instructions for Broichan to drink a certain type of water and to free his stolen concubine. Broichan followed Columba's instructions and overcame his illness. This encounter helped motivate the Picts of northern Scotland to accept the gospel (Hale 1976, 89, 92–93).

Columba's Mission Strategy

The Picts believed in a world where demons inhabited every part of creation from trees to the weather. The physical environment was capable of holding the presence of evil and causing harm to people. Columba combated this fear of the spirit world by creating songs to replace incantations (sidebar 3.4). The poems encouraged the people to trust in God's protection as the Irish missionaries blessed the sacred wells and land, bringing them under the authority of Christ. "Traversing corries and forest wild, down winding glen, up mountain side, the fair white Mary still uphold me, the shepherd Jesus be my guide" (Hale 1976, 86) is one such work.

Anecdotes of Columba's encounters with spiritual forces abound in popular folklore. On one occasion, Columba washed and drank from a demonized well and, unharmed, declared the majesty of Christ. He blessed a herd of cows, and they increased from five to over one hundred; he gave an angry farmer a sack of barley, and it unseasonably produced a bountiful crop; he brought sweetness to bitter fruit; he cleared snake-infested lands. In all these efforts, Columba demonstrated that the Creator God cared about the well-being of people.

Columban's Mission to Europe

Another remarkable Irish monk who wandered beyond his homeland was Columban (also known as Columbanus, the Latinized form of *Columbán*, meaning "the white dove"). He was in his forties when, accompanied by twelve followers, he traveled to Europe to share the gospel. With his twelve Irish monks, Columban traveled to Brittany around 590 and preached to the inhabitants with such success that the local king, Sigebert, gave them land to build a monastery. The monastery at Luxeuil became a center of learning for Christianity and Western culture. There, scholars and artisans worked side by side. For Columban, the teaching of the Christian worldview included the secular sciences as well as theological subjects. Unfortunately, the king became offended by his preaching against immorality and forced the Irish monk to leave Luxeuil as well as the other monasteries Columban had founded at Burgundy and Fontaines in Gaul.

Columban's Mission Strategy

In spite of Columban's discharge, monks from Luxeuil established another fifty-three monasteries and influenced the establishment of two hundred more. Jonas, Columban's biographer, claims that 620 French missionaries left Luxeuil in one generation alone, scattering monasteries throughout France, Switzerland, and Italy. Columban also inspired the French missionary Ansgar, who witnessed to ninth-century Denmark and Sweden and saw many come to Christ.

Columban traveled farther into the Continent, where he established a monastery that dominated the European intellectual scene for nearly a thousand

Portrait of Ansgar (801–865)

"Born in northwestern France, Ansgar became an early French missionary to Sweden. Known for his humility, courage, and initiative, he displayed serious Christian commitment at an early age. His missionary zeal came most likely from the Corbey monastery, which found its spiritual roots in Columban and Irish monasticism. Later he helped found a monastery in Westphalia (New Corbey) for newly converted Saxons; there he held the office of preacher and first master.

"Ansgar's first mission was to Denmark (c. 823) accompanying recently baptized King Harald to establish converts in Schleswig. In 829 Swedish officials arrived at the court of Louis the Pious (successor to Charlemagne) asking for missionaries. Ansgar responded, leaving Denmark. He and his companions endured hardships and piracy, and finally arrived in Birka on the island of Bjorko in Lake Malar, west of present-day Stockholm.

"Among Ansgar's first acquaintances were Christian slaves, brought to Sweden from Viking raids. These and others (including members of the royal court) became Ansgar's first congregation. He then left Sweden to assume the archbishopric of Hamburg. Delayed nearly twenty years by pagan reactions to Christianity, he eventually went back to Sweden. Upon returning, he reorganized the congregation, which later dissolved when commerce moved from Birka to Uppsala. Ansgar's legacy is that of a forerunner. Although his efforts yielded little lasting fruit, some 250 years later Christianity eventually came to Sweden with the destruction of the pagan temple at Uppsala."

S. J. Pierson (2000, 65–66)

Reflection and Discussion

1. What forms of Christian service to others did Ansgar engage in during his life?
2. In what ways may your personal history be leading you to specific forms of missionary service?
3. How do you balance service with other dimensions of Christian life?

years. Bobbio, in northern Italy, became a center of education with an international reputation due to the work of the Irish monks. Here, scholars devoted themselves to studying, writing, and teaching in both the spiritual and the natural domains. They studied doctrine and creeds and memorized Scripture, while learning the fundamentals of Latin grammar. In addition, these monks considered rhetoric, classical writings (such as Virgil, Homer, and Ambrose), mathematics, music, and astronomy. The monastery became an academy of theologians, historians, artists, poets, and musicians—living in ascetic devotion to God.

The abbey of Saint Gall (Saint Gallen in present-day Switzerland), the sister monastery to Bobbio, is described by J. M. Clark as being full of both scholarly and cultural activities. Established by Gall, a disciple of Columban, this monastery had become the intellectual center of Germany by 610 and remained so for three hundred years.

Books were written, copied, and illuminated in the scriptorium. Musical works were composed, and the theory of music was taught. The monks observed the sun and the stars to calculate the dates of church festivals. All the sciences known in that day were diligently studied, nor were the more practical arts and handicrafts neglected: painting, architecture, sculpture in wood, stone, metal, and ivory, weaving, spinning, and agriculture were all objects of assiduous attention. (Clark 1926, 91)

It was not, however, the intellectual aroma of Gall that brought people to Christ but the fragrance of Christ, who manifested himself through the miracles that occurred there. The monastery was having little success with the disinterested locals of Annegray in the Vosges Mountains of Gaul until a man arrived who gave the monks food and requested prayer for his sick wife. Upon returning home, the man found his wife healed. Based on this one miracle, many people brought their sick to Annegray for healing, and many more converted to Christianity. In fact, so many young men requested instruction to become monks that the leaders opened two more monasteries in the region. By the end of the seventh century, ninety-four monasteries in Europe had sprung into existence—directly attributed to the Irish invasion.

Columba and Columban, as well as those who followed them, were only the first of thousands of Irish missionaries who came to educate Europe. By the beginning of the seventh century, Irish monks were the preeminent scholars and educators on the Continent. From Britain to Germany to northern Italy, they trained the leaders, developed the educational systems, and spread the Christian message to faraway places such as Iceland, Greenland, and Russia. The monks even had extensive influence in the courts of the Carolingian and Merovingian Empires. The majority of church leaders were Irish monks, including a number of bishops in Austria, France, and Gaul. Slowly but steadily, the monks and their students assumed dominion over the scholarship of Europe, as well as the leadership structure of the Roman Catholic Church. As the Irish *peregrini* grew in number, so grew their fame. Many were inspired to missions in their wake, including Boniface, the renowned English missionary.

Boniface's Mission to Germany

A century before Boniface, Irish missionaries had spread Christianity throughout Europe by instituting monasteries in Belgium, France, Holland, Italy, and northern Germany. Geographically isolated, lacking communication networks, and deficient in knowledge of the local languages, the Irish missionaries struggled in their evangelistic endeavors. Boniface played a key role in evangelizing eighth-century Germany. He used his organizational skills to initiate linguistic and evangelistic communication systems between the trained men and women and the Christian communities.

Boniface, whose birth name was Winfrid, was born to a noble Anglo-Saxon family in southern England around AD 675. When he was five years old, a group of Benedictine monks visited his family; two years later, his parents placed him in their monastery at Exeter. There he learned to study, work, preach, and care for the sick and the needy. The monks then moved him to a monastery at Nutshell, where Abbot Winbert helped him increase his understanding of the Bible, history, grammar, rhetoric, and poetry. Though Boniface was given the task of running the monastic school, his truest desire was to preach the gospel in his ancestors' land of Saxony (Sladden 1980, 19).

His first missionary journey was not to Saxony, however, but to Germany. Boniface traveled there with a group of men—training them along the way. The first venture was unsuccessful due to political issues. Therefore, he undertook a second mission trip the next year and traveled to Rome with another group of disciples. In that year, 719, Pope Gregory II gave Boniface authority to preach the gospel in Germany and down the Rhine River. After Boniface proved his knowledge of Scripture, morals, and purity over an eight-month period, the pope declared:

> We now place your humble and devout work upon a secure basis and decree that you go forth to preach the Word of God to those people who are still bound by the shackles of paganism. You are to teach them the service of the kingdom of God by persuading them to accept the truth in the name of Christ, the Lord our God. You are to instill into their minds the teaching of the Old and New Testaments, doing this in a spirit of love and moderation, and with arguments suited to their understanding. (Talbot 1954, 68)

From Rome, Boniface and his followers went through Innsbruck and Salzburg and on to Fulda, where he labored for three years under the direction of a fellow Anglo-Saxon missionary, Willibrord of Holland. From there, the two men worked together in itinerant preaching, destroying pagan temples, and training priests and teachers. After returning to Rome in 722, Boniface became a bishop, and the pope changed his name from Winfrid. There, he received new missionary direction to "preach the word of faith, so that by his preaching he may teach them the way of eternal life" (Hillgarth [1969] 1986, 171), bringing salvation and the teachings of the Catholic faith to the people.

Boniface's Mission Strategy

After returning from Rome, Boniface discovered that the people in Germany were worshiping both the pagan gods and the Christian God. To change the allegiance of the people, Boniface decided to cut down a sacred oak tree that had been the worship site for Thor, the god of thunder. As Boniface struck the first blow, people stood in fear, expecting the god to act in vengeance at

Portrait of Willibrord of Holland

Willibrord (658–739), first Archbishop of Utrecht, was born in Northumbria in England and studied in France and Ireland. In 690 he was sent by the Anglo-Saxon Christians with twelve companions to preach to the pagans of Frisia (present-day Friesland in the Netherlands).

Willibrord was a pupil of Wilfrid . . . at the monastic center Wilfrid established at Ripon. He later became one of the outstanding Northumbrian missionaries to the Continent, specifically following up work Wilfrid had begun in Frisia and laying important groundwork for Boniface, an Anglo-Saxon scholar-missionary. Beyond Boniface were Willibald and Alcuin, other Northumbrians, who contributed in eventually bringing northern Europe into the sway of the Latin-Roman Christian tradition.

Earlier missionaries like Columban had been ethnically Celtic and stood for a crusading emphasis on morality and spirituality. They were ethnically and linguistically more remote than this later Anglo-Saxon group, which combined both Celtic and Roman (Gregorian) missionary zeal and, most of all, had impeccable Roman credentials to influence the people at the top.

Thus, this series of sturdy Anglo-Saxon missionaries reached their distant cousins, spread Celtic zeal and Roman order, championed the Benedictine rather than the more austere Irish monastic model, and furnished a crucial biblical and spiritual foundation for the later role of Charlemagne in the expanding Frankish kingdom and the entire Carolingian Renaissance.

Ralph Winter (2000, 1017)

Reflection and Discussion

1. What was the significance of education and mentoring to the English missionaries of the seventh century?
2. What were the important contributions made by the Northumbrian missionaries to continental Europe?

this violation. The tree fell, and the god of thunder was silent. The people were awed, and the Christian faith won the day. On the site of the victory, the people built a monastery in the present-day town of Fritzlar in northern Hesse. Through Boniface's preaching, great numbers converted to Christianity.

Boniface went on to establish a number of monasteries in Germany, which trained monks for mission. Modeled after the English monasteries, the core foci included study, manual labor, preaching, and the care of the sick and the needy. Boniface placed particular importance on copying books for use by his disciples. In a letter to Abbess Eadburga, he thanked her for sending him some books. "To my dearest sister, who has brought light and consolation to an exile in Germany by sending him gifts of spiritual books. For no man can shed light on these gloomy lurking places of the German people and take heed of the snares that beset his path unless he have the Word of God as a lamp to guide his feet and a light to shine on his way" (Talbot 1954, 88).

While ministering in Europe, Boniface kept in touch with a number of nuns in England, including his cousin, Leoba. To Leoba he would write about his struggles and sorrows. When thirty English nuns came to Germany to help in the mission, she became abbess of the convent at Tauberbischofsheim and a counselor in the courts of Charlemagne.

When Boniface was about sixty years of age, he began to focus his missionary endeavors on the Bavarian region. The monks Rupert, Emmeram, and Cobinian had already started churches and monasteries in the area, but they lacked organization. Boniface reorganized the region into four sections and created a centralized administration. Between AD 740 and 778, nearly one hundred monasteries began in Bavaria (G. W. Greenway 1955, 43). In 742 Boniface began the monastery at Fulda, in the southeast of Thuringia, which served as the mother monastery for the Bavarian region. Boniface described the situation: "There I have placed a group of monks living under the rule of St. Benedict who are building a monastery. They are men of ascetic habits, who abstain from meat, wine, and spirits, keeping of servants, but are content with the labor of their own hands" (Talbot 1954, 136).

By 779 more than four hundred monks lived at the Fulda monastery—all of whom were under the direct supervision of the pope, rather than the local bishop. Boniface had requested this arrangement to safeguard the center against political interference. From Fulda, at the age of seventy, Boniface and fifty other monks launched a mission to the Saxon region. Finally, his dream of preaching in the land of his ancestors came to fruition. As a result, thousands were converted. He had hoped to die a martyr's death in this land, and he did—at the hands of an angry mob in 754.

Conclusion

This chapter witnesses to Patrick's burning love of Christ. The love of God in his heart meant that no sacrifice was too great to endure. He yearned to win all to Christ, and many Irish and English missionaries such as Brigit of Kildare, Columba of Iona, Columban of Luxeuil and Bobbio, and Boniface of Germany carried this same passion to spread the gospel throughout Britain and Europe. They left their own monastic schools and planted monasteries to propagate faith and learning. Dying to self by leaving their own countries allowed them to reach a greater degree of personal obedience to the divine call. Monks and nuns alike healed the sick, cared for the poor, and ministered to the needy and the outcast alongside their academic pursuits and mission travel.

Recognized as the best scholars and educators on the Continent, Irish monks had extensive influence for more than five hundred years following Patrick's work. As the Celtic Christian faith spread throughout Ireland, Britain, and Europe, it exhibited community, literacy, and spiritual awakening. As Irish

Christians traveled to Europe in the midst of opposition and threats, they brought with them these staples of a faith-based life. Furthermore, they were able to work within the worldview of particular societies and help the people incorporate the gospel into a unique type of Christianity without destroying the culture. Education and literacy, healing and servanthood, and devotion and perseverance to God's call combined to form a powerful Christian heritage.

4

Encountering
Orthodox Missions

From the Celts of Europe's western tip to the east coast of Japan, God was at work in his church during the Middle Ages. In particular, the Orthodox Church produced lasting fruit throughout this time that became evident in the vibrant lives of its missionaries. From harsh living conditions to fighting against spiritual warfare to resistance of the local government, these missionaries faced extraordinary challenges. Two brothers from Thessalonica translated the Scriptures into indigenous languages and suffered imprisonment because the religious leaders believed that only Hebrew, Greek, and Latin were appropriate to share the Christian faith. A well-educated monk confronted the animistic beliefs of a savage far-northern tribe by destroying their false gods and initiating a power encounter. A layperson lived for over four decades in a rudimentary hut eating only turnips, radishes, potatoes, and fish to serve the people of Alaska for Christ.

In this chapter, we expound Orthodox mission strategy by examining four key case studies: Cyril and Methodius of Moravia, Stephen of Perm, Herman of Alaska, and Nicholas Kasatkin of Japan. We unfold the success and methodology of these missionaries as well as offer a brief critique of Orthodox history. Before addressing the details, we must first gain historical perspective through an overview of the two main eras of Orthodox missions: the Byzantine and the Russian.

Orthodox Byzantine Missions

In the one thousand years of its existence, the Byzantine Empire was concerned with propagating the Christian faith to the nonbelievers within its boundaries as well as neighboring tribes. There were two periods of intense theological and mission fervor: from the fourth to the sixth centuries and during the ninth and eleventh centuries. In the first period, mission-oriented bishops such as John Chrysostom and monks such as Hilarion, Euthymios, and Sabbas evangelized the peoples on the borders of the empire: the Goths, the Huns, the Iberians, and the peoples of the Caucasus and Colchis, as well as parts of north and east Africa (Nubia). The conversion of the Slavs by such missionaries as Cyril and Methodius forms the second period.

Byzantine missions exercised certain basic principles. The prime desire was to establish an authentic local eucharistic community, and to this end, much missionary effort focused on translating the Bible, liturgy, and patristic writings into the vernacular and building aesthetically pleasing churches that would broadcast that God had come to live with humanity. This "incarnational approach has long been a hallmark of the Orthodox Church. Missionaries from Byzantium consistently employed this method in their efforts to bring the message of salvation to the heathen tribes. Whereas the Roman Catholic Church insisted on the universal use of Latin as the language of worship, Orthodox theology dictated the use of the living language of the people" (Stamoolis 1986, 62).

Greek missionaries also endeavored to fuse their Christian worldview (Byzantine liturgy and tradition) with the people's culture, which helped to preserve the national dignity and identity—spiritually, socially, and politically—of the converted tribes. Further, Orthodox Byzantium witness concerned itself with decentralizing the church and emphasizing local parishes while involving the full continuum of believers in missionary work—from bishops and monks to nobility, merchants, soldiers, and slaves. Due to the inclusive nature of the Byzantium mission method, the gospel spread rapidly during this era. The success of this mission and its methods of evangelizing became influential to the next era, that of Orthodox Russian missions.

Orthodox Russian Missions

The Russian missionary era has four major periods. The first phase extended from the baptism of Prince Vladimir Svyatoslavich and the people of Kiev to the Mongol conquest (988–1240). It concentrated on the conversion of the northern Slavic tribes—mainly through bishops, priests, and monks such as Sava in Serbia at the turn of the thirteenth century.

The building of isolated monasteries marks the second period: from the invasion of the Mongols to the end of the fifteenth century. These monastic institutions became cultural and missionary centers, which produced exemplary missionaries such as Stephen of Perm. Between the fourteenth and the sixteenth centuries, the Mongol Empire divided into a multiplicity of smaller states, eventually becoming separate ethnic groups such as the Crimean and Volga Tatars, the Uzbek, the Kazakh, and other groups. The Mongols (Tatars) became predominantly Muslim during this era. The Russians during this time began to centralize and demonstrate their military might, culminating in the sixteenth century with the reign of Ivan IV (the Terrible), who overthrew the Tatar regions of Kazan, Astrakhan, and Siberia. This conquest was partly in response to the fall of Orthodox Constantinople (1453) to the Ottoman Turks. Muscovite Russia was responsible for the leadership of Orthodox Christendom, with the czar viewed as divinely appointed to preserve the nation and the Orthodox Christian faith. Ivan, when rebuked for his oppression of the poor, instigated conflict with Philip, the metropolitan of Moscow (1568). This resulted in the murder of the church leader six months later.

The third era—the sixteenth to the eighteenth century—saw thousands of Muslims from the regions of Kazan and Astrakhan enter the Orthodox Church. A burgeoning of churches and monasteries in Siberia followed. In 1555 Bishop Gouri and his colleague Germanus went to the conquered Kazan and in nine years saw thousands of Tatars convert to Christianity (Smirnoff 1903, 11). It was difficult work for these pioneering missionaries, considering the region's cultural diversity (numerous languages, lifestyles, and beliefs); the vast, barren topography; the nomadic life of the Tatars; the harsh climate; the enmity of an oppressed people; and the psychological battles with loneliness and depression.

Peter the Great continued the harassment of the church when in 1700, on the death of the patriarch of Moscow, he dissolved the ecclesiastical courts and twenty-one years later declared himself supreme ruler of both church and state. During the reigns of the eighteenth-century czars Elizabeth and Catherine II, the state increased its supremacy over the church, coercing the church to become only an agent of "civilization" to the Russian colonies (Johnstone et al. 2007, 66–67).

In spite of the continued hostility of the government toward the mission of the church, there were notable missionaries such as Trifon of Novgorod (sixteenth century), who brought Christ to the Lapps, and Filotei of Tobolsk (eighteenth century). Yet Eugene Smirnoff recognizes that stagnation pervaded from 1756 to 1824, with missionaries having little organizational structure or desire to learn indigenous languages, and converts often persuaded by money or tax exemptions rather than real faith (1903, 15).

The fourth period ranged from the middle of the nineteenth century to the Russian Revolution in 1917. This epoch bore such fruitful missionaries as Macarius Gloukharev in the rugged Altai Mountains; Nicholas Ilminski, a theologian and linguist who introduced new methods of translation and mission among the Tatars of central Asia (Johnstone et al. 2007, 68–69); Brother Herman and Innocent Veniaminov, who labored among the people of the Aleutian Islands in Alaska; the merchant Sidenikoff among the Samoyeds; Innocent Figourovsky in China; Paul Ivanovsky in Korea; and Nicholas Kasatkin in Japan (see Gallagher 2012a–f and h).

Inspired by the principles of Byzantine Orthodox missions, Russian missionaries created alphabets for unwritten languages, translated the Bible, and celebrated the liturgy in the vernacular. The cross-cultural workers selected and trained indigenous clergy for pastoral care and evangelism as quickly as possible. The local culture was valued together with educational, agricultural, and artistic development. "Continuing the Orthodox tradition, they gave importance to liturgical life, to the harmonious architecture of the churches, to the beauty of worship, and to its social consequences. Certain fundamental principles, only now being put into use by western missions, were always the undoubted base of the Orthodox missionary efforts" (Yannoulatos 1989, 68). The remainder of this chapter will explore the following Orthodox missionaries and their work in appreciation of the characteristics of Orthodox missionary methodology: Cyril and Methodius of Moravia, Stephen of Perm, Herman of Alaska, and Nicholas Kasatkin of Japan.

Cyril and Methodius of Moravia

Theophylact, the archbishop of Ohrid in Bulgaria (now Macedonia) in the eleventh century, wrote these words about the subjects of our first case study:

> The saints [Cyril and Methodius] . . . felt an inconsolable sorrow over the fact that the lamp of the Scriptures had not been lit in the dark region of the Bulgarians. . . . They looked to the Paraclete . . . [and] entreated him . . . that letters be invented suited to the rudeness of the Bulgarian language, and that they be enabled to translate the Holy Scriptures into the language of the people. And they obtained their desire by devoting themselves to persistent fasting and continuous prayer. (*The Life of St. Clement of Ohrid* in S. Scott 1989, 78–79)

Historical Background

The ninth century was a time of social and political transition in the Byzantine Empire. The Arab threat from the eastern frontier disappeared; pressured by migrating eastern tribes, the Slavs and Bulgars migrated to the Balkan Peninsula in search of new land and natural resources; restoration of Orthodoxy followed the defeat of iconoclasm; and there was a revival of secular education and missionary resurgence. The empire also enjoyed a time of relative peace with the Arab Muslim forces, which had twice (674–678 and 717–718) besieged and nearly conquered Constantinople (Obolensky 1971, 69, 71).

Iconoclasm was the movement of certain bishops of Asia Minor against the customary Orthodox veneration of icons. Byzantine emperor Leo II (717–741) briefly forbade icons and ordered their destruction. Yet at the Seventh Ecumenical Council of 787 icons became an acceptable means to honor Christ's incarnation: "We declare that one may render to icons the veneration of honor, not true worship of our faith, which is due only to the divine nature." John of Damascus explained the issue: "In former times, God, who is without form or body, could never be depicted. But now [that] God is seen in the flesh conversing with men, I make an image of the God whom I see. I do not worship matter; I worship the Creator of matter who became matter for my sake" (Nassif 1997, 23).

With the official end of iconoclasm in 843, the Byzantine Church and society were free to engage in an intellectual revival sponsored by Emperor Theophilus (829–842). He restored the university in Constantinople and gathered scholars such as Leo the mathematician; Photius, a renowned theologian and philosopher; and Constantine (Cyril), the future missionary to the Slavs. The reorganization of the university played a central role not only in education but also in the ecclesial and cultural expansion of the empire. It became the training ground for a new generation of diplomats, leaders, and missionaries equipped in theology, international politics, and ethnography, and influencing both the educated and the uneducated (Obolensky 1971, 72–73).

Also during the ninth century, growing political tensions between the patriarchate in Constantinople and the papacy in Rome came to a head. The Orthodox Church rejected a Western change to the Nicene Creed, disagreeing on the Spirit's "double procession" from the Father "and the Son" (known as the *filioque* clause). The Church of Rome was also exerting its papal authority over Constantinople and claiming apostolic succession. Nor did it help that both realms were competing in the "civilization" of the Byzantine neighbors such as the Slavs and Bulgars (Cunningham 2002, 35–36). The Slavic people in the central and southern regions of the Balkan Peninsula began to succumb to the control of Constantinople, while in the north they gravitated toward either the Bulgarian regime or the new political entities of Serbia and Croatia. Economic and cultural revival accompanied the political situation, with domestic and foreign trade increasing as Slavic immigrants returned from military service to repopulate farming communities.

Against this backdrop, the brothers Cyril and Methodius grew up in a prominent family in multicultural Thessalonica, at the northern border of Greece. Each received a privileged education and distinguished himself in both academics and politics, Cyril serving as an ambassador, librarian of the Hagia Sophia, and professor of philosophy at the Imperial Academy of Constantinople, and Methodius serving as governor of a Slavic province.

Missions to the Slavs

In the early ninth century, Irish and German missionaries worked for fifty years among the Slavs north of the Balkans, using Latin to explain Christianity and conduct the liturgy. Prince Rastislav of Moravia (present-day Czech

Republic and Slovakia), however, disliking the encroachment of the Western church and desiring to escape the allied Bulgarians and Franks (Germans), sought ties with the Byzantine Empire. In 862 he appealed to Emperor Michael III to send missionaries to Greater Moravia:

> Many Christian teachers have reached us from Italy, from Greece, and from Germany, who instruct us in different ways. Our people have renounced paganism and observe the Christian law, but we do not have a teacher to explain to us the true Christian faith in our own language in order that other nations even, seeing this, may imitate us. Send us therefore, Master, such a bishop and teacher, because from you emanates always, to all sides, the good law. (Dvornik 1970, 73)

After attacking Bulgaria and halting the advance of Latin Christianity, the Byzantine emperor commissioned Cyril and Methodius to fulfill the Moravian royal request. The brothers already spoke the Macedonian dialect of the Slavs around Thessalonica, and since these people had no written language, they desired to develop an alphabet so that the Slavic people might "be counted among the great nations which praise God in their own language" (Dvornik 1970, 103).

Theology of Bible Translation

The brothers supposed, with the Eastern church, that at Pentecost the apostles received the gift of speaking and understanding foreign languages. This meant that people of all cultures were able to hear and understand the gospel in their own language. Likewise, the fulfillment of the Great Commission of Matthew 28 was to come about via the various languages of the people groups. All languages are equal in God's sight, and through speech, he connects with the human soul, a person's most intimate possession (Obolensky 1963, 12). Thus Cyril poetically wrote of an illiterate person who cannot see because there is no light. Then when the person receives letters and language, he is able to understand the law of God and his promises.

> As without light, there can be no joy
> For while the eye sees all of God's creation,
> Still what is seen without light lacks beauty
> So it is with the soul lacking letters,
> And ignorant even of God's law
> The law that reveals God's paradise.
> Obolensky 1986, 114–15

In translating the Bible for the Slavic people, Cyril developed a unique writing system. The Glagolitic alphabet was adopted from Hebrew, Greek, and oriental characters and expressed all the sounds of the Slavic language. Eventually the Cyrillic alphabet evolved, which became the basis for several Eastern European languages and is to the present day the liturgical idiom of the Russian and the Slavonic Orthodox Churches.

Missions in Moravia

The brothers from Thessalonica traveled in 863 to Rastislav's court in Moravia, where Cyril began translating the Byzantine liturgy into Old Church Slavonic (still the exclusive language of the Croatian Orthodox Church).

Because God's Word was spreading, the evil envier from time immemorial, the thrice-accursed Devil, was unable to bear this good and entered his vessels. And he began to rouse many, saying to them: "God is not glorified by this. For if this were pleasing unto Him, could he not have ordained that they should glorify God from the beginning, writing their language in their own script? But He chose only three tongues, Hebrew, Greek and Latin, which were appropriate for rendering glory unto God."

Methodius (Kantor and White 1976, 45)

Within a few years, he had finished the entire ecclesiastical office: Vespers, Compline, Matins, the Hours, and the Divine Liturgy. He then began to translate the four Gospels, which became the first Bible translation in a Western vernacular. Using the biblical Greek to maintain the original meaning with accuracy, he often rendered the text with dynamic equivalence so that it was culturally appropriate.

As they competed for the religious loyalty of the Slavs, the Bavarian Catholic missionaries opposed Cyril's and Methodius's emphases on the vernacular and insisted that only Hebrew, Greek, and Latin were suitable for sharing the Christian faith with the Moravian people. This "heresy of the three languages" evidently arose from the trilingual inscription on the cross of Christ (John 19:19–20). Cyril and Methodius also recited the Nicene Creed in its original form, while the papal missionaries inserted the *filioque*. Furthermore, the Macedonian brothers trained the Slavic clergy to read and write the new script. Their goal was not conversion but rather the instruction of the Slavic leaders. They mentored and ordained the most promising converts as soon as possible, affecting both the native population and the selfhood of the local church (Stamoolis 1986, 22). Methodius alone taught over two hundred indigenous priests (Veronis 1994, 54).

"In their apostolic labours throughout the Balkans, the holy brothers were slandered by certain Germanic bishops who opposed the use of the vernacular in the church services" (Greek Orthodox Archdiocese of America 2013). To resolve the language conflict, the brothers journeyed to Rome in 867 and 868 (this action shows that they still regarded East and West as united in one church). While they were there, they "presented their Slavonic translations to Pope Adrian II, who received them with love and full approval" (Greek Orthodox Archdiocese of America 2013), affirming the Slavonic language for the mass and translation. Placing the work in Moravia directly under the papacy, the pope ordained Methodius and three of the Slavic priests and invited them to celebrate Mass in the Church of Saint Peter using the Slavic liturgy (Lacko 1963, 132–33). After Cyril died in Rome in 869, Methodius returned to the Slavic people, appointed as bishop of Moravia by Adrian II, and continued his translation and education work.

The German bishops, however, ignored the papal endorsement and hampered Methodius's ministry. In 870 King Louis the German and Prince Sviatopolk imprisoned Methodius in Swabia for two and a half years, until Pope John VIII released him and consecrated him archbishop of Pannonia and Moravia, removed from the authority of the Franks (Germans). Conflicts continued, and, following Methodius's death in 885, the Germans imprisoned, enslaved, and expelled his followers from Moravia in an attempt to counter his influence. Led by Methodius's successor, Clement, his followers carried on their work of evangelism and translation among the Poles, the Bulgars, the Bohemians, and other Slavic peoples, even after Pope Stephen V had outlawed the Slavic liturgy. Although the effects of the Slavonic mission remained for over two hundred years, Latin Christianity eventually replaced the Byzantine missions (Ware 1993, 75). James J. Stamoolis concludes, "From the missiological point of view, it can be argued that the Western Church missed an opportunity to gain the allegiance of the Slavic peoples. . . . Even more important was the loss of a significant input to the mission practice of the Roman Church. It [was] only in the mid-twentieth century that Roman Catholicism [was] experimenting with an idea presented to the papal court in the ninth century, that of liturgy and Scripture in the vernacular" (1980, 44–45).

Missions Results

While immediate events in Moravia seemed to counter the brothers' mission efforts, their ministry became the foundation of Slavic culture in eastern and southeastern Europe and of the missionary advancement of Eastern Orthodoxy for future centuries. "The body of literature in Slavonic, including the Bible and the liturgy, played an important role in the Christianization of Russia. The influence of Sts. Cyril and Methodius far outlasted their own efforts.

It is no wonder that they are commemorated in the liturgy as 'equals to the Apostles, evangelizers of the Slavonians'" (Stamoolis 1986, 21).

Followers of Cyril and Methodius continued their evangelistic work of spreading Slavic culture and preaching the gospel in the vernacular in Bulgaria, Serbia, and Russia. The development of Old Church Slavonic was significant in preventing the absorption of these nations by the Greeks in the south and the Latin Franks in the west. It enabled them to create their own literature and national identity. Until the 1920s, Old Church Slavonic remained the official language of the Bulgarian Orthodox Church for liturgy and Bible readings.

The ability to read and hear the Scriptures in their own language opened a new spiritual world to the Slavic people, as they were able to deepen their relationship with God. Their faith became more understandable and real. Through the invention of the unique Slavic alphabet, the translation of liturgy and Scripture into the vernacular, and the performance of the Mass in the local language, Cyril and Methodius recognized the cultural dignity of the Slavic people (Olson and Torrence 2001, 7).

A written language also enabled the translation and promotion of Greek patristic literature and Byzantine secular learning among the Slavic people. Literacy gave the people the ability to interact with the rest of the world. Connection with the nations around them made them cultural equals, as they better understood their national contribution and identity. "By acquiring the Scriptures and the liturgy in their own language, the Slavs entered a privileged and chosen society within which every nation has its own peculiar gifts and every people its legitimate calling" (Obolensky 1986, 110).

Stephen of Perm

Another successful and dynamic missionary of the Russian Orthodox Church is Stephen of Perm. Stephen's mission was to the Zyrian people of Perm, a nomadic Finnish tribe in the Ural Mountains, northwest of Siberia. Stamoolis claims that "the most outstanding example of an Orthodox missionary in the Middle Ages is Saint Stephen of Perm (1340–1396). Well educated, he left the quiet of the monastery to bring the gospel to the savage Zyrians of the northern forest" (1986, 26). The Zyrians were animistic in faith, believing in the spirits of trees, wind, and earth, and they had no written language. By the time of Stephen's death, he had left a deep impression on this people, through his holistic aid and the lasting impact of an indigenous church.

The Early Years

Stephen grew up in the Orthodox city of Veliki Ustyug on the Dvina River in northwestern Siberia during the Mongol period. A gifted language-learner,

Stephen entered Saint Gregory of Nazianzus's monastery (famous for its Hellenistic library) in Rostov on the Black Sea at age twenty-five. He aspired to study New Testament Greek and patristics under Hieroschemamonk Parthenios and become a missionary to Siberia. In the monastery he not only deepened his understanding of Scripture and became an authority on the Greek language but also developed a spiritual life of prayer and fasting. Thirteen years later

SIDEBAR 4.1

Portrait of Stephen of Perm

As Stephen traveled through Zyrian villages, he became alarmed and saddened at the people's veneration of idols such as a "sacred birch tree. Immense in its thickness and height, the birch tree grew on an elevated spot. The Zyrians gathered there and brought wild animals [and expensive furs] for sacrifice. St Stephen's cell was not far from the birch tree. He prayed and set fire to the tree in order to end the superstition." The destruction of this false god occurred in the midst of his teaching against such idols. The saint said to the people, "Your idol could not defend itself against me, a weak man. Are all your other gods so powerless?" Stephen launched a campaign to destroy such objects by fire, which annoyed the local people. The Zyrians believed that it was wrong to start a fight, although finishing a fight was culturally acceptable. Since Stephen was aggressive only toward the gods, then it was up to the gods to defend themselves, without the intervention of the people, against whom Stephen did not fight. The people complained that "he has a bad habit of not starting the fighting" (Hatch 1980, 16; Stephens 1991, 9–10).

Finally, Pam, the head shaman, confronted Stephen as recorded by Epiphanius:

"By what power do you do this?" Pam demanded. "You have insulted our gods. . . . Those who do this in my court deserve the sentence of death,

which you will experience at my hand. I shall not fail to work miracles for your destruction and let loose many gods to kill you." Stephen replied, "The gods of whom you are boasting have perished. . . . The word of Moses has been fulfilled: gods who did not create heaven and earth shall perish." (Fedotov 1966, 238)

Pam challenged Stephen to walk through a burning hut and swim under the ice of the frozen Vychegda River to prove that Christ was all-powerful. Though each was supposed to participate in the trial, Pam pulled back in fear from each challenge. Although Stephen only proved his willingness to pass through fire and water, it was enough to win the admiration of the people and convince them of Christ's power over local gods. Pam, driven from the region as a coward, resettled in a village beyond the Ural Mountains. Other Zyrian believers then continued the destruction of local shrines, building churches like Saint Michael's in Perm on the former sacred sites (Hatch 1980, 19).

Reflection and Discussion

1. Is this aggressive missional approach helpful, or does it do more harm than good?
2. What are the positives and the negatives of Stephen's methods?

he left the monastery and traveled north toward the White Sea to live among the Finno-Ugric Zyrian tribes between the Pechora and Vychegda Rivers at Ust-Vim. "The servant of God felt a great pity that men created and honored by God were enslaved by His enemy" (Fedotov 1966, 233).

Stephen settled in the Zyrian village of Kotlas among the Komi people, and his message and simple lifestyle attracted many people normally suspicious of Russians. Inspired by the example of Cyril and Methodius, and having learned the local language as a child in a nearby Russian town, he began to translate the gospel for the Zyrians. For an alphabet, Stephen adapted cultural runes found on clothing, beads, embroidery, carvings, and instruments in daily use, rather than adapting the Greek or newly created Cyrillic letters (Struve 1963, 32). Stephen believed that the Zyrian people had the right to worship in their language and in doing so preserve their cultural heritage and identity as a people. Soon he carried with him Zyrian translations, including the daily and weekly order of service, the Psalter, the Gospels, and parts of the Old Testament together with several sermons, which he used as he lived among the Zyrians (Hatch 1980, 18; Stephens 1991, 8–9). Dominant in his teaching were the themes of human sin, God's forgiveness through Christ, and the kingdom of heaven.

Many politically motivated leaders in the Russian Orthodox Church opposed Stephen's translations, claiming that only the Hebrew, Greek, Latin, and Slavic languages were holy. Stephen wanted to disassociate the Christian message from Russian colonialism, and he finally received the blessing and protection of Metropolitan Gerasim of Moscow for his new alphabet and translation. As Zyrians learned to read and write in their own language, using the Bible as a primer, several became followers of Christ (Veronis 1994, 59).

The Indigenous Church in Mission

Converts to Christianity received baptism, as well as encouragement to read the Bible and pray in their language. By 1379 Stephen was training his better students to assist him as leaders in the newly formed church. A church of some one thousand people soon formed along the banks of the Vychegda River in Perm. Within five years, the work became so successful that Stephen traveled to Moscow and asked the Holy Synod to appoint a bishop. In 1383 Stephen was consecrated as the first bishop of Perm and returned to another fourteen years of translating the Scriptures and liturgy into Komi, organizing the church into parishes and monasteries, and teaching adults and children in their native language. He ordained some as deacons, priests, readers, and chanters, teaching them to write Permian books (Hatch 1980, 19; Stephens 1991, 9).

Stephen built churches, monasteries, and schools to train local leaders and used his icon paintings to express his internal relationship with God through

SIDEBAR 4.2

The Lamentation of Perm on Stephen's death (1396)

"Had we lost but gold and silver, these we could regain. But we shall never find another like you. . . . We had only one bishop; he was our lawmaker, our baptizer, our apostle, our preacher, our confessor. We have lost our patron and intercessor. He prayed to God for the salvation of our souls, and presented our complaints to the prince; he worked to obtain benefits for us and was concerned for our welfare; he was our zealous protector before the boyars and the superiors; many a time did he deliver us from violence, heavy labor, and the titun's bribery, alleviating our taxes. Even the Novgorod river pirates, those robbers, heeded his instructions and did not rob us. We used to be jeered at by our heathen neighbours . . . but he rid us also of them."

Hatch (1980, 24)

an external art form. He built and decorated the first church in Ust-Vim, the main Zyrian settlement, and filled it with elaborate works of art as if adorning a bride for her groom. Stephen stated that people came "not yet for prayer, but desiring to see the beauty of the church," and left believing that "great is the God of the Christians" (Stephens 1991, 9).

Beyond striving to demonstrate God's truth in the Holy Scriptures, this Russian missionary also served the people by importing food during times of famine and speaking against unjust government taxation. He used money given by wealthy Christians to build an almshouse for the poor of Perm and travelers in the area. On behalf of the Zyrians, Stephen successfully protested to the government authorities against the unjust Muscovite taxation system and the invasion of the Novgorod river pirates.

Stephen sought to train indigenous leadership and mentored trainee priests as he moved from village to village. Some of his leaders even crossed the Ural Mountains and found the descendants of Pam, the exiled sorcerer and his followers. In 1713 the 3,500 descendants of these people finally became followers of Christ because of Zyrian evangelism (Bolshakoff 1943, 32). Yet, Stephen's work toward a national Zyrian church ended abruptly when, shortly after his death, the Zyrian language he promoted was replaced by Russian following political and military invasions. His dying words were, "Live godly lives, read the Scriptures, and obey the Church" (Veronis 2000, 907).

Herman of Alaska

Almost four hundred years later, and on the other side of the world from Perm, another young Orthodox monk distinguished himself by his service to another remote and exploited people group. Herman brought the Orthodox faith to North America using many of the same missionary methods as Stephen did in northern Russia.

Pathways to Missions

Born in 1756 to a merchant family in Serpukhov, near Moscow, at sixteen Herman entered the Troitsko Sergiev Monastery in Zagorsk, close to Saint Petersburg, Russia. After six years at the hermitage, he transferred to the more rigorous Valaam Monastery, on an island in Lake Ladoga, Finland. There he developed the ascetic practices of the desert fathers as revived by Ukrainian monk Paisii Velichkovskii. Here Herman was taught that "the head of a monastery must be knowledgeable in the Holy Scriptures, just, capable of teaching his pupils, full of truly unhypocritical love for all, meek, humble, patient, and free from anger, and all other passions—greed, vainglory, glut-

---

A sin for a person loving God is nothing more than an arrow fired by an enemy during battle. The true Christian is a warrior, fighting his way through hosts of unseen foes to his place in Heaven. For, in the words of the Apostle, Our Kingdom is in Heaven, and about the warrior he says: our battle is not with flesh and blood, but with ideas and authorities.

Herman of Alaska (Oleksa 1987, 44)

---

tony, etc." (Oleksa 1987, 14). While at Valaam, Herman devoted himself to a life of simplicity, prayer, worship, and service.

Gregorii Shelikov, the Russian co-owner of the principal fur company in North America (in present-day Alaska), the Russian American Company, visited the Valaam Monastery and requested that missionaries be sent to the inhabitants of the Aleutian Islands. Earlier attempts to evangelize the Aleutian Islands often involved traders baptizing the locals to enhance their monopoly on the fur trade (Starr 1987, 127). Upon this appeal by Shelikov, Empress Catherine II in 1794 commissioned ten Orthodox monks to the island of Kodiak to minister to the native people. These missionaries, though under the authority of the Valaam Monastery, received a salary from the company. This was a normal practice of imperial Russia since monasteries obtained state funding. This policy provided an incentive to the clerics to serve in such inhospitable regions (B. Smith 1980, 9).

Herman and the other nine Valaam monks and hieromonks were the first overseas mission team of the Russian Orthodox Church. They arrived on the island of Kodiak at Three Saints Bay after traveling "for almost a whole year." The missionary group met resistance from the Russians "because he [Herman] revealed many of them as leading a life of drunkenness, as being revoltingly sinful and oppressing the Aleuts" (Letter from Simeon Ianovskii to Igumen Damascene of Valaam, November 22, 1865, quoted in Oleksa 1987, 48). Despite the opposition, within the first few years of the Orthodox mission the monks baptized over seven thousand people and performed marriage ceremonies for more than two thousand Russian and Aleutian couples (Barkey 1988, 19). As Archimandrite Ioasaph observed in a letter, "There is such a press of people waiting to be baptized or married, or who have come to learn God's laws, and we do not want to grieve or hurt anyone by refusing them. In addition the Russians here have various needs of their own: they wish to talk to us and for us to hear confessions" (Letter to Igumen Nazarii, May 1795, in Oleksa 1987, 39).

Servant Leadership

By 1799 nine of the original monks had either perished or simply moved back to Russia, leaving Herman alone to minister to the Aleuts. Because Herman repeatedly declined priestly ordination on the grounds of his unworthiness, his lay status restricted his work so that he could not administer the sacraments to converts. Yet for forty-three years Herman faithfully served the Alaskan natives. He taught the basics of the Christian faith, improved agricultural practices, and offered instruction in simple crafts to the native Koniag Eskimos and the transplanted Aleuts. He lived in the manner of an Eastern ascetic monk on the small wooded Spruce Island, northeast of Kodiak, showing little regard for his own welfare and the greatest concern for the welfare of others. Herman's spiritual life was the product of traditional Orthodox monasticism, with daily study of the Scriptures and the Holy Fathers of the church, strict observance of the liturgical order, no ownership of private property, and consistent care for the sick, weak, and elderly.

On Spruce Island, Herman established New Valaam, which included a schoolhouse, a guesthouse, a wooden chapel, and a small, hand-dug cave where Herman lived during his first summer in Alaska. By winter's onset the Russian American Company had built him a small cell (his living quarters), where he would live the rest of his life. Living simply, he grew only turnips, radishes, and potatoes, since nothing else would ripen in the short growing season, using kelp as a fertilizer; he also preserved mushrooms and fish for winter. Herman's ascetic practices extended beyond his meager food rations to his clothing, sleeping habits, prayer vigils, and service. In an 1819 letter to Igumen Jonathan of Valaam, Herman concluded with these words: "For all somber circumstances and adventures we live happily and peacefully on our own; our only worry is to gain entry to the Kingdom of Heaven. For this we pray and beseech you, kind Reverend Father, to help our humble selves with your holy prayers—in hope of which I remain your Reverence's obedient servant and fervent subject humble Herman" (Oleksa 1987, 43–44).

In all his simplicity, *Apa* (a Kodiak term for "uncle/father") Herman became as Christ to the Sugpiaq people. On November 22, 1865, his Russian convert, Simeon Ianovskii, described his daily life:

> More than anything he liked talking about eternity, salvation, the next life, and God's miracles, the Holy Martyrs; here he never added an empty word. . . . He was very pleasant to listen to, and the ordinary Aleuts and their womenfolk loved to do so. . . . Aleuts of both sexes with their children often came to visit him—for advice, with complaints against the authorities, seeking his protection, and with various other needs; sometimes they brought him fish and helped him with his work. He always welcomed them, pacified them, and helped them as best he could. On Sundays and feast days many people came to him to pray. Father Herman told the hours, the Acts and the Gospel, and sang and preached. He would give the children biscuits or bake them cracknels. The children loved him, and he loved them. (Oleksa 1987, 48, 54)

Herman interceded on behalf of the Sugpiaq people before the civil authorities, defending those who were being hurt and helping the needy ones in any way he could. He influenced the lives of others by his personal example, as well as his teaching. The Russian authorities objected to his defense of the indigenous people against the shameful treatment by the fur traders and twice exiled him to Spruce Island. On one occasion, a Russian ship from Sitka brought a contagious disease that in three days had killed hundreds of Aleuts and Russians alike. Simeon Ianovskii, the company manager, reported, "The energetic elder Father Herman ceaselessly, tirelessly and at great personal risk visited the sick, not sparing himself in his role as priest—counseling those suffering to be patient, pray, repent and prepare themselves for death" (Oleksa 1987, 50). After the epidemic Herman and Ianovskii organized an orphanage for the children left without family. "Herman's legacy best represents the Orthodox Church's understanding of 'passive missions,' where holy people preach the gospel more with their life than with their actual words" (Veronis 2000, 430).

Mission Methods

The Valaam monks aligned themselves from the beginning with the Alaskan native peoples. In the journey across the Urals to the Pacific, they had witnessed the mission strategy of the Orthodox Church in establishing Christian communities among shamanistic tribes more by example than preaching. The goal was to establish a self-governing American church in Alaska, which would respect and use the native languages and creative arts and enjoy administrative independence within the Orthodox community.

The early success of the Orthodox mission was due to the monks sharing the gospel in the native languages and desiring "to present Christianity as the fulfillment of what the Alaskans already knew rather than its replacement" (Oleksa 1987, 13). Some Aleut men who had been sent to Russia for training in company and church leadership helped them toward this end. For example, one such coworker helped the missionaries by preaching to the Sugpiaq people without directly undermining their native shamanistic worldview. By presenting Christianity as the fulfillment of what the people already knew rather than as its replacement, the monks walked a thin theological line, since "at that time the Aleuts were all idol-worshippers of the Shaman sect and made human sacrifice, even of children" (Letter from Simeon Ianovskii to Igumen Damascene of Valaam, November 22, 1865, in Oleksa 1987, 47–48).

The similarities between the Russian and the Aleut worldviews seemingly created a suitable path for the presentation of Christ. Both cultures valued mystical religious experience, oral tradition, rites filled with symbols, feast days and celebrations, religious images, and baptism. Other similarities existed between the Orthodox veneration of Christ and the Aleutian honoring of warriors, the ornate priestly vestments and those of the shamans, obedience to the Ten Commandments and to the traditional Aleutian taboos, and the Russian acceptance of the Holy Scriptures compared to the belief in Aleutian mythology (Barkey 1988, 79).

Indigenous Education

Education for the native people was a priority for Alaskan Orthodox missions. Plans for a school at Kodiak had to wait until the 1805 arrival of Cathedral Hieromonk Gideon as the personal representative of the emperor. Two years later a school for both boys and girls was attracting as many as

---

We, on our journey through life, must call on God for help, and we have to shed this filth and clothe ourselves in new desires and new love for the coming ages, and thereby come to know our nearness or distance from our Heavenly Father.

Herman of Alaska (Oleksa 1987, 45)

---

one hundred children. As a result, Gideon composed the first grammar of Sugpiaq (Kodiak) Aleut and began translation of biblical and liturgical texts. In 1824 he devised an alphabet for the Ungangan language, which allowed for translations of a small catechism and the Gospel of Matthew and for the first Aleut book, *Indication of the Pathway into the Kingdom of Heaven* (Oleksa

Miracles of Herman of Alaska

In 1970 the Alaskan Orthodox Church officially recognized the exemplary model of the Christlike life of Herman as one for all believers to emulate. Herman received canonization; "the ascetic Elder, the monk Herman, [was] glorified as [a] 'wonderworker of all America' for his miracles of healing, his words of consolation and prophecy, and his life of joyful service, humility, and love" (Oleksa 1987, 340). In a life of humble service to the Kodiak people, Herman also performed miracles of healing and prophesied concerning the future of the land and the Orthodox Church.

In a September 9, 1867, letter from Bishop Petr of Yakutsk to Igumen Damascene of Valaam, the following prophecies and miracles concerning Herman were recorded (Oleksa 1987, 72–80):

- Prophesied regarding the brutal ax slaying of the Russian Ponomar'kov (74).
- Performed a miracle in holding back the floodwaters by placing an icon on the ground in prayer (72–73).
- Prophesied concerning the promotion of Ferdinand Petrovich to the rank of admiral (74).
- Foretold the death of the Moscow metropolitan a year before he received the news (74).

- Prophesied the unpleasant transfer of the administrator V. Ivanovich Kashevarov, "whom he loved and respected" (75).
- Prophesied concerning the building of a monastery on Spruce Island (75–76).
- Prevented a bush fire on Spruce Island from devastating the people and buildings by drawing a boundary mark on the forest ground among the moss.
- Prophesied that after his death there would be an epidemic among the Aleuts causing many deaths and that later the Russians would gather the natives into one community (76–77).
- On the night that Herman died (December 13, 1837), many people witnessed from various places "an unusually bright column of light rising into the air above Spruce Island" (78). "On the same evening from other villages, and also from Afognak, a figure was seen in the sky below the clouds over Spruce" (79).

Reflection and Discussion

1. What were the foundational principles of Herman's mission?
2. What was the result of the miracles and prophecies?
3. How was Herman's life reflective of Christ?

1987, 15). Though the school program dwindled when Father Gideon returned to Russia, Herman resumed the work at his orphanage and school on Spruce Island. With the help of a native couple, "he taught them to read and write and sing the litanies, [using] the girls and boys to replace reader and choir" (Oleksa 1987, 80). Consequently, still more national leaders received theological instruction in Russia (Barkey 1988, 99, 147).

One of the key objectives of Orthodox missions was the selection and training of indigenous leaders for the local churches. The ordination of the first Ungangan priest, the Creole Iakov Netsvetov, occurred in 1828, and the pattern of ordaining indigenous leaders continued past the sale of Alaska to the United States in 1867. Trained by the Orthodox mission's school system, within Herman's lifetime, Aleuts were leaders in the community, the company, and the church, as they became teachers, choirmasters, priests, rectors, deans, wardens, and evangelists to their own people (Barkey 1988, 111–17).

The Kodiak missionaries "were far ahead of their western contemporaries in stressing indigenous leadership development, treasuring the native culture and language, developing worship and catechetical materials in the vernacular, and carrying on their ministry in the same incarnational approach that was exemplified in the life and ministry of Christ" (Barkey 1988, 103). They were "not simply trying to translate Scripture, catechetical materials, and the liturgy into the vernacular. The incarnational approach was the determination that the life of the missionary must also be in the vernacular of the people" (Barkey 1988, 62).

Nicholas Kasatkin of Japan

Episcopal bishop Henry St. George Tucker called Nicholas Kasatkin "the outstanding missionary of the nineteenth century" (H. Tucker 1938, 103), and Richard Drummond summarizes his work as follows:

> The life and life fruits of Nicholas compel us to recognize him as one of the greatest missionaries of the modern era. In accordance with Orthodox tradition, he respected highly the language and cultural traditions of the people among whom he served. He respected the people and loved them as persons. He went beyond the common traditions of Orthodoxy in freeing his work to an extraordinary extent from the political aims and interests of his homeland. His apostleship was remarkably non-polemical for the day; he was in singular fashion an apostle of peace among men. His method of evangelization was concentrated upon the family, and he stressed above all the raising up of national workers and the indigenization of the Church, even as he urged it to remember its distinctive association with the kingdom of God. (Drummond 1971, 354)

Call to Missions

Nicholas Kasatkin entered the Smolensk Seminary and graduated in 1857 with a scholarship to Saint Petersburg Theological Academy, Russia. There he demonstrated an aptitude for foreign languages and church history, and he was ordained to the priesthood after three years of study. During his studies, Kasatkin's reading of Vasilii Golovnin's *Narrative of a Captivity in Japan* and the memoirs of British navigator Will Adams, both imprisoned by the Japanese, fostered an interest in Japan (Bartholomew 1987, 5). At twenty-four Kasatkin volunteered to serve as chaplain of the Russian consulate in Hakodate, Japan.

After wintering with veteran missionary Innocent Veniaminov and armed with his advice, Kasatkin arrived in Japan in 1861 at a time of political upheaval. Since the middle of the seventeenth century, Japan had prohibited foreign immigration. At that time, some thirty-seven thousand Christians had died, and those who remained had gone underground. Japan had reopened the ports of Nagasaki, Shimoda, and Hakodate to Western trade only six years earlier. The first Russian consulate at Hakodate (on the island of Hokaido) had lost its priest due to sickness, and Kasatkin was commissioned to take this position at age twenty-seven.

Unfortunately, the young missionary was not very warmly received either by the Russians in Hakodate, or by the Japanese who, because of the nation's previous isolationism, were not well disposed to hear the Gospel. The situation was discouraging. However, on September 9, 1861, he received a visit from Archbishop Innocent, Apostle to America, who rebuked him for his waning enthusiasm and advised him to study the Japanese language. Thus, his missionary zeal was rekindled and Father Nicholas began to apply himself in earnest to the study of Japanese. (Takahashi n.d.)

Language Learning and Translation

In the midst of these political changes, Kasatkin spent his first seven years in Japan learning the Japanese language and culture while performing priestly duties for the Russian community at Hakodate. Since converts to Christianity were executed and foreigners who evangelized deported, the young priest focused his ministry among the Russians, anticipating that the Japanese religious restrictions would change. Emulating the mission strategy of Veniaminov, Nicholas prepared himself for cross-cultural work by studying the Chinese classics, Buddhism, and Japanese language, history, and literature. "He studied diligently with a private tutor and also visited the Buddhist temples to listen to the sermons and study the vocabulary necessary to preach about virtues" (Takahashi n.d.). After this rigorous preparation, Kasatkin began his lifelong work of Bible translation by comparing each verse he translated with the Chinese Bible, in addition to the Vulgate and the Greek and English texts, while consulting the commentaries of John Chrysostom for help with difficult passages. "Blessed Nicholas' greatest talent is universally recognized as his ability to translate" (Takahashi n.d.). Striving for perfection, it took the Russian priest four to five hours to translate some fifteen verses, and for the last thirty years of his life, he spent most days giving more than seven hours to translation work. While in Hakodate, he translated the Gospels, Acts, several other books of the New Testament, a Chinese prayer book, catechetical materials, and several other religious works. He then formed a translation team of nine Japanese scholars to expand the number of publications so that by 1893 they had produced fourteen theological books and in the next nine years another seventy-five.

For a time the Orthodox translators used the Protestant version of the New Testament. However, Nicholas composed a new translation when he found that the Protestant edition was too conversational and connected to the English language. He achieved a more dignified translation by using more Chinese expressions and antiquated forms (Cary 1909, 421). In addition, he obtained from Russia a printing press that by 1900 had produced three monthly periodicals: *Reverse Brocade* (women's literature), the *Orthodox Messenger* (family guidance), and *Sea of the Spirit* (theological and philosophical discussion). Even during the Russo-Japanese War, Nicholas continued his work on the translation of religious literature into Japanese.

Development of Indigenous Leadership

In 1868 Takuma Sawabe, a patriot and samurai Shinto priest, with two of his friends, the physician Sakai and Urano, became Kasatkin's first Japanese converts. Baptized in secret, they studied the Scriptures with the priest and told friends about the good news. A church began to develop, and "within a year the number of baptized Christians had grown to twelve and twenty-five more were preparing for conversion" (Barkey 1986, 115). By 1871 the mission station consisted of an archimandrite (Kasatkin), three priests, and a catechist. Anatolii Tikhai, a graduate of Kiev Theological Academy, arrived in Hakodate in 1873, and Kasatkin immediately appointed him to lead the work in northern Japan. This released Nicholas to concentrate his efforts in Tokyo, the geographic and political center of the nation.

In Tokyo Kasatkin started preaching to fifteen people in a small two-room house in Tsukiji while continuing his study of the Japanese language and culture. He wandered the streets talking to people, listening to the public storytellers, and establishing relationships with Buddhist monks. Realizing the need for theological education, he purchased a residence at Surugadai Hill in Tokyo, which eventually became the site of the Orthodox cathedral. There he began a Russian-language school, a chapel, and a school for girls, as well as providing training opportunities for laypeople and evangelists. Following the pattern of the Buddhist schools, the Russian leader established Sunday schools rather than day schools, as did the Catholics and the Protestants. The schools were so successful that many non-Christian children attended.

Tokyo saw four new missions built in 1874, and musician Dimitrii L'vovskii arrived to train choirs and lead worship. A year later, a seminary opened in the same city to train the converts for leadership roles. The first Japanese national to be ordained to the priesthood was Sawabe, with Sakai ordained as a deacon; the ordination was performed by a visiting Russian bishop. Five more

Japanese men traveled to Vladivostok for ordination so that they could serve the mission that opened in Osaka in 1878. The number of Japanese priests continued to increase, and by 1883 there were eleven and by 1890 eighteen.

Indigenous Orthodox Church

Kasatkin's original goal was to create an indigenous church, Orthodox in faith yet Japanese in form. Not wanting the Japanese to associate Christianity with European politics, Kasatkin believed that the number of Russian missionaries should be kept to a minimum. Therefore, in the entire history of Orthodox missions in Japan, there have never been more than four foreign missionaries at any one time. He believed that the spread of Christianity in Japan should occur by the efforts of indigenous believers and not by Russian missionaries. "The plan he presented [before the Holy Synod in Moscow] demonstrates his conviction that the new converts must be active in evangelism. It is this principle, as much as Nicholas' own character, that accounts for the success of the work in Japan, for it enabled the gospel to be spread by the learners themselves without relying on extensive missionary support" (Stamoolis 1986, 36).

The believers were encouraged to share their faith, meet for small group Bible study, and give to those in need, including special offerings for famine relief in Russia. Each parish had a women's missionary society, which conducted ministry to the poor, especially abandoned children.

> Soon after Nicholas returned [from Russia for authorization and funds], a group gathered under him for instruction in Christian doctrine. Some of these were the inquirers who had previously studied with Sawabe. After a number of them had received baptism, three went back to their home area of Sendai as evangelists. It is characteristic of the zeal and faith of the converts that they went without arrangements having been made for their financial support. The evangelists, unwilling to burden others, anticipated providing for themselves by their own labor. (Stamoolis 1986, 38)

These evangelists would hold two types of meetings each week: they read and explained the New Testament to believers, and they taught the Creed, the Lord's Prayer, and the Ten Commandments to new believers (Cary 1909, 383).

In 1872 five hundred people applied for baptism. Further, Kasatkin established an organization that provided continued leadership through a parish system using full-time indigenous workers to evangelize and teach others the Christian faith while they themselves were still learning. Every two years representatives from each parish sent delegates to the general synod, with the priests attending a conference in alternate years. The first synod in 1874 saw eight parish representatives; the following year the number grew to forty from throughout Japan.

SIDEBAR 4.4

Kasatkin's Rules for the Mission's Organization

"Besides conducting the two kinds of meetings already mentioned, the evangelists shall go about the city every day trying to win new enquirers. If among those interested are persons unable to attend the meetings, the evangelists shall go to their houses in order to explain the Creed, the Lord's Prayer, and the Ten Commandments. This is to be regarded as of prime importance and should be done even if, for lack of time, the evangelist is obliged to omit the meeting for reading the New Testament. When persons have thoroughly learned the Creed, the Lord's Prayer, and the Ten Commandments, and are established in the faith, they shall be presented to the priest for baptism."

Cary (1909, 383–84)

Reflection and Discussion

1. How would you describe Kasatkin's mission strategy and discipleship methods?
2. Would they work in your mission context? Why or why not?

The Orthodox Christians of northern Japan suffered persecution in 1873 because the government was suspicious of the church's rapid growth. Sawabe and Sakai, with six other believers, were imprisoned. Other Christians underwent interrogation, and those employed by the government lost their jobs. Kasatkin appealed to the government authorities and four months later obtained release for the imprisoned eight (Cary 1909, 394–404). Later Sakai again endured incarceration simply because he was a Christian, but he was soon exonerated, as the prison became a church. After a year of persecution, officials decreed the removal of the anti-Christian edict from public notice boards. With the easing of the religious conflict and the Orthodox missionary work receiving prominent national press coverage, a renewed mission vigor arose in the Orthodox community. In the midst of these unsettled times, there was a greater receptivity to new ideas.

In 1880 Kasatkin revisited Russia, this time to raise funds to build the Cathedral of the Holy Resurrection, unofficially called by the Japanese Nicolai-Do, House of Nicholas (Meyendorff 1962, 184). After four years of raising support and seven years of construction, the Tokyo Cathedral was complete. With a bell tower 125 feet high and a dome with a 115-foot circumference, covering an area of 1,053 square feet, the church became a Tokyo landmark. A choir of more than one hundred sang each Sunday, together with a special children's choir.

The Orthodox Church in Japan continued to grow rapidly "with 6,099 members in 1888, and 20,048 members, 22 priests, 219 churches and chapels in 1891. In 1903 there were 38 native priests, 8 deacons, 144 evangelists, and 1,063 people baptized that year. In 1904 they had increased to 28,230 members" (Barkey 1986, 116).

Orthodox Mission in Japan

The following excerpt shows Nicholas Kasatkin's breadth of vision for the Orthodox mission in Japan:

The money first collected [by the Association of Evangelists] shall be used for the propagation of Christianity. When sufficient money has been gathered, a young man shall be taught the Russian language and sent to a theological school in Russia. On the completion of his education, he shall return to Japan and there establish a school for teaching Christian doctrine and the sciences. He shall also translate religious books. Another young man shall be sent to a medical school in Russia, and on completing his studies shall return to found a hospital and a medical school. When the number of baptized believers reaches five hundred, one of the evangelists shall be chosen for sending to Russia that he may be ordained to the priesthood. Afterwards, one person shall be ordained for every additional five hundred converts. When there are five thousand believers, a request shall be made for the appointment of a bishop.

Otis Cary (1909, 383–84)

Reflection and Discussion

1. Given the rapid increase of church members in Japan from 1888 to 1904, why was this an effective leadership development method?
2. How could this method be adapted for contemporary intercultural missions?

Separation of Orthodoxy and Nationalism

Japan and Russia declared war against each other in 1904. At the unanimous decision of the Orthodox council of Japanese workers and leaders, Kasatkin remained in Japan with his church, enduring open hostility and even suspicion of being a Russian spy. All the while Nicholas admonished the Japanese believers to pray and fight, not out of hatred for the Russian enemy but out of love of their country, thereby following the example of Jesus's patriotism and loyalty to his people. Kasatkin's teachings and writings reinforced his belief in the separation of the Orthodox Church from political nationalism, which won favor with the Japanese government. He declared, "We Christians have also another country . . . which is the Church, and in which the children of the Heavenly Father really form a family. This is why I do not leave you, brothers and sisters, but I remain in your family as though in my own" (Barkey 1986, 118).

On the question of whether an Orthodox Japanese should fight against Russia, Nicholas responded:

From now on, I will not take part in public services of the Church. Until now, I have prayed for the prosperity and peace of the Japanese empire. Now with the declaration of war between Japan and my homeland, I as a Russian subject, cannot pray for the victory of Japan over my homeland. Since I too have responsibilities to my homeland, I am happy to see you fulfill your responsibilities to yours. (Bartholomew 1987, 53)

Withdrawing from public affairs, Kasatkin watched his Japanese spiritual family pray for the defeat of his homeland while helping to organize a ministry to some seventy-three thousand Russian prisoners of war detained in Japan. Although the church's progress stagnated during the war years, twenty Russian-speaking Japanese priests served as chaplains in the prisons with the indigenous church, dispensing gifts, icons, vestments, and religious and secular literature to those confined. At the end of the conflict, the Russian authorities built a number of chapels for the Orthodox Church out of gratitude (Stamoolis 1986, 39).

In 1912, after fifty-one years of Orthodox ministry in Japan, Kasatkin died, leaving a heritage of "33,000 members in 266 parishes, with 35 priests, 22 deacons, 116 catechists, and 82 students in seminaries" (Barkey 1986, 119).

Characteristics of Orthodox Missions

In looking at missionaries Cyril and Methodius of Moravia, Stephen of Perm, Herman of Alaska, and Nicholas Kasatkin of Japan we recognize patterns in Orthodox missionary work. The three main characteristics of Orthodox missions were use of the local language, selection and training of national leaders, and formation of an indigenous church.

Use of the vernacular in worship and Bible translation was a hallmark of most Orthodox missions. That is, the missionaries preached the gospel and the converts worshiped in the local language. The Orthodox Church believed that it was the right of all people to use their own language to worship their Creator. This perception stems from the view that at Pentecost the miracle of speaking in tongues showed God's blessing on vernacular languages and his desire to redeem all peoples (Acts 2). Unfortunately, this gift of direct access to Scripture and the liturgy in the mother tongue sometimes led to nationalistic ecclesial fragmentation (e.g., the Slavic countries in the Byzantine Empire) and a multiplicity of sects.

The usual Orthodox process of evangelism was to have the most promising indigenous Christian leaders ordained as soon as possible. If there was a delay in consecration, it was generally due to the lack of a bishop in an inaccessible region, and this deficiency was subsequently righted when the Orthodox missionary returned home. The clergy were trained more informally than formally, with emphasis on the fundamental doctrines of the faith, especially the liturgy, since it was the center of Orthodox faith and theology. The goal was the establishment of local churches with a strong thrust for self-government. Of course, there was often disagreement between the mother church and the local members over when independence should occur.

With these three characteristics in mind, Orthodox mission practice had its own identity and was not a copy of Western methodology. Though not all Orthodox missions followed this approach, it does demonstrate a missional attitude that obtained acceptance. For example, some missionaries did not learn the language of the people among whom they ministered, while others used political power to bring about conversions.

There were also low periods in Orthodox missionary activity. The lack of sustained interest in missions during much of the Byzantine Empire led to the spiritual void that Islam filled. If in the fourth to the sixth centuries the Byzantine Church had made a careful translation of the Bible into Arabic to foster an Arabic cultural identity, as was done by Cyril and Methodius for the Slavs in the ninth and tenth centuries, perhaps Islamic expansion from Saudi Arabia to northern Africa would have taken a different course.

Furthermore, many centuries of Orthodox Church life were spent under the domination of Muslim regimes, such as in the Balkans, the Middle East, Syria, and Egypt, hampering missions by forcing the churches in these places to focus solely on protecting and maintaining their existing membership. In the twentieth century this missionary resistance continued as the Orthodox Church protected itself against antireligious states such as the former Soviet Union. Could it be that the complacency of the Russian Orthodox Church, its indifference to social change, and lack of applicable Christian ethics both socially and politically contributed to the development of communism?

The missionary work of the Orthodox Church in non-Christian arenas, though existent, remained limited. The call to missions arose in certain eras as a spiritual flame yet dwindled when there was no organizational vehicle to continue the Orthodox presence. To some extent, the fault may be with the excessive nationalism of the local church. National Orthodoxy has certainly strengthened the cultural identity and dignity of a people group, yet it has often led to an inward focus that has restricted missions within cultural boundaries, even when exported to other countries through immigration. The responsibility for missions was often restricted to a particular ethnic group.

Nonetheless, out of an imperfect Orthodox mission arose our five missionaries, Cyril and Methodius of Moravia, Stephen of Perm, Herman of Alaska, and Nicholas Kasatkin of Japan, whose work was effective and whose legacy is still influential. These missionaries were among a host of Orthodox cross-cultural workers who created alphabets for unwritten languages, translated the Bible, and celebrated the beauty and importance of liturgical life within vernacular worship. Together with selecting and training indigenous clergy for pastoral care and evangelism, these missionaries valued the local culture alongside educational, agricultural, and artistic development. Western missions are only now fully appreciating the fundamental principles that were the base of Orthodox missionary efforts.

5

Encountering Dominican and Franciscan Missions

The beginning of the thirteenth century was a time of social and political upheaval as the Mongols invaded from the East, and although the major Crusades in the Holy Land had ended, the holy wars against the Saracens (Muslims) continued. During the Crusades new trade routes forged opportunities for social mobility as merchants increased in wealth and prominence. The European feudal system continued to dominate the masses by manipulating them into military service in return for refuge and security. The church was blasé concerning its responsibility to protect its members from these nationalistic passions of violence and power, and it merely practiced similar means of suppression via the Holy Crusades. The papacy of the medieval period was politically corrupt, immoral, and abusive of power, as well as devoid of religious and spiritual authority. From this European milieu emerged two movements that set the stage for an explosion of Catholic mission efforts throughout the thirteenth century until today. In this chapter, we will explore the theological foundations in addition to the mission focus and efforts of both societies: the Dominicans and the Franciscans.

The Dominicans

Clouded in mystery, Dominic Guzman left behind only three small letters and some legal documents. One of the most prominent church leaders in the Middle Ages, he launched a student movement of preachers that produced one of the most dynamic missionary forces in history. In the Basilica of Saint Peter in Rome, a statue pays homage to Dominic alongside Francis, Bernard, Benedict, and Ignatius of Loyola.

Born around 1170 in Caleruega, Spain, Guzman trained for the priesthood at the University of Palencia and developed a deep concern for the poor. To raise money for the socially marginalized, he sold his books and commentaries and even twice attempted to sell himself into slavery to use the funds to liberate others (O'Connor 1913, 234). He believed that to be a follower of Jesus meant to lead a life engaged in service to others.

In 1204, as assistant to the bishop of Osma, Diego d'Azévédo, Guzman accompanied his leader on a diplomatic journey to Denmark. During the trip the young priest was disturbed by the way in which various heresies were used to manipulate the population of southern France. On one occasion, the travelers stayed with a nobleman in Toulouse, only to discover that their host was a member of the Albigensian sect. This group believed that there was an evil creator of the material world and a benevolent one of the spiritual realm; Christ came as both an evil savior in the physical and a good savior in the spirit. Dominic spent the night using the New Testament to refute the Albigensian heresy, which resulted in the conversion of the host family by morning (Butler 1868, 108–13).

Throughout the Spanish pair's tour, the various heretical groups they observed so troubled them that on their return to Spain they visited Pope Innocent III in Rome to seek permission to evangelize the northern regions of Europe. The pope declined their request, instead redirecting their energies to southern France to support the Cistercians (a religious order focusing on the observance of the Rule of Saint Benedict) in their efforts to win the population back to the church (Tugwell 1982, 53–54). Upon their arrival in southern France in 1204, Diego and Dominic joined the Cistercians and convinced them to change their evangelistic strategy from physical intimidation to theological debate with key leaders. The interreligious dialogue proved successful, and several heretical leaders converted to Christianity (Walsh 1985, August 8).

After two years, Diego returned to Spain, while Dominic continued to preach in southern France, believing that the Albigensian heretics would convert if shown the biblical truth in ways they could understand. Relying primarily on the New Testament and following the example of the heretics themselves, he and his followers went humbly into the streets and shared their faith. After returning to Rome in 1215, Dominic petitioned a cautious Innocent III for permission to found a new order. After experiencing a dream that revealed a collapsing church supported on Dominic's shoulders, the pope reluctantly gave approval, but only if the order submitted to an existing monastic rule. Back in southern France, Dominic and sixteen followers (eight Frenchmen, seven Spaniards, and one Englishman) chose the Rule of Saint Augustine and formed the Order of Preachers, also known as the Dominicans.

One year later Guzman returned to Rome to confirm the rule only to find Honorius III as the new pope. Their discussions on theology and the need to protect the doctrinal integrity of the church led to Dominic's appointment as the first Master of the Sacred Palace, a position that the Dominicans held for many years. After returning to southern France in 1217, Dominic developed a progressive plan to send his preacher-theologians to the universities (Tugwell 1982, 18–19). Within fifty years after his death in 1221, there were more than four hundred Dominican houses throughout Europe. In the next section, we explore the outworking of the Dominican vision beyond Europe into Latin America together with a case study of Bartolomé de Las Casas of Spain.

Dominican Missions in Latin America

The Spanish incursion into the New World in the sixteenth century, as Spaniards searched for gold and brought Christ to the native peoples through military conquest and forced conversions, spread from the Caribbean Islands to Central and South America. The theology of mission at the time embraced the divine right to Christianize a naturally inferior people, with theologians such as Fernández de Oviedo claiming, "All attempts to convert the Indians required prior conquest by the Spaniards" (*La Historia general de las Indias* [General History of the Indies] 1535, quoted in Brading 1997, 124). For instance, Hernán Cortés invaded the Aztec lands of Mexico in 1520 with a small contingent of soldiers and subdued the Aztecs thanks to advanced weaponry, horses, cultural circumstances, and resistance to smallpox. He then requested twelve Franciscan mendicants from Charles V, who had succeeded Ferdinand II on the Spanish throne in 1516, to guide the spiritual life of the conquered peoples and to educate the children of the Indian nobility.

In their greed for gold, the Spaniards disregarded the rights of the indigenous peoples. "In the name of Christ, the natives were dispossessed of their lands by means of *Requerimiento* . . . and the natives were dispossessed of their freedom by means of the *encomiendas*" (Gonzalez 1992, 32). *Requerimiento* refers to the church's belief that only indigenous people who acknowledged Christ should remain free since non-Christians had no rights. This crusade mentality justified forced conquest and focused exclusively on salvation and conversion without concern for the physical and social circumstances of the convert (Floristan 1992, 132). Since the Spanish believed that the natives were subhuman, the settlers stole the lands of the Amerindians and enslaved them to work in the fields and mines on *encomiendas* (estates granted to Spanish colonists) in exchange for instruction in Spanish customs, the value of diligence, and Christian doctrine. In a twisted irony, the natives became the reward granted by the Spanish Crown to the conquering settlers in this semifeudal institution imposed on the indigenous people that required them to give part of their crop as tribute to the Europeans and perform arduous labor. Spain had followed this practice in previous centuries when it had used the conquered Moors as laborers in Spanish *encomiendas* (Chasteen 2001, 52–53).

In 1493 Pope Alexander VI had entrusted sovereign lordship of the New World (any conquered land three thousand leagues west of the Cape Verde Islands) to the Spanish monarchy to spread the gospel to its inhabitants; accompanying this right was a hidden Spanish royal agenda of gaining economic supremacy. The combination of Spain's declining economy and the promise of New World wealth with a massive indigenous workforce, together with Catholic missionaries seeking refuge from European persecution, led to ever-increasing conquests of the land and its natives. Luis N. Rivera charges, "Hidden behind the evangelizing cross, faintly veiled, was the conquering sword. . . . The hostile medieval dichotomy between Christians and infidels assumed the shape of a crusade in the very heart of the discovery and acquisition of America" (1990, 9).

Eighteen years after the Italian Christopher Columbus (representing King Ferdinand II and Queen Isabella of Spain) arrived at the island of Hispaniola in the West Indies in 1492, the Dominicans sent missionaries under the leadership of Pedro de Córdoba from Saint Stephen's in Salamanca, Spain. On arrival, the Dominicans found "children torn to shreds by hungry dogs, women tortured, men burned alive, tropical roads lined with corpses of Indian porters dead of exhaustion, and Indian villages pillaged and burned" (Daniel-Rops 1959, 73). They immediately spoke against such atrocities. Called to a life of serving the poor, the Dominicans believed that Jesus's example showed that human equality and the love of all people were biblical principles that they needed to follow; they thought that, given a peaceful opportunity, the indigenous peoples would choose the truth of Christ in preference to their animistic beliefs (Gutiérrez 1993). The following excerpt is taken from a sermon that Dominican Antonio de Montesinos preached (from Matt. 3:3, "A voice calling in the wilderness") on December 21, 1511, denouncing the mortal sin of the *encomienda* system to a congregation that included the governor of Santo Domingo, Diego Columbus, the son of Christopher Columbus:

> In order to make your sins against the Indians known to you I have come up on this pulpit, I who am a voice of Christ crying in the wilderness of this island, and therefore it behooves you to listen. . . . This voice tells you that you are in mortal sin: that you not only are in it, but live in it and die in it, and this because of the cruelty and tyranny that you bring to bear on these innocent people. Pray tell, by what right do you wage your odious wars on people who dwell in quiet and peace on their own lands? By what right have you destroyed countless numbers of them with unparalleled murders and destruction? . . . You kill them with your desire to extract and acquire gold every day. And what care do you take that they should be instructed in religion? . . . Are these not men? Have they not rational souls? Are you not bound to love them as you love yourselves? (Gonzalez 1992, 33)

Angered by the sermon, which every Dominican on Hispaniola signed, Governor Diego Columbus communicated his concerns to the king of Spain. One year later, the king supported the Dominican cause by passing the Laws of Burgos to protect the rights of the indigenous people: the natives were free; they were to be taught the Christian faith; and their forced work could not be "detrimental to their physical or spiritual wellbeing" (DiSalvo 1993, 90). These laws were difficult to implement in the New World due to settlers' greed for land and gold, the difficulty of communication with Europe, and the Dominicans' lack of governmental authority. We will now examine the outworking of Las Casas's missionary efforts to protect the rights of the native people in Central and South America, especially the effect of his publications and legislative appeals to Europe (see Gallagher 2005b, 109).

Bartolomé de Las Casas

Bartolomé de Las Casas of Seville, Spain, originally came to Hispaniola in 1502 (when he was eighteen years old) with the family heritage that his father and uncle had sailed with Columbus on his second voyage to the Americas. As a "gentleman cleric," he served the religious needs of the Spanish military for four years and then returned to Salamanca for priestly ordination (1510), whereupon he received a papal commission to bring the gospel to the natives in New Spain. Las Casas was also in the congregation and influenced by Montesinos's sermon on human rights for the indigenous peoples. Furthermore, having witnessed the Caonao massacre of five hundred Cuban Amerindians in 1513, this twelve-year *encomendero* (a labor system rewarding conquerors with the labor of a particular group of people) set his Indian slaves free the next year (Las Casas 1992b, 51–53).

Las Casas then began traveling between the New World and the Spanish monarchy, lambasting the Spanish conquistadores' injustices: "Everything done to the Indians in these Indies was unjust and tyrannical" (Las Casas 1992b, 74). In 1515 Las Casas (with Antonio de Montesinos) sailed from New Spain to Seville to expose the unjust treatment of native people to the Spanish monarchy in the hope of saving Cuba from a fate similar to Hispaniola's.

> The island of Cuba is almost as long as the distance from Valladolid to Rome; it is now almost entirely deserted. The islands of San Juan [Puerto Rico] and Jamaica . . . are both desolate. The Lucaya Isles lie near Hispaniola and Cuba to the north and number more than sixty. . . . The poorest of these . . . contained more than 500,000 souls, but today there remains not even a single creature. . . . We are assured that our Spaniards, with their cruelty and execrable works, have depopulated and made desolate the great continent. . . . The reasons why the Christians have killed and destroyed such infinite numbers of souls is solely because they have made gold their ultimate aim. . . . In this way have they cared for their lives—and for their souls: and therefore, all the millions above mentioned have died without faith and without sacraments. (Las Casas 1992b, 145)

Las Casas's defense of the Amerindians persuaded King Charles V, the Holy Roman emperor, to adopt a welfare reform to replace the oppressive *encomienda* structure. "Indians would be settled in villages of their own, grouped around a central Spanish town, and would work under a few carefully chosen Spanish supervisors mutually sharing profits of each other's labor" (Las Casas 1992b, 132). The king granted land in Guatemala to establish a colony to implement the idea. After seven years, Las Casas abandoned the venture because Cuban *encomenderos* had invaded the settlement and enslaved most of the inhabitants. After repeated protests to the Santo Domingo authorities failed, he considered the project "a divine judgment, punishing and afflicting" (Las Casas 1992a, 88).

Attracted by the Dominicans' purpose of intellectual study, writing, and preaching to correct the nominal in belief and practice, Las Casas joined the order in Santo Domingo in 1522. From his ten years of studying theology and writing he formed his mission to work among the indigenous peoples to share Christ and protect their human rights. His order silenced him for two years, however, because of his controversial action of refusing absolution to those who declined to renounce ownership of their slaves and *encomienda* (Las Casas 1992a, 30). Nevertheless, he did not change his mind. He declared in *Respuesta al Obispo de Charcas* (1553) that *encomenderos* who did not do penance and restitution for their actions "will go to hell, along with the confessors who have absolved them and the bishops who appointed them" (Gutiérrez 1993, 227). Those who spread the gospel with the sword, likewise, are "precursors of Antichrist and imitators of Mahomet, being thus Christian only in name" (Brading 1997, 131). According to Las Casas, Christlike faith, love, and justice were inseparable and led to the salvation of both the Amerindian and the so-called Christian.

Las Casas's Writings

Las Casas strengthened his focus on justice and compassion missions by publishing. He wrote a three-volume history of the early colonization, *History of the Indies*, and the *Apologetic History* (1527–1561). In 1530 Las Casas penned a missionary tract in Latin, *The Only Method of Attracting All People to the True Faith*, which became a guideline for his missionary method. In summary, he advocated "the spread of the Gospel by peaceful means alone, the need for understanding of doctrine and clear catechesis prior to conversion, the need to respect and utilize native cultures as part of the missionary enterprise" (Gutiérrez 1993, 263).

Through Las Casas's many court appearances and publications, such as his 1542 work, *De Unico Vocationis Modo* (*The Only Way*), he persistently presents the case for the indigenes of the Americas. In this publication he reasons that the natives have rational minds and that all peoples need to follow the divine laws in the Bible rather than those set by monarchs. The only way to evangelize is through peaceful persuasion and dialogue. He argues that God appointed one way of conversion "common to men throughout the world . . . by persuading the understanding through reasons and by gently attracting . . . the will" (Las Casas 1992b, 138). Las Casas elaborates on this method: "This conclusion will be proved in many ways by arguments drawn

---

The aim which Christ and the Pope seek and ought to seek in the Indies—and which the Christian Kings of Castile should likewise strive for—is that the natives of those regions shall hear the faith preached in order that they may be saved. . . . And the means to effect this end are not to rob, to scandalize, to capture or destroy them, or to lay waste to their lands, for this would cause the infidels to abominate our faith.

Bartolomé de Las Casas (Hanke 1951, 561, 617)

---

from reason; by examples of the ancient Fathers; by the rule and manner of preaching which Christ instituted for all times; by the practices of the Apostles; by quotations from holy teachers; by the most ancient tradition of the Church; and by her numerous ecclesiastical decrees" (Las Casas 1992b, 138). He continues, "There is no other reason why Saracens, Turks, and other unbelievers refuse to embrace our faith than the fact that we deny them with our conduct what we offer them with our words" (Gutiérrez 1993, 155–56).

It was the responsibility of the missionaries to protect the oppressed and lead them to Christ. Las Casas writes, "They [the natives] are most submissive, patient, peaceful, and virtuous. Nor are they quarrelsome, rancorous, querulous, or vengeful. . . . Surely these people would be the most blessed in the world if only they worshipped the true God" (Neill 1964, 146). Finally, in 1542 Charles V of Spain established the Laws of the Indies, advancing the previous attempt at rectifying colonial oppression. The indigenous peoples were free subjects of the king of Spain: they should learn the Catholic faith; they were not slaves; they should receive the rights to life, health, and self-preservation; and they owned themselves and their possessions (Tinker 1993, viii).

Hindrances of Application

Despite the Spanish royal decrees of 1512 and 1542, the colonizers continued to deny the indigenous peoples their basic human rights. The laws were difficult to enforce in the New World primarily because of the greed of the Spanish settlers and government, who relied on the natives to work the land and the mines. Too invested in their growing wealth and convinced of their racial superiority and natural right to rule, the settlers resisted the new laws.

The independent colonists advocated rebellion before they would submit to laws against their interests, and the government was unwilling to lose any colonies to revolution (Caroazza 2003, 87).

At one point, Las Casas even suggested, as an alternative, that African slaves replace the natives of the Americas in the *encomienda* labor system to maintain the newly founded Spanish economic interests. Although Thomas E. Skidmore and Peter H. Smith accuse the Dominican of being responsible for initiating the African slave trade in the Indies (2001, 291), Las Casas quickly

---

Your majesty will find out there are no Christians in these lands; instead, there are demons. They are neither servants of God or of the King. Because in truth, the great obstacle to my being able to bring the Indians from war-making to a peaceful way of life, and to bring the knowledge of God to those Indians who are peaceful is the harsh and cruel treatment of these Indians by the Spanish Christians. For which scabrous and bitter reason no word can be more hateful to those Indians than the word Christian, which they render in their language as Yares, meaning Demons. And without a doubt they are right, because the actions of these Governors are neither Christian nor humane but the actions of the Devil.

Bartolomé de Las Casas (1974, 100)

---

and permanently repented of this idea. Further, not all Catholic religious leaders agreed with Las Casas's belief that the establishment of social justice was a necessary requirement for the propagation of the gospel. Toribio de Motolinia, a Franciscan missionary to Mexico, protested to Charles V against the Dominican's portrayal of the conquistadores since the military force of the Spanish settlers had prevented "pointless martyrdom" (Brading 1997, 135–36).

Even though the Dominican campaigns did not bring immediate results, many Europeans became aware of the terrorism, thousands of indigenous people received salvation, and Las Casas formed the *reduccion*. The practice of *reduccion* throughout Latin America provided indigenous peoples a peaceful opportunity to accept Christianity with freedom from Spanish slavery, yet in the process it "enabled, simplified, and enhanced the ultimate conquest of their tribes" by placing them in European cultural and social systems (Tinker 1993, viii).

In 1543 Las Casas accepted the bishopric of Chiapas, Mexico, and brought with him forty-five Dominican friars. Because of the new laws, hostile Spaniards in Santo Domingo and Chiapas continually rejected the Dominicans on arrival. In addition, Juan Ginés de Sepúlveda (the emperor's chronicler and Renaissance humanist), in Valladolid, Spain (1550), debated the legality of the reforms in the Spanish occupation of the Americas. Sepúlveda argued that the Indians were "slaves by nature" (Gutiérrez 1993, 217). He reiterated the belief of many Europeans: "With perfect right do the Spanish exercise their dominion over these barbarians of the New World . . . who in prudence, natural disposition, and every manner of virtue and human sentiment are as inferior to Spaniards as children to adults, women to men, cruel and inhuman persons to the extremely meek . . . in a word, as monkeys to men" (Las Casas 1992b, xiv). On the other hand, Las Casas contended, "It clearly appears that there are no races in the world, however rude, uncultivated, barbarous, gross, or almost brutal they may be, who cannot be persuaded and brought to a good order and way of life, and made domestic, mild, and tractable, provided . . . the method is properly and naturally used; that is, love and gentleness and kindness" (Las Casas 1992b, 174).

The next year, the "Protector of the Indians" resigned from his bishopric and focused on writing for the courts in defense of the indigenous peoples. In a year he produced eight treatises denouncing the "Black Legend" of Spanish cruelty in the Indies, which resulted in a growing respect for his ideas in the Spanish court and throughout Europe. In 1552 Las Casas wrote one of his most renowned publications, *A Brief Account of the Destructions of the Indies*, in which he unfolds a "grisly description of Spanish cruelty, rhetorically exaggerating a slaughter that was horrible enough in reality" (Chasteen 2001, 61). The pamphlet saw forty-two editions in seven languages. Three days before his death in 1566, he wrote the following in his will:

> In His goodness and mercy, God considered it right to choose me as his minister, though unworthy, to plead for all those peoples of the Indies, possessors of those kingdoms and lands, against wrongs and injuries never before heard of or seen, received from our Spaniards . . . and to restore them to the primitive liberty of which they were unjustly deprived. . . . And I have labored in the court of the kings of Castile going and coming many times from the Indies to Castile and from Castile to the Indies, for about fifty years since the year 1514, for God alone and from compassion at seeing perish such multitudes of rational men, domestic, humble, most mild and simple beings, well fitted to receive our holy Catholic faith. (Las Casas 1992a, 16)

Las Casas and the Dominicans traveled through much of Latin America preaching the gospel in the vernacular and establishing indigenous churches and schools. According to Gustavo Gutiérrez, "Salvation of unbelievers and believers, proclamation of the gospel to both, and defense of the Indians' life and liberty: here are Las Casas' great concerns" (1993, 194). In 1522, for example, the Dominicans opened in Lima, Peru, the first of a series of

SIDEBAR 5.1

"Monsters" in Medieval Europe

Motivated by the love of God and humanity, the Franciscans were not content to confine their message to continental Europe. The instigator of the Friars Minor became the first Christian leader to devote a section of his "Rule of Life" to Muslim mission, where he projected, "Loving all that God loves leads the Franciscan to love every man, woman, and child as brother and sister" (Richstatter 2001, 206). This love of all peoples was all the more remarkable since the common view toward non-Europeans (non-Catholics) in thirteenth-century Europe was a series of concentric circles. Europeans occupied the center, the non-Christian barbarians were in the next circle, and in the outer circumference were "disorder, fears, and fantasies," which, in the medieval imagination, were "monstrous races" who were hairy, naked, cannibalistic, and sexually perverted. The term *monster* in medieval times applied specifically to

non-Christians since they failed to embrace the Christian faith. Hence, the Western medieval viewpoint saw Jews, Muslims, Mongols, and black Africans as "monstrous." Debra Higgs Strickland has expounded the consequences of what being a "monster" meant in the later Middle Ages: "The non-Christian 'monsters'—Jews, Muslims, and Mongols—were believed legitimate targets of destruction owing to their failure to embrace the True Faith, a failure that Christians were convinced was the ultimate cause of monstrosity" (2003, 241).

Reflection and Discussion

1. Compare and contrast the European medieval worldview regarding non-Christians with that of the early Franciscans.
2. In what ways does this "monstrous" attitude toward non-Christians carry over in today's world?

twenty-five universities as well as fifty-six secondary schools and numerous hospitals (Maust 1992, 35). As a result, the mission methods of the Dominicans influenced other mission groups as well. In California the Spanish Franciscan friar Junipero Serra used the Dominican model with the Native Americans of that territory, as did the Puritan John Elliot with the Algonquians, Henry Benjamin Whipple with the Sioux, and the Moravian David Zeisberger with the Delaware Indians.

The final section of this chapter investigates the Franciscans, a thirteenth-century mission group contemporary with the Dominicans. The founder of the Franciscan order, Francis of Assisi, led his followers in early preaching trips throughout Italy, where he taught his "little brothers" to spread the gospel by living in the world instead of withdrawing from it. As martyrdom goaded Francis to convert others to Christ, his message of joyous peace went beyond the religious and political strife of his home country (Thomas of Celano 1999, 229). From the inception of their order in 1210, the Franciscan mendicants abounded in mission energy. They were the first religious group of the time, for example, to have a written missions goal to reach the Muslims. They believed that Christian outreach to Muslims should occur through peaceful dialogue rather than the violence of the Crusades (Ingvarsson 2004, 311).

The Franciscans

Giovanni di Pietro di Bernardone (later renamed Francesco by his father, or Francis in English) was born at Assisi in Umbria, Italy, around 1181 to a cloth merchant family of seven children. From sixteen to twenty years of age, Francis, attracted by the ideas of "romantic chivalry," joined his city's army to fight in the regional class wars over land and property between the new bourgeoisie and the old nobility. After he was imprisoned in the neighboring town of Perugia for a year, the authorities released Bernardone due to a severe illness. Afterward, through a series of dreams and visions, he underwent a radical conversion to Christ and exchanged his frivolous behavior for an ascetic lifestyle.

Historical Background

The Crusades had established new trade routes, and opportunities arose for merchants and artisans to gain wealth and power. Feudal nobility controlled the common people through wealth and power, using them as soldiers in return for security and protection. The church did little to safeguard the people from these nationalistic passions of violence, merely using similar methods of subjugation during the international series of Crusades against Islam to spread the gospel's message of peace. Corruption had infiltrated the papacy in the form of immorality and abuse of power, with the church acting more in a civil than a religious capacity. Roger P. Schroeder sheds light on the historical context:

> The church and mission of the Latin West were at a low point in the year 1000. Many if not most of the clergy were caught up in moral and political corruption, in addition to having little to no biblical/theological training. In an attempt to escape from the corruption of the Church, most of the reform movements which arose at this time emphasized isolation from the world, resulting in almost no impetus for mission. (2000, 412)

A New Mendicant Order

In contrast to this prevailing perspective was Francis of Assisi. Foremost in his life was the desire to imitate Christ's poverty in the world and "rebuild his church." He felt God's call to preach to "kings and rulers and great crowds," and in turn the Lord would "multiply and increase his family throughout the entire world" (Galli 2002, 72). Bishop John of Sabina, who gained Pope Innocent III's favor for Francis to create a new mendicant order in 1210, declared, "I believe that the Lord wills, through him [Francis], to reform the faith of the holy church throughout the world" (Galli 2002, 77). Francis had not intended to found an order, but his winsome habits and his message proclaiming a rejection of possessions found a response among those who were ashamed of the earthly church. "Francis' originality consisted in his lack

---

The Lord has shown me that God will make us [Franciscan brothers] grow into a great multitude, and will spread us to the ends of the earth. I saw a great multitude of people coming to us, wishing to live with us in the habit of a holy way of life and in the rule of blessed religion. Listen! The sound of them is still in my ears. Their coming and going according to the command of holy obedience. I seem to see highways filled with this multitude gathering in this region [Umbria] from nearly every nation. Frenchmen are coming, Spaniards are hurrying, Germans and Englishmen are running, and a huge crowd speaking other languages is rapidly approaching.

Francis of Assisi (Thomas of Celano 1999, 206)

---

of originality. He drew his spirituality directly and entirely from the Gospels without addition or subtraction" (Lynch 1982, 91).

Francis's Earlier Rule (1221), which governed the order, states, "The rule and life of these brothers is this: namely to live in obedience, in chastity, and without anything of their own, and to follow the teaching and footprints of our Lord Jesus" (Francis of Assisi 1982a, 117). Along with his friars, Francis ventured to the fields, homes, marketplaces, and vineyards in gentle humility and sincere piety, dispensing his message of joy and holy living for Christ using words "well-chosen and chaste for the instruction and edification of the people" (Francis of Assisi 1982b, 143). They traveled in pairs; taking no money or extra clothing; working with their hands; singing hymns and poems of praise to God; using Italian, the common language, in "preaching the kingdom of God and penance"; and alternating between itinerant speaking and prayer in remote places (Galli 2002, 57). Francis desired above all else to obey God and "took the Gospels as a manual for Christian life" (Harkins 1994, 40).

Francis copied the communication technique of the troubadours popular with the uneducated—an attention-getting action followed by a short poetic explanation often incorporating a song or chant (Dries 1998, 6). He believed that "all the brothers should preach by their deeds" (Francis of Assisi 1982a, 122); and if speaking were necessary, it should be "in a discourse that is brief because it was in a few words that the Lord preached while on earth" (Francis of Assisi 1982b, 143). Francis and his disciples imitated the humility and poverty of Christ by living among the powerless, sick, and lepers, proclaim-

---

The flesh desires and is most eager to have words but [cares] little to carry them out. It does not seek a religion and holiness in the interior spirit, but it wishes and desires to have a religion and holiness outwardly apparent to people.

Francis of Assisi (Dries 1998, 6)

---

ing peace in a war-torn Italy. Bestowing dignity rather than shame, Francis respected the poor and desired to be more like them (Thomas of Celano 1983, 432). "Anyone who curses the poor insults Christ whose noble banner the poor carry, since Christ made himself poor for us in this world" (Thomas of Celano 1999, 248). For the Franciscans, "the preaching of the word availed little without the sermon of one's life" (Schroeder 2000, 413). They were to live as a presence and witness of Jesus.

With only twelve brothers at its beginning, the order expanded to five thousand men within the first decade. The followers of Francis spread the gospel beyond Italy (Ugolino di Monte Santa Maria 1998, xxxvi): from Tunis (in 1217

In the fervor of his [Francis's] love he felt inspired to imitate the glorious victory of the martyrs in whom the fire of love could not be extinguished or their courage broken. Inflamed with that perfect love "which drives out fear" he longed to offer himself as a living victim to God. . . . He would repay Christ for his love in dying for us and inspire others to love God.

Bonaventure (1983, 701)

---

with Giles, one of the first disciples) to England (1224), and from Syria (Elias in 1217) to Germany (in 1219 with John of La Penna leading sixty friars) and France (the troubadour Pacifico in the same year). Continuing in mission, the Franciscans established houses stretching from Russia to the Mongol court of China (1254) and on to India. In India, for example, they translated the New

Hymn of Saint Francis

Praises of the Most High

You alone are holy,
Lord God, wonder of wonders.
You are strong.
You are great.
You are Most High.
You are omnipotent,
Our Holy Father,
Lord of Heaven and earth.
You, Lord God, are one and
    three, are our every good.
You, Lord God, are good, all
    good, our highest good,
Lord God living and true.
You are charity and love.
You are wisdom.
You are humility.
You are patience.
You are a firm anchor.
You are peace.
You are joy and happiness.
You are justice and temperance.
You are fullness of riches.
You are beauty.

You are gentleness.
You are our protector.
You are our guardian and
    defender.
You are our strength.
You are refreshment.
You are our great hope.
You are our faith.
You are our most profound
    sweetness.
You are our eternal life, great
    and admirable Lord,
Omnipotent God.
Holy and merciful Saviour!

Francis of Assisi (Thomas
of Celano 1983, 125)

Reflection and Discussion

1. As you read this hymn, consider what it communicates about Francis's relationship with God.
2. With what characteristic(s) of God's character portrayed in the hymn do you most closely resonate? Why?

Testament and Psalter into the common language and converted six thousand to Christ (Ellens 1975, 490). By 1260 there were approximately 17,500 Franciscan brothers; forty years later there were about 30,000 friars in the order in more than 1,100 houses. We now turn to Franciscan mission expansion in Africa with a particular spotlight on Ramon Llull.

Franciscan Missions to Africa

Ramon Llull closely followed the footsteps of Francis and similarly dedicated his life to bringing Muslims to Christ by way of his apologetic writings, the establishment of missionary training colleges, and his willingness to embrace martyrdom. In an age influenced by the Crusades to consider that the only way for infidel conversion was by the sword, Llull's strategy of Muslim outreach was a unique alternative to the predominant brutal interactions, and this strategy allowed for the opportunity of increased affiliations and reconciliation.

HISTORICAL BACKGROUND

Thirteenth-century Europe commonly portrayed non-Europeans (non-Catholics) as a series of concentric circles. Europeans occupied the center, the non-Christian barbarians were in the next circle, and the outer circumference was reserved for "disorder, fears, and fantasies" where in the medieval imagination "monstrous races" existed who were hairy, naked, cannibalistic, and sexually perverted (Strickland 2003, 157–65). Followers of Islam were not in the center of the European worldview.

By the end of the seventh century, the Islamic Empire was on the rise, and although Muslims condemned forced conversions, they believed that the "faithful" should govern the world. In 638 Jerusalem surrendered to the Muslims, and at first the conquerors allowed Christians to visit the holy places. By 714 an Arab-Berber army had control of Spain, establishing the western border of the Islamic world for three hundred years. During those centuries, Islam

> If speaking is necessary then it should be "in a discourse that is brief because it was in a few words that the Lord preached while on earth."
>
> Francis of Assisi (1982b, 143)

experienced significant internal conflict as well as prosperity until the end of the 900s, when economic growth shifted from North Africa to Europe. In 1031 the domination of the Umayyad Caliph of Córdoba ended and was followed by a period of anarchy until James I of Aragon gave the Catalan people power over the western Mediterranean region, some two hundred years later. Islamic rulers employed the Catalans as mercenaries during this time—even as the royal guard of the caliph of Tunis.

A change of leadership from the Arabs to the Turks in the Middle East saw an increase in Christian persecution. In reaction, the Byzantine rulers appealed to Pope Urban II, who in 1095 aroused an avenging missionary spirit in Europe and launched a series of Crusades over the next 250 years. The pope declared, "A race from the kingdom of the Persians, an accursed race, a race wholly alienated from God have taken what belongs to us. . . . Let the holy sepulcher of our Lord and Saviour, which is possessed by unclean nations, especially arouse you, and the holy places which are now treated, with ignominy and irreverently polluted with the filth of the unclean" (Munro 1901, 6).

The beginning of the thirteenth century was a time of social and political upheaval as the Mongols invaded from the East, and although the major Crusades in the Holy Land had ended, the holy wars against the Saracens (Muslims) continued. For instance, James I of Aragon regained Majorca, conquered by the Saracens in the eighth century, in 1229. A city strategically located in the western Mediterranean and an important commerce center with Catalan as a language of trade and diplomacy, it had a dominant Muslim culture with a population that was one-third Muslim and included Jews in prominent financial and political positions (Bonner 1985, 3–10).

Ramon Llull

Born to an aristocratic family in Palma, Majorca, in 1233, Ramon Llull became chief administrator to James II of Majorca. At thirty-three years of age he became a follower of Jesus after a series of five visions of the crucified Christ and receiving inspiration from the life of Francis of Assisi; he eventually became a member of the Franciscan third order. In a conversion poem he wrote, "But Jesus Christ, of His great clemency, five times upon the Cross appear'd to me, that I might think upon Him lovingly, and cause His name proclaim'd abroad to be through all the world" (Peers 1969, 21). When he dedicated his life to serving Christ, he pledged to bring the gospel to the Muslims because of their continuing influence in Spain, the church's lack of success in overcoming Islam by the sword, and the insidious effect of Islamic teaching on Christian theology. His other two ministry objectives were to write a book addressing the errors of other faiths and convincingly present the gospel, and to establish monasteries where monks could learn the languages of nonbelieving peoples and receive appropriate instruction to preach the gospel.

He then spent the next nine years in Majorca learning contemporary science, Latin, and Arabic with a Muslim slave as his teacher, as well as studying Christian, Muslim, and Jewish theologies and philosophies. In all this preparation, he felt inadequate in knowledge, education, and mastery of the Arabic language (Llull 1985a, 15–17). The Catalan influence in southern Europe together with Llull's aristocratic connections enhanced his emergence as a respected scholar and prolific writer in interdisciplinary fields and enabled him to gain access to ecclesiastical leaders and monarchs.

Conversion of Unbelievers

During the Middle Ages, the prevailing attitude toward Islam was one of "gross ignorance and great hatred," and in spreading or defending Christianity, violence and torture were considered justifiable (Zwemer 1902, 50). In general, Llull believed that the first attempts to convert the unbeliever should be with love and compassion and called himself the advocate of unbelievers [*procurator infidelium*] (Lorenz 1985, 20). In his *Book of Contemplations*, he avowed that the conquest of the Holy Land should "be attempted in no other way than as Thou [Christ] and Thy apostles undertook to accomplish it, by love, by prayer, by tears, by the offering up of our own lives" (Mackensen 1920, 29). Moreover, attempts at such conversion should be through apologetics and dialogue by using principles common to Islam, Judaism, and Christianity.

Dominican apologists such as Ramon Martí (missionary to North Africa) and Ramon de Penyafort (the Dominican minister general) held debates with Jewish and Arabic scholars at Paris in 1263, using reason to try to prove that the opposition's suppositions were false. In contrast, Llull promoted true debate by insisting that each of the faiths, including Christianity, needed to prove by reason its own faith as well as engage with each of the other belief systems (Hames 2000, 2–3, 8–9).

Llull's Communication Methodology

Llull tried to communicate in a way that was most appropriate to his audience. His novel *Libre de Blanquerna*, written in Catalan, incorporated narrative with theology and philosophy; he wrote *The Book of Contemplation* first in Arabic and then later translated it into Catalan. Not only did Llull use the vernacular in written communication (Arabic, Catalan, and Latin; his writings were also translated into French and Italian), he also sought to use a commonality of thought in style and content. For instance, he styled *The Book of the Lover and the Beloved* after the style of Muslim Sufi writings; well versed in the Qur'an and Islamic doctrine, he wrote on Islamic beliefs in his *Book of the Gentile* (Bonner 1985, 20).

In the Middle Ages, the intelligentsia of the different religions influenced one another and had much in common in their ways of thinking. Since the strength of Islam and Judaism in the age of Scholasticism was their philosophy, Llull engaged the Saracen and Jewish philosophers where they were intellectually, using Augustinian reason and logic to understand faith. He held that if a scholar could be overwhelmingly convinced of the truth of the gospel through philosophy and rational debate, then that person would convert. This approach was at odds with Llull's own complex conversion process, which unfolded not through philosophical debate but because of a series of supernatural interventions and traumatic encounters with people. He held firmly to the belief, however, that divine reason had placed in God's creation an order that he could discover through the disciplines of language, mathematics, and poetry, in addition to music, geometry, and astronomy. Since the educated, wealthy aristocrats were the shapers of society, Llull was convinced that if these elites were converted, a mass conversion of Jews and Muslims would follow.

In practice, Llull, under government sponsorship, debated with the minority Majorcan Jewish intellectuals in their synagogues with some success, although in Muslim-majority Bugia, Algiers, he spent most of his time imprisoned with limited opportunity for debate and only then with the intervention and protection of the Catalan royal mercenaries. Samuel M. Zwemer concedes that

Llull "perceived the possibilities (though not the limitations) of comparative theology and the science of logic as weapons for the missionary" (1902, 127).

Llull appeared unaware of the controlling influences within the Islamic world. Because of past heresies and fear of Hellenistic influences, Muslim theologians, such as Al-Ghazzali (d. 1111), exhorted the Ummahs (communities of believers) to restrict study and teaching to the revealed knowledge of the Qur'an, which was to be accepted without question (Saunders 1965, 197). Doubting or questioning Allah's composition was sin and resulted in a believer losing any hope of salvation. The fear this inspired severely limited the importance of reason in the conversion process. Further, political instability created by Islamic heretical sects in the Middle Ages produced a controlling cooperation between religion and politics. The Shiite and Ismailian heresies with their Greek philosophical persuasions had almost engulfed Sunni theological tradition, which responded by establishing the madrassa educational system to subjugate unorthodoxy (Talbani 1996, 68–69). Unlike his Muslim counterparts, Llull had freedom of thought and expression, which he used without reciprocal responsiveness.

Well acquainted with Arabic theology and philosophy, Llull wrote about the Trinity and the incarnation in the *Book of the Gentile* and *Felix, the Book of Wonders*. Because Islamic theology considers these ideas idolatrous—since God is one and does not have a son (a relationship between Mary and God being an abomination)—they were not addressed as such in Llull's writings. Not having lived within the Islamic worldview, which preconditioned resentment against these doctrines and restricted critical reflection, Llull remained ignorant of the ineffectiveness of his rational missional methods.

Llull wrote some 256 books; nevertheless, it was in his major work of apologetics that he developed a complex instrument of logic to demonstrate the truth of Christ. He wrote this work to explain the superiority of the Christian faith to Jews and Muslims based on the attributes of God common to all three major religions. He spent years redeveloping a witnessing technique that he called "the Art" (*Ars General, Ars Brevis,* and *Ars Demonstrativa*). The Art was a series of mnemonic charts, which he used to classify all aspects of knowledge, science, and theology, believing that such a system of truth would ultimately support Christian doctrines.

Derived from Jewish theological reflection on how an infinite and perfect God could have a relationship with his finite creation, he synthesized a Christian Neoplatonist understanding of creation. Aware of the questions of both the Jewish and Muslim academic communities, Llull designed the Art to answer them using their own cognitive frameworks.

Missionary Training Schools

For Llull, missionary training was essential in reaching the unbeliever, especially in language, theology, geography, and ethnography. Similar to the

Dominicans, his desire was to establish monasteries to train monks and laypeople to learn Arabic, Hebrew, and other languages of unbelievers to share "the holy truth of the Catholic faith, which is that of Christ." In *Felix, the Book of Wonders*, he expresses his hope that God would send apostles who

---

Wherefore, it appears to me, O Lord, that the conquest of that sacred land will not be achieved . . . saved by love and prayer and the shedding of tears as well as blood.

Ramon Llull (Peers 1969, 30–31)

---

knew science and languages to convert unbelievers and set an example for the church (Llull 1985b, 781).

Although Llull spent some fifty years endeavoring to gain financial support from papacies and monarchies, he only partially succeeded in diverting the church's attention from the Crusades to his peaceful mission techniques. Through the assistance of James II of Majorca and the support of the Portuguese pope John XXI, he founded his first school, Trinity College at Miramar, Majorca, in 1276. There Llull established a curriculum in the liberal arts, theology, Oriental languages, Islamic doctrines, and his own Art for thirteen Franciscans and taught there for a time. It is unclear what happened to the students trained in this institution (Lorenz 1985, 20).

Llull continued to seek endorsement for other missionary training facilities in various cities without success, since popes such as Nicholas IV were more interested in fighting the Saracens than in saving them. This continued until at Pope Clement V's Council of Vienne in 1311 his proposal aroused support for academic chairs in the study of Arabic, Chaldean, and Hebrew in cities where the papal courts resided and at the universities of Bologna, Oxford, Paris, and Salamanca. The council's decision died with Llull in 1316. The insufficient support of the church for Llull's missionary training colleges was one of his major disappointments and the catalyst for his missionary trips to North Africa.

Missions to Africa

Thirty years after his conversion, Llull embarked from Genoa for Tunis, North Africa, on his first mission journey to bring the gospel to Muslims. Desiring to serve Christ unto death yet fearful that the Saracens would imprison or martyr him on landing, Llull claimed, "I want to preach in the land of the Infidels the incarnation of the Son and the three Persons of the Trinity. The Mahometans do not believe in this, but in their blindness think we worship three Gods" (Barber 1903, 46). Despite his good intentions, Llull was so fearful of Muslim persecution that he disembarked from the ship. Then, racked by shame and remorse over his disobedience to God's call, he became physically ill. In 1292, restored in health and courage, he once again set sail for Tunis (Llull 1985a, 30). Upon arriving he decided to "experiment whether he himself could not persuade some of them [Saracens] by conference with their wise men and by manifesting to them, according to the divinely given Method, the incarnation of the Son of God and the three Persons of the Trinity in the divine unity of essence" (Zwemer 1902, 82). A contemporary biographer describes this occasion: "When he [Llull] had answered these [arguments in defense of Islam] readily and given satisfaction therein, they were astonished and confounded" (Peers 1969, 242).

The volatile situation in Tunis caused Llull to flee within a year and focus his energies on obtaining church partnership for a unification of the three monotheistic faiths—Judaism, Christianity, and Islam—which he hoped would defeat the Mongol invaders then threatening Europe and the Middle East. Returning to the Muslim port of Bugia, Algiers, in 1306 he brought his arguments to the city's chief judge, only to suffer imprisonment for six months and then expulsion for proposing to write a book proving the Christian faith. He returned to this city two years later on a reconnaissance mission for a crusade planned by Pope Clement V. He returned to Europe in 1308 and reported that the pope should achieve conquest through prayer, not through military force. Llull again traveled to North Africa and lived peacefully in Tunis, where he debated with the city's intelligentsia, five of whom converted. In this city in 1315 while he was preaching in the market square an angry mob fatally stoned him.

Conclusion

In this chapter we have highlighted early Franciscan missions to the thirteenth-century world via Francis of Assisi and Ramon Llull by underscoring the inspiration of martyrdom and efforts to contextualize the message of Christ. This strategy of Muslim mission was "certainly an alternative to the prevailing model of interaction, which was a battle of words and disputation that brought rancor, ill will, separation, and death, rather than strengthened relationships and healing" (Dries 1998, 6). It also deemphasized the prevailing missionary method of military conquest and forced mass conversions. The Franciscans fostered the belief that it was necessary in mission to respect what was best and central in other religions and use those beliefs as a connecting point to "announce the word of God . . . in order that [unbelievers] may believe in God, the Father, the Son, and the Holy Spirit" (Francis of Assisi 1982a, 121).

Two main religious convictions guided Franciscan missionaries such as Francis of Assisi and Ramon Llull: to present the gospel of Christ in an intellectual manner, which would confound the errors of the nonbeliever; and to attain martyrdom for their beloved Lord. In an age in which the power-obsessed Crusades taught that the only way to convert infidels was by the sword, the Order of Friars Minor demonstrated the love of God by its members' sacrificial lives and compassionate communication—a distinctive mission approach to thirteenth-century Islam that still speaks to the church today.

6

Encountering Medieval
Renewal Missions

Frequently people identify the nailing of Martin Luther's Ninety-Five Theses to the door of the Castle Church at Wittenberg in 1517 as the beginning of the Protestant Reformation. Yet few realize that many earlier medieval renewal movements identified and supported Luther's fundamental disagreements with the Catholic Church. This chapter explores three such groups and their founders: Peter Waldo of southern France in the thirteenth century, John Wycliffe in fourteenth-century England, and the Bohemian Jan Hus of the fifteenth century.

Peter Waldo (1140–1218), who started the Waldensian movement, was a converted merchant whose itinerant preaching stressed a passion for voluntary poverty and spreading the gospel of Christ. Known as the "Poor of Lyons," his followers dispersed throughout Europe. They proclaimed the errors of the Catholic Church and adamantly pushed for the sole leadership of Christ and the need for evangelism. Waldo was excommunicated by Pope Lucius III, but his teaching and the persecution of his followers continued well beyond his lifetime.

The Waldensians were not alone in their dissatisfaction with the church. John Wycliffe (1320–1384) was an English theologian who spoke against the church's abuses of power. Convinced of the need for people to be able to read the Bible for themselves, Wycliffe was the first to translate the entire Bible into English. His followers, the Lollards, were laypeople who preached the gospel and spread Wycliffe's teachings throughout England. Like the Waldensians, the Lollards were also persecuted by the church despite their popularity among the masses.

Further, in Bohemia (now the Czech Republic), Jan Hus (1373–1415) followed Wycliffe's example and boldly preached for church reform and social change. After Wycliffe's writings were banned in Europe, Hus was burned at the stake for heresy against the doctrines of the Catholic Church and became a martyr of the early Reformers. Unlike earlier groups, which only focused on ecclesiastical reform, Hus's followers began a political and religious uprising; they rebelled against their Catholic rulers, defeating five consecutive papal crusades (1420–1431), and formed a national Hussite Church in Bohemia.

The fundamental disputes that the leaders of the Protestant Reformation had with the Catholic Church—dissatisfaction with spiritual impotence and abuses of authority—were already the central foci of many medieval pre-Protestant movements throughout Europe. Hence, in this chapter we further expand on the impact of the Waldensians, the Lollards, and the Hussites to demonstrate that sparks from these movements helped light the explosive Protestant Reformation of the sixteenth century.

Waldensian Missions

While scholars debate the origins of the Waldensians, most credit Peter Waldo with the movement's formation. Itinerant preaching and voluntary poverty characterized this medieval alliance. Linked to the political and economic restlessness of the changing society, this association of poverty earned the condemnation of the Roman Church, which sought to preserve institutional unity. Persecuted as heretics for over six hundred years, the Waldensians influenced later Protestant Reformation groups through their biblical interpretation of Scripture, advocacy of the priesthood of all believers, and personal devotion. Even Martin Luther's German translation of the Bible found its medieval origins in the Waldensian Bible (P. Schaff 1910, 202).

Historical Background

There is no clear consensus on the Waldensians' origins. Some trace them back to Irenaeus, who served as bishop of Lyons at the end of the second century. While Voltaire claimed they were the remnant of Gallic Christians who preserved true Christianity, most credit their formation to the leadership of twelfth-century merchant Peter Waldo (1140–1218). Furthermore, the recent recovery of Waldensian writings that were preserved by famous French theologian Peter the Chanter (d. 1197) has provided scholars new information on the early stages of Waldo's life; these scholars have, in turn, generated further evidence for his ownership of the movement (Biller 2006, 18). Regardless of Waldo's role, scholars "agree on the essential point, that the founder of the movement was a rich layman, who suddenly decided to abandon all his wealth and seek a life of perfection through apostolic poverty" (Cameron 2001, 12).

Peter Valdés ("Waldo" in English) was born in the village of Vaux on the Rhone River in eastern France around 1140. He moved to Lyons as a young man, became a wealthy merchant in the city, and like any respected citizen attended church regularly (De Blois 1929, 37). Around 1170, three incidents changed Waldo's attitude toward Christ and his life's vocation: he witnessed the sudden death of a close friend after a dinner party; he heard a commemorative song of Saint Alexis sung in the city streets; and he received the counsel of a wise priest. Through these events and the teaching of Christ, Waldo experienced a radical conversion whereby he renounced his previous business practices, paid his debts, and distributed his wealth.

While questioning the meaning of life, the transformed merchant turned to the Bible and found solace in the Gospel story of the rich young ruler whom Jesus directed to sell his material wealth and follow him (Matt. 19:21). Waldo heeded Christ's words to the ruler and dedicated his life to following Christ, preaching his story, and attracting a following that he called the "Poor in Spirit" or the "Poor of Lyons." Unlike mendicants of the time, Waldo did not donate his wealth to a monastery but continued in his working profession, sharing the gospel of Jesus as the sole authority of the Christian faith in his community. He distributed his estate to his wife and established dowries for his daughters to attend the convent school at the Abbey of Fontevraud. He later directed the rest of his fortune toward personally giving out food and clothing to the poor at the public square of Lyons, even starting a soup kitchen.

While the Poor of Lyons were receiving assistance from Waldo's social welfare program, he read the Scriptures in the local vernacular and attracted many followers with his simple gospel message. Later, he commissioned two priests to translate the Latin Vulgate Bible into the French provincial language, aiding the movement's message of "repentance, good works, and an authentically Christian life" (Tourn 1980, 8). Waldo advocated that the life of poverty and discipleship was required of all followers of Christ, not just religious professionals, and so began his itinerant preaching. This resulted in his excommunication by Pierre Scise, the archbishop of Lyons, who removed Waldo from the church for preaching without ordination. However, following an appeal to Pope Alexander III and the Third Lateran Council of 1179, it was decided that Waldo and his laypeople could preach their poverty gospel if they received approval from the local ecclesiastical authorities. In response, Waldo proclaimed before Rome, "We have decided to live the words of the Gospel, essentially that of the Sermon on the Mount and the Commandments, that is, to live in poverty without concern for tomorrow. But we hold that also those who continue to live their lives in the world doing good will be saved" ("Prophet without Honor" 1989, 7).

Even though the church designed the ruling to inhibit the merchant leader and his followers, the Waldensians were so convinced of their calling to preach to the poor that they continued to proclaim Christ, resulting in the movement's expansion throughout southern France and into Italy. Archbishop Scise used this blatant disregard for church authority to force Pope Lucius III at the

SIDEBAR 6.1

Waldensian Doctrine

Four original Waldensian documents (*Noble Lesson, Ancient Confession of Faith, Catechism of the Ancient Waldensians*, and *Treatise of the Antichrist*) were retrieved by English ambassador Morland in 1658 for Oliver Cromwell to advocate on behalf of the Waldensians before the Duke of Savoy and Louis XIV of France. Unfortunately, the documents later disappeared from the University of Cambridge.

The *Ancient Confession of Faith*, written in 1120, for example, shows their significance. It denied the belief in the authority of the Apocrypha, the existence of purgatory, the efficacy of holy water, prayers to the saints, and the sacraments (except baptism and the Eucharist).

Later church movements also used Waldensian doctrine as confirmation of their reforms. A little over a century after Luther nailed his theses on the door of Wittenberg's cathedral, Huguenot pastor Jean-Paul Perrin published a defense of the Reformation by arguing that Waldensian doctrine had supported the movement's tenets four centuries earlier. Writing from exile in Switzerland, Jean Léger recorded the Waldensian massacres at Piedmont, Italy, in 1655 and, in pleading for assistance, claimed that Protestant beliefs have apostolic connection to ancient Waldensian dogma, which strengthened the legitimacy of Luther and Calvin (1669, 177).

Reflection and Discussion

1. Why did the Reformers believe that appealing to Waldensian doctrines justified their own reforms?
2. Where do you see traces of Waldensian doctrinal influence in contemporary Protestantism?

Council of Verona in 1184 to excommunicate Waldo and his group from the Catholic Church (Shelley 1995, 208; Irvin and Sunquist 2001, 412).

Waldensian Practice

Giorgio Tourn, a Waldensian historian, argues that there were two distinctive characteristics of the Poor of Lyons: they acknowledged only the leadership of Christ in the church and lived out Christ in the world rather than in isolation (1980, 7–9). The catechism of the Waldensians emphasized salvation through faith in Christ alone, obedience to the teaching of the Gospels, and the belief that only the elect of God comprised the true church. When the Waldensians refused to obey the order of the council of Pope Alexander III and continued to preach without the approval of the archbishop of Lyons, the church feared dissent and authorized the nobility to imprison those who defied the ecclesiastical governance. This culminated in the Fourth Lateran Council (1215), which sanctioned mass execution of the Waldensians. In this environment the Dominicans attempted to win back the Waldensian "heretics" in southern France and save them from the papal wrath by preaching and living a simple gospel similar to their lifestyle.

A Dominican mendicant, on returning to the bishop of Cavaillon from a mission to convert the heretics, was so impressed with the group's biblical knowledge that the bishop commissioned a group of scholars from the University of Paris to challenge the Waldensians. The scholars likewise returned extolling the dissenters' concept of salvation, which proved more insightful than all their "disputations of divinity" at the Sorbonne (Perrin 1624, 30).

Their biblical knowledge was not surprising, for a prerequisite of Waldensian ordination was a minimum of three years serving as an itinerant tentmaker apprenticed to a seasoned minister. Waldensian pastors oversaw their congregations, preaching throughout the week, often in the open fields, and living in simplicity and piety. Even their enemies recognized that "they lived very religiously in all things, their manners well-seasoned, and their words wise and polished, by their wills always speaking of God and his saints, pervading to virtue and to hate sin, to the end that they might be in greater esteem with good men" (Perrin 1624, 29).

Waldensian ministers also memorized "all the chapters of St. Matthew and St. John with all the Epistles called canonical, and a good part of the writings of Solomon, David, and the prophets" (Mitchell 1853, 375). The Waldensians did not recognize the legitimacy of a minister based on his appointment from Rome. They believed that ministers obtained their authority from "the true sense of faith; by sound doctrine; by a life of good example; by the preaching of the gospel; and a due administration of the sacraments" (Mitchell 1853, 381–82). It is important to note, however, that while the Waldensians often found themselves in opposition to the Catholic Church, they still held to much of the piety and doctrine of medieval Catholicism, unlike the other early Reformers (Accardy 2001, 47).

Expansion in the Midst of Persecution

In spite of avid persecution, the Waldensian movement dispersed throughout Europe and by 1315 had led to the establishment of over four thousand societies throughout Germany, Bulgaria, Croatia, Dalmatia, and Hungary (Perrin 1624). Manuscripts recovered by Alexander Patschovsky in 1979 from a Cistercian monastery at Heiligenkreuz, Austria, revealed records of a Waldensian inquisition trial held in Bohemia during the mid-fourteenth century. These manuscripts showed that the inquisition was not limited to France and northern Italy, as had been previously believed, but was also intensely active in Bohemia. Patschovsky's research indicated that Waldensians and their doctrine were rife in that region in the 1350s, with approximately ten thousand Bohemian Waldensians active at the time (Lerner 1986, 238).

Accounts of Waldensian persecution drew sympathy from many in Europe. Bohemian refugees, for example, presented a sympathetic John Wycliffe with a statement of faith. Swiss ambassadors wrote letters to German princes urging them to grant asylum to Waldensians, which eventuated with the allocation of lands near Brandenburg. Furthermore, the Protestant cantons of Switzerland assisted the Waldensians fleeing from Italy and France, especially in Geneva, the center of the Reformed movement (Muston 1875).

Extended Influence

The Waldensians played an active role in shaping the Protestant faith. An Austrian Waldensian bishop ordained by the Catholic Church provided a legitimate episcopate succession to the first ministers of the Unitas Fratrum, or Bohemian Brethren (P. Schaff 1919, 567). The Puritan John Milton admired Waldensian piety and perseverance so much that he references them in his sonnet "On the Late Massacre in Piedmont": "Avenge, O Lord, thy slaughtered saints, whose bones / lie scattered on the Alpine mountains cold; / e'en them, who kept thy truth so pure of old" (Tourn 1980, 125). Furthermore, in the early part of the eighteenth century, Count Ludwig Nikolaus von Zinzendorf established a refuge at Herrnhut for the Waldensians and the Bohemian Breth-

---

In the name of the Father, Son, and Holy Spirit, and of the blessed and ever Virgin Mary. Be it noted by all the faithful that I, Valdesius [Peter Waldo], and all my brethren, standing before the Holy Gospels, do declare that we believe with all our hearts, having been grasped by faith, and that we profess openly that Father, Son, and Holy Spirit are three Persons, one God.

Peter Waldo (Tourn 1980, 13)

---

ren who formed the Moravian missionary movement. In turn, these groups greatly influenced the early Methodists.

Methodist circuit preachers in Great Britain and the American colonies modeled their strategy after the Waldensian ministers, who, because of persecution, traveled in circuits to minister to their scattered congregations (Muston 1875). The Waldensian Church still exists today in parts of Piedmont, Italy, where, around a century after Calvin's death, his understanding of Scripture had become the church's official creed (Accardy 2001, 55).

Summary

Though the mist of history still shrouds its precise beginnings, most scholars believe that the Waldensian movement emerged through Peter Waldo. A successful merchant, he advocated a biblical platform of simplicity of living, meeting the needs of the poor, and pursuing godly discipleship. Waldo's desire "to live in poverty without concern for tomorrow" reflected the Waldensian doctrine of salvation through faith, practicing lifestyles of piety, and the importance of biblical truth ("Prophet without Honor" 1989, 7). The influence of the Waldensians extended beyond Waldo to help shape the future of Protestantism. Another medieval renewal movement that assisted in determining the Reformation was that of the Lollards of England.

Lollard Missions

After William Cameron Townsend translated the Bible for the Cakchiquel Indians of Central America, he returned to the United States in 1934 and, with the assistance of two students, established a training camp to prepare translators of Latin American indigenous languages. The camp, named "Camp Wycliffe" in honor of John Wycliffe, grew into the renowned organization now known as Wycliffe Bible Translators, which currently has over six thousand members from nearly fifty nations, working in over one thousand languages around the globe. Wycliffe, who in 1384 was the first to translate the whole Bible for English speakers, was not only a translator but also an influential Reformer and missionary. His bold views on religious and civil authorities often put him in disfavor with the church. His writings, however, proved to be extremely persuasive in the lives of his followers, the Lollards, and their mission to preach the gospel of Christ.

Historical Background

John Wycliffe entered Oxford University as a student in 1345 and completed an arts degree in 1356. After receiving his doctorate in theology in 1372, he became a lecturer at the university in addition to serving as the rector of three different local parishes (1361–1384). In 1372 he entered the service of King Edward III and liaised on his behalf regarding the papal provisions of Pope Gregory XI; four years later, he became clerical advisor to John of Gaunt, duke of Lancaster, who became his political patron in theological conflicts with William Courtney, bishop of London, later the archbishop of Canterbury (Farr 1974, 7).

Operating within the papacy, Wycliffe continually opposed the abuses of the clergy, which shaped his theology as he interacted with both state and church authorities. Wycliffe condemned the moral laxity of the friars, poor education of the clergy, accumulation of wealth by bishops, and secular employment of priests. He also preached against pilgrimages, relic worship, and the sale of indulgences, together with the cult of the saints, masses for the dead, and the movement of money from England to Rome. Likewise, he did not accept the infallibility of the pope and even declared that the vicar of Christ be called the "Antichrist" (D. Wood 1984, 113). Wycliffe did not reject the seven sacraments or the belief in purgatory but felt strongly that confession to a priest and confirmation were unnecessary.

In his writings, Wycliffe made a distinction between the church of Rome and the elect. He believed that the church included only the elect, with Christ, not the pope, as its head, and that the laws of Christ had authority over the corrupt laws of the church. From this belief, Wycliffe derived two main resolutions: the church should not allow priests to perform functions if they were living in sin; and the church had the responsibility to reform itself. Furthermore, since God placed governments in power, Wycliffe believed they should take the role of reforming society and act as a watchdog of the church.

Because Wycliffe lived between the two eras of Scholasticism and the Reformation, his writings were highly controversial, especially his views on civil and religious authority. So contentious were the Englishman's writings that the Blackfriar Synod in London in 1382 condemned them, as did antipope John XXIII in 1410. In *On the Church* (1378), Wycliffe maintains that the right to hold secular or ecclesiastical office rests on grace, and specifically those whom God sanctifies by his grace. He goes on to say that a civil authority can remove clergy from their positions if they are not living in a state of grace, claiming that there is no distinction between laity and clergy and that all the elect of God are priests. The Oxford professor's major divergence with the accepted practices of the established church concerned the role of tradition in orthodox interpretation. Wycliffe accused the church leaders of behaving as Pharisees: letting traditions be the source of church authority instead of Scripture, which prevented the people from truly knowing Christ. Indeed, the Papal Schism in 1378 evidenced that papal power had ceased and that the Bible was the predominant source of authority.

Wycliffe also challenged the church's "superstitious" understanding of transubstantiation in the Eucharist. In his works *On Apostasy* (1379) and *On the Eucharist* (1380), he maintains that Christ's genuine presence is in the bread and the wine, yet rejects the notion that the substance of the elements is completely annihilated when consumed. It is not a magical rite, he argues, but needs to be received in faith by having "a love of Christ, peace with one's neighbor, and actual devotion" (*De Eucharistia* in Stacey 1958, 358).

Scripture Translation

One of the most distinctive features of Wycliffe's theology was the *lex Christi*, which concluded, "No (th)ing untouchid in (th)is lawe shulde be dun or axid to do" (Stacey 1958, 357). That is, he viewed the Scriptures as the final religious authority, which fueled his criticism of various practices of the Roman Church. He believed that the "Holy Scripture is the highest authority for every Christian and the standard of faith and all human perfection" (Mackinnon 1939, 90). He was angered by the unfair hierarchal advantage that priests took over their congregations, corrupting the law of God to benefit themselves (Marsden 2011, 287). He wanted laypeople to have access to Scripture so that they might recognize the distortion of the church, which Christ had instituted for them (MacCulloch 2009, 568).

Influenced by Augustine of Hippo's *On Christian Doctrine*, Wycliffe believed in a fivefold rule for interpreting the Bible: (1) start with a reliable text, (2) trace the logic, (3) interpret difficult passages by comparing with clearer passages, (4) maintain humility, and (5) allow the Holy Spirit to guide (*De Veritate*, I, c. 9, 194–205, quoted in Mallard 1961, 51). Anyone prayerfully seeking guidance of the Spirit, therefore, could understand the plain meaning of Scripture. Wycliffe used this process in his personal life; "all his discoveries of scriptural truth were obtained by a study of the Bible and the writings of old theologians (mainly the church fathers)" (D. Wood 1984, 113). The "elect," chosen by God and not the church, had immediate access to Christ through the Bible; no one could enter heaven or know God without his election. This was a revolutionary idea for the time, placing the practice of biblical interpretation and the promise of being a part of God's elect in the hands of everyday people, instead of being restricted to the professional religious. Wycliffe insisted that the Bible was the daily guidebook for every Christian and that everyone had the right to read it for himself or herself.

In 1395, under Wycliffe's supervision, two of his disciples, Nicholas of Hereford (doctor of divinity and an Oxford canon) and John Purvey (Wycliffe's church secretary at Lutterworth), completed translating the Latin Vulgate Bible into Midland English (the idiomatic Wycliffe Bible for the ordinary people), making this the first time that the entire Bible had been translated into English.

Wycliffe's Movement: The Lollards

Wycliffe produced numerous short tracts for the English people, including a series of sermon outlines, which emphasized the exposition of Scripture. Itinerant preachers, commissioned by Wycliffe in 1381, employed these outlines to disperse knowledge of the Bible among the commoners (Hudson 1985, 145). This band of "poor priests" spoke wherever they could find an audience, teaching the Scriptures as well as the Lord's Prayer, the Ten Commandments, and the seven deadly sins. These men, predominantly Oxford graduates, were sent barefoot, two by two, and armed with a long staff to minister to the people in the local vernacular. Wycliffe charged his followers, "Go and preach, it is the sublimest work; but imitate not the priests we see after the sermon sitting at the ale house, or at a gambling table. . . . After your sermon is ended, do you visit the sick, the aged, the poor, the blind, and the lame and succor them?" (D. Wood 1984, 87). *Lollards* was the term used to

SIDEBAR 6.2

Translating the Bible into English

In the fifteenth century, Wycliffe penned these words about translating the Bible into English:

[Say] that the truth of God stands not in one language more than in another, but who so lives best and teaches best pleases most God, of what language that ever it be, therefore the law of God written and taught in English may edify the common people, as it does clerks in Latin, [say] it is the sustenance to souls that should be saved. And Christ commanded the gospel to be preached, for the people should learn it, know it, and work thereafter. Why may we not then write in English the gospel and all holy Scripture to edification of Christian souls, as the preacher shows it

truly to the people? For, if it should not be written, it should not be preached. This heresy and blasphemy should Christian men put from their hearts, for it is sprung from the fiend, father of lies (John in the 8th chapter).

John Wycliffe (Hudson 1978, 107)

Reflection and Discussion

1. What were Wycliffe's motives for translating the Bible into English? Do you believe that they are still relevant today?
2. In what ways might this characterize how people think about the English language today? In what ways does it differ from contemporary thinking about English?

describe the followers of Wycliffe, a word derived from the Dutch language meaning "mumblers or mutterers of prayers" (Estep 1986, 67).

The poor preachers had three main centers of operation: Leicester, London, and the west district of England, from which they dispersed into the surrounding counties of Berkshire, Gloucester, Hereford, Monmouth, Northampton, Sussex, Warwick, Wiltshire, and Worcester. They even reached beyond England as well. One Lollard, William Thorpe, when questioned by Archbishop Thomas

---

And Christ commanded the gospel to be preached, for the people should learn it, know it and work thereafter. Why may we not then write in English the gospel and all Holy Scripture to edification of Christian souls, as the preacher shows it to the people?

John Wycliffe (Hudson 1978, 107)

Arundel of Canterbury in 1407, admitted to preaching north of England for twenty years (D. Wood 1984, 87–89). The followers of Wycliffe often discussed his heretical views in secret meetings, yet they lacked the organizational skills to create a set of Lollard values and beliefs such as those of the Lutherans and the Anabaptists. Using the Bible as the criterion of judgment, the Lollards opposed the wealth of the clergy and the weakened asceticism of the mendicant orders. The Lollard movement began as a "product of academic speculation but moved out of the academic world to become a popular movement" (Hudson 1988, 62).

Response to Lollard Ministry

While the church and the Crown resisted Wycliffe and his movement, the public favored the Lollards. In Walsingham's 1382 records, he connects Wycliffe's escape from censure in 1377 with his sermons that "charmed the ears of Londoners with his perverse doctrines" (Hudson 1985, 75). Soldiers were often found in the crowds listening to the Lollards preach, which brought security to the movement as well as the support of the gentry. Great examples are Thomas Latimer of Leicestershire and Northamptonshire, who protected the poor preachers and gave them hospitality, and the mayor of Northampton, who hired Lollard students from Oxford to preach in his city (Hudson 1988, 153).

In 1382 the Blackfriar's Council condemned ten of Wycliffe's propositions as heretical and fourteen as erroneous. This action prompted the termination of Wycliffe's professorship at Oxford and the confiscation of all his literature. Consequently, he retreated to his duties as the Anglican parish vicar of

SIDEBAR 6.3

The Internal Mission of the Lollards

Drawn mostly from the common people, the Lollards spread beliefs among their own society to such an extent that the Peasants' Revolt of 1381 (three years before Wycliffe's death) was blamed on the views expressed in Wycliffe's teachings. The leader of the revolt, John Ball, admitted to being a disciple of Wycliffe from his two years as a student at Oxford University. Certainly, Wycliffe's teachings attacking the church's hierarchy and stirring commoners to unshackle themselves from their feudal lords fueled the popular reform movement. "Popular opinion was hostile to the clergy and ready to help bring the Church out of the Middle Ages into modern times" (Cowie 1970, 71). Wycliffe's opinion of the revolt was that, although the peasants acted illegally and cruelly, the clergy were to blame and received their rightful punishment (Stacey 1962, 327–28).

Reflection and Discussion

1. Why were Wycliffe's teachings so attractive to the local community, yet rejected by the church authorities?
2. Do you believe there are civil situations when acts of violence and disorder are justifiable, contrary to public law and order? Why or why not?

Lutterworth in Leicestershire. Furthermore, King Henry IV supported the conviction of the Lollards, giving the archbishops of York and Canterbury the authority to arrest and imprison anyone who followed Wycliffe's beliefs. Almost a decade later, in 1395, John Montague, Thomas Latimer, and Richard Stury—all of English nobility—proposed to Parliament the Twelve Conclusions, outlining reforms for the church. Although the Crown and Parliament rejected their request, the movement continued to grow as Lollard preachers spread their beliefs in the rural areas, often obtaining support and protection from the local authorities. Continued growth led Archbishop Arundel to succeed in persuading Parliament to pass the De Haeretico Comburendo Act in 1401, which allowed the execution of the heretical Lollards. Furthermore, the archbishop of Canterbury published the *Constitutions of Arundel*, which forbade the translation and reading of the Bible without the bishop's permission. While the Lollards received local support, they suffered unyielding persecution from the church.

Summary

John Wycliffe's ministry left a legacy of Bible translation and a movement, which helped to foster the rise of Protestantism. While the Lollards failed to accomplish everything they envisioned, they did play a significant role in setting the stage for the Reformation. William R. Estep writes, "While the reformation [the Lollards] attempted to generate was stillborn, it did provide the seeds of dissent that prepared the masses for the more dynamic movements of reform that arose out of the Reformation of the sixteenth century" (1986, 68). Paul S. Seaver even credits the Lollards as the source of Protestantism, serving as an early answer to the "Catholic question of where the true church was before Martin Luther" (1998, 33). Wycliffe and his teachings served as a vital predecessor to Heinrich Bullinger, John Calvin, John Knox, Martin Luther, Philipp Melanchthon, and Huldrych Zwingli and the subsequent theological and social revolution. Jan Hus was another radical activist directly affected by Wycliffe whose influence also reached into the sixteenth century.

Hussite Missions

On July 6, 1415, in Constance, Germany, bitter religious differences between the Catholic Church and a Reformer came to a dramatic finale. Jan Hus, a Bohemian Catholic priest, while mocking the heretical accusations of his accusers, was soaked in tar and bound to a thick post atop a massive pile of firewood. Wearing a heavy chain around his neck and a paper miter on his head, he echoed Jesus's words of Luke 23:46 before the flames consumed him, "Father, into your hands I commit my spirit."

121

Unfortunately, this tragic episode of Reformation history almost disappears in the shadow of Calvin, Knox, Luther, and Zwingli. Emerging from beneath the oppression of the Holy Roman Empire, the Bohemian Hus was a passionate theologian and preacher who continued the work of his Reformer predecessors in advocating scriptural authority and the revival of the church. Despite a number of suppressive ecclesial actions, Hus continued to preach biblical truth even into exile, eventually forfeiting his life at the stake. His sacrifice was not in vain, however, since it ignited a Bohemian uprising, which led to the collapse of the Catholic Church in Bohemia and the establishment of national Protestantism.

Tentacles of the Holy Roman Empire

During the reign of Emperor Charles IV (1316–1378) of the Holy Roman Empire (which at the time consisted of Upper and Lower Lusatia, Silesia, Moravia, and Bohemia), the independent kingdom of Bohemia (the present-day Czech Republic) experienced a period of extraordinary financial growth and prosperity. The German emperor of the Luxembourg lineage aimed to make Bohemia the central power of his empire, incorporating German culture into the lives of the Bohemian people. This was not difficult, since Bohemia was surrounded by German-speaking nations, and its population included many Germans who had immigrated to the state. The influence of Germany was evident even in the church, as the majority of the priests in Bohemia were German or of German descent and spoke only their mother tongue. However, the forced integration of culture on the Bohemians began to create socio-cultural issues, which led to ethnic tensions between the two people groups.

In addition to reshaping the state's culture, Emperor Charles IV brought about many political innovations to enhance the prosperity of Bohemia, including religious reform. One such reform was the Golden Bull of 1356, which denied the papacy's right to give consent to the election of the Holy Roman emperor. This provided protection and support for the Reformers and bold preachers, such as Conrad Waldhauser and Jan Milic of Kroměřiz, despite persecution. Two other Reformers, Mathias of Janow and Thomas of Stítné, writing in Czech, pronounced the Bible to be the standard of faith and attacked the immorality of the clergy.

Political Papacy

The Papal Schism (1378–1417) divided Europe in its allegiances to the papacy between three popes: Benedict XIII, Gregory XII, and Alexander V (followed by the Pisan antipope John XXIII). Each claimed to be the true heir to Peter's Holy See at the same time, creating much havoc and confusion within the church. Each pope controlled armies that crusaded against each other with the support of secular kingdoms that were vying for influence over the church. Church corruption was ubiquitous, as recorded by Archdeacon Pavel of Janovic, who depicted priests in Prague as drunkards who engaged in promiscuous acts and disregarded the poor (Fudge 1998, 16–17). Charles H. George has commented on this socioeconomic situation, revealing the rampant corruption and injustice at the time:

> The ecclesiastical hierarchy controlled about one third of the arable land and vast wealth in buildings and gold; in the towns the churchmen were exempt from taxes, yet collected heavy interest on loans to the burghers; and in the villages the Church was not only a staunch opponent to manumission of servile labor, but also was the hated collector of fees for every moment of religious ceremony from baptism to burial. (1971, 19)

Hus's Preaching in Prague

Born in 1373 to farming parents in Husinec (in Czech the word means "goose town") in southern Bohemia, Jan Hus moved to Prague at seventeen to attend the city's local university. He excelled in school, obtaining a bachelor of sacred theology and a master of arts. After graduating, Hus went on to become a member of the university's faculty in 1396 and lectured as dean of philosophy at Charles College. He joined the clergy in 1400 because it brought him both wealth and status. Two years later, he became the rector and preacher at the Chapel of the Holy Innocents of Bethlehem in Prague. Hus's preaching was not the beginning but rather a part of a long tradition of Reformation ideas. Jarold K. Zeman concludes, "The tradition of public reformist preaching in the language of the people, Czech and German, was thus firmly established in Prague and other Bohemian and Moravian urban centers for at least a generation prior to the career of Jan Hus" (1976, 5). While Hus was not the first to introduce reformation, his ideas expanded to have extreme influence on future Reformers.

Hus's Theology

In 1382 Anne of Bohemia married Richard II of England, which began an open exchange of both students and ideas between the universities of Prague and Oxford. This exchange introduced the writings of John Wycliffe in Bohemia, which fanned the flames of reform. Hus then further urged Rome to rescind the ban on Wycliffe's writings, pleading, "Therefore most compassionate father, we beseech on bended knees . . . that Your Holiness design to remove . . . the illegal aspersion by annulling the sentence" (Spinka 1972, 41). Although the ban remained, the writings of Wycliffe provided Hus with the philosophical framework for the Czech reformation. In contrast to the

English priest, however, Hus preferred the transformation of society through the church, since his native government under King Václav was administratively incompetent and morally corruptible.

Though more conservative than Wycliffe, Hus recognized the discrepancies between Scripture and the operation of the Catholic Church and declared that the Scriptures were "the supreme rule of faith and conduct." He viewed the church as composed of the elect with Christ, not the pope, as the head; and the Scriptures, not the church, as the ultimate authority in life's conduct. This, in turn, influenced his view of the church's role in social change. The Bohemian Reformer did not want to subvert the authority of the local church but rather strove for reformation within the church. He saw the church as the perfect agent for

> While the prelates of the Church, both high and low, were aiming only to grow rich and at times were bequeathing fabulous wealth to sons and nephews, the heretic Huss, like Christ, left nothing but those few poor garments. Huss had not only preached, he had also practiced, and like Saint Francis of Assisi, he had wed coram populo, Dame Poverty.
>
> Benito Mussolini (1929, 74–75)

stirring social change rather than waiting on the broken government to intervene, believing that it was the church's responsibility to reach out to the community. Hus argued that the renovation of the church preceded the transformation of society. Evaluation of church doctrine needed biblical scrutiny since "the law of God" was the guiding principle of all theology and life (Fudge 1998, 95).

Hus's reflective return to the Scriptures initially concerned social reform of the European medieval feudal system in regard to its hierarchical structure of nobility, including merchants, artisans, clergy, and peasants. In the midst of a growing nationalistic awareness that the church was "the one institution with a foreign head, expensive, arrogant, and remote," Hus concerned himself with the physical and spiritual welfare of the peasants. He was more interested in the moral reform of the church than ecclesiastical revolution, believing that the church was composed of more than the clergy (C. H. George 1971, 20). This was in staunch opposition to Stanislav of Znojmo (Hus's revered teacher), who defined the church as consisting of only the pope and the cardinals, even excluding the bishops (Spinka 1968, 51). The outworking of Hus's belief manifested itself at Bethlehem Chapel, where he preached in the vernacular and administered both the bread and the wine of the Eucharist to common people. This was in direct opposition to the Catholic Church, which strictly separated the cup from the laity to reinforce clerical authority.

Heresy Condemned

When Rome condemned Wycliffe's writings as heretical in 1410, Archbishop Zbyněk sought an injunction from the newly elected pope, Alexander V. His request was to "root out all heresy in his diocese, to prevent at all hazards the spread of Wycliffe's doctrines, to require all those possessed of copies of his writings to deliver them up, and to forbid all preaching except in places privileged by the Church" (Kuhns 1907, 64). Hus's refusal to comply with this direction resulted in the censorship of Bethlehem Chapel, forbidding his preaching despite the protests of his two thousand congregants. In 1411 Rome declared Hus's writings heretical and afterward excommunicated him for the third time, along with a number of King Václav's palace officials. Hus wrote to Zbyněk: "Your Paternity should therefore know that it has never been my intention—and I trust in the Lord it will never be—to desist from obedience of the Holy Mother Church; on the contrary, in accordance with the precept of the blessed apostle Peter, my intention is to obey not only the Roman pontiff and Your Paternity, but also to submit 'to every human creature for God's sake'" (Spinka 1972, 36).

King Václav then entered the fray and confronted the archbishop about his decisions. This stand forced Zbyněk to use the "most powerful weapon in the arsenal of the church"—a ban on both public worship (blessings and preaching) and the administration of the sacraments, such as marriage, burial, and the Eucharist—and an interdict was placed on the city of Prague (Fudge 1998, 74). Through judicial support, the king triumphed and pressured Zbyněk to clear Hus and his supporters of all their accused heresies.

Preaching in Exile

After Pope Alexander V died in 1410, the antipope John XXIII became pope and inaugurated the sale of indulgences to fund a crusade against a papal rival. Hus preached against the ordinance, charging that the sale of indulgences supported the immoral lifestyle of the priests. King Václav viewed Hus's reaction as interfering with his royal financial interests, and the faculty of the University of Prague denounced him as disobedient to the papacy. Hus was excommunicated for the fourth time, and Prague was again under interdict with the king's consent.

In 1412 Hus voluntarily went into exile at the castle of Krakowec so that the city of Prague could maintain its divine services. He continued preaching for two years in the Bohemian countryside, as well as to his Bethlehem congregation via letters and occasional visits (Spinka 1941, 46). People came from as far as Germany and Poland to hear Hus preach in the fields, barns, forests, and rural villages (Kuhns 1907, 81). He wrote of this time, "I have preached in towns and market-places; now I preach behind hedges, in villages, castles, fields, and woods. If it were possible I would preach on the seashore, or from a ship, as my Savior did" (Workman 1904, 86). Hus was determined to proclaim the gospel wherever he could gain an audience. During his exile, Hus wrote *De Ecclesia (The Church)*, in which he criticized papal authority, revised a Bohemian translation of the Bible, translated Wycliffe's tracts into the vernacular, and wrote letters accusing the church and city leaders of hindering the spread of the gospel. He pleaded, "Give heed to God's cause for a great wrong is being done to Him; for they [those in authority] wish to suppress His holy Word, to destroy the chapel useful for the preaching of God's Word, and thus to obstruct the salvation of the people" (Spinka 1972, 77). In a letter "to a certain nobleman," he wrote:

> I presume that they likewise incited Your Nobility against me. Shall I be terrified at that to keep still about the truth of the gospel? Certainly no; for they themselves are opposed to the gospel of Jesus Christ, desiring to constrict it so that it could not be freely preached, as the most merciful Lord commanded. Truly the prelates have now assumed the spirit of the pagans and the Pharisees prohibiting the preaching of the gospel in chapels and in other appropriate places. (Spinka 1972, 77)

Hus's Imprisonment and Martyrdom

In 1414 Emperor Sigismund requested that Hus appear before a church council in Constance and explain his views, with promised safety throughout. Despite the warnings of many Bohemian nobles not to trust the invitation, Hus was eager to convince the German religious officials of his genuine concern for the church. On arrival, however, the church leaders imprisoned Hus in the Dominican monastery for several months. Asked to write an explanation of his beliefs, he instead requested an open hearing. Hus's friend, Jan of Chlum, represented his case before the tribunal. When asked by the presiding cardinal, Pierre d'Ailly, to recant his beliefs, Hus replied, "I John Hus . . . fearing to offend God and to fall into perjury, am not willing to

---

If anyone seeks . . . peace with the flesh, the world, and the devil, he will not have it.

Jan Hus (Spinka 1972, 75)

---

recant all or any of the articles produced against me in the testimonies of the false witnesses. Furthermore, fearing to offend against the truth and to speak against the opinions of the saints, I am not willing to recant any of them" (Spinka 1972, 206).

Tried at the Council of Constance as a heretic, Hus was burned at the stake on July 6, 1415. Seemingly, his martyrdom came as a blessed surprise to him since he considered suffering for Christ something to embrace yet did not consider himself commendable of such an honor. He had written, "For alas! It cannot be found that I would be worthy of the sufferings of the martyrs, which the holy fathers endured for the Lord" (Spinka 1972, 44).

Reformation after Hus

It only took a short time for Hus's death to cause political and social turmoil in Bohemia and Moravia. Thomas A. Fudge describes this immediate influence: "Within a year of his death, the memory of Jan Hus gained commemorative status and liturgical observance. In short order, he was elevated to the status of a popular saint and was thus venerated by some Hussite communities" (2011, 45). At the Bohemian Diet, 452 Bohemian and Moravian nobles sent an official complaint to the Council of Constance and formed a Hussite League to ensure religious freedom in Bohemia. Sigismund, a vigorous opponent of Hus, became king of Bohemia in 1419, and a civil war broke out. Pope Martin V declared a crusade against the Hussite militant resistance. This resistance comprised two groups: the Calixtines (or Utraquists) and the Taborites. The Utraquists were composed of many upper-class Hussites due to their disapproval of certain church practices, while the Taborites attracted the lower classes with their antigovernment sentiments. The Taborites experienced great military success due to their development of new war technologies; six campaigns ended with the superior papal forces unable to defeat the combined Hussite armies (De Schweinitz 1885, 88; D. Schaff 1949, 393; Heymann 1955, 75).

At the Council of Basel in 1433, Utraquists compromised with the Catholic Church to reform unbiblical practices in the church (Kaminsky 1967, 369). The Taborites, however, were not satisfied with the agreement and continued fighting until the Utraquists joined forces with the Catholic armies; they eventually defeated the Hussite radicals in 1452 (D. Schaff 1949, 397).

> Though only extreme Taborites anticipated Protestant doctrine by actually questioning the dogma of transubstantiation . . . the identification of the sacrament as a political as well as a theological symbol tied together and made tangible otherwise abstract beliefs. . . . [They] used sacramental symbols for organizational purpose to rally support to a mass movement and attack the spiritual pretensions of the clergy. (Baskerville 2004, 198)

The Creation of the Hussite Church

Following the Council of Basel in 1433, the Utraquists became the national church of Bohemia under the leadership of Jan Rokycana, the minister of the Týn Church in Prague. Rokycana and his nephew, Gregory the Patriarch, were leaders in another movement that followed the teaching of Hus. Peter Chelčic, a partner of Rokycana and Gregory, refused to side with either the Utraquists or the Taborites and was appalled at the violence done in the name of Christ. In his writings, Chelčic quoted both Wycliffe and Hus and, at the closure of the Hussite Wars, began forming groups called the Brethren of Chelčic.

Gregory the Patriarch led some of the Brethren to the village of Kunwald in northeast Bohemia, and in 1457 they officially left the Catholic Church. Rokycana objected and instigated persecution of the group that continued until his death four years later. At that time, Peter Chelčic and Gregory founded the Unitas Fratrum (Unity of the Brethren), a formal union between the Moravians, the Bohemians, and the Waldensians, which was the first fully organized Protestant church.

In 1495, however, at the Synod of Reichenau, they decided to "no longer honor the memory of Peter [Chelčic]. . . . Instead of regarding Peter as the founder of their Church, they began to regard themselves as the disciples of Hus, 'even though previously the reformer was only viewed as the "causer of a terrible war"'" (Hutton 1909, chap. 6, 1). The Hussite church was committed to follow the teachings of Christ according to the traditions of the early church; it used the Czech language, allowed laity to partake of the Eucharist cup, and acknowledged Christ as head of the church since the pope, as a sinful human being, was capable of fallible doctrinal and theological decisions. Scripture was the Hussites' ultimate source of authority and the only dictate of people's theology in life, reflecting the heart of the man who had sacrificed himself at the stake for the cause of the reformation (Spinka 1966, 160, 198, 292; Kaminsky 1967, 97, 123).

By 1500 the Unitas Fratrum in Bohemia and Moravia had over four hundred churches and 150,000 members. It survived as an underground remnant until after the Thirty Years' War ended in 1648 (De Schweinitz 1885, 90–99).

Summary

Jan Hus focused on the social injustices of the medieval feudal community in pastoral humility and service yet was condemned for his ecclesiastical challenges to the church of Rome. He believed that while governments were morally corruptible, the church stood as a beacon of hope, justice, and life, none of which could ever come from humans alone. For this reason, he spent his life prodding the church to live up to its responsibility to people and God. Hus's martyrdom was not in vain, for his death sparked an uprising that brought lasting change to the Bohemian church. Leaders such as Jan Rokycana, Gregory the Patriarch, and Peter Chelčic continued the struggle of the Hussite national church based on Hus's passion for the authority of Scripture.

SIDEBAR 6.4

Contemporary Discussion of Hus

The Hussites have received mixed reviews by historians. In the process of Catholic and Protestant scholars together reevaluating Hus, Pope John Paul II on December 17, 1999, supported eastern European unity by stating, "Today, on the eve of the Great Jubilee, I feel the need to express deep regret for the cruel death inflicted on Jan Hus." Although Hus's martyrdom sponsored repentance, his views still engender skepticism. Stephen Baskerville writes,

> [Hussites'] fanaticism, brutality, intolerance, and moral rigidity are not likely to win many fans in an academic environment whose fashions currently require us to extol values such as tolerance, democratization, and the "open society." Yet if we consider them within the context of their own time it is likely we may better come to understand what moved them. (2004, 201)

Reflection and Discussion

1. What made Hus's teachings attractive to the people of his time?
2. How would the Hussites be treated if they lived in our contemporary world?

Medieval Renewals: Conclusion

In this chapter, we addressed the doctrinal beliefs of three medieval renewal movements and their involvement in both ecclesiastical and political reform. While each endured persecution from both the Catholic Church and local government authorities, their passion for spreading the biblical gospel to the common people established the platform of protest that helped launch a global transformation of the Christian faith. The Waldensians, the Lollards, and the Hussites uniquely contributed to the accumulation of disapproval and action against the Catholic Church, which in turn influenced the Protestant Reformation of the sixteenth century.

7

Encountering
Reformation Missions

The Protestant Reformation was a religious, political, and cultural movement in sixteenth-century Europe that brought into question many beliefs and practices of the Catholic Church. Reformers protested Catholic orthodoxy and doctrine that they deemed unbiblical—such as selling indulgences and clerical offices. The evidence of corruption in the church's hierarchy caused the Reformation to enact new ways of thinking in the hope that reform might take place and to address the pressing issues of the church. Catholicism, however, did not accept the reorganization, which caused conflict and schism. In Poland, Hungary, and France, for instance, Martin Luther's reformed followers suffered intense persecution from the papacy. Further, the Netherlands Lutheran Church began with former Dutch Augustinian monks who became Luther's disciples, some of whom the Catholics martyred for their new beliefs (Swihart 1960, 263–68).

Motivated by the glory of God, John Calvin played a crucial role in the spiritual reawakening of Europe with a passion for the church and the pastorate and a desire to see the kingdom of Christ restored in Europe. To this end he established the Academy of Geneva to educate pastor-missionaries who upon graduation went forth with confidence to teach others throughout Europe and abroad. The result was that Calvinism came to dominate most of the thinking of northwestern Europe. Moreover, conveyed by Reformers from England, France, Germany, and Holland to the ends of the earth, Calvin's teachings consequently formed the substance of much of contemporary Western culture (Reid 1955, 21).

Despite the suppressing efforts of the Catholic Church, the Protestant ideas of Luther and Calvin spread throughout much of northern and central Europe. Ignited in the minds of the Reformed ministers and laity, these new ideas resulted in a movement of Protestant expansion. In this chapter, we will consider the work of Calvin and Luther and their successes and struggles in spreading the reformed message throughout Europe.

Predecessors of the Reformation

Leading up to the sixteenth century, France's involvement in wars with the Italian states drained the country's resources, resulting in heavy taxation of the common people. The government used the church structure to boost its economic straits. In the Concordat of 1516, Pope Leo X endowed King Francis I of France with the authority to appoint bishops, abbots, and priors in the church in France, which in turn profited the Crown through payment of political favors. These *bénéfices* had little to do with religious zeal, spiritual worthiness, or service to the church. In fact, the church could appoint a bishop to more than one region, which led to nonresidential privileges. In Brittany at this time, for example, not one priest out of fifty parishes occupied his church (Neale 1943, 13).

In the midst of this spiritual apathy, some called for reform. In 1507 the son of Cardinal Guillaume Briçonnet, also named Guillaume Briçonnet, succeeded his father as abbot of Saint-Germain-des-Prés. As the leader of the monastery, he successfully reformed moral abuses, enforced discipline among the monks, and inspired learning in his clergy. Later, as bishop of Meaux, he continued his improvements. "He supported the French translation of the Bible by Jacques Lefèvre d'Étaples, a fellow reformer, and the promotion of vernacular biblical preaching" (Benedetto 2008, 104). He also developed the "Meaux Group" of Reformers, which included Lefèvre d'Étaples. This group supported individual study of the Bible and a return to early church theology. King Francis I eventually sent Briçonnet to Pope Leo X in Rome, where his support of Jacques Lefèvre d'Étaples and other Reformers caused consternation with the pope. Opposition from the monarchy, Parliament, and leaders of the Sorbonne University in Paris eventually forced Briçonnet to recant his support of the Reformation and combat the preachers he had once sponsored (Baird 1896, 81).

Persecution ensued at Meaux, where church authorities arrested fourteen men for conducting a home Bible study and burned them at the stake for heresy (Winters 1938, 16). Guillaume Farel, a disciple of Lefèvre, escaped the town, going first to Neuchâtel, Switzerland, where the city accepted the Reformers' message. He then went to his home region in the Alps of southeastern France, where he met with Waldensian leaders and convinced many to join the Reformation. Finally, Farel traveled to Geneva, where his preaching again influenced the city leaders to adopt Reformed ways, as well as challenged John Calvin, a young French refugee.

John Calvin and Missions

On All Saints Day in 1533, Nicolas Cop, the rector of the University of Paris, gave a sermon on the First Beatitude, interwoven with the Reformers' message of forgiveness of sin and eternal life as gifts of God's grace only through the sacrifice of Jesus Christ. Opposition arose against the sermon and the preacher, which led to Cop and his writer, John Calvin, fleeing Paris.

Calvin was born at Noyon in the northern French province of Picardy in 1509. He attended the University of Paris at fourteen (at the same time as Ignatius of Loyola and Francis Xavier). He began studying law at nineteen and had a conversion experience at twenty-four years of age. Subsequent to the persecution following Cop's sermon, Calvin escaped to Basel, Switzerland, where, in 1536, he published *The Institutes of the Christian Religion* (in Latin), which explained his Protestant beliefs to the king of France, Francis I. From Basel, Calvin's path tacked its way to Geneva (en route to Strasbourg), where William Farel persuaded him to stay and pastor the Church of Saint Pierre to help create a model reformed city. Calvin spent the rest of his life in Geneva (except from 1538 to 1540, when he married and ministered to French refugees in Strasbourg) until his death in 1564.

Calvin arrived in Geneva in 1536, during a chaotic period in the life of the city of thirteen thousand people (Terry 1994, 78). It was free from papal political and episcopal control and as such had experienced a time of political, educational, and religious decline before becoming a refuge for Protestants. Half of its inhabitants were refugees, yet Geneva had no police (McNeill 1954, 193). "Genevan authorities could rely on the public fear of scandals to ensure that laws were kept most of the time," together with the fear of God's wrath on their city (Monter 1967, 101). Because of the city's chaotic state, Calvin was able to help politically reconstruct the new Geneva, although this work was not without challenges, including his expulsion from the city and the plague epidemic of 1538–1542. Calvin desired to structure the church and the state into true Protestantism. For instance, he helped the city write Christian guidelines on business ethics, charging interest, and establishing industries.

Calvin believed in the importance of reform through means of preaching repentance and belief to the church and the city. Through a prayerful synthesis of theology and evangelism, he reached his goal. As C. George Fry states, "A lifetime of theological labor and biblical preaching saw a sensual, secular city reformed. From an approximation of Babel, Geneva was changed into an anticipation of the New Jerusalem" (1970, 60). Christopher Elwood concurs: "[Calvin] transformed this border city on the edge of the Alps into what one observer called a Protestant Rome. It became, that is, the center of a vital movement and ministry on behalf of a new vision of the church" (2002, 139–40). For example, Calvin formed the Genevan Consistory, a governing body that monitored the spiritual life of the people. The Consistory expected the citizens of Geneva to recite the Lord's Prayer and the Apostles' Creed in their national language, instead of Latin, to demonstrate their understanding of the faith. In this way, Calvin hoped that the hearts of the people of God would transmit the true reformation to others.

Academy of Geneva

With this sentiment to convey God to the masses, Calvin founded an institution of higher learning. The Academy of Geneva was an important contributor to the Reformed mission movement. According to Calvin, as long "as this objective was not realized, no permanence was assured for the work of reform" (McNeill 1954, 192). In 1557 Calvin entreated the city council for land and a building, and two years later he conducted the inaugural service. With the establishment of the Academy of Geneva, "Calvin had achieved his task: he had secured the future of Geneva making it at once a church, a school, and a fortress. It was the first stronghold of liberty in modern times" (McNeill 1954, 196).

The academy's aim was to make the church educationally self-perpetuating, and as such, it established a school for children run by Antoine Saunier. The city ordinances of 1541 spoke "of the need to raise seed for the time to come, in order not to leave the Church a desert to our children and an obligation to prepare youth for the ministry and civil government" (McNeill 1954, 132). The opening of the academy gave permanence and stability to the Reformed mission that it previously did not possess. Without such an institution, the Reformation may have died with its Reformers.

The school began with an enrollment of 162 students, mainly young Frenchmen, yet in six years the numbers had increased tenfold. In the first four years, out of 160 students, 13 were Swiss (3 from Geneva), 10 Dutch, 10 German, 13 Italian, and 114 French (G. Lewis 1994, 49–50). For these students, "the purpose of the academy was mainly preparation for the ministry, with law and medicine as secondary interests" (McNeill 1954, 194). This institution trained them to understand and propagate Calvin's teachings. The academy divided the pupils according to their location within the four sectors of the city, and each sector arranged into seven grades. In the style of a Renaissance school, they studied French, Latin, and New Testament Greek, along with the works of Virgil, Ovid, and Cicero, and rhetoric and dialectic from classical texts. In addition, the students sang psalms in French daily for one hour, beginning at eleven in the morning (McNeill 1954, 194).

Knowledgeable in theology and preaching, the alumni of the academy, many of whom had come from various parts of Europe, returned to their homelands to share the Reformers' message and affect their societies. "The establishment of education in Geneva . . . [was] the beginning of a hugely successful missionary undertaking" (Elwood 2002, 140). The first five years of the academy "were the great years of the Academy's contribution to the missionary effort, which had been in full swing since 1556" (G. Lewis 1994, 51). W. Stanford Reid observes, "Those who graduated went forth, convinced of their position, to teach others, the result being that Calvinism came to dominate most of the thinking of northwestern Europe and was carried by the Dutch, the English, the Scots, the Germans, and the French to the far places of the earth, with the consequence that today it lies, to a large extent, at the basis of western culture" (1955, 21).

Calvin believed that once leaders grasped a proper appreciation of the truth, they then could train those in their churches, who in turn would continue to spread the Reformed doctrines. He wrote, "The biblical faith must be put into words so that people can know and confess what they experience, so they can teach and minister to others" (Calvin 2001, 22). To this end, the Reformer wrote the Geneva Catechism (1542), in addition to numerous tracts, pamphlets, and scriptural commentaries, which he printed in Geneva and distributed throughout Europe, especially in France. Calvin also wrote letters to other Reformed leaders and royalty to communicate and encourage unity in the cause of the Reformation.

Calvin's Motivation for Missions and Beliefs

Motivated by the glory of God, Calvin played a crucial role in the spiritual reawakening of Europe with a passion for the church and the pastorate and a desire to see the kingdom of Christ restored in Europe. Rather than the normal tendency to regard the happiness of humanity as the central point of mission, Calvinism emphasized the furtherance of God's glory, together with the notion that the lordship of Christ extends to every part of human life and the created world. Kingdom values were to be applied in every area of life, which is why in Geneva Calvin designed a sewer system, inaugurated a financial fund to help poor refugees, composed the laws of the city, and supported a weaving industry to enhance the people's welfare.

Calvin believed that God is able and willing, by virtue of his omniscience, omnipresence, and omnipotence, to do whatever he desires with his creation. Humanity is completely sinful, and, by God's grace, he predestines people to salvation based not on their worthiness but by the kind intentions of his will. Jesus's death was only for those predestined, and hence God regenerates the individual so that he or she chooses to follow him always in eternal salvation. Some theologians argue that Calvin's view of God's sovereignty discourages missions, and in fact, God's predestination of specific persons necessitates that human missionary endeavors are unnecessary.

Contrary to that view, Calvin focused his teaching on affirming that God called and equipped people to join him in his work while underscoring that, first and foremost, missions was about the work of God and not of humanity. "God alone can cause sinners to respond to the gospel's call" (R. Greenway 2000, 155–56). Predestination does not make the preaching of the gospel unnecessary; indeed, it makes preaching more important as a means to save those who are predestined.

Charles Chaney identifies four principles of Calvin's philosophy of missions: the calling of the gentiles, the progress of the kingdom, the gathering

134

of the church, and personal Christian responsibility (1964, 25–33). Regarding the last principle, Calvin believed that after the ascension of Christ, the gospel was to spread throughout the world via the preaching of God's word. He understood that this expansion of the church was accomplished using the apostles, yet believers should continue the work "until the gospel [has] reached the farthest bounds of the earth" (Chaney 1964, 28).

Calvin believed that Christians should disclose their faith since the act of evangelizing expresses their gratitude to God for sparing them, God commands it, and it leads to compassion for others who need salvation. For example, Calvin, in his *Commentary on the Prophet Isaiah*, encourages believers to desire the salvation of the world based on their understanding of God's deliverance in their lives. His exposition of Isaiah 12:4 states,

> Hence, it is evident what is the desire, which ought to be cherished among all the godly. It is that the goodness of God may be made known to all, that all may join in the same worship of God. We ought especially to be inflamed with this desire, after having been delivered from some alarming danger, and most of all after having been delivered from the tyranny of the devil and from everlasting death. (1999, 403)

Again, in his commentary on Micah 2:1–4, Calvin maintains, "The Kingdom of Christ was only begun in the world when God commanded the gospel to be everywhere proclaimed and . . . at this day its course is not as yet complete" (Beaver 1973, 56–57). In other words, the apostles did not complete the Great Commission, and Christians still have the responsibility to preach the gospel.

Furthermore, in Calvin's notes on 1 Timothy 2:4 he states, "There is no people and no rank in the world that is excluded from salvation, because God wishes that the gospel should be proclaimed to all without exception" (1970, 12:2, 172). Not that everyone will obtain salvation, yet certain people from various parts of the world will receive Christ's redemption. Finally, in Calvin's comments on Ezekiel 18:23, he proclaims, "God certainly desires nothing more than for those who are perishing and rushing toward death to return to the way of safety. This is why the gospel is today proclaimed throughout the world, for God wished to testify to all ages that he is greatly inclined to pity" (1963, 402). God desires humanity to accept salvation and by his election ensures that some will do so.

Methods of Missions

Preaching and Teaching

Calvin taught at the Geneva Academy and preached at the Church of Saint Pierre with the desire to help people express their worship of God, find personal salvation, and live their days as worthy of Christ. He preached in his church twice on Sundays and once every day on alternate weeks. These opportunities to teach and preach became a powerful factor in the conversion of individuals and the changing of social customs in the Geneva community.

Writings

During the early days of the Reformation, the Protestant churches needed organization in dogma and practice, since they were structurally and doctrinally loose and heavily persecuted by the Catholic Church. Calvin's *Institutes of the Christian Religion* provided this stability as the Reformed movement spread. The work was first published in 1536, and Calvin revised it three times in the next twenty-four years. What began as a six-chapter booklet ended as four volumes with eighty chapters.

In this publication, Calvin teaches his understanding of the biblical topics of sin, redemption, faith, God's will, and his dealing with humanity, in an attempt to return to first-century teaching. In his missional statement he makes known his motivations: "These were my reasons for publishing *The Institutes*: first, that I might vindicate from unjust affront my brethren whose death was precious in the sight of the Lord; and next, that some sorrow and anxiety should move foreign peoples, since the same suffering threatened many" (Walker 2005, 108).

Calvin also wrote against the beliefs of the Catholic Church, such as the veneration of relics, in the satire *Admonition, Showing the Advantage Which Christendom Might Derive from an Inventory of Relics* (1543): "For it [the Catholic Church] clearly is a hundred times more corrupt than it was in the times of Gregory and Bernard [former popes], though even then it greatly displeased those holy men" (Calvin 1960, 2:1141).

In other writings Calvin encourages believers to pray for those not following Christ, that they would attain faith. He maintains that a proper understanding of God's sovereignty will encourage the church to prayer even if there are few results. God promised that the church's work would not be in vain. In his *Institutes of the Christian Religion*, his teaching on "hallowed be thy name" in the Lord's Prayer expounds, "We [the church] are bidden to request that [God] subdue the whole race of mankind to reverence [His name]" (1960, vol. 2, book 3, chap. 20, section 41). In simpler terms, he viewed the Lord's Prayer as a petition to God for the salvation of the world.

Ecclesiology

In addition to teaching, preaching, and writing, Calvin was also a successful evangelist. Fry writes of him: "While it has been traditional to consider

Calvin a master theologian, an excellent church administrator, an ardent professor, and a powerful author, it has been less common to recognize him as one of the major modern evangelists. Yet, together with Martin Luther and John Wesley, Calvin stands out as one of the most successful evangelists in modern church history" (1970, 3).

Calvin believed in the invisible church, where only God knew the membership. Yet he felt there was a need for the visible church with its observable membership and activity. He considered the church as missions' structure and therefore sent out pastors rather than evangelists of missions. He believed that church preaching was the means of hearing the gospel. This contrasts with much of contemporary evangelism. "Calvin was more intentional [than Luther] in encouraging mission. In some areas Calvinism became the religion of the state; in other areas local churches were established amidst persecution. Pastors were trained in Geneva and sent as missionaries; many were martyred" (P. Pierson 2000a, 814).

Missions to France

Among the refugees in Geneva, many were Catholics from France. The majority of Huguenots, French Protestants influenced by Calvin's teachings, fled after King Louis XIV revoked the Edict of Nantes in 1685, which had permitted the basic rights and religious toleration of the French Reformers. Approximately one hundred thousand refugees left France during this time (Rothrock 1979, 178–79). In Geneva, Calvin trained immigrants at his academy in ethics, homiletics, and theology and sent them back to France as pastor-missionaries ("the gatekeepers of the kingdom") as early as 1555. Calvin believed that for proper gospel proclamation, trained ministers needed to establish churches. Carl D. Stevens writes, "Calvin's interest was not the sending of men into France to preach the gospel to anyone who might listen; rather, Calvin's intention was to restore the church in France as a gospel-preaching institution" (1992, 201).

Between 1555 and 1562, the Geneva Reformers sent 142 men to France. These men caused such a stir that in 1558 Calvinist (Huguenot) minister Jean Macar of Paris wrote in a letter to Calvin, "The fire is lit in all parts of the kingdom and all the water in the sea will not suffice to extinguish it" (De Jong 1995, 8). The missionaries of Geneva created such an impact that King Henry II of France in 1559 described Geneva as "the cause of all France's misfortunes," declaring "guilty of high treason all who [had] any relation whatever with Geneva," and stating that he "would have no ease until [Geneva had] been reduced to impotence" (De Jong 1995, 9). This was not an empty threat, and many suffered under the ruling. The Reformed pastors in France were in such danger that the Genevan Consistory agreed not to keep records of the missionary activity in France.

The Reformation message of Luther first reached the French universities and influenced the professors, private tutors, and students, followed by other professional people such as doctors, lawyers, and notaries. The lower classes were conservative and more resistant to change. The next group influenced by the new message was the lower clergy and friars, many of whom were already moving away from papal control. Finally, many of the noble women, spiritually attuned and tired of rampant immorality, followed the Huguenot movement and encouraged their husbands (who desired freedom from the oppression of both state and church) to join also, which provided protection for the small Reformed congregations (Neale 1943, 24–27).

Although heavily persecuted, these Reformers proclaimed their faith, and the Protestant church grew from five underground groups in 1555 to nearly one hundred by 1559, when it held its first national synod in Paris. In only three more years the growth of the Huguenot movement bourgeoned to 2,150 churches through the efforts of the 142 missionaries (Laman 1989, 59). It is estimated that in 1562 there were nearly three million members of the French Reformed churches, with half of the French nobility committed to Calvinism (Haykin 2001, 42). As George A. Rothrock explains, "They constituted, of course, a tiny minority in a population of fifteen or sixteen million people, but in the face of intensifying repression their simple survival was a considerable achievement" (1979, 40).

Missionary correspondence of this period discovered by Peter Wilcox confirms the rapid church growth: in Bergerac the church had grown to between four and five thousand people, in Montpelier the church had an attendance of five to six thousand members, and in Toulouse the Reformed church attracted eight to nine thousand people (1993, 689–95). "Calvin didn't just plant fledging churches; he planted mega churches that in turn planted more churches" (James 2001).

Many French cities, including Annonay, Bourges, Grenoble, La Rochelle, Mâcon, Orleans, and Toulouse, had received Huguenot missionaries (De Félice 1851, 43). The movement also took root in Lyons and southern France, with their close proximity to Geneva; in the east at Metz near the Reformed center of Strasbourg; and in Brittany and Normandy on the west coast, as they connected with international trade in England and the Netherlands. In Metz the two foremost proponents of the French Huguenot movement, François Lambert and Jean Châtellain, were former Catholic priests who saw the need of reform in the church (Winters 1938, 51).

Martin Luther and Missions

Another powerful Reformer was Martin Luther of Germany. Born November 10, 1483, Luther (the son of a copper miner) was an educated theologian from Eisleben, Saxony, who dedicated his life to the purposes of God. His revolutionary teachings irreversibly changed the religious and social fabric of Europe. As a result, Lutheranism came to dominate most of the thinking of northern Europe and was carried by the Danes, the Finns, the Germans, the Norwegians, and the Swedes to the far places of the earth; consequently, it became one of the pillars of Western civilization.

In the midst of a fierce electrical storm, Luther called on the name of Saint Anne (the patron saint of miners), bargaining for his life in exchange for the existence of a monk. After his survival, he entered the Augustinian order as a friar on July 17, 1505, devoting himself to fasting, long hours of prayer and vigil, pilgrimage, and confession. Luther was not satisfied as a monk, however, and described his time in the monastery as one of deep spiritual despair. He said, "I lost touch with Christ the Savior and Comforter, and made of him the jailor and hangman of my poor soul" (Kittelson 1986, 78–79). On April 4, 1507, Luther was ordained to the priesthood, yet he still found no peace in his tortured soul. In 1508 Johann von Staupitz, Luther's superior, sent Luther to teach theology at the monastery at Wittenberg. It was through the reading and teaching of God's word at this time that Luther developed his Reformed theology and nailed his Ninety-Five Theses, a Latin document stating his grievances with the Catholic Church, on the Wittenberg church door. Thus began a radical spiritual journey of rejecting the papacy and Catholicism that ripped Europe into political and theological pieces.

Luther's Rejection of Monasticism

Because of Luther's rejection of Catholic monasticism, Lutheranism was devoid of a vehicle for missions. Kenneth Scott Latourette argues that in the newly formed Protestantism, Luther, in forsaking monasticism, lost a valuable form of missionary expansion. The slow start of Protestant missions resulted from their lack of a committed community, such as the monks, who were the "ready-to-hand machinery" for propagating the faith (1975, 92). James A. Scherer, a Lutheran missiologist, agrees with this assessment, acknowledging that Luther's teaching of Scripture needed real-life practice: there was a disconnection between Luther's missions theology and praxis. In other words, the absence of mission practice can be attributed largely to Luther's rejection of monasticism and its accompanying framework for cross-cultural outreach, and no replacement mission structure for early Protestant missions existed (1982, 3).

The reality of the situation concerning Luther was that he rejected European monasticism because of what he viewed as its exaggerated emphasis on spiritual superiority and works righteousness, as well as begging and almsgiving (Bainton 1952, 246–47). Regarding the dangers of religious professionalism and embracing elitist perfectionism, he writes:

139

If the monasteries do not serve this purpose (turning out learned men and chaste women, etc.) it is better to let them go to ruin or to tear them down than to keep them. Their blasphemous services, invented by men, should not be considered something better than the ordinary Christian life and the offices and positions ordained by God. For all such notions are contrary to the first, chief article of the redemption wrought by Jesus Christ. (Smalcald Articles of 1537, WA 50:212, cited in Lindquist 1990, 50)

The former Augustinian monk further disapproved of monasticism because it threatened biblical salvation by moving the source of holiness away from the cross to the religious life and established structures that substituted faith in Christ with the works of the religious rule and vows. Luther continues,

This is the chief abomination: we had to deny the grace of God and put our trust and hope in our holy monkery and not in the pure mercy of Christ, as we had promised and begun to do in Christian Baptism. For relying on works in order thereby to be justified and sanctified is in reality denying God's grace, as St. Paul clearly says (Gal. 5:4): "Christ is become of no effect unto you, whosoever of you are justified by the Law, ye are fallen from grace." (WA 38:159, cited in Lindquist 1990, 51)

Luther was an advocate of Christian action, which was exemplified in the spread of Lutheranism in early sixteenth-century Germany and other regions. "Luther was never forgetful of the Gospel's universal goal, and so he declared that, 'It is necessary always to proceed to those to whom no preaching has been done in order that the number [of Christians] may become greater'" (Koschade 1965, 235). The lack of mission-sending institutions, such as monasteries, was not a reflection of the missional situation. Scherer asserts, "God needs no special missions agencies to accomplish his purposes. He is able to make use of persecution, the dispersion of believers, the travels of merchants, the captivity of believing soldiers, and the acts of rulers to bring about universal witness" (1994, 21). Although Luther rejected monasticism, the methods mentioned by Scherer played a large role in the organization's successful progress throughout northern Europe.

Luther's Mission Theology

Luther believed that preaching was the missional purpose of the church and that preaching renewal of the gospel inside the church itself would propel the believing community into the world. The duty of every Christian was to teach the Scriptures to those who had not heard. He taught that all Christians were to be missionaries as they lived for their neighbor in consideration of his or her needs. Luther used the following metaphor to describe his mission theology: "As if one threw a stone into the water; the stone causes ripples, circles, and streams round about it; and the ripples always roll them farther and farther; one drives the other until they come to the shore. Although the water becomes calm in the center, the ripples do not rest but keep on flowing" (Elert 1962, 392–93). In simpler terms, each believer placed within a circle of non-Christians should "preach to the erring heathen and must teach the Gospel because brotherly love makes it his duty to do so" (Lindquist 1990, 48).

All believers were compelled to do good works according to their faith in Christ; they were to use their gifts to serve the kingdom of God wherever they found themselves, whether as carpenters, farmers, homemakers, poets, or preachers. Luther moved the concept of "vocation" from the cloister to the workshop (Bainton 1952, 246). All Christ-followers were to serve with their gifts in whatever capacity they could.

The ministry of the gospel belonged first to Christ and then to all believers in the church. Luther asserts, "The gospel itself equips and impels the whole church into the whole world" (Lindquist 1990, 57). For Luther mission was for the church and was the essential task of the church.

The German theologian alleged that Christians needed to rely on the guidance and power of God to spread the gospel, which necessitated only

---

We must also go to those to whom Christ has hitherto not been proclaimed. We must teach the people who have not known Christ, so that they, too, may be brought to the spiritual kingdom of Christ.

Martin Luther (Porter 1974, 124)

---

obedience and a willingness to serve. The growth of God's kingdom was divinely controlled. Humans were powerless without God's Spirit to do his work through them. "For Luther, mission is always the work of the triune God—missio Dei—and its goal and outcome is the coming of the kingdom of God" (Scherer 1994, 18). Luther believed that although the apostles began missions, the church was to continue and include the whole world as its responsibility. God was unfolding his mission purposes, and Christians should spread the gospel among non-Christian people.

Luther had a theology of mission and called others to be involved in the missio Dei. The real issue beyond these facts is how Luther's views on mission played out in his life and the lives of his followers. The evidence of missionaries from Wittenberg, publications that spread the gospel, music, and missions work among the Scandinavian peoples, Jews, and Muslims all attest to Luther's heart for missions.

Wittenberg's Missionaries

Luther was involved in training young men for Christian ministry and dispersing them from the university at Wittenberg. Conversion of the unsaved was paramount for Luther, and he was convinced that the universities would play an important role in this goal (Coates 1969, 603). At Wittenberg, Luther emphasized knowing true doctrine and at the same time took a personal interest in the students, knowing that on leaving the university they would face many hostile forces. His mentoring of students even included finding their first and subsequent positions.

Between 1520 and 1560, approximately five thousand of the sixteen thousand at Wittenberg were from nations other than Germany, making the university an important center for mission training (Bunkowske 1985, 170). Through his teaching at the university, Luther promoted a renewed interest in the gospel, and his mentorees carried the Reformation teachings of their mentor to their home regions. This was especially true of Scandinavia, which, similar to Germany, wanted to discard Rome's dominance. The influence of Wittenberg missionaries in this region was profound and played a large role in the spread of Lutheranism. These missionaries were proof that Luther's mission theology was more than concepts: it led to a successful and flourishing cross-cultural movement (Gallagher 2005a, 131–32).

Scandinavian Distress

The complex and turbulent history of medieval Scandinavia was a key component in the propagation of the Reformation. From 1397 to 1523, the royal Union of Kalmar united Denmark, Finland, Iceland, Norway, and Sweden. Throughout its history, power struggles peppered this northern region, so much so that by the beginning of the sixteenth century the union was on the verge of collapse. Against this background of political volatility and insecurity the Protestant Reformation flourished in Scandinavia.

EXPANSION IN DENMARK

In the early sixteenth century Denmark was undergoing economic and social change, with the expansion of the merchant classes in the towns and the nobility seeking to secure and expand their aristocratic power. By 1518 Luther's influence had reached the courts of Denmark, where Wolfgang von Utenhof, a Wittenberg graduate, tutored the future king, Christian III. Intrigued by his tutor's witness to Reformation ideas, the young prince attended the Diet of Worms in 1521 and heard Luther's defense before Emperor Charles V (Grell 1995, 14).

Frederik I (r. 1523–1533), father of Christian III, began his reign with Reformation rumblings on the rise. Influenced by Lutheran teaching, the new king declined to interfere with the "preaching of God's word," even though at his coronation he had promised the Danish hierarchy that he would deal with heretics: "[We will] not allow any heretics, disciples of Luther or others to preach and teach, either openly or secretly, against God, the faith of the Holy Church, the holiest father, the Pope, or the Catholic Church, but where they are found in this kingdom, we promise to punish them on life and property" (Grell 1992, 104).

The city of Viborg in Jutland became the center of the Danish Lutheran Reformation under the direction of Hans Tausen (a former member of the Order of Saint John of Jerusalem and a graduate of Wittenberg) and Jørgen Jensen Sadolin. In 1526 they formed a school to train Protestant preachers. To evade growing pressure from the Catholic bishops, Frederik I appointed Tausen that same year as his personal court chaplain. Also in 1526 and 1527, a council of nobles in Odense, Denmark, officially severed relations with the papacy. Under the rule of Frederik, religion became a matter of personal conscience, with Lutherans permitted to preach "the word of God." Beginning in 1527 the king closed Franciscan houses and monasteries in twenty-eight towns and sporadically offered small stipends to retiring monks. Tausen's preaching at Saint Nicholas Church in Copenhagen and a printing press established at Viborg in 1528 aided the dissemination of Protestant views throughout the nation. In the meantime, due to skillful propaganda, King Frederik weakened the power of the Catholic Church and averted a religious war.

Frederik permitted his eldest son, Christian III, to establish over sixty Lutheran parishes around Haderslev and Tönning. Two German Wittenberg theologians, Eberhard Weidensee and John Wendt, were leaders in this Protestant movement, creating the first Lutheran church diocese in Scandinavia in 1528 (modeled after Wittenberg). The ministers pledged allegiance to Christian, the Duke of Schleswig.

In Copenhagen and Skåneland (present-day Sweden), another Lutheran awakening occurred through the influence of Paul Helie (a Carmelite provincial who taught biblical humanism at the University of Copenhagen) and his students Peder Laurentsen, Claus Mortensøn, Christian Pedersen, and Frans Vormordsen. The first Danish version of the New Testament appeared in 1524, followed by a plethora of other Bible translations and theological literature from Malmø in Skåneland, one of the first cities in Scandinavia to convert (1527–1529). In 1528 Mortensøn produced the first Danish hymnal for church use, including translations of a number of Luther's hymns (Dunkley 1948, 45). Moreover, the publication of the first Danish Bible based on the Wittenberg Bible of 1545 occurred in 1550.

By 1530 the reform movement had established itself in the majority of towns and cities throughout Denmark. At the Diet of Copenhagen that same year, the Lutheran pastors presented "Forty Three Articles," which outlined their Protestant beliefs. These articles became immensely popular with the people, and when Frederik died in 1533 most of Denmark was Lutheran (Skarsten 1985, 31–32). The full realization of a Lutheran national church, however, occurred in 1537, after Christian III won the civil war with the Catholic nobles (1534–1536). He then removed the Catholic bishops from office and nationalized the monasteries, even though many Catholic priests continued their ministry as Lutherans. As the supreme head of the church, Christian III appointed Luther's pastor, John Bugenhagen, to lead the ecclesiastical reorganization for two years (1537–1539). This task included modeling the University of Copenhagen after Wittenberg and placing national education in the hands of the church, supervised by the Lutheran bishops and the king's pastor.

As Christian III corresponded with Luther and other Wittenberg Reformers, especially Peder Palladius (a Wittenberg graduate who became the first Lutheran bishop of Zeeland), Danish Lutheran theology aligned with Wittenberg. Tausen, who became bishop of Ribe in Jutland, drafted the first Lutheran church ordinance in 1537 and adopted Philipp Melanchthon's Augsburg Confession of 1530 as normative for Danish Lutheran theology (Gritsch 2002, 50–52).

Expansion in Finland

Under Swedish political authority, Lutheranism influenced Finland. The Swedish authorities dissolved Catholic churches and promoted vernacular services so that sermons could fulfill their purpose. This led to a disruption in education that detrimentally affected the training of clergy, and as the academic language moved from Latin to Swedish, Finnish was bypassed. In spite of this predicament, in 1548 Mikael Agricola published a Finnish New Testament, which he had begun as a student at Wittenberg. Not until 1583 was the first Finnish hymnal produced (Wuorinen 1965, 65). Christian II, who converted to Lutheranism while in exile in the Netherlands after visiting Wittenberg, supported the national importance of the Bible, sermons, and hymns in the vernacular. He directed the first two publications of the Danish New Testament, in 1524 and again five years later in 1529.

Expansion in Iceland

Iceland was under Danish domination and content to stay Catholic. Slowly and reluctantly, the Icelandic people accepted Lutheranism in the 1530s in this remote outpost of the Danish monarch with resultant Catholic uprisings and ecclesial reforms by Christian III. Despite the turbulent beginnings of Protestantism in Iceland, the emphasis on the word of God became compelling in the lives of the people through the efforts of bishops Guðbrandur Þorklasson and Jón Vídalín and the hymns of Séra Hallgrímur Pétursson (Fell 1999, 2). An Icelandic translation of the New Testament published in Denmark in 1540 assisted in the revitalization of the indigenous language in the midst of Danish supremacy. A complete translation of the Bible produced in Iceland followed in 1584 and within five years the first Icelandic hymnal as well.

EXPANSION IN NORWAY

Although Norway was politically under the dominance of Denmark and therefore its allegiance to Lutheranism, Norway presented its loyalty to Frederik I of Denmark as conditional on the king allowing Catholicism to remain the Norwegian ecclesial authority. Yet the agreement was not upheld, and Lutheran ministers arrived in the late 1520s with Christian III officially declaring Norway Lutheran in 1537 (Wilson 1903, 307–8).

There were few trained clergy, which resulted in a mixture of styles in services and ministry, a situation exacerbated by a lack of Norwegian literature. The Danes finally produced a Norwegian catechism in 1541, but the sparse number of copies meant many churches went without. The first Norwegian printing press was not operational until 1644; in the following years, the spread of Lutheranism accelerated. When the first vernacular hymnal for the Lutheran churches of Norway was published in 1569, it contained only Danish and Latin compositions, yet "congregational singing [was] the most appealing feature in the new order" (Larsen 1948, 271).

EXPANSION IN SWEDEN

There were strong cultural and economic ties between Germany and Sweden in the early sixteenth century, which contributed to the flow of Protestant ideas. German merchants first introduced Lutheranism to the German colony in Sweden, with Nicholas Stecker, a Wittenberg graduate, becoming their first Lutheran minister in 1524 (Senn 1997, 401–2). Other Wittenberg graduates followed into the courts of King Gustav Vasa, namely Laurentius Andreae and the brothers Olaus and Laurentius Petri. The influence of these three men infected the nation with the Protestant message. It was amid economic and nationalistic malaise that the spark of the Swedish Reformation originated and spread, fanned by Luther's Wittenberg students.

Olaus Petri and his younger brother, Laurentius, were educated in a Carmelite monastery in Örebro (their place of birth), and in 1516 Olaus went to Wittenberg to study for his master's degree. There he witnessed the events that unfolded after Luther nailed the Ninety-Five Theses to the cathedral door, and in 1518 he returned to Strängnäs, Sweden, to teach at the cathedral school.

In 1524 King Gustav Vasa invited Olaus Petri to be the secretary of Stockholm and preach at Storkyrkan (in the Cathedral of Saint Nicholas), with his brother Laurentius as the king's counselor, and Laurentius Andreae, who had studied canon law in Rome, as his principal advisor. Andreae became the political engineer of the king's Reformation ideas, Laurentius Petri the conductor of ecclesiastical transformation, and Olaus the propagator of the

Protestant message, or, as Altman Swihart contends, the "intellectual leader of the Reformation in Sweden" (1960, 224–38). Stirred by the polemical writings of Olaus Petri against the doctrines of the Catholic Church, a Riksdag (parliament of nobles) gathered at Västerås in 1527 and agreed with King Vasa (after his tears and threats of resignation) to establish a Swedish Lutheran Church modeled after the Wittenberg reform. The king then pressured Petrus Magni, the Catholic bishop of Västeras, to appoint three other bishops without papal consent; he also installed Laurentius Petri as a professor of theology at the University of Uppsala in 1527 and then four years later as the archbishop of Uppsala.

The work of Andreae and the Petri brothers continued to influence the nation with the Protestant message. Together they published the New Testament in Swedish in 1526; in 1531 Olaus printed a manual for a Swedish Mass and five years later a Swedish translation of the Old Testament. In addition, Olaus edited vernacular hymnals because he believed that they were edifying and instructive, and "expressed the prayer of the heart" (Bergendoff 1928, 160), even though Latin hymnals continued to be published. In 1541 Laurentius Petri translated the entire Bible into Swedish, and its use in every parish influenced religious education (Woodward 1910, 205–66).

Throughout these reforms, the popular cause of Protestantism was strongest in Stockholm. The king had contended with repeated agrarian uprisings before 1540, as the people, sponsored by the Catholic priests, objected to excessive royal taxes (to pay for the war with Denmark) and supported traditional Catholicism. Plagued by constant financial troubles, King Vasa readily appropriated Franciscan and Dominican monasteries for secular use at places such as Viborg to buttress the national treasury to pay for defense expenses; in so doing, he also inadvertently facilitated the reform movement (Te Brake 1998, 54–55). During this time of disorder, one of the students of German nobility at Wittenberg was Georg Norman, whom Luther had sent as a tutor to the Swedish prince Eric. Between 1539 and 1544 German Lutheran views held sway in Sweden because of Norman's ministry to the prince. After Vasa died in 1560, subsequent royal political intrigues hindered the complete formation of Protestantism for the next forty-five years. A full Protestant church order finally occurred in 1571, whereby Laurentius Petri defined the practice of the church, followed by a complete embrace of Lutheran theology in 1593 (Gritsch 2002, 52–53).

Publications and Missions

Luther's German translation of the Bible became the example as other European nations considered translating the Scriptures into their languages. He published some 350 works and 3,000 letters to people throughout Europe. In particular, his Large and Small Catechisms have been extremely influential, even to the present day. In addition, Luther's speeches, sermons, and hymns in the vernacular set a standard for others to follow. Due to all the different forms Luther used to reach people, Ji Won Yong has claimed that Luther was a missionary to Germany and the rest of the world (1996, 148).

Among their congregations, Lutheran laity and ministers promoted Luther's publications, which raised awareness of missions. With large numbers of people promoting Luther's message, his teaching spread effectively and rapidly.

Music and Missions

The cathedral school at Magdeburg, which Luther attended for one year in his youth in 1497, developed his love for choral singing. Four years later, he began attending the University of Erfurt, where he studied music theory and learned to play the flute. Later, at the Augustinian monastery in the early sixteenth century, Luther formed his theology of music following Augustinian thought. For Luther, music expressed biblical truths in service to theology but was secondary to Scripture. The vernacular sermon was of primary importance (Guicharrousse 1995, 20–27, 67–68). Nonetheless, he believed that music, as a gift from God, should be used to adore God and share biblical truth, whether the style was traditional rural, urban, or humanist.

Despite popular music's questionable morality, Luther adapted it to serve theological purposes. "After all, the gift of language combined with the gift of song was only given to man to let him know that he should praise God with both words and music, namely, by proclaiming [the word of God] through music and by providing sweet melodies with words" (Luther 1965, 323–24).

> **Within his [Luther's] lifetime his hymns became a national possession, so that his enemies said he had destroyed more souls by them than by all speeches and other writings.**
>
> Eva Mary Grew (1938, 72)

Luther reorganized the musical sections of the Reformed order of service, believing that worship was both an outward and an inward expression achieved by truly appreciating the benefits of God (Luther 1884, 296). The vernacular communicated biblical truth throughout the service in both sermon and song. Modified chants avoided obscuring the words with music, different pitch tones indicated various speakers within the song, and altered chorales reflected his appreciation of the Netherlands' polyphonic music—all molded to suit his theological purposes (Bainton 1950, 341–42).

Luther's most significant contribution to church music was in the area of congregational singing. Since all believers are priests unto Christ, all followers need to participate in corporate song. For Luther, "all of the music of worship—including the hymnody—was in reality the song of the royal priesthood confessing and proclaiming to the world the good news of God in Christ" (Schalk 1983, 133). Luther himself wrote thirty-six hymns: fifteen metrical renditions of biblical passages, ten adaptations from Latin hymns, six modified German hymns, and five originals (Grew 1938, 72). These hymns were sermons set to music, with the notes giving life to the text (Grindel 2006, 179). Luther aimed "to make German Psalms for the people, i.e., spiritual songs so that the word of God even by means of song may live among the people" (Luther 1965, 221). Luther's use of music was just one more way he spread the Protestant message to others. This missional tactic of creating vernacular worship music spread to many other countries, drawing in and passing on Reformed ideas.

SIDEBAR 7.1

Massacre of French Lutherans in the New World

In the middle of the sixteenth century, the king of France, with a party of French Lutherans led by explorer General Jean Ribault, believed that planting settlers in Florida would aid in defusing religious conflicts in France and strengthen the king's own claim to a part of North America. The Crown wanted to discover silver and gold, as the Spanish had done in Central and South America. The political and religious hostilities that existed between the Spanish Catholics and the French Protestants resulted in a naval skirmish off the coast of the New World. Don Pedro Menéndez de Avilés, the Spanish governor of Florida at the time of the conflict, proclaimed, "I am Captain-General of the fleet of the King of Spain, and I am come into this country to hang and behead all Lutherans I may find by land or sea, and in the morning I will board your ships; and if I find any Catholics they will be well treated; but all who are heretics shall die" (Marshall 2011, 59).

Subsequently, on September 20, 1565, Menéndez captured Fort de la Caroline, La Florida (present-day Jacksonville, Florida), without loss to the Spaniards of a single person; of the 240 French in the fort, 132 died in the military exchange. Menéndez then hung the remaining male prisoners on trees and placed above them the Spanish inscription, "I do this not to Frenchmen, but to Lutherans" (Marshall 2011, 60). The only survivors of the massacre were about 50 women and children.

Reflection and Discussion

1. How would you have responded to this massacre had you been alive at the time?
2. Does such religious intolerance between Catholics and Protestants exist today? As Christians, how should we behave when exposed to such hatred?

Conclusion

Even with the backdrop of theological, social, and political chaos, Lutheranism and Calvinism flourished in Europe during the sixteenth century. Luther's message swept through Scandinavia, promoted by former Wittenberg students carrying Luther's writings, Bible translations, and hymns. Parallel to this expansion was the spread of Calvin's Protestant gospel. Similar to Luther, Calvin distributed his message during a time of intense difficulty for Protestant churches. Much energy was concentrated on survival of the fledging Protestant movement via organizing church governance, establishing theological doctrine, and training pastors. The immediate pressing need was for the church and its message to be safely established. Even so, preaching Reformation doctrine in Catholic regions inevitably ensured the death sentence.

In such a milieu of violence and unrest, we could possibly excuse Calvin or Luther if they neglected evangelism or missions. The immense social pressures and difficulties, however, did not immobilize the evangelistic efforts of the Reformers and their followers. In addition, the consequence of their efforts was far more than reforming the thinking of established believers. In light of the situation of the world around them, their missionary activity and that of their colleagues was remarkable. Even though both Luther and Calvin never traveled much farther than their homeland, their message infectiously spread throughout Europe and beyond to the corners of the world, bringing tens of thousands of new believers to Christ.

8

Encountering
Jesuit Missions

The Spaniard Ignatius of Loyola had a radical conversion to Christ the King while recovering from wounds in the battle of Pamplona against the French in 1521. He stated, "Here it will be to ask for an intimate knowledge of our Lord, who has become human for me, that I may love him more and follow him more closely" (Ignatius of Loyola 1991, 89). He became the founder of a sixteenth-century Catholic missionary order that produced pathfinders for Jesus. Europeans belonging to this papal society showed notable faithfulness to Christ and flexibility in presentation as they took the good news to the ends of the earth. The pioneering legacy of such men as Francis Xavier in India and Japan and Matteo Ricci in China to the history of Christian expansion remains that they presented the gospel to non-Europeans without promoting Western culture and thus provided ways of contextualizing the Christian faith outside Europe. This movement began with one man on the periphery of the church: Ignatius of Loyola (see Gallagher 2005b, 108–16).

Loyola was born in 1491, one of thirteen children of a noble family in northern Spain. As a young man, aroused by the ideals of courage and courtly romance, he dreamed of doing great exploits. A cannonball had shattered his right leg in the battle against the French and his leg was not setting properly. The bone protruded in an ugly way that showed through the tight hose that a courtier wore. Loyola insisted on having his leg rebroken and set again at a time when there was no anesthetic. This resulted in one leg being shorter than the other, and he limped for the rest of his life. While recuperating he read an illustrated *Life of Christ* (*De Vita Christi*) by Ludolph of Saxony and a book of saints' legends, which provoked his desire to do great things for God, similar to Francis of Assisi and Dominic.

Seventeen years later, with six student friends at the College Sainte-Barbe in the University of Paris, he formed the Society of Jesus—commonly known as the Jesuits—to undertake hospital and missionary work in Jerusalem or to go without questioning wherever the pope might direct. In 1540, with ten men in the society, Pope Paul III gave his approval for its formation as a new order based on education and missions. Over the years, Ignatius collected his

> At all events, love of God (or God Himself, and not of a human theory about Him), is the ultimate reason for a love of man's neighbour.
>
> Ignatius of Loyola (Rahner and Imhof 1979, 19)

insights and prayers in his book *Spiritual Exercises*, one of the most influential books on spiritual formation ever written.

Ignatius and Education

As Ignatius began his work in education in the Society of Jesus, he identified the need for Christian education to address ignorance among both clergy and

SIDEBAR 8.1

Soul of Christ

The Soul of Christ, or *Anima Christi*, is often attributed to Saint Ignatius of Loyola because Ignatius included the prayer in his teaching, placing it at the beginning of the *Spiritual Exercises*. However, the prayer appears in early fourteenth-century texts and prayer books, far earlier than the sixteenth-century inclusion by Ignatius. The prayer is Christ centered, asking Christ for comfort, strength, and guidance.

> Jesus, may all that is You flow into me.
> May Your body and blood be my food and my drink.
> May Your passion and death be my strength and life.
> Jesus, with You by my side enough has been given.
> May the shelter I seek be the shadow of Your cross.

> Let me not run from the love, which You offer,
> But hold me safe from the forces of evil.
> On each of my dyings shed Your light and Your love.
> Keep calling me until that day comes
> When, with Your saints, I may praise You forever.
> Amen.
>
> Frisbee (1907)

Reflection and Discussion

1. In what way does the central figure of the suffering Christ serve as an anchor in meditation?
2. What word or phrase is meaningful to you? Why?

laity and open new mission opportunities. He stated, "As you know my great desire was to 'help souls' as I put it in my diary to tell people about God and His grace and about Jesus Christ, the Crucified and Risen, so that their freedom would become the freedom of God" (Rahner and Imhof 1979, 11). He seems to have realized that teaching could be a powerful means to form the minds and the souls of those who in turn would influence many others. Requests for schools multiplied, and the society began to build colleges throughout Europe, in cities such as Coimbra, Portugal (1541); Messina, Sicily (1547); Palermo, Sicily (1549); Rome (1551); Vienna (1553); and Billom, France (1556). In his lifetime Ignatius founded thirty-five colleges across Europe, developing a unified educational system with shared objectives, procedures, curriculum, and evaluations, all administered from Rome.

Characteristically, Jesuits adopted the best available educational models and adapted their own practices to the needs of the people they wanted to help. They implemented the curriculum of other academies: the works of Latin and Greek authors, rhetorical analysis, writing, public speaking, and the study of these materials as guides to moral character and practical action, in addition to study of the natural sciences and mathematics. F. C. Cesareo summarizes Ignatius's objective in Jesuit education: "[It] seems to have been twofold: to form a good, solid Christian leader who could exert a positive influence on the social, political, and cultural environment in which he lived and by means of this, to allow for the spiritual program of one's soul on its pilgrimage toward salvation" (1993, 20).

Ignatius and Missions

At first, the Society of Jesus believed that its mission field would be among the Muslims of the Holy Land. This focus changed as the society embraced Ignatius's idea of action and mobility: to be willing to go anywhere in the world for the pope. Created to be a mobile missionary army, the members of the order were soldiers of Christ, for the immobile church. Ignatius believed that "the members of this Society ought to be ready at any hour to go to some or other parts of the world, where they may be sent by the sovereign pontiff or their superior" (Ignatius of Loyola 1970, 262).

Jesuit missionary strategy involved reviving and nurturing faith among Catholics, winning back those who had become Protestants, converting the unbaptized, training the order's members for social service and missionary work, and establishing educational institutions, spiritual devotion, academic excellence, and missionary zeal. In a 1550 papal bull, Pope Julius III stated, "The Company is founded to employ itself entirely in the defense and the spread of the holy Catholic faith, and to help souls in Christian life and doctrine by preaching, public reading of the Scriptures and other means of teaching the word of God, by giving spiritual exercises, teaching Christian doctrine to children and the ignorant, hearing confessions, and administering the sacraments" (Van Dyke 1926, 175). In the strategic vision of Ignatius, "preference

> **My devotion to the Church had in general one imperative motive for me, which was my desire "to help souls," a desire which only reaches its true goal when those "souls" grow in faith, hope, love, and nearness to God.**
>
> Ignatius of Loyola (Rahner and Imhof 1979, 26)

ought to be shown to the aid, which [was] given to the great nations, such as the Indies, or to important cities, or to universities, which [were] generally attended by numerous persons who by being aided themselves [could] become laborers for the help of others" (1970, 74).

As the Jesuits grew in number, so did their diversity of ministry in the life of the church: diplomatic assignments for the papacy, teaching at universities, theological counseling at the Council of Trent, reform of religious communities, administration of schools, and foreign missions.

The early Jesuits also worked with the poor and oppressed as well as with prominent figures such as kings and bishops. They spoke against the social injustices of the day and were successful in banning Catholic clergy who indulged in gambling and relationships with concubines. Ignatius showed special sympathy to the Jewish people, defending them in public and even obtaining a legal brief that prohibited confiscating the possessions of Jewish converts. Further, he founded a house for repentant prostitutes in Rome, and

> **From among those who are now merely students, in time some will depart to play diverse roles: one to preach and carry on the care of souls, another to the government of the land and the administration of justice, and others to other callings. Finally, since young boys become grown men, their good education in life and doctrine will be beneficial to many others, with the fruit expanding more widely every day.**
>
> Ignatius of Loyola (O'Neal 2000, 19)

one for girls whose mothers were prostitutes, so that "the evil one" would not influence them. Ignatius believed that he fulfilled God's purpose if he kept even one of the prostitutes out of sin for just one night. Moreover, he

opened houses for orphans, ministered to the sick, and provided free schooling for many who were illiterate. He performed some of his social activism
with public consent, yet often he went against societal opinion (Dalmases
1985, 181, 220). He asserted, "What they [the Jesuits] should especially seek
to accomplish for God's greater glory [the Jesuit motto was *ad maiorem dei*

**Their [the Jesuits] assignment came to be called "mis-
sion" (a term first used in this sense by Ignatius of
Loyola), and they themselves "missionaries." Previously,
various terms were used such as "propagation of the
faith," "preaching the gospel," "augmenting the faith,"
"expanding the church," "planting the church," "propagation of the reign of Christ," and "illuminating the nations."**

David J. Bosch (1991, 228)

---

gloriam, "to the greater glory of God"] is to preach, hear confessions, lecture,
instruct children, give good example, visit the poor in the hospitals, exhort
the neighbor according to the amount of talent . . . so as to move as many as
possible to prayer and devotion" (Ignatius of Loyola 1970, 65).

"By 1556 [the year of Ignatius's death] the Society of Jesus had well over
3,000 members, dispersed in many countries of Western Europe [Italy, Spain,
France, Germany, and Ireland] as well as in India, Japan, Brazil, and other
exotic places [Malacca and the East Indies]" (O'Malley 1993, 51). Ignatius
maintained the unity of the members of the society, scattered in distant lands,
through letter writing and general assemblies every three years. He wrote nearly
seven thousand letters and required all members of the society to write to him
regularly in Rome. He argued, "The chief bond to cement the union of our
hearts among the members . . . is the love of God our Lord. . . . We should not
break this divinely constituted oneness and fellowship, but rather strengthen
and consolidate it ever more, forming ourselves into one body" (1970, 279).

Eastern European Expansion

Long before Ignatius formed the Society of Jesus, the Portuguese had claimed
Goa on the west coast of India in 1498, when Vasco da Gama reached that
territory during his first voyage. The city then became the center of the Portuguese Empire in the East, with trading extensions in Malacca, Macau, and the
island of Timor. The Europeans were mainly interested in trade and not land
acquisition, so the influence of Christendom remained small but not without

controversy. Trading centers were often acquired through military force. A Portuguese Franciscan made the following observation in 1638: "The two swords of the civil and the ecclesiastical power were always . . . close together in the conquest of the East. . . . For the weapons only conquered through the right that the preaching of the Gospel gave them, and the preaching was only of some use when it was accompanied and protected by the weapons" (Boxer 1978, 75).

The Portuguese method of evangelization in their colonies consisted of preaching, social work, and support for intercultural marriages among European men. The Hindus and the Muslims in the trading ports became marginalized citizens. Social and financial tensions, together with the destruction of temples and the prohibition of Hindu festivals, coerced non-Christians to conversion. For converts this meant the acceptance of Portuguese customs and culture, which was especially repulsive to high-caste Brahmins, who did not want to associate with the Portuguese because the Europeans did not wash, drank alcohol, ate meat, and interacted with the lower castes. To counter this adverse reaction to Christian conversion, baptisms celebrated at Goa were full of pomp and ceremony; the candidates wore elaborate clothing and paraded down the decorated streets to the church in the presence of the city's highest officials (Thekkedath 1988, 317–18, 349).

Xavier's Mission to Asia

In contrast to these strategies of evangelism were the methods of the sixteenth-century Society of Jesus. The king of Portugal, John III, appointed Francis Xavier, one of the seven original members of the order, to evangelize the people of the East Indies. Arriving in Goa, India, in 1542, he found the native cultures, customs, languages, and institutions suppressed by the policies of Portuguese colonialization. The colonizers forced the natives to accept European names, clothes, and rites as well as to learn Portuguese in order to study Christian doctrine. Xavier wrote to a Jesuit missionary in Japan:

> Take diligent care never to speak harshly of the native Christians in the presence of the Portuguese; rather always defend them and take up their cause when they are accused, making excuses for them, and commending them as much as you are able. . . . If we knew the language, do not doubt that a great many Japanese would become Christians. God grant that we may soon acquire it well, as we have already for some time begun to understand it. (J. D. Young 1980, 2–3)

Xavier spent his first five months preaching in the streets and ministering to the sick in the hospitals. His approach was to go through the streets ringing a bell and inviting the children to hear the word of God. When he had collected a crowd, he invited them into his church, where he explained the catechism and taught them to sing rhymed lessons and recite prayers. The Jesuit believed that the repetition of the Catholic teachings enabled the youth to remember the lessons more easily. Later that first year, he moved to the pearl fisheries of the far southwest coast of India, where he spent three years preaching. His journeys even reached the island of Sri Lanka. The Spaniard faced many hardships and difficulties during this time from petty kings and the Portuguese military.

Xavier wrote the following from Cochin in Kerala, India, on January 27, 1545, to the Mission Society at Rome, explaining his missionary method.

> This is the method I followed. As soon as I arrived in any heathen village where they had sent for me to give them baptism, I gave orders for all men, women,

SIDEBAR 8.2

The Prayer of Francis Xavier for the Conversion of the Infidels

Francis Xavier, who with Ignatius of Loyola cofounded the Society of Jesus, led a Christian mission into Asia and was influential in evangelization work, most notably in southern India. He also ventured into Malacca, the Molucca Islands, Borneo, and Japan, although in these regions he struggled to learn the local languages and in the face of opposition had less success than he had enjoyed in India. The prayer below, which still speaks to us today, reveals his theological message and motivation for missions as he encountered non-Christian peoples in Asia.

Eternal God, the Maker of all things, remember that the souls of unbelievers have been called into existence by Thee, and that they have been made after Thy own image and likeness. Behold, O Lord, to the dishonour of Thee, with these very souls hell is filled. Remember, O God, that for their salvation Thy Son Jesus Christ underwent the most cruel death. Let it not then, I entreat Thee, Lord, be any longer permitted by Thee that Thy Son should be despised by the unbelievers; but, appeased by the prayers of holy men and of the Church, the Spouse of Thy most holy Son, do Thou remember Thy own pity, and, forgetting their idolatry and their unbelief, bring it to pass that they too may sometime acknowledge Thy Son Jesus Christ, who is our salvation, life, and resurrection, through whom we are saved and set free; to whom be glory from age to age without end. Amen.

Francis Xavier (in Lasance 1911, 766–67)

Reflection and Discussion

1. How might Francis Xavier's experience with multiple cultures, religions, and individuals have shaped this prayer?

2. How would you describe Xavier's theological message and motivation "for the conversion of the infidels"? How does this compare with your understanding of missions to non-Christians?

and children to be collected in one place. Then, beginning with the first elements of the Christian faith, I taught them there is one God, Father, Son, and Holy Ghost; and at the same time, calling on the three divine Persons and one God, I made them each make three signs of the Cross; then, putting on a surplice, I began to recite in a loud voice and in their own language the form of the general Confession, the Apostles' Creed, the Ten Commandments, the Lord's Prayer, the *Ave Maria*, and the *Salve Regina*. (Kuriakose 1982, 32)

He continues in his letter, "In this region of Travancore, where I am now, God has drawn very many to the faith of His Son Jesus Christ. In the space of one month I made Christians of more than 10,000." In two years, he translated and memorized a series of Catholic prayers written in the language of the region. Xavier stated, "[I] recited them slowly so that all of every age and condition followed me in them. Then I began to explain shortly the articles of the Creed and the Ten Commandments in the language of the country." After this accomplishment, he would instruct the people to confess their sins "to touch the hearts of the heathen and confirm the faith of the good." He asked each baptismal candidate whether he believed each of the articles of faith. After baptism, he then gave the convert a new name written on a ticket and allowed him to bring his wife and family for baptism. Xavier explained, "When all are baptized I order all the temples of their false gods to be destroyed and all the idols to be broken into pieces. I can give you no idea of the joy I feel in seeing this done, witnessing the destruction of the idols by the very people who but lately adored them."

Missions to Japan

Xavier sailed away from India on a Portuguese ship in 1545 and stopped in Malacca (on the west coast of present-day Malaysia) to evangelize the people of that port. A year later, he left Malacca and went to the Portuguese settlements in the Molucca Islands (present-day Indonesia), where he continued to preach the gospel to the inhabitants. After he returned to Malacca in 1547, he met a Japanese man, Han-Sir, and thereafter desired to introduce Christianity to Japan. In August 1549, Xavier and two other Jesuits arrived in Kagoshima, Japan; they devoted their first year in the country to learning the Japanese language and translating into the vernacular the principal articles of faith and short treatises, which would be employed in preaching and catechizing.

In the two and a half years that Xavier spent in Japan, he focused on preaching the gospel in the center and southern parts of the country. He changed his mission strategy after recognizing the sophistication of Japanese culture. Instead of dressing poorly to connect with the common people, as he had done in India, Xavier wore the finest clothing and gave expensive gifts in hope of winning the favor of the local leaders. During his time in

Japan, he realized the need to present the gospel in the Japanese language and in a way that affirmed the culture (Ross 1994, 26–27). His methods of contextualization became a missionary model for the Jesuits of Asia, yet not without serious debate among European Christians. At the time of Xavier's death, "over seven hundred Japanese had joined the church; by the 1580s, there were seventy-five Jesuits at work in Japan and perhaps 150,000 converts" (M. Noll 1997, 216).

Alessandro Valignano, an Italian Jesuit who was appointed to help supervise the Jesuit missions in the East Indies (including Japan and China) in 1573, continued with the reforms that his predecessor had initiated. He embarked on three trips to the Jesuit mission in Japan (1579–1582, 1590–1592, and 1598–1603), during which he met with several Christian daimyo (Japanese feudal lords) and indigenous leaders. He reorganized the Jesuit mission and founded a novitiate at Usuki (in what is now Oita Prefecture) and two boys' schools, at Funai and Azuchi. In promoting Christianity, he supported the ruling classes, all the while instructing his missionaries to master the Japanese language and adapt to Japanese customs, etiquette, and culture. Valignano brought to Japan a European printing press, which produced grammars and dictionaries for the Jesuits and works of instruction and devotion for Japanese Christians.

The "visitor to the East" understood that foreign missionaries by themselves were incapable of converting the Japanese to Christianity. One of his main concerns was to train Japanese Jesuits and priests to break down the barriers between the Asians and the Europeans. Eight years after Valignano's death in 1606, Christianity was banned in Japan, missionaries were banished from the country, and Japanese Christians were ordered to renounce their faith, prompted by fear of a Spanish invasion from the Philippines. In 1614 persecution broke out, many of the three hundred thousand Japanese Christians were martyred, and the church went underground. As the Jesuit work ended in Japan, however, other opportunities opened for the gospel witness in Asia (Jennes 1973, 216–24).

Missions to China

Portugal in Macao and Spain in the Philippines were expanding their political and economic influences with the pope's blessing. Wherever the colonial powers expanded, Christian missions followed close behind, with converts forced to become European in practice in order to be Christian. Valignano believed that Japan and China were not places to be conquered and that any such approach would be to the detriment of Christianity. Furthermore, both these cultures contained elements of truth and morality that could serve as a foundation for the Christian faith. His aim was to create a genuine Japanese and Chinese church, and the imperial greed of Europe was harmful to such a goal.

Xavier had desired to enter China in 1552 from the small island of Sancian, near the coast of China, but the Chinese officials refused him entry, and he died a few months later. Following Xavier's death, attempts to enter China with the Christian message failed. The Franciscan Pedro de Alfaro expressed the frustration of the missionaries when he said, "With or without soldiers, to wish to enter China is to attempt to reach the moon" (Dunne 1962, 16–17).

Valignano employed a method of cultural adaptation in Asia, an approach of humility and cultural sensitivity. Finding the Jesuits in Macao not suited to such a method, he sent Michele de Ruggieri in 1579 and Matteo Ricci in 1582 to the Portuguese colony. Valignano instructed Ricci to prepare a report on China in which he was to describe its peoples, customs, and government; he was also to learn the Chinese language. With the help of Chinese interpreters, Ricci was able to write the first extensive report about China received in the West. "Without Valignano there would have been no Ricci. It has been noted, however, that perhaps no one could have carried out Valignano's ideas in China with such intellectual daring and perception as Matteo Ricci" (Ross 1999, 510).

Ricci's Mission to China

Sixteenth-century China was a closed world. The Chinese people believed that they were the "Middle Kingdom," the greatest of all civilizations, while others were barbarians. The Chinese dynasty and culture were ancient, and the Chinese were suspicious of anything that was not as old. However, the Ming dynasty, while achieving a unified political entity, was weak and in decline as well as isolated from Western science, though the Chinese used the printing press.

SIDEBAR 8.3

Attitude toward Foreigners in China

"The Chinese look upon all foreigners as illiterate and barbarous, and refer to them in just these terms. They even disdain to learn anything from the books of outsiders because they believe that all true science and knowledge belongs to them alone. . . . Even the written characters by which they express the word foreigner are those that are applied to beasts, and scarcely ever do they give them a title more honorable than they would assign to their demons. . . . They [foreigners] are never permitted to see the King. . . . No one in the whole kingdom is ever permitted to do business with foreigners, excepting at certain times and in certain places, as on the peninsula of Macao. . . . Anyone carrying on foreign trade without official sanction would be subject to the severest punishment."

Matteo Ricci (1953, 88–89)

For the Jesuits, the study and adaptation of Chinese culture were important to their strategy of reaching the higher-class literati. They believed that it was necessary to be an intellectual equal to gain acceptance with the Chinese philosophers. These were the people at the head of China's hierarchy, those in control of the government. Ricci believed that if they became Christians, the impact on the nation would continue well beyond his lifetime (Peterson 1988, 129–52).

> Another remarkable fact and quite worthy of note as marking a difference from the West, is that the entire kingdom is administered by the Order of the Learned, commonly known as The Philosophers. The responsibility for the orderly management of the entire realm is wholly and completely committed to their charge and care. The army, both officers and soldiers, hold them in high respect and show them the promptest obedience and deference, and not infrequently the military are disciplined by them as a schoolboy might be punished by his master. (Ricci 1953, 363)

Ricci's Beginnings

Three years after studying law at the University of Rome at the age of sixteen, Ricci became a novice in the Society of Jesus at Saint Andrew's Quirinale in Rome. At twenty-five, he left for India from the Lisbon palace of King Sebastian in Portugal. In 1578 he arrived in Goa, India, with thirteen other Jesuits to study theology and teach Latin and Greek at Saint Paul's College. Two years after Ricci became an ordained priest in Cochin, India, in 1580, Valignano invited him to Macao. In Macao he produced the first edition of his map of the world, *Great Map of 10,000 Countries* (annotated in Chinese), showing China's geographic position in the world.

Then, in 1583 the Jesuits had the opportunity for permanent residence in Zhaoqing, China. Ricci responded to the request knowing that Valignano had ordered him to remain in China with the goal of reaching the capital, Peking (present-day Beijing), to interact with the rulers (Ricci 1953, 142). Expelled from Zhaoqing by hostile Mandarins, he settled in Shaozhou six years later when the prefect of the province, Wang Pan, invited him after learning of his expertise in mathematics, astronomy, and geography. Shaozhou became a starting point for a mission that spread within eighteen years to Nanchang, Nanjing, and eventually Peking. The earlier mission centers had six to ten priests and a number of converts, yet after the Peking mission opened "the number of Jesuit priests rose to seventeen, and conversions rose to 150 a year or more, many of these coming from rich and influential families" (Spence 1984, 179). Ricci spent twenty-seven years of his life in China, never returning to Europe. Rosalie Judith Ford explains, "Imbued with the spirit of the Italian Renaissance, its humanistic emphasis and intense interest in ancient cultures, Ricci entered China with an attitude of open-mindedness, respect, and curiosity" (1985, 206).

Ricci's Mission Strategy

In 1584 Valignano received direction from Rome that only Jesuits were to work in Japan and China. He had confidence that they were adopting the right approach, which would be successful if not interfered with by other orders. This move disturbed the Dominicans and the Franciscans in the Philippines, who opposed the Jesuits' accommodating style of missions, especially their attitude toward ancestral ceremonies and the veneration of Confucius.

When Ricci and his colleague Ruggieri first entered China, they began adapting to the culture. For instance, they performed the Chinese kowtow with three kneelings and nine prostrations to show respect to the appropriate officials and began wearing the gray cloak of a Buddhist monk as well as shaving their heads and beards. After eleven years, they realized that they needed more prestige and respect than that accorded a typical Buddhist monk, whom many people despised. Their guiding principle then became to draw close to Confucianism yet repudiate Buddhism. After 1594 Ricci and the other Jesuits in China lived as Confucian literati, changing their dress to a full-length robe of purple and blue silk (Rule 1968, 112; Spence 1984, 114–15). By 1601 Ricci had reached Peking, the capital of the Chinese Empire, established a Jesuit house, and moved closer to his goal of influencing the educated classes.

Confucian scholars were well-educated and respected teachers in Chinese society, and Ricci wanted to be associated with them. His house became a gathering place for these Chinese literati, where he not only improved his understanding of the language and culture but also reaffirmed how important these philosophers were to Chinese government and society. This became the key to his mission strategy:

> Because of the high regard for the educated class, Ricci sought to befriend and accommodate himself to this group. . . . It was essential for Ricci to understand the government and to operate in it according to its many rules, for many foreigners had been expelled because they were suspect to the officials and the Emperor. Ricci used this knowledge to gain respect and entrance into the country that had been closed and resistant to the gospel. (G. Williams 1996, 38)

Learning the Language and Literature

Ricci believed that the way to reach the Chinese was to learn their language, and he was one of the first missionaries to have such an approach. He became fluent in speaking and writing Chinese, which gained him respect with the people. Realizing the importance of the written word in China, Ricci wrote to a friend, "In China more can be done with books than with words" (Covell 2004, 44). Encouraged by Valignano, he studied the Chinese classical *Four Books*, the foundation of Confucianism, in preparation for writing an effective Christian catechism, and in 1594 he finished translating them into Latin. Ricci translated many Chinese works for European readers. Conversely, he translated European writings into Chinese, including the first six books of Euclid's *Elements of Geometry* (1607) and a catechism. There was a constant exchange of books and letters between East and West. Seventy-two-year-old Chinese scholar Li Zhi wrote of Ricci:

> Now he can speak our language fluently, write our script, and act according to our rules of conduct. He is an extremely impressive man—a person of inner refinement, outwardly most straightforward. In an assembly of many people, all talking in confusion with each holding to his own point of view, Ricci keeps his silence and cannot be provoked to interfere or to become involved. Amongst the people of my acquaintance, no one is comparable to him. All those who are either too overbearing or too flattering, or those who parade their cleverness or are narrow-minded and lacking in intelligence are inferior to him. (Franke 1976, 1140)

In addition, Ricci wrote on science, mathematics, memory, astronomy, and European culture. Some of his publications in Chinese were *Treatise on Friendship* (1595), *Treatise on Mnemonic Arts* (1596), *Fundamental Christian Teachings* (1605), *Twenty-Five Sayings* (1605), *Ten Discourses by a Paradoxical Man* (1608), and *Historia* (1610). His intent was to form the Jesuit mission in such a way that it would be a part of Chinese society. It would then be possible for the Chinese church to evangelize the nation. He was preparing the ground for a great harvest. "To Westerners, Ricci and his companions were the first sinologists, while to the Chinese they were the first occidentalists" (McNaspy 1993, 83).

Not only was Ricci a prolific author, but he wrote with excellence. Still appreciated for its literary style in China nearly two centuries later was his book *The True Meaning of the Lord of Heaven* (Dunne 1962, 94, 96). Begun in 1593 and completed in 1603, this volume introduced Christianity to Chinese leadership using the format of a dialogue between Chinese and Western scholars. It was his attempt to use Chinese thinking to introduce Christianity to Chinese intellectuals. Douglas Lancashire, Peter Hu Kuo-chen, and Edward Malatesta state, "The book . . . stressed self-cultivation, equated God with *Shang-ti*, and used the Chinese classics to prove that some of the basic religious concepts of Catholicism were already to be found in the China of ancient times. The work provided Christian thought with an entrance into Chinese culture" (Ricci 1985, 39–40). Described as a "pre-evangelistic dialogue," this apologetic work was Ricci's legacy (Ricci 1985, 15). Of this work, Andrew C. Ross writes, "It was this book that finally convinced the scholar community that Ricci was someone who could be respected as a Chinese scholar, someone who had overcome his unfortunate origins to become one who could be treated as if he were Chinese" (1994, 131).

Teaching European Knowledge

Ricci shared his expertise in Western mathematics, science, and astronomy with the Chinese scholars. He had studied philosophy, mathematics, cosmology, and astronomy at the Jesuits' Roman College under Christopher Clavius, a friend of Kepler and Galileo and one of the most widely recognized mathematicians of the day. Ricci's secular studies "later opened a door for him among the *literati* of China" (R. Tucker 2004, 67).

The Chinese literati were attracted to Ricci and the Jesuits because they wanted to learn Western mathematics, the mnemonic system, and how to turn mercury into silver. Mnemonics was a fundamental part of Jesuit training in Rome, and Ricci's memory skills impressed the intellectuals. Mention of Ricci, whose Chinese name was Li Ma-tou, is in the official records of the Ming dynasty. "Li Ma-tou, surnamed Hsi-t'ai, was a man of the Great West Ocean, with a curly beard, blue eyes, and a voice like a great bell. . . . He was intelligent, witty, and of manifold ability, understanding Chinese books and documents, and able to repeat what he had once glanced at. Famous nobles and great officers of that day all held him in high regard" (Rule 1968, 106). In addition, the Jesuit respected Chinese scientific discoveries. "The Chinese have not only made considerable progress in moral philosophy but in astronomy and in many branches of mathematics as well. At one time, they were quite proficient in arithmetic and geometry, but in the study and teaching of these branches of learning, they labored with more or less confusion. They divide the heaven into constellations in a manner somewhat different from that which we employ" (Ricci 1953, 30).

Supporting Confucianism

In studying Confucianism to understand the Chinese culture, the Jesuits grew in their appreciation of this philosophical religion and used it as a framework for their mission strategy. In 1595 Ricci wrote, "I have interpreted with the help of the good masters, not only the *Four Books* but also all *Six Classics*, and I have noted many passages in all of them which favor the teachings of our faith, such as the unity of God, the immortality of the soul, and the glory of the blessed" (Wu 1983, 113). All members of the society were required to study these Confucian classics to acquire understanding of the culture and train their minds to enter the Chinese intellectual arena. In this way, they hoped that they would be able to communicate the gospel in a meaningful manner.

Ricci found in Confucianism many beliefs that were compatible with Christianity—such as filial piety, respect for authority, the concept of a supreme

God, and moral cultivation (Wu 1983, 112). He believed that Buddhism had corrupted this ancient religious philosophy, and thus it displayed an incomplete view of God and humanity based on natural religion. His aim was to complete Confucianism and to do away with Buddhism. His converts always saw themselves as followers of Confucius and never abandoned the truths of their tradition. The Jesuit leader emphasized to these followers of

---

The most renowned of all Chinese philosophers was named Confucius. This great and learned man was born five hundred and fifty-one years before the beginning of the Christian era, lived more than seventy years, and spurred on his people to the pursuit of virtue not less by his own example than by his writing and conferences. His self-mastery and abstemious ways of life have led his countrymen to assert that he surpassed in holiness all those who in times past, in the various parts of the world, were considered to have excelled in virtue.

Matteo Ricci (1953, 30)

Confucius that in their attempt to better themselves they needed a belief in and service to God.

Although Confucian ancestral rites originated with primitive animism, Ricci included them since they complied with his beliefs of filial piety. The Jesuits saw the rites as social and not religious because they gave continuity and dignity to the ancient society. The Chinese were greatly concerned with achieving harmony between human events and the heavenly bodies. Respect, obedience, and service between parents and child brought such harmony and thus stability to the social order. Ricci believed that the Chinese burned incense as a gesture of respect, not worship, and that food was given symbolically as a sign of ongoing care for the family member.

Furthermore, Ricci required that the Chinese Christians make no prayers to the dead, burn no money, and understand that the spirits were not receiving sustenance in the offering of food. Believers were encouraged to give money to the poor instead of offering food to the ancestors. The Jesuits allowed ancestral tablets (wooden plaques bearing the names of the ancestors) to be kept along with other items showing honor such as flowers, candles, and incense. Chinese Christians participated in the ancient rituals that reinforced filial piety, central to Chinese morality, with the hope that Christian maturity would modify these ceremonies in the light of Scripture. The idea was to wean the Christians from these deeply rooted customs rather than to demand that they cease to observe such practices (Ross 1994, 151–52).

After Ricci's death in 1610, Jesuits continued to have influence in China. In 1623 German Jesuit Johann Adam Schall von Bell found himself at the bureau of astronomy in Peking, where he assisted the grand minister of the Ming dynasty, Xu Guangqi (a Christian convert who had studied under Ricci), in revising the Chinese calendar. Through Schall's Christian witness in the imperial court, by 1640 fifty imperial concubines and more than forty eunuchs had become converts. At the time of the Qing government's overthrow of the Ming dynasty in 1644 (resulting from the Manchu invasion of the capital), there were between 100,000 and 150,000 Chinese Catholics. This number included members of the royal family and some learned scholar-officials such as Xu Guangqi (Paul), Li Zhizao (Leon), Yang Tingjun (Michel), and Wang Zheng, who became leadership pillars in the early Chinese Catholic Church during the late Ming dynasty (Sunquist, Sing, and Chea 2001, 140, 734).

Likewise, Belgian Jesuit Ferdinand Verbiest served in the court of Emperor Kang Xi, of the Qing dynasty. In 1660 he joined Schall in Peking, and after a brief imprisonment with his predecessor, he succeeded the German Jesuit as chief director of the astronomical bureau. For over fifty years, Verbiest and the Jesuits enjoyed the favor of the emperor, who learned Western science from them. Verbiest helped new missionaries enter China, encouraged the training of indigenous clergy, and published scientific and religious books in Chinese.

The Rites Controversy

During the almost one hundred years between Ricci's entry into China and Verbiest's death in 1688, there were many Catholic missionaries in China from different orders. In particular, the Dominicans and the Franciscans criticized

SIDEBAR 8.4

Chinese Annual Funeral Rites

"The most common ceremony practiced by all the Literati, from the King down to the very lowest of them, is that of the annual funeral rites. . . . As they themselves say, they consider this ceremony as an honor bestowed upon their departed ancestors, just as they might honor them if they were living. They do not really believe that the dead actually need the victuals, which are placed upon their graves, but they say that they observe the custom of placing them there because it seems to be the best way of testifying their love for their dead departed. . . . This practice of placing food upon the graves of the dead seems to be beyond any charge of sacrilege and perhaps also free from any taint of superstition, because they do not in any respect consider their ancestors to be gods, nor do they petition them for anything or hope for anything from them."

Matteo Ricci (1953, 96)

the Jesuits' mission strategy before Pope Innocent X; as a result, in 1645 he declared a moratorium on Chinese believers participating in any ancient rites ceremonies. In the debate that lasted for centuries, some European Catholics sounded the call for Asian Christianity to reject Western cultural norms. For instance, Rome's Sacred Congregation for the Propagation of the Faith (1659) directed three new French missionaries in Tonkin and Cochin concerning cultural adaptation.

> Do not try to persuade the Chinese to change their rites, their customs, their ways, as long as these are not openly opposed to religion and good morals. What would be sillier than to import France, Spain, Italy, or any other country of Europe into China? Don't import these, but the faith. The faith does not reject or crush the rites and customs of any race, as long as these are not evil. Rather, it wants to preserve them. (R. Noll 1992, 6)

Emperor Kang Xi studied Ricci's *The True Meaning of the Lord of Heaven* for six months and in 1692 issued an edict of toleration for Christianity:

> The Europeans are very quiet; they do not excite any disturbances in the provinces, they do no harm to anyone, they commit no crimes, and their doctrine has nothing in common with that of the false sects in the empire, nor has it any tendency to excite sedition. . . . We decide therefore that all temples dedicated to the Lord of heaven, in whatever place they may be found, ought to be preserved, and that it may be permitted to all who wish to worship this God to enter these temples, offer him incense, and perform the ceremonies practised according to ancient custom by the Christians. Therefore, let no one henceforth offer them any opposition. (Neill 1964, 189–90)

A similar edict had resulted in the conversion of the Roman Empire under Emperor Constantine, and it seemed that China was moving toward another such Christian awakening, with around 200,000 Catholics by 1700. Kang Xi "was arguably the most powerful ruler in the world at the time, ruling perhaps 150 million subjects," a population equivalent to Europe and Russia combined (Jenkins 2002, 32).

Nevertheless, even with the emperor's edict together with the first native Catholic bishop, Luo Wenzao (consecrated in 1685) and many Christians in positions of political power, the issue was reexamined by Rome a year after the proclamation. Over the next ten years, the arguments raged, with Kang Xi siding with the Jesuits. In 1704 and 1715, the Roman Inquisition under Pope Clement XI enforced the decree that Chinese Catholics stop venerating the ancestors and Confucius, and using the terms *T'ien* (heaven) and *Shang-ti* (Sovereign Lord) as names for God, permitting only *T'ien chu* (Lord of Heaven). Further, the Vatican ruled that religious services were to be only in Latin and suppressed recent Bible translations.

Emperor Kang Xi in 1720 forbade missionaries to preach in China when Pope Benedict XIV insisted on the total ban on any participation in ceremonial rites.

> Reading this proclamation, I [Kang Xi] have concluded that the Westerners are petty indeed. It is impossible to reason with them because they do not understand larger issues as we understand them in China. There is not a single Westerner versed in Chinese works, and their remarks are often incredible and ridiculous. To judge from this proclamation, their religion is no different from other small, bigoted sects of Buddhism or Taoism. I have never seen a document which contains so much nonsense. From now on, Westerners should not be allowed to preach in China, to avoid further trouble. (Li 1969, 22)

Upon the emperor's death, his son Yung Cheng ascended to the throne and relentlessly enforced the judgment by commanding Chinese Christians to renounce their faith, seizing church property, banishing missionaries (except those in government positions), and forbidding indigenous clergy. This reprisal

---

Ancestor worship is a very ancient custom, older than Confucius. Ricci proposed not to antagonize it. Unfortunately, the Spanish Dominicans who came later to China disagreed with Ricci and initiated what was called the "rites controversy" which lasted for almost a century. It led the papal court in Rome to ban the Chinese rites. This made the Chinese Emperor very angry as it was regarded as an interference in China's internal affairs. Emperor Kang Xi issued a decree to forbid any mission work in China. This controversy almost caused the disappearance of Christianity in China for the third time.

Wenhan Jiang (1983, 260)

---

against the Catholic Church originated from the new emperor's prophetic concern for the ambitious political role of the papacy in his country. The following conversation between the emperor and a Jesuit priest demonstrates this anxiety.

> What would you say if I sent a troop of Bonzes and Lamas into your country to preach their doctrines? You want all Chinese to become Christians. Your law demands it, I know. But in that case, what will become of us? Shall we become subjects of your king? The converts you make recognize only you in time of

trouble. They will listen to no other voice but yours. I know that at the present time, there is nothing to fear, but when your ships come by thousands, then there will probably be great disorder. (Boxer 1991, 46)

Finally, in 1742, Pope Benedict XIV gave all Catholic missionaries an order: agree to abide by the prohibition of rites. The tensions that resulted from the clash between the Qing dynasty and the Vatican proved detrimental to the growth of the church in China for over two hundred years. Not until 1939 did Pope Pius XII finally revoke the papal restrictions on Chinese Catholics (Loewe 1988, 207).

Missions Results in China

What was the Jesuit influence in China? The order's interpretation of Christianity gained them access among many of the Confucian literati and other higher-class groups. This continued missionary access to the emperor, and their role as official scholars aided in increasing the impact of Christianity on the educated classes. Concerned for the christianization of China, Ricci commented, "We desired to build something solid, so that converts would answer to the name of Christian, and in these beginnings, spread the good odor of our faith" (Dunne 1962, 105).

As they assimilated with the academic class that governed the country, the Jesuits were so successful in bringing about a Confucian-Christian synthesis that other Catholic orders, following them to China, accused them of syncretism. European political conflicts finally caused the church to condemn the Jesuit policy, an act that the Qing emperor Kang Xi refuted by imperial endorsement of only Ricci's Christianity. As a result, Christianity moved from being an option for all ranks of Chinese to being a peripheral sect for the marginalized.

Although the Jesuits were successful in reaching many key leaders among the literati, some traditional Confucian scholars opposed them, and Taoists and Buddhists were apathetic to their teaching (Ricci 1985, 44–45). Nevertheless, C. J. McNaspy claims that there were some 50,000 Christians in China at the time of Ricci's death in 1610 (1993, 82). William V. Bangert asserts that after Ricci died there were only 2,500 Chinese Catholics in the country, and in the next five years, the number grew to 5,000. By 1627, 13,000 had been received into the church, 40,000 by 1636, 65,000 in 1640, and by 1651 some 150,000. In 1617 there were eight priests and six Chinese brothers staffing the mission stations. By 1664 there were thirty priests in forty-two stations (1986, 23). C. R. Boxer concedes, "Exact figures for the number of converts are lacking, but all reliable authorities agree that the total of native Christians never exceeded 300,000 for this period" (1991, 47).

Other estimates of the Jesuits' impact are more restrained. James F. Lewis claims, "At his [Ricci's] death advances were modest: eight foreign priests, eight Chinese lay brothers, missions in four cities, and 2,500 'neophytes.' His grave was the gift of the emperor himself, a testimony to his stature as one of the most respected religious figures ever to come from the West" (2000, 834). D. J. Adams places these conversion figures in perspective when he admits that "Ricci had confidence in God's grace, and refused to yield to the pressure of time for immediate results. For him it was more important to be accepted by the Chinese on their terms than it was to make converts" (1980, 96).

Conclusion

The Jesuit mission in Asia begun by men such as Francis Xavier and Alessandro Valignano was short-lived and seemed to fail in the end. Nonetheless, missionaries were able to provide a bridge between cultures, for example Matteo Ricci, who introduced European science and traditions to the Chinese and brought Europe knowledge of Chinese life. His courage and vision enabled him and his colleagues to win the respect of many of China's most eminent scholars. Their method of operation was in contrast to that of other religious orders as they sought to come to terms with Chinese culture. The Jesuits attempted an accommodation, and though they failed to transform the thinking of the Middle Kingdom, their attempts were still noteworthy in their distinctiveness of method.

In 1926 Liang Qichao, an influential reformer and opponent of Marxism, wrote,

> The seed of late Ming and early Qing science came from the hands of the Jesuits. . . . The missionaries of that society had a clever way of preaching Christianity; they understood the psychology of the Chinese. They knew that the Chinese did not like any religion of extreme superstition so they used science as a lure, since the Chinese lacked science. On the surface evangelism was their sideline and the converts were allowed to worship the Chinese *T'ian* (Heaven) and ancestors. Such a method was carried out for years, and both sides were satisfied. (Whyte 1988, 50)

This appraisal does not consider, however, the main purpose of the Jesuit presence in China: the conversion of the Chinese people to Christianity. "The purpose of the Jesuits in coming to China was neither for political power nor for social status; it was to spread a spiritual Gospel" (Wang, Wang, and Kwong 1999, 31). Not all Jesuit missionaries were good missionaries, and often early Catholic missions seem shallow, theologically thin, and sometimes syncretistic, effortlessly melting Catholicism into the local religions. Still, the Jesuit record

SIDEBAR 8.5

Matteo Ricci and Music

Ricci used music to further his missionary goal. He did not care for Chinese music, with its five-tone scale. He missed the sweet four-part harmonies of his native Italy and the keyboard instruments used to support these sonorities. Ricci composed music such as this song for Emperor Wan Li to impart ethics, morals, and virtues in a simple story.

> A shepherd boy fell sad one day,
> Hating the hillside on which he
> stood;
> He thought a distant hill he saw
> More beautiful by far,
> And that going there would wipe
> away his sorrows.
>
> So he set off to that distant hill,
> But as he drew near it
> It looked less good than it had
> from afar.
>
> O shepherd boy, shepherd boy,
> How can you expect to transform
> yourself
> By changing your dwelling place?
>
> If you move away, can you leave
> yourself behind?
> Sorrow and joy sprout in the
> heart.
>
> If the heart is peaceful, you'll be
> happy everywhere,
> If the heart is in turmoil, every
> place brings sorrow.
>
> A grain of dust in your eye
> Brings discomfort speedily;
> How can you then ignore this
> sharp awl
> That pierces your heart?
>
> If you yearn for things outside
> yourself,
> You will never obtain what you
> are seeking.
> Why not put your own heart in
> order
> And find peace on your own
> hillside?
>
> Old and new writers alike give
> this advice:
> There's no advantage to roaming
> outside,
> Keep the heart inside, for
> That brings the profit.

Matteo Ricci
(Spence 1984, 198–99)

Reflection and Discussion

1. How did Ricci effect the spread of the gospel message in China through the use of music?
2. Describe how Ricci uses phrases in the song to convey Christian ethics, morals, and virtues. What Scripture passages correlate to the lyrics in this song?

shows remarkable faithfulness to Christ and flexibility in expression. The Jesuits' pioneering legacy to the history of Christian expansion remains that they presented the gospel to non-Europeans with the realization that it need not be a manifestation of Western culture, providing ways of contextualizing the Christian faith outside Europe.

Letter from India (1543)

(Source: McNeil and Iriye 1971, 4–11)

Below is a letter written by Francis Xavier to the society at Rome in 1543 describing the conversion and teaching of Christian converts of Comorin, Mozambique. As you read this letter, contemplate how its content fits with current approaches to missiology.

May the grace and charity of Christ our Lord always help and favor us! Amen.

It is now the third year since I left Portugal. I am writing to you for the third time, having as yet received only one letter from you, dated February 1542. God is my witness what joy it caused me. I only received it two months ago, later than is usual for letters to reach India, because the vessel, which brought it, had passed the winter at Mozambique.

I and Francis Mancias are now living amongst the Christians of Comorin. They are very numerous, and increase largely every day. When I first came I asked them, if they knew anything about our Lord Jesus Christ; but when I came to the points of faith in detail and asked them what they thought of them, and what more they believed now than when they were Infidels, they only replied that they were Christians, but that as they are ignorant of Portuguese, they know nothing of the precepts and mysteries of our holy religion. We could not understand one another, as I spoke Castilian and they Malabar; so I picked out the most intelligent and well-read of them, and then sought out with the greatest diligence men who knew both languages. We held meetings for several days, and by our joint efforts and with infinite difficulty, we translated the Catechism into the Malabar tongue. This I learnt by heart, and then I began to go through all the villages of the coast, calling around me by the sound of a bell as many as I could, children and men. I assembled them twice a day and taught them the Christian doctrine; and thus, in the space of a month, the children had it well by heart. And all the time I kept telling them to go on teaching in their turn whatever they had learnt to their parents, family, and neighbors.

Every Sunday I collected them all, men and women, boys and girls, in the church. They came with great readiness and with a great desire for instruction. Then, in the hearing of all, I began by calling on the name of the most holy Trinity, Father, Son, and Holy Ghost, and I recited aloud the Lord's Prayer, the Hail Mary, and the Creed in the language of the country; they all followed me in the same words, and delighted in it wonderfully. Then I repeated the Creed by myself, dwelling upon each article singly. Then I asked them as to each article, whether they believed it unhesitatingly; and all, with a loud voice and their hands crossed over their breasts, professed aloud that they truly believed it. I take care to make them repeat the Creed oftener than the other prayers; and I tell them that those who believe all that is contained therein are called Christians. After explaining the Creed I go on to the Commandments, teaching them that the Christian law is contained in those ten precepts, and that everyone who observes them all faithfully is a good and true Christian and is certain of eternal salvation, and that, on the other hand, whoever neglects a single one of them is a bad Christian, and will be cast into hell unless he is truly penitent for his sin. Converts and heathen alike are astonished at all this, which shows them the holiness of the Christian law, its perfect consistency with itself, and its agreement with reason.

As to the numbers who become Christians, you may understand them from this, that it often happens to me to be hardly able to use my hands from the fatigue of baptizing; often in a single day I have baptized whole villages. Sometimes I have lost my voice and strength altogether with repeating again and again the Credo and the other forms. The fruit that is reaped by the baptism of infants, as well as by the instruction of children and others, is quite incredible. These children, I trust heartily, by the grace of God, will be much better than their fathers. They show an ardent love for the Divine law, and an extraordinary zeal for learning our holy religion and imparting it to others. Their hatred for idolatry is marvelous. They get into feuds with the heathen about it, and whenever their own parents practise it, they reproach them and come off to tell me at once. Whenever I hear of any act of idolatrous worship, I go to the place with a large band of these children, who very soon load the devil with a greater amount of insult and abuse than he has lately received of honor and worship from their parents, relations, and acquaintances. The children run at the idols, upset them, dash them down, break them to pieces, spit on them, trample on them, kick them about, and in short heap on them every possible outrage.

Reflection and Discussion

1. Describe the methods that Francis Xavier used to convert the indigenous people to the Christian faith. Which of these methods could you use in your mission context? Which of these would you reject? Why?

2. Why did Francis Xavier emphasize the recitation and teaching of the Creed to recent converts? What role do creeds play today in Christian teaching?

3. How might children be utilized in spreading the gospel in today's context? Is there a line to be drawn when working with youth?

9

Encountering
Pietist Missions

Two hundred years had elapsed since the Reformation, with little Protestant cross-cultural expansion. A unique historical amalgamation of circumstances changed this lapse: a Danish monarchy influenced by a foreign Pietist chaplain called for student volunteers from a German university to share the gospel with his colonial people in southern India. This combination of events catalyzed an eighteenth-century mission movement that continues today.

Pietism emphasized the practice of Christianity from a subjective and emotional perspective in contrast to a rational and intellectual manner. These post-Reformation German Lutherans met after church for Bible study and personal "cultivation of holiness" and "edification in Christian living." Pietists desired to transform society by improving the living conditions of the poor, reforming the prison system, abolishing slavery, reducing class distinctions, reforming education, increasing mission activity, and fostering programs for social justice. The key principles of Pietism were personal conversion, holy living, group fellowship, and responsibility for witness. They saw themselves as "the church within the church" and not as a separatist movement (see Gallagher 2005b, 116–21).

This chapter explores the early beginnings of the Pietist movement through the lives of Philipp Jakob Spener and August Hermann Francke of the University of Halle before moving on to the endeavors of Pietist missionaries such as Bartholomäus Ziegenbalg, Heinrich Plütschau, and Christian Schwartz in India and Hans Egede in Greenland. Throughout the treatise, the question arises: what can we learn for modern cross-cultural work from these historical precedents?

Historical Background

The Thirty Years' War had left Germany with one-third of the urban and two-fifths of the rural population dead. People were traumatized, the countryside was devastated, and its inhabitants were living in poverty. The war had uprooted people and destroyed entire villages. Twenty years after the end of the war, soldiers still wandered the countryside, robbing farms and villages of food and clothing. With an increased rift between upper and lower classes, there was great distrust among people.

This was a world of incessant violence and social upheaval. From 1616 to 1748, Germany's Rhine Valley had uninterrupted war—including the devastating Thirty Years' War, the French wars, and the wars of Frederick the Great. The Treaty of Westphalia in 1648 ended the Thirty Years' War, but Germany was left divided and in political and social disarray. At this time there were some three hundred territories, each governed by a prince who decided his people's religious affiliation: Catholic, Lutheran, or Reformed. Bibles were scarce, and most of the population was uneducated. Church attendance was often legally enforced, and the continuing civil wars led to changes in political control and subsequent changes in denominational affiliation. Although most of the German states were Lutheran, the rulers—even though they appointed the clergy—were not necessarily Christian or trained to argue their region's theology and doctrine. The clerics' focus was on theological debate, which made for irrelevant sermons and contributed to an increasing gap between congregations and ministers.

Philipp Jakob Spener (1635–1705)

Seventeenth-century Reformer Philipp Spener instituted small groups that focused on personal conversion, intimate fellowship, and trust in the empowerment of the Holy Spirit. Through his pastoral ministry in Frankfurt am Main in Germany, his Lutheran church experienced a renewal. Spener emphasized the importance of basing doctrine on the Bible, personally experiencing the transforming power of the gospel, and developing the clergy.

In Spener's early years, his readings of the Bible, Johann Arndt's *True Christianity*, the English Puritans, Emanuel Sontham's *Golden Treasure of the Children of God*, and Lewis Bayly's *The Practice of Piety*, all of which concentrated on personal holiness and morality, influenced him. First published in 1610, Arndt's *True Christianity* would later have the greatest impact on Spener. This student of Reformation theology and disciple of Martin Luther proposed the need to practice faith and godly living over against the prevailing practice of theological polemics. The book became the launchpad for Spener's most influential publication, *Pia Desideria* (Pious Desires).

Spener was an assistant minister in Strasbourg for a short time and moved on to a senior minister position at Frankfurt am Main, the leading publishing center of Germany. Here he focused on church renewal by giving his time to children's catechization and adult pastoral care. Although there was opposition from the civil authorities against church reform, he pressed on and in 1670

Complete pleasure [is] in the knowledge that through your ministry the name of God is hallowed, his kingdom extended, and his will [is] done, and that the salvation of many souls, the peace of your own consciences, and ultimately your eternal glory are achieved to the honor of his holy name.

Philipp Jakob Spener (1964, 31)

---

initiated within his parish the *collegia pietatis*, or small groups (Snyder 1989, 78). As Spener states in *Pia Desideria*, he sought to "reintroduce the ancient and apostolic kind of church meetings." He held Monday and Thursday night meetings in his home, where his parishioners could study the Bible, discuss sermons, ask questions, pray for one another, and experience the love of God in community. He describes these gatherings: "In addition to our customary services with preaching, other assemblies would also be held in the manner in which Paul describes in 1 Corinthians 14:26–40. One person would not rise to preach . . . , but others who have been blessed with gifts and knowledge would . . . speak and present their pious opinions on the proposed subject to the judgment of the rest, doing all this in such a way as to avoid disorder and strife" (1964, 89).

Spener did not intend to leave the Lutheran Church but rather wished to be a catalyst for church renewal. His desire was for parishioners to apply the doctrine of the church, to participate in church government, and to live according to the Scriptures. Believers were first to have a personal conversion experience and then continue in their devotion to Christ as members of the Christian community. In *Pia Desideria*, he declares:

We preachers in the ecclesiastical estate cannot deny that our estate is also thoroughly corrupt. . . . Behold how they seek promotions, shift from parish to parish, and engage in all sorts of machinations! Look with ever so loving eyes, illuminated by the light of the Spirit! One will surely discover that many, of whom in Christian love one would like to think differently, are at the bottom the same, that although they themselves do not realize it they are still stuck fast in the old birth and do not actually possess the true marks of a new birth. (1964, 45–46)

Spener taught from the Bible, preaching on the necessity of personal salvation and sanctification. He asserted, "Where the Word of God is neglected, real, and true religion collapses" (1964, 79). In "On Hindrances to Theological Studies," he defends mysticism, stating that "the working presence of the Holy Spirit, the sealing, the illumination (by virtue of that which the Spirit brings to us from the truth created from the Word), the Spirit's consolation, and the loving taste of eternal things. All these things indicated in the Holy Scripture are promised to believers, and thus, are not empty names or fantasies" (Erb 1983, 69). Spener longed for Christians to grow in their relationship with Christ.

The Holy Spirit

For Spener, the work of the Holy Spirit accomplished the essential goals of holy living and personal conversion. Luther had focused on justification as the starting point of the new person, whereas Spener centered on regeneration. According to Spener, "it is the same Holy Spirit who is bestowed on us by God who once affected all things in the early Christians, and he is neither less able nor less active today to accomplish the work of sanctification in us. If this does not happen, the sole reason must be that we do not allow, but rather hinder, the Holy Spirit's work" (1964, 85). Holiness for the individual and the church was the foundation of mission. Spener argued, "In order for the Jews to be converted, the true church must be in a holier state than now if its holy life is to be a means for that conversion, or at least the impediments to such conversion (which, as we have seen . . . , have hitherto consisted of offenses) are to be removed" (1964, 77).

Spener's hope was in the power of the Holy Spirit to revive the Lutheran Church. In his article "Christian Joy," he states that it was "Christ's appearance which does not come visibly but through a powerful working of his Holy Spirit in us so that he allows us to know and taste his being in a special manner in our souls" (Erb 1983, 94). It is not good enough to hear the Scripture with natural ears. The word of God needs to penetrate the heart of a person so that he or she may hear the Spirit. The Spirit brings illumination to the word of God. "Indeed the Scripture is a light for our enlightenment, but it is a word of the Spirit and if we could separate the Holy Spirit from the Word (which we cannot do); the Scripture would no longer work" (Erb 1983, 72). God has promised his Holy Spirit to all who call on him in sincerity, not just the educated. By the anointing of the Spirit, "the proper teacher," comes all necessary understanding of salvation and Christian growth. With teaching such as this, Spener endeavored to shorten the gap between the social classes, much to the consternation of those in social and religious power.

Spener's Pietist legacy included not only the empowerment of the laity and emphasis on the Holy Spirit's power but also welfare programs that he worked to establish in Frankfurt and Berlin for those still suffering the effects of the Thirty Years' War. He also published over one hundred books and was a prolific correspondent with people of all classes. He helped in the formation of Halle University, which became a formative location for many missionaries and Pietist leaders in the next century.

August Hermann Francke (1663–1727)

August Francke trained and sent out missionaries from Halle to India, and his published correspondence inspired others in Europe and North America to be involved in cross-cultural ministry through prayer, giving, and fieldwork (Sattler and Francke 1982, 78). Francke saw himself as "a poor and wretched worm" who had a "natural inability" except through total dependence on God's grace (Francke 1770, 9). He confessed that he would be nothing "but a poor unprofitable servant, and undone worm, if the Lord withdrew himself from [him]" (Francke 1705, 157). Francke loved learning, yet he was very aware of his own inadequacies and pointed to the mercy and faithfulness of God to explain the success of Halle. Among those he inspired in faith and social activism were George Whitefield, George Müeller, and Hudson Taylor.

Leipzig

Francke began the well-attended Society for the Study of the Bible at Leipzig with another private teacher. Even in the midst of his own spiritual struggles and questions about the faith, Francke redirected people's views of theology to the Bible, which was at that time much neglected. After Leipzig, he went to

---

In the faith of Jesus are my beginning, middle, and end.

August Hermann Francke (1774, 18)

Lunenburg, which became the place of his spiritual awakening, and his pious views began to form. He wrote "The Christian's Life of Faith," in which he describes the deep reality of Christ's salvation and its implications for daily living. Honor of God and his gift of salvation to all peoples became the guiding principle of his life.

University of Halle

Exiled from Erfurt on false accusations, Francke was so full of joy resting in the guidance of God that he wrote a hymn during his journey to Halle to accept the invitation to be a professor of theology (Guerike 1837, 34). Because of Francke, Halle became a center for social ministry, cross-cultural mission, and Jewish mission and for the distribution of the Bible and other Christian literature; under his influence, many students converted to Christ and were inspired to serve God to the ends of the earth. He became a professor of Greek and Oriental languages at Halle and the pastor of Saint George Church at Glaucha, a poverty-stricken suburb of Halle. Noted for "great plainness of speech" in his preaching, the town consequently became more spiritually aware and transformed by his reforms (A. Brown 1830, 70). He preached the importance of union with Christ and continuous fellowship with the Holy Spirit (A. Brown 1830, 62). The effectiveness of his faith centered on prayer. Many viewed him as a heretic and a fanatic, yet that did not stop his daily evening prayer meetings continually seeking God's blessing. Here he established a Bible society to study and apply the word of God as he had done in Leipzig and Erfurt. At Halle, he upheld the Bible as the only rule of faith and doctrine. He shared from the Scriptures and taught the application of the Bible. He was not without his critics at the university, since many of the professors believed that their task was to make students more learned and not more pious.

Institution

Francke's concern for the poor began in 1694, when he organized the beggars who visited him into weekly catechism classes to share the Bible with them before giving them money. His school was of such quality that wealthy people also began to send their children. Francke charged them tuition and used the funds to increase the number of poor children who attended school at no cost. The institutions at Halle included a free elementary school, a trade school, a classical school that prepared people for university, a royal school

---

His living Spirit will work constantly and without ceasing; and whoever does not suffer his streams to flow continually, cannot say that he does not resist his operations.

August Hermann Francke (1774, 25)

---

for the nobility, a teacher's seminary, the Oriental College of Divinity (where Eastern languages were studied for Bible translation), an orphanage, a drugstore, a museum and bookstore, a house for widows with chaplains, and a Bible society. With his goal of bringing Scripture to every part of the world,

Francke established the Canstein Bible Institute in 1712, and in one hundred years it had printed and distributed two million Bibles and one million New Testaments. Francke maintained a tolerant attitude toward Roman Catholicism, Reformed denominations, and Eastern Orthodoxy, which allowed the spread of his ideas to many countries.

Within ten years of the founding of the orphanage, it served 250 students and 64 orphans. When Francke died in 1727, the numbers had increased to 2,196 students in the schools and 134 orphans (A. Brown 1830, 135). In addition, there were 130 teachers employed by the schools, with 600 receiving daily food at the hospital. He was one of the first to take an interest in the education of girls. Francke believed that the success of his institutions was to be measured not by numbers alone but also by the spiritual impact that he had on his students.

Goals

The institution and everyone who worked there were to have as their chief goal the glorification of God and the welfare of their neighbor. The main object of the schools was to instruct the children in the vital knowledge of God and Christ. All wisdom must have as its end the glory of God. Effective faith is in obedience to God's providential call. Francke advised his students: "Never, under the pretext of faith in God to engage in undertakings, or place themselves in dangers, where there was no clearly marked call of Providence: but with their loins girt about to wait the directions of their Master, both where, and how they should labor" (A. Brown 1830, 139). He was a father to the students and children at the orphanage, often calling them "my dear children." Francke treated each person as an individual with dignity. Everyone was educated according to his or her abilities and gifts, and the teachers were encouraged to cultivate these talents. He trained the poor in trades, so they could become self-sufficient, and the city's guilds even accepted apprentices from Halle.

Provision

Through prayer, God supplied the needs of the Halle institutions to care for the needy. Not once did Francke solicit funds, although his work was well known. There is no record of any children going without meals or enduring poverty of any kind. Evidence of God's past faithfulness increased the faith of Francke and his colleagues to believe that God would provide further. In *Pietas Hallensis*, Francke cites twenty-two occasions when God miraculously provided at exactly the right time. Repeatedly he says that they were "in straits," or that "all was spent," or that they "saw no support," and then the Lord moved people to give.

Holy Spirit

Francke encouraged his students to depend on the Holy Spirit in preparation for their ministry: "Think not, however, that you will love him of yourselves. This is the work of the Spirit of God, without whose influences, your own efforts, your reading of the Bible, and your thinking on the love of God to you will be without effect" (A. Brown 1830, 151). He believed that a person could not love God or understand Scripture without the help of the Spirit.

Correspondence

Until Francke's death, he continued to appoint missionaries who went out from Halle, to correspond with them, and to publish accounts of their missionary endeavors. This interest in mission included the Jewish people. Even today, there are remnants of the missional work of the Halle institutions still functioning to aid the poor, orphans, widows, the elderly, and the uneducated. Because of Francke, Halle University became the center of Pietistic mission, sending young men out from its halls to minister to German soldiers of the Thirty Years' War, settlements in eastern and southeastern Europe, and people around the world.

Bartholomäus Ziegenbalg (1682–1719)

Based on his person, Bartholomäus Ziegenbalg's missionary influence in the early eighteenth century seems improbable. He was a depressed and frail German university student, asked by a powerful foreign king to speak to his royal subjects at the ends of the earth about the Christian God. The account of his adventures set into motion missional consequences that reverberated in the European courts of ecclesial and political power.

Pietistic Influences

Ziegenbalg was born to pious Lutheran parents in 1683 in the Saxon farm village of Pulsnitz near Dresden, Germany. The hardships of the Thirty Years' War (1618–1648), the plague and a severe fire that his village suffered, and the death of both parents and two sisters before he turned six caused Ziegenbalg to think much about death, heaven, and hell. At ten, he left home and the care of Anna, his eldest sister, to attend grammar school at Custrin in Prussia and seek answers to his questions in theological study. At twelve, he moved to the gymnasium in Görlitz, Saxony, where the rector concluded that he had little to offer physically or mentally. Inner turmoil, physical weakness, and depression played a debilitating role in his life, as did the later cycle of rigorous study and emotional breakdown at the University of Berlin. At eighteen, in the midst of wrestling with questions of God's purpose for his life, he found comfort in God's saving grace (Scherer 1999, 488).

In 1703 Ziegenbalg enrolled at the University of Halle in Prussia under the tutelage of August Hermann Francke and thrived in the understanding of Pietistic values and beliefs. His studies confirmed his own beliefs in per-

---

"For this reason we are made Christians, that we should be more bent upon the Life to come, than upon the present." This is my daily memorandum, lest I should perhaps forget, entirely to consecrate my life and actions to an invisible eternity, minding little the world either in its glory and smiles, or in its frowns and afflictions.

Ziegenbalg's motto (Beach 1904, 163)

---

sonal conversion, faith, study, and witness. At the university he met Heinrich Plütschau and founded the Order of the Grain of Mustard Seed, a group of students who met daily for scriptural meditation, prayer, and singing and whose members were pledged to the Pietistic ideal of a life of religious devotion and Christian service. He continued to battle physical ailments and depression and withdrew from Halle after one semester to become a private tutor of children in Merseburg and then in Erfurt. In both places, he started Pietistic meetings and led people to Christ. Despite his own doubts and feelings of inadequacy, his interest in missions continued through the influence of leaders in the Pietist movement such as Halle's Joachim Justus Breithaupt, a friend of both Spener and Francke (Zorn 1933, 27–30). At Merseburg, Ziegenbalg made a vow with a friend: "We two will seek nothing in this world but the glorification of the name of God, the extension of His Kingdom, the spread of the divine truth, the salvation of our fellow-men, and the continued sanctification of our souls, in whatever part of the world we may be and no matter what amount of cross and affliction may befall us on account of it" (Zorn 1933, 31).

These pious desires were about to be fulfilled in a surprising way.

Mission to India

At the beginning of the eighteenth century, national princes governed the southern peninsula of India, with a scattering of Portuguese, French, Dutch, English, and Danish trading settlements. In 1621 Denmark obtained from the rajah of Tanjore the town and surrounding territory of Tarangambadi, or Tranquebar, on the east coast of southern India. Eighty-four years later, the king of Denmark, Frederick IV, concerned for the spiritual care of his

181

colonial subjects, commissioned the Danish court chaplain, a German Pietist named Franz Julius Luetkens, to conduct a national search in Denmark to find suitable ministers to go to southern India. Having found none, Luetkens contacted Francke at Halle, who suggested Ziegenbalg and Plütschau as worthy candidates. The invitation was at first received with timidity and indecision on the part of Ziegenbalg, but he accepted it nonetheless.

After an eight-month voyage on the *Princessa Sophia Hedwiga*, Ziegenbalg and his companion arrived at the Danish port of Tranquebar on the Coromandel Coast on July 9, 1706. At that time, Tranquebar comprised fifteen square miles, twenty small villages, and about thirty thousand inhabitants (Zorn 1933, 34). These two former tertiary students were to become the first Protestant missionaries to India for the express purpose of evangelizing the indigenous people. Putting into practice the principles and teachings learned at Halle, they sought to share the Scripture with cultural sensitivity. Their message was a blend of Lutheran theology and Pietistic relevance based on the belief that the word of God was "efficacious and powerful" for personal conversion and holiness. In a letter of November 15, 1713, regarding the mission church and school, Ziegenbalg wrote:

> We try to [deeply plant] in these young minds . . . the true Christian doctrine. We pay special attention in the daily instruction to catechization. We have several catechists who go from house to house and catechize our people. . . . We are not satisfied merely with an outer appearance of the Christian religion, but press for a real change of heart and an implicit obedience of faith, and we look not so much for large numbers but that all who accept our religion should attain a living knowledge of the truth unto godliness and . . . the true way of Christianity. (Quoted in Lehmann 1956, 109)

The two German missionaries immediately met opposition from the Tranquebar Danish chaplains, local Hindu leaders, the Danish East India Company, and the Danish governor, Johann Sigismund Hassius, who later imprisoned Ziegenbalg for four months (1708–1709) for "rebellion against [his] authority" (Hieber 1905, 9). The imprisonment concerned Catholic-Protestant rivalries rather than political matters.

Five Missional Principles

Stephen Neill, the Anglican bishop of Tirunelveli in southern India from 1939 to 1944, has claimed, "At point after point, with hardly any precedent to guide him, Ziegenbalg made the right decision, and showed the way that has been followed ever since by the best and most successful among the Protestant missions" ([1964] 1990, 194). Neill recognizes five principles that characterized the missionary effort as follows ([1964] 1990, 195–96):

1. *Church and school are to go together.* Education links the propagation of the Christian faith—children need to be educated to read the word of God.

To this end, the two Pietists began schools for the Portuguese, the Danish, and the Tamils a year after arrival. They also founded the first girls school in India (for Europeans), orphanages, and a Tamil seminary, which in 1716 had eight students training as national teachers and pastors. They believed it was critical to teach children the Scriptures before they grew hardened to spiritual truth (Lehmann 1956, 103). Concerning the connection between church and school, Ziegenbalg asserted: "It is a thing known to all persons of understanding that the general good of any country or nation depends upon a Christian and careful training of children in schools, due care and diligence in this matter, producing wise governors in the State, faithful ministers of the Gospel in the Church, and good members of the Commonwealth in families" (Sabiers 1944, 6).

2. *If Christians are to read the word of God, that word must be available to them in their own language.* Translation of the Scriptures into the indigenous language is important. The word of God needs to be available in the vernacular to build a native church and facilitate a noncolonialist approach to mission.

During the voyage to India, the two Germans studied Danish, not realizing that the trade language of Tranquebar was Portuguese. Upon arriving, Ziegenbalg began to learn Portuguese and Plütschau Tamil, but then they switched, with Ziegenbalg studying the more difficult language. Learning languages was a gift to Ziegenbalg, and he quickly mastered colloquial and written Tamil.

In learning the language Ziegenbalg devoted himself to studying Tamil literature; he explained, "I chose such books as I should wish to imitate, both in speaking and writing and had such authors read to me a hundred times, that there might not be a word or expression which I did not know, or could not imitate" (Holcomb 1901, 21). Yet in Tranquebar alone, there were three Tamil dialects (Kerendum, Damul, and Wardagu), so Ziegenbalg learned both Kerendum and Damul by hiring tutors such as the high-caste Hindu Ellappar. Within eight months the German preached his first sermon in Tamil, exclaiming, "With God's grace I was able to read, write, and speak in this very difficult language and even understand the conversation of others" (Lehmann 1956, 24).

Although Kerendum was the Tamil dialect of the Brahmins, together with that of the sacred literature and scholarship, the missionaries chose the language of the common people, Damul, for their pamphlets, books, and translations (Singh 1999, 65–66). By 1708 Ziegenbalg had compiled a forty-thousand-word Malabar dictionary, *Grammatica Damulica* (published at Halle eight years later), and a poetical dictionary, *Lexicon Poeticum*, of some seventeen thousand words. Less than five years after his arrival in Tranquebar, Ziegenbalg, with the help of Halle's Johann Ernest Gründler, had translated the entire

New Testament into Tamil. This was the first translation of the Bible into any Indian language.

3. *The basis of preaching the gospel is an accurate knowledge of the mind of the people.* An understanding of the worldview of the people makes dissemination of Christianity possible. Missionaries need to understand the culture of the indigenous people to share the gospel.

As Ziegenbalg traveled around southern India and shared the gospel, he was continuously aware of the importance of understanding the customs of the people. He set out to study their Hindu beliefs and values, asserting, "Hardly an hour passes that I do not have an opportunity to speak with the heathen on the way" as he visited villages and towns (Lehmann 1956, 31). For example, he asked Kanabadi, a Tamil poet, to translate some Christian literature, and upon his subsequent conversion, the local artist wrote poems using Christian themes in place of Hindu legends. In turn, the schoolchildren learned these poems.

The Halle missionary wrote his cultural discoveries in a number of monographs—such as *Malabarian Gods* (1711) and *Genealogy of the Malabar (South-Indian) Gods* (1713). On receiving this material, Francke wrote to Ziegenbalg, objecting that such studies were "not to be thought of, inasmuch as the missionaries were sent to extirpate heathenism, and not to spread heathenish nonsense in Europe." Thus, the Halle director deliberately hid the ethnographies in the archives of the university (Germann's preface in Ziegenbalg [1713] 1869, xv). This material remained concealed for 154 years until Wilhelm Germann, a Leipsic Missionary Society scholar, discovered the volumes and subsequently published them in both German and English. Further, the Lutheran Pietist translated hymns using both European and Tamilian melodies for corporate worship and instructing children in the catechism. Published in 1715, Ziegenbalg's first hymnal contained forty-eight hymns (Lehmann 1956, 26).

Ziegenbalg publicly criticized some members of the Brahmin caste for their disregard of the lower castes in Hindu society. Yet "his impressive knowledge of Hinduism, high regard for Hindus as human beings, desire to preserve the integrity of the Tamil language and culture as he presented Christianity, and the lack of racist attitudes, coupled with his repudiation of the racism of other Europeans towards Indians" gained him the respect of many Hindus (Singh 1999, 22–23).

4. *The aim must be definite and personal conversion.* The spread of Christianity should focus on individuals rather than on mass movements.

The Halle missionaries avoided mass conversions and prayed for individual transformation. They tried to work with not only the indigenous people but also the German and Portuguese inhabitants employed by the Danish monarchy, and they invited them to a church service especially for them in the local Danish church. Within the first few months, the slaves of the settlement assembled for religious instruction in the fundamentals of the Christian faith for two hours every day. One year after their arrival, the German missionaries, after publicly examining five slaves on the Articles of the Christian Faith, baptized them and built Jerusalem Church to conduct Tamil services. Church membership grew; the church building erected in 1707 quickly became too small, so Ziegenbalg built a new one, New Jerusalem Church, eleven years later.

Ziegenbalg held conferences with Hindu priests, Muslim clerics, doctors, and poets. From these meetings the German missionary wrote three collections of conversations in which he argued the truths of Christianity. In 1719 Mr. Philipps made an English translation of Ziegenbalg and Gründler's *Thirty Four Conferences between the Danish Missionaries and the Malabarian*

As the body is bound to the soul, so precisely is the service of the body connected with the service of the soul, and these cannot be separated from each other. This work demands the service of the whole [person]. If I deny such service, I deny that in which the Scripture places the proper manner of faith and love. . . . The more one devotes to the service of [neighbors], and gladly helps in bodily and spiritual needs, the stronger one must be in Christianity.

Bartholomäus Ziegenbalg (Lehmann 1956, 87)

Bramans (or *Heathen Priests*) *in the East Indies, concerning the Truth of the Christian Religion* and published it in London. This work was an account of the German Lutheran missionaries' religious discussions in Tranquebar with Hindus. The Pietists founded mission stations in Srirangam, Tanjore, Madura, Kanchi, Chidambram, and Tirupathi, and as they traveled around, they established contacts with the Brahmanas and held fifty-four conversations with them. From 1715 onward, Halle published a record of the dialogues. In addition, a select group of Hindu Brahmanas and non-Brahmanas received a large number of letters with different questions. The missionaries translated the answers to the questions into German and forwarded them to Halle. Before moving to our last cross-cultural principle, the following notion needs highlighting: "Every phase of Ziegenbalg's conversations (and dialogue with Hindus) reveals that, notwithstanding his untiring attempts to meet the Hindus on their own level, the uncompromising proclamation of the free saving grace of God in Jesus Christ was the heart and center of his evangelism" (Genischen 1957, 841).

5. *At as early a date as possible an Indian church, with its own Indian ministry, must come into being.* Dissemination of Christianity must result in an indigenous church.

Ziegenbalg insisted on developing a church with Indian characteristics. The Society for Promoting Christian Knowledge (SPCK) in England desired to establish Christian schools for the indigenous children from Madras to Calcutta. A number of the young men who became followers of Christ through these schools in Tranquebar became valuable teachers and preachers for Ziegenbalg. Three years after his arrival, he petitioned the Danish authorities to ordain a native, so that the ministry would not be dominated by Europeans. Aaron, an Indian catechist of fifteen years, became the first Lutheran Tamil pastor in 1733 (fourteen years after Ziegenbalg's death) and was pastorally responsible for several congregations in the Māyāvaram area until his death in 1745. Even though only fourteen pastors were ordained in the mission's first one hundred years, the Europeans chose carefully, and few failed (Neill [1964] 1990, 196–97). Caution still seems to be the dominant selection criterion, however, since the consecration of the first Indian bishop of the Evangelical Lutheran Church in Tamil occurred at Tranquebar on the 250th anniversary of Ziegenbalg's arrival. James Scherer summarizes, "Ziegenbalg appears to have grasped the principle of inculturation, developing an indigenous church with Indian characteristics in architecture, music, caste, and customs. Here also he was clearly ahead of his time" (1999, 493).

Promoting Missions

King Frederick IV instructed Ziegenbalg and Plütschau to send letters whenever a ship returned to Denmark (Fenger [1863] 1906, 238). Accordingly, Ziegenbalg sent out annual letters reporting on the Tranquebar mission, which Anton Wilhelm Böhme, the Lutheran chaplain at Saint James's Palace in London, translated into English and published in Berlin in a book titled *Notable News.* Later, the SPCK published the letters as *A Propagation of the Gospel in the East* and distributed them to Pietist communities in Germany, Denmark, and England (Zorn 1933, 101, 103). This compilation of letters reached the courts of Denmark and England, the archbishop of Canterbury, and John and Charles Wesley, to name a few, and served as a catalyst to encourage financial giving and sending to the mission field.

The Danish prince George, the husband of Queen Ann of England, with Böhme, his Lutheran chaplain, had a great interest in the Danish Tranquebar mission. Böhme suggested to the SPCK that it should send a printing press to India for the service of the mission to translate the Scriptures into the languages of southern India. In ecumenical collaboration, the Tamil New Testament eventually resulted from a translation by a German Lutheran in the service of a Danish monarch, printed on an English press, and funded by an Anglican mission society.

Missions Legacy

Upon Ziegenbalg's death in Tranquebar in 1719 at the age of thirty-six (thirteen years after arriving in India, after a lifelong struggle with poor health), there were 250 members of the church. In addition to a study of the Hindu religion and culture that aided later missionaries, his legacy included two church buildings and a seminary for the training of national leaders together with the New Testament and Genesis to Ruth in the Tamil language. Both the New Testament Tamil translation of 1715 and the church building constructed in 1718 are still in use today by the Tamil Evangelical Lutheran Church.

Ziegenbalg's reputation for excellence and his blameless lifestyle added to his effectiveness in India. During an age when colonialization and prejudice were normal, he had a respect and empathy for the host culture that focused on the people over the task and an ability to maintain flexibility. With a deep love for the Indian people, he shared God's message wherever he could—at festivals, at work, and at play. The young Saxon did not merely speak words of love but also demonstrated that the "service of souls" and the "service of the body" were connected; Christian ministry could not be effective without social action.

Halle Missional Influences

Francke used the Tranquebar mission to promote missions and raise support. For instance, he published letters from his Halle missionaries in Germany and England that generated interest and financial assistance, especially among nobility and royalty (Stoeffler 1973, 34–35). In 1713 Francke began to send Bibles, hymnals, and scriptural tracts, in addition to money, to Swedish prisoners of the Thirty Years' War in Siberia. In succession, Pietism established itself among the prisoners, and, upon returning to their homeland, they formed schools modeled after Halle, including the Copenhagen Royal College of Missions, which was the first Protestant missionary training center (D. Brown 1978, 155).

Other Halle missional influences followed. The university sent teachers to the courts of Peter the Great in Russia, where Francke cultivated friendships with several ministers in the tsar's government. As mentioned previously, Halle graduate Anton Böhme became the chaplain in the court of Queen Anne of England and translated many Pietist devotional tracts into English. Furthermore, the Lutheran churches of the American colonies in the eighteenth century lacked trained pastors, and Halle supplied the need. For example, Justus Falckner, who trained under Francke, served in New York for twenty years (Stoeffler 1976, 14–15). The Halle zeal for missions did not end with Francke's death in 1727. Halle continued to train and send people all over the world, including the missionary to India Christian Friedrich Schwartz.

Christian Friedrich Schwartz (1749–1798)

Christian Friedrich Schwartz was a Pietist missionary in southern India in the late eighteenth century. For over forty-eight years he witnessed to non-Christians, discipled new believers, studied languages, committed himself to the physical needs of the people, trained indigenous pastors, and served in various diplomatic roles. With his unique ability to forge friendships with Muslims, Hindus, and English settlers and soldiers alike, Schwartz sought to transform society one person at a time, as had his predecessor Francke (Genischen 1998, 606).

FAMILY DEDICATION

Born in Sonnenburg, Germany, in 1726, he was dedicated to Christ by his mother, who vowed that her son must receive training for Christian service. By eight years of age he had been inspired by the writings of August Francke and the stories of missionaries in India and confirmed in the Pietist Lutheran faith. This led him to study at the University of Halle in 1746. There he grew in his understanding of Pietism under the guidance of Benjamin Schultz, who had been a missionary in southern India, and dedicated himself to serving Christ in that part of the world (Frykenberg 1999, 130).

In 1750 Schwartz arrived in southern India and began his missionary career as chaplain in the English garrison. The pioneering work of Ziegenbalg and Plütschau had created a strong Christian influence in Tranquebar, yet the Danish government restricted missionaries to that particular region. Schwartz arrived in India at a time of political unrest in the southern part of the country, especially between the English East India Company and the French colonialists.

DISCIPLES OF CHRIST

Schwartz's passion was to make disciples of Christ in all segments of Indian society. Thus he spoke about his Savior with farmers cleaning their newly harvested rice, gardeners tending their fields, the Byragess (professional beggars in the caste system), and the rajah and his family in the palace of Tanjore. In a letter to a friend he wrote, "Be sure that if you are instrumental in converting a soul, you have gained more than if you got the treasures of both Indies" (Pearson 1835, 217).

The German missionary's motivation was not to convert large numbers quickly, but rather he desired a genuine faith in those who received the Lord

Jesus. He treated new converts with a "kind severity" and did not immediately trust the newly saved, since he realized that people could have mixed motives. Schwartz took an active role in discipling new believers as he helped prepare

---

You read, you pray, you sing hymns; but take care that all these excellent things may improve your hearts and lives, that by your reading you may grow in the knowledge of Jesus, in faith, in a sincere love towards him, in willingness to follow him, in hating and rejecting all things which hinder you in your desire of winning Christ, and the happiness of being found in him.

Christian Schwartz (*Church Missionary Gleaner* 1850, 52)

---

them for water baptism. This he did four hours every day for a number of months, teaching them the basic doctrines of Christianity as well as encouraging them to tell others about their newfound faith. Having spent the morning with Schwartz in prayer and meditation on God's word, the new converts shared the gospel in the villages for the rest of the day. Upon returning, they would report their experiences to Schwartz and spend further time in prayer and meditation. Sathyanathan, one of the early catechumens nurtured under Schwartz, in 1785 became the first Indian superintendent of the Tirunelveli mission (Richter 1908, 117).

LANGUAGE STUDY

Even before Schwartz left for India, he had learned from his secondary education Greek, Latin, and Hebrew, and under Benjamin Schultz he had spent some time studying English and Tamil at the University of Halle. Less than four months after his arrival in India, he had preached his first sermon in Tamil, on Matthew 11:25–30. So that the Indian intellectuals might regard him as a properly trained scholar, he learned Hindustani (the language of the court of the nawab of the Muslim ruler), Arcot, and Persian. For five years Schwartz studied the mythological writings of India so that he could understand its system of theology in order to present the gospel intelligently to the people. Altogether Schwartz learned Tamil, Telugu, Sanskrit, Marathi, Dukhni-Urdu (southern Hindustani), Persian, and Portuguese (Frykenberg 1999, 131). He believed that he could best share Christ with people through the vernacular. His diligent study of languages provided opportunities for Schwartz to witness to people of high and low castes, together with foreigners in the region.

Church Planting

The Pietist missionary served as the English army chaplain for several years, providing Christian instruction, leading prayer meetings, and offering spiritual leadership to many of the European missionaries. In a systematic manner of discipleship derived from his chaplaincy experience, Schwartz sought to strengthen the Indian churches. His desire began to unfold in church planting. In 1766 he built Christ Church in Trichinopoly at the foot of a mountain dedicated to idolatry; then in 1780 the missionary established a new chapel at Tanjore for the English garrison to replace the one destroyed during the war. Schwartz also founded another chapel for the local people, together with a mission house, homes for the catechists, and a school on land donated by the rajah of Tanjore and funded by the British officers. He longed to give each group a place to gather and worship.

Social Concerns

During times of war and hardship in southern India, the German Pietist used his influence to help relieve the distress of the indigenous people. Beginning in 1767, Hyder Ali, the de facto Muslim ruler of the kingdom of Mysore in southern India, began a three-year siege of Madura (under British rule). Many English soldiers lost their lives, which left their children fatherless. In response, Schwartz founded a school for the orphans and taught there himself when there was a shortage of teachers. Furthermore, before the siege he foresaw the inevitability of war and began to store rice while it was affordable. Later, when the war caused drastic food shortages, Schwartz was able to use the accumulated twelve thousand bushels to give relief to those without food, especially his catechists and schoolmasters. When General Munro, to whom Schwartz was chaplain and translator (Danish and German), asked the governor of Madras, Thomas Rumbold, to reimburse the missionary for the food expenses, Schwartz declined the offer for himself but asked for financial assistance to build a new church in Tanjore (Muthuraj 2006, 63).

Political Involvement

Since the Indian rulers respected Schwartz, the English often used their German friend as a political liaison. The Maharaja Sirfojee, rajah of Tanjore, for example, memorialized his friend in a poem:

> Firm wast thou, humble and wise,
> Honest, pure, free from disguise,
> Father of orphans, the widow's support,
> Comfort in sorrow of every sort.
> To the benighted, dispenser of light,
> Doing, and pointing to that which is right.
> Blessing to princes, to people, to me;

Christian Schwartz's Epitaph in Tanjore

The following epitaph was written in 1798 for Christian Schwartz by the Maharaja Sirfojee in southern India.

> To the memory of the
> Reverend Christian Frederic
> Swartz,
> born at Sonnenburg of Neumark
> in the Kingdom of Prussia,
> the 26th of October 1726,
> and died at Tanjore the 15th of
> February 1798,
> in the 72nd year of his age.
> Devoted from his early manhood
> to the office of
> missionary in the East,
> the similarity of his situation to
> that of
> the first preachers of the Gospel,
> produced in him a peculiar re-
> semblance to
> the simple sanctity of the
> Apostolic character.
> His natural vivacity won the
> affection
> as his unspotted probity and pu-
> rity of life

alike commanded the reverence of the Christian, Mahomedan, and Hindu, for sovereign princes, Hindu, and Mahomedan, selected this humble pastor as the medium of political negotiation with the British Government. And the very marble that here records his virtues was raised by the liberal affection and esteem of the Raja of Tanjore Maha Raja Sirfojee.

Reflection and Discussion

1. From reading the epitaph, what do you learn about Christian Schwartz's impact in southern India?
2. In what ways might missionaries today act as reconcilers, bringing together different nationalities and religions?

> May I, my father, be worthy of thee!
> Wisheth and prayeth thy Sarabojee.
> (Richter 1908, 123)

Indeed, after the death of the raja, Schwartz cared for the monarch's adopted son for two years without payment (Muthuraj 2006, 63).

Toward the end of the Madras siege, the British governor Rumbold asked Schwartz to be a peacemaker between British forces and Hyder Ali since Schwartz was uncorrupted by money. He agreed because he desired peace and went to Serirangapatnam for discussion; Schwartz offered another reason for accepting Rumbold's request: "This would enable me to announce the gospel of God my Savior in many parts where it had never been known before" (Pearson 1835, 196). In his faithfulness to provide political guidance to Hyder

Ali, Schwartz had an opportunity to proclaim Christ; in a letter afterward he acknowledged, "In Hyder's Palace, high and low came, inquiring of me the nature of the Christian doctrine; so that I could speak as long as my strength allowed" (Pearson 1835, 204). Hyder gave him money to defray the costs of his travels, which the missionary accepted reluctantly; Schwartz used the money to fund a school for orphans in Tanjore, which employed twelve catechists. In the words of the German, "I resolved to keep my hands undefiled from any presents . . . and I have not accepted a farthing excepting my travel expenses" (Rutherford 1896, 53). Following his wishes, upon his death all his possessions were used to further the progress of the mission, which enabled it to function for three decades (Pearson 1835, 408–11).

Hans Poulsen Egede (1686–1759)

Hans Poulsen Egede was a colonist and trader for the Danish monarchy in early eighteenth-century Greenland. His main motivation to travel this country was to shepherd the possible offspring of forgotten Norwegian settlers. In subsequent interaction with the indigenous people, however, he found them to be immoral and their customs and food distasteful. After fifteen years, Egede had few converts, never learned their language, and even proposed that Europeans should enslave the natives to bring discipline. Yet, people call him "Greenland's Apostle." How could such a person as Hans Egede be so highly regarded in missions history?

FRUSTRATED CALLING TO MISSIONS

The Norwegian Lutheran Egede was born in 1686 in Harrestad, Norway (at the time a territory of Denmark). At nineteen he received his bachelor of theology degree from the University of Copenhagen. While he was studying at the university he acquired an interest in missions and connected with Pietist believers in the court of the Danish king Frederick IV. Commissioned by the king, Danish Protestant missions began work in their colonies in southern India in 1705 with the German Halle university students Ziegenbalg and Plütschau. Egede witnessed their ordination and departure, which influenced his own mission desires.

At twenty-one he was appointed the Lutheran pastor at Vaagen, Norway, a coastal town near the Arctic Circle. His interest in Greenland began when he read a history of tenth-century Norsemen in Iceland, North America, and Greenland titled *Torfai Groenlandia Antiqua*. In the account, he discovered that Eric the Red had fled from Iceland in AD 985 to the western section of Grønland (Greenland) to evade a murder charge, and ultimately he established a Nordic Viking settlement by producing enticing reports of a "fertile country"—a green land. Even though the colonialists did not communicate beyond their society for three hundred years, Egede believed that there might be some Nordic people living in Greenland without the gospel. He wrote in his journal:

> Anno 1708 in the month of October or thereabouts when newly arrived at Vaagen parsonage in the Norlands, one evening towards dusk I walked by myself, and it occurred to me that once long ago I had read in a description of Norway, which also included Greenland, that in that place there were churches and monasteries, but from those who at a later period had been there for purposes of whaling I had not been able to learn anything of the kind, and therefore I became curious to know how they now fared. . . .

> Dear Lord and Father, if it is true that our brothers and sisters are living in Greenland like wild people, having neither Word nor Sacraments, possibly like the heathen, not knowing you or Jesus Christ whom you have sent, then, Lord, send me to them to preach anew your most holy name. Amen. (Bobé 1952, 20)

From his brother-in-law, Niels Rasch, he learned that "there [were] no human beings to be seen there, but in Greenland towards the south there [were] savages" (Bobé 1952, 22). Still Egede felt a passion to be a witness to the Norwegian people in Greenland.

> This relation called forth in me a commiseration for the miserable state of these poor people, who in former times had been Christians and enlightened in the Christian faith, but who now for lack of teachers and instruction had again fallen into heathen blindness and savagery. I therefore wished with all my heart that my circumstances had been such that I could regard it as my greatest bliss and joy, if I were able again to preach the Gospel to them. (Bobé 1952, 22)

When in 1710 Egede appealed to the Danish court to evangelize Greenland in a pamphlet titled "A Proposition for Greenland's Conversion and Enlightenment," he received opposition from King Frederick IV, who thought his proposal idealistic and impractical. In his request he desired that Christianity be "re-established, and the poor inhabitants, the offspring of the old Northern Christians, if through God's mercy any such may yet be found there, as true subjects to Denmark and Norway, might be assisted and comforted both as to body and soul" (Egede [1741] 1973, preface). He believed that "all Christians have a duty towards the mission, as long as any heathens exist, and all should be ardent in spirit for that task and pray to God to send 'apostles'" (Bobé 1952, 25).

Finally, the Danish king granted Egede the opportunity to establish a Bergen Trading Company post in Greenland after ten years of denied proposals to the royal court; continued opposition from his wife, Giertrud Rask; and ignored pleas to Bishop Krog of Drontheim and Bishop Randulf of Bergen. The catalyst for the change was the availability of funds after the defeat of Sweden in the Great Northern War (1700–1721). In Bergen, Egede eventually raised financial support for his mission, including a gift from the monarch, which allowed him to buy equipment and a ship called the *Haabet* (Hope).

After a voyage of eight weeks, Egede, his wife, and his four children along with twenty-five colonists arrived in Greenland in July 1721, landing on the west coast near the estuary of Ball's River. They began building their new settlement, Haabets Ø Godthåb ("Harbor of Good Hope"). Instead of finding the Catholic descendants of Norsemen, he found ancient ruins and a superstitious and immoral Inuit tribe. The Inuits were jealous of and hostile toward Europeans, giving rise to the rumor that they had cannibalized the original Norwegian settlers (Tweedie 1884, 93; Lenker 1896, 279).

Language Struggles and Strategy

As he worked to establish his trading post for the Danish Crown, Egede also began learning the language of the local people in order to evangelize them. He struggled in his studies and, after a few years, translated a rudimentary catechism that "on the whole . . . must have been incomprehensible to a monolingual Greenlander" (Bergsland and Rischel 1986, 13). The Norwegian missionary concluded that even though some words were of Norse origin, because of the Inuit accent whereby they "speak very thick and in the throat," it would be of greater benefit for colonization and missions for the indigenes to learn Danish (Egede [1741] 1973, 167; Bobé 1952, 85). Therefore, he began to teach the Inuit children Danish, but he soon met resistance from the uninterested youth when their parents concluded that they did "nothing but stare at a book and scrawl with a feather" (Crantz 1767, 290).

Egede's hope was to succeed in establishing a trading post, which would maintain his royal grant. In doing so, Danish Christians would then be attracted to the area and would positively influence the Inuit population. Egede reasoned that teaching the indigenous people Danish would prepare them for this future interaction. Coupled with this strategy, he believed that indigenous teachers would enhance the propagation of the Christian faith. To this end, the Lutheran colonizer invited young boys into his home to instruct them in Danish, religion, and European etiquette. His two eldest children, Paul and Petronella, acted as translators, but the experiment did not last long.

Hardships of the Colony

A severe famine and an outbreak of smallpox transmitted by European sailors occurred in 1726 at the colony of Haabets Ø, and many Inuits died. The people appreciated the missionary's sacrifice: "Thou hast buried our dead who would have been devoured by the dogs, foxes, or the ravens; thou has instructed us in the knowledge of God and of a better life to come" (Crantz

1767, 334). Egede finally received relief assistance from King Frederick IV, who also built a fort to establish a more permanent colony.

Egede was certainly a colonizer. In the preface of his first report to the Bergen Company (1729), *A Description of Greenland*, he promoted the region as "not so despicable and wretched . . . a country worthy of keeping and improving" ([1741] 1973, 122). The Norwegian spoke of the abundance of plant and animal life, aware of the financial benefits of trading the pelts of polar bear and arctic fox together with whalebone and walrus tusks. Likewise, he highlighted the Inuit culture, commerce, and shamanic religion, speaking disparagingly of the people as "commonly of a phlegmatic temper, which [was] the cause of a cold nature and stupidity" ([1741] 1973, 122). Yet he was not without Christian hope, believing that by civilizing the Inuits they would come to an acceptance of Christ. He posited, "It is a matter which cannot be questioned, that if you will make a Christian out of a mere savage and wild man, you must first make him a reasonable man, and the next step will be easier" ([1741] 1973, 216).

Although trade growth slowed, in 1730 Egede proposed to the newly crowned King Christian VI the establishment of ten new settlements or trading posts near Hope Island. Not only would this increase wealth for the Danish monarch but also more missionaries would come with each new post and the Inuits would be "kept under some discipline." Furthermore, he argued, the indigenes "must decidedly be brought under the yolk and treated as slaves, with the only exception that those who were converted and those who showed proper obedience to the word of God should be treated with greater clemency" ([1741] 1973, 217). In 1731 the king denied the request from the failing Greenland mission and ordered the colonists to return home, including the settlement's army garrison. Though threatened with starvation after a poor trading season, Egede and his family stayed on without government support, even though the majority of Europeans left.

Then, in 1732, the king sent supplies and money to Egede's mission as well as financial backing to launch the Bergen Trading Company in the region. As trade improved, the Danish king approved Egede's proposal for ten new trading posts and continued missions support. Egede's son Paul returned to Greenland after studies in Denmark, bringing with him missionaries from Herrnhut.

In the early 1730s a number of Christian Inuits visited Copenhagen, and unfortunately some died of smallpox. Those who returned brought the disease back to their people, and another smallpox epidemic occurred in 1733. This resulted in the death of some two hundred Christian families, which left only three families remaining in the settlement (Lenker 1896, 279). After the death of Egede's wife in 1735 from the continuing smallpox epidemic, the grieving missionary struggled with the realization that his work had made little impact on the people. Yet he believed that what was due him was in the

Lord's hand, and his reward was with God. Egede returned to Denmark the following year, leaving his son Paul in charge. He expressed his distress in his farewell sermon, from Isaiah 49:4, in which he alleged that he had labored to no purpose, having spent his strength in vain. After fifteen years of hardship and sacrifice, only two men, Poek and Keperok, had come to Christ.

On his return to Copenhagen, the former colonizer of and missionary to Greenland was appointed the superintendent of Mission Collegium, a royal missionary training institution, and continued promoting missions to Greenland, campaigning that language study was of paramount importance. Persistent disagreements over the quality of the missionary candidates and the growing recognition of governmental trade ambitions led to Egede's resignation and his son Paul's succession to his position in 1747.

CONTROVERSY

Was Hans Egede truly a missionary for the kingdom of God or primarily a colonist and trader for the kingdom of Denmark? Many have seen him as a pioneer of business as mission because of his efforts to join trade with his passion for mission. Despite his aversion to the native customs and foods, Egede designed pictures of biblical scenes to share the gospel, tried to learn the native language, and lived and ate with the people. He worked to the best of his ability to teach the Inuits about Christ, while at the same time establishing a trading presence to support his homeland and family. Although the intentions and effectiveness of Egede's missionary work are debatable, his efforts are a memorable part of Pietist missionary history.

Conclusion

The cultural sensitivity of Pietism was paramount, with the primary exception being Hans Egede. While supporters of Pietism desired that it would not be a separate movement from the rest of the church, its emotional ideals and values were clearly different from the Lutheran theology of Germany at the time. Philipp Spener, August Francke, Bartholomäus Ziegenbalg, and Christian Schwartz all made more uncontested mission contributions than Egede. This chapter has shown that Spener's heritage centered on enabling the laity, empowerment of the Spirit, social activism for the poor, and the establishment of the University of Halle. Francke carried Spener's passion to new levels by extending social ministry to include schools and orphanages, establishing publishing houses for Christian literature, and influencing Halle to become a sending base of Pietist mission. As a missionary in southern India, Ziegenbalg was a product of Halle as he began schools, translated the Scriptures into the local languages, studied the customs of the people, proclaimed Christ for individual conversion, and selected and trained indigenous leaders for the church. The Halle zeal for mission continued in Schwartz some thirty years later, also in southern India, where he witnessed to non-Christians, studied the indigenous languages and cultures, mentored converts, served the social needs of the people, and developed local church leaders. Affected by Francke and Spener, Pietist missionaries of the eighteenth century—such as Ziegenbalg and Schwartz—worked toward the transformation of society one disciple at a time.

August Hermann Francke's Admonition

(Source: Erb 1983, 165–66)

Prior to their departure for Lapland in 1722, twelve students received words of encouragement and instruction from August Hermann Francke for their daily living: from entering into daily conversation with God, to living humbly, and speaking the truth of God from the gospel.

Prayer during travel and at all times.

Abrahamitic walk before God.

Humility, modesty with decorous *Parrhesie* [openness] toward all men.

Edification of neighbors during travel and at other times.

Shunning all contention while traveling, according to the counsel of Joseph and his brothers.

No unnecessary curiosity, but necessary observation of necessary matters.

In the vocation: the *dic cur hic* [say: why am I here?].

True denial of self, in particular if one cannot have everything according to one's own *Commodität* [comfort] and otherwise according to one's wish. Again: if one notes that one will be loved and preserved. Again: if better *Conditiones* [conditions] and promotions are offered.

Shunning dangerous and idle conversation even if it has a good appearance and *Praetext* [pretext]

so as not to be directed into great temptations, sins, and shame.

To shun the supposed *Indifferentismus* [indifferentism] of the world, if one is invited as a guest and dinner companion or in some other capacity.

No day without food from God's Word and pouring out the heart before God; both with constant observation of oneself.

To remain with pure *tigniden* [building] truths; to shun paradoxes, meanings strange and difficult to explain to others.

To fill the mouth with the pure truth, in which is sap, power, and life, from the gospel of Christ, for example, *Lutherus redivivus* of [Martin] Statius [d. 1655].

To attend to God's way, not to deny the opportunities to promote the good, and to arm oneself for this with firm faith.

To count each day as the last and, so far as possible, to keep a diary.

Reflection and Discussion

1. How would you respond to these admonitions?
2. What types of admonitions or instructions would you offer if you were to send people into the mission field?

10

Encountering
Moravian Missions

The Moravian missionary movement was founded by Count Nikolaus Ludwig von Zinzendorf, a Lutheran Pietist, at Herrnhut ("the Lord's Watch"), near Dresden in Saxony. His ancestors were feudal lords in the Wachau region of the Danube Valley in Lower Austria and occupied positions of influence in the Habsburg Empire. During the Reformation, they became Lutherans. In 1721 Nikolaus von Zinzendorf became a legal counselor at the Dresden court of August II, the elector of Saxony, king of Poland, and Grand Duke of Lithuania. The next year, Nikolaus offered a part of his estate as a refuge for a group of persecuted believers from Bohemia and Moravia. From these United Brethren came the Moravians, the first organized Protestant mission, which in its first twenty years commissioned more Protestant missionaries than in the previous two hundred years.

Zinzendorf's passion was cross-cultural mission, with the Moravians often embracing suffering by associating themselves with destitute people groups. For instance, two years after sending the first Moravian missionaries to the West Indies, a group of eighteen arrived for service. Within a year, ten of them had died. In replacement, another eleven volunteers came from Herrnhut, and again nine of them died within a short time after their arrival. By 1736 Zinzendorf had recalled the remaining survivors back to Europe. By the time he died in 1760, however, after only twenty-eight years of cross-cultural ministry, the Moravians had sent out 226 missionaries and entered ten different countries.

Historical Background

In the early eighteenth century, European colonialism was reaching the height of its global political power. In contrast, the influence of Protestantism outside Europe was minimal. From within Lutheran Scholasticism, with its tendency toward a concern for structure and theological polemics, emerged the spiritual renewal of Pietism, led by Philipp Jakob Spener and August Hermann Francke, which emphasized the emotional and mystical aspects of the Christian faith. German Lutheran Pietists together with Moravian and Bohemian Brethren formed the early Moravians. The suppressed Unity of the Brethren (Unitas Fratrum) came from the followers of Jan Hus, who were widely persecuted by both Catholics and Protestants in Bohemia and Moravia during the Thirty Years' War (1618–1648). The outcome of the war was devastating in terms of the economic burden on the common people and the number of lives lost. The Bohemian population had declined from three million to eight hundred thousand because of death and exile. From the ashes of the war arose a longing for true godliness that led to the Pietist movement in the German Lutheran Church (Hutton 1909, 160).

Zinzendorf's Early Development

Zinzendorf was born in Dresden in 1700 into a Pietistic family. His grand-mother, Baroness Henrietta Catherine von Gersdorf, and his aunt Henrietta raised him in the Pietist-Lutheran tradition in Upper Lusatia. The baroness studied the Bible in its original languages, composed hymns in German and Latin, and corresponded in Latin with the likes of Spener and Francke. From an early age, Zinzendorf showed a strong inclination toward spiritual matters, as evidenced by the following description of his childhood in his own words. "I firmly resolved to live for him alone, who had laid down his life for me. My very dear Aunt Henrietta endeavored to keep me in this frame of mind by often speaking to me loving and evangelical words. I opened all my heart to her, and we then spread my case before the Lord in prayer" (Weinlick 1956, 19).

In these early years, the count shared Lutheran Pietism's belief that Christians have a biblical responsibility to evangelize those without the knowledge of Christ as Savior. Francke at Halle University had transformed that college into a center not only for European Pietism but also for overseas mission. In 1705 the University of Halle and the Pietist community of Berlin in partnership with King Ferdinand IV of Denmark sent the first Pietist missionaries from Europe. Commissioned by the king, Bartholomäus Ziegenbalg and Henry Plütschau evangelized the Danish colonialists and the indigenous people in Tranquebar, along the southeast coast of India. Pietist missionary letters from Tranquebar were read in meetings at Zinzendorf's grandmother's castle at Gross-Hennersdorf. Reflecting on the first time he heard about the work of Ziegenbalg in India, Zinzendorf stated, "I know the day, the hour, the spot in Hennersdorf. It was in the Great Room; the year was 1708 or 1709. I heard items read out of the paper about the East Indies, before regular reports were issued; and there and then the missionary impulse arose in my soul" (Hutton 1895, 179).

Francke influenced Zinzendorf while the young boy attended the Royal Paedagogium at Halle University from ten to sixteen years of age. In Francke's home, he met Ziegenbalg and Plütschau. Later he wrote that these conversations "with witnesses of the truth in distant regions, and the acquaintances with several missionaries . . . increased my zeal for the cause of the Lord in a powerful manner." During this time he joined, with four of his friends, a small group known as the Order of the Grain of Mustard Seed, which focused on prayer and the cause of Christ. With one of these university friends, Count Frederick von Watteville, Zinzendorf vowed to "do all in our power for the conversion of the heathen, especially for those for whom no one cared, and by means of men whom God, they believed, would provide," even if they could not be missionaries themselves (Hutton 1922, 7).

The Halle Pietists shaped the young count's theological views. They emphasized the heartfelt religious devotion of the individual, belief in the Bible as the Christian's guide to life, and a complete commitment to Christ that would manifest itself in ethical purity and charitable activity. In doing so, they stressed the importance of experiencing God.

After Halle, Zinzendorf attended the University of Wittenberg and studied law to prepare himself to be a judicial counselor in the Dresden court of August II the Strong, the Saxon elector. Yet service for Christ's kingdom was his ultimate goal. August Gottlieb Spangenberg quotes Zinzendorf regarding this career divergence: "My mind inclined continually toward the cross of Christ . . . and since the theology of the cross was my favorite theme, and I knew no greater happiness than to become a preacher of the gospel, therefore subjects not related to that I treated superficially" (Spangenberg 1838, 236). At Wittenberg Zinzendorf became a "strict Pietist" by establishing a stringent prayer, fasting, and devotional life; studied hymns and theological lectures; and read the Bible in Greek. He believed that a Christianity of the heart with its personal, intimate experience of Christ the Savior transcended the denominational divisions between Orthodox, Catholic, Reformed, and Lutheran. At Wittenberg he promised to follow his Savior in humility and to abandon the world.

At nineteen years of age, after graduating from Wittenberg, Zinzendorf traveled through Germany, Holland, and France—as was the custom for men of his social rank and status as a German imperial count—visiting royalty, religious leaders, and museums. He had the opportunity to gamble, dance, and live the life of high society. He recalled, "I went upon my travels but the more I entered into the world, the more firmly did the Lord retain his hold of me; and I sought out those amongst the great of this world, to whom I could speak upon the grace and goodness of my Saviour. I found them frequently where it would not have been expected" (Spangenberg 1838, 18). At an art museum in Dusseldorf he viewed a painting of Jesus crowned with thorns (*Ecce Homo*) by Italian artist Domenico Fetti. The inscription below the painting read: "All this I have done for you; what have you done for me?" Though he loved Christ, the count realized that he had done little for him. He knelt in front of the painting and rededicated himself for the service of Christ, vowing, "From now on I will do whatever he leads me to do" (Moore 1982, 9).

The Herrnhut Community

Following his marriage in 1722 to Countess Erdmuth Dorothea von Reuss, Zinzendorf began his work in the court at Dresden and moved to his estate of Herrnhut at Berthelsdorf near the Bohemian border in Saxony. Erdmuth was the sister of Duke Heinrich XXIX Reuss of Ebersdorf, who was a friend of Zinzendorf. The newly married couple vowed to put aside all favors of rank, to win souls, and to hold themselves in readiness to go immediately wherever the Lord might call. That same year he met Christian David, who asked permission for groups of Unitas Fratrum refugees from Bohemia and Moravia (present-day Czech Republic) to seek asylum on his estate. Five years later, three hundred Moravians were living at Herrnhut as well as other religious dissenters such as German Pietists. The decades of religious persecution with their pilgrim life had made them spiritually resilient and ready for any service for their Savior.

After five years, Zinzendorf left the Dresden court to concentrate on shepherding the growing settlement at Herrnhut. Visiting each home, Zinzendorf tried to bring unity to the fledgling community; having learned the historical background of the Moravians, he began to organize the settlement into a Christian community. Zinzendorf discovered Comenius's *Account of Discipline*, which validated his own attempt at guiding Christian community living in *Manorial Injunctions and Prohibitions* and *Brotherly Agreement of the Brethren from Bohemia and Moravia and Others* (Weinlick 1956, 74). There were forty-two items in the agreement that guided the community in promoting spiritual growth and the knowledge of God. This agreement was drafted following an attempt by the count to end a dispute over end-time teaching between Christian David and Pastor John Rothe of the nearby Berthelsdorf Lutheran Church.

Experiencing the Holy Spirit

One of the motivations for the early Moravians to be involved in missions was the love of Christ through the Holy Spirit. Mission was an extension of their personal love relationship with the Lamb of God. The desire to share this love of the Lamb with others and bring them into his saving arms formed the catalyst for mission. Two key events explain this impulse. On May 12, 1727, Spangenberg reported that Zinzendorf made a covenant with the Moravians at Herrnhut whereby they committed themselves to the Savior, confessed the sin of their religious quarrels, and "sincerely renounced self-love, self-will, disobedience and free thinking . . . and each one wished to be led by the Holy Spirit in all things" (Spangenberg 1838, 83).

Then, in August, the Moravians gathered for a week of prayer and fasting and experienced an outpouring of the Holy Spirit. There was a sense of the presence of the Holy Spirit moving among the people, immersed by the Holy Spirit himself into one love. This movement was in response to an earlier increase in unity and spiritual renewal experienced during the summer. Zinzendorf called it the Moravian Pentecost and stated: "The whole place represented truly a visible tabernacle of God among men, and till the thirteenth of August there was nothing to be seen and heard but joy and gladness; then this uncommon joy subsided, and a calmer sabbatic period succeeded" (A. Thompson 1885, 53).

> As the Brethren were learning, step by step, to love each other in true sincerity, Pastor Rothe now invited them all to set the seal to the work by coming in a body to Berthelsdorf Church, and there joining, with one accord, in the celebration of the Holy Communion. . . . The sense of awe was overpowering. As the Brethren walked down the slope to the church all felt that the supreme occasion had arrived; and all who had quarreled in the days gone by made a covenant of loyalty and love. . . . They entered the building; the service began; the "Confession" was offered by the Count; and then at one and the same moment, all present, rapt in deep devotion, were stirred by the mystic wondrous touch of a power which none could define or understand. There in Berthelsdorf Parish Church, they attained at last the firm conviction that they were one in Christ; and there, above all, they believed and felt that on them, as on the twelve disciples on the Day of Pentecost, had rested the purifying fire of the Holy Ghost. (Hutton 1909, 209)

After these two events the Moravians desired to carry the gospel to the ends of the earth to win souls for the Lamb. Now at Herrnhut there were love feasts, foot washings, festival days, song services, and hymn writing—all manifestations of the love of the Holy Spirit.

Because of the Moravian Pentecost, Zinzendorf structured the community into bands to provide discipline, fellowship, and worship with group accountability. Out of these bands arose an emphasis on prayer. Zinzendorf became involved with the single men's band and inspired them to consider mission service. More and more the community desired to spread this love of the Spirit to other Christians. Both men and women traveled to other churches and Pietistic small groups throughout continental Protestantism, bringing needed renewal (see Gallagher 2008a, 190–91).

Mission Beginnings

In 1731 Zinzendorf traveled to Copenhagen to attend the coronation of King Christian VI of Denmark. There he met two Christian Inuits from the Danish government-sponsored mission in Greenland founded in 1721 by Norwegian Lutheran Hans Egede, as well as Anton Ulrich, a former slave from Saint Thomas in the Virgin Islands who spoke of the great spiritual need of his homeland. Several weeks later both the Inuits and Ulrich spoke at Herrnhut. Ulrich addressed the community on behalf of his enslaved sister Anna about the possible need of selling themselves as slaves to gain access to the slaves' quarters (Bossard 1987, 270–71). Tobias Leopald and Leonhard Dober, members of the Moravian church at Herrnhut, felt called to go to the Caribbean, so the community waited on God for direction. They endeavored to understand God's desire for Tobias and Leonhard through their prayer life, the casting of lots, and their philosophy of "firstfruits." Each of these three methods contained significance in Moravian church life.

Prayer Life

The mission movement observed three main principles, known as the "Brotherly Agreement of the Moravian Church": salvation by the blood of Christ, sanctification through the work of the Holy Spirit, and love for one another, upheld through Bible readings and three set prayer times daily. Following the Pentecost event at Herrnhut, on February 10, 1728, the Moravians began an hourly intercessory prayer time with twenty-four men and women taking turns on a "Watch of the Lord" that was continuous for over one hundred years. That day, discussion and prayers included such countries as Turkey, Ethiopia, Greenland, and Lapland. Spangenberg described this prayer vigil as an "intercession for the church of Christ collectively, for the community . . . for individuals, for the missionaries, the land in which they dwelt . . . the whole of Christendom, and the human race in general" (Spangenberg 1838, 88).

Casting of Lots

The Moravians trusted the guidance of the Holy Spirit through the casting of lots. This approach decided who should serve in different roles in the community, whether someone should go as a missionary, how to ratify a person appointed as a clergy, what part of the Bible to read daily, resolutions to church problems, and whether an offer of marriage was to be accepted. After the consultation of the lot, the decision was binding, since God's Spirit had spoken.

For instance, Leonhard Dober and Tobias Leopold both believed that they should be the first missionaries sent out from Herrnhut to Saint Thomas.

Eighteen months after Ulrich's visit to Herrnhut, the leadership cast lots following the usual ritual to determine the next step. The process confirmed that Dober, a potter, was to go, but Leopold was to remain; David Nitschmann, a carpenter, took Leopold's place.

In August 1732, Nitschmann and Dober set out as the first missionaries from Herrnhut. So sure was their trust in the Spirit's guidance that they began their journey to the West Indies with little plan or provision. After prayer, hymn singing, and the charge to "do all in the Spirit of Jesus Christ," they rode with Zinzendorf in his carriage for the first fifteen miles. The potter and the carpenter then walked for two months to a Danish port and eventually boarded a ship to Saint Thomas. Upon arrival on the island, they joined the slaves in cutting sugarcane. This eventually won the respect of the workers but also the wrath of the European landowners, which resulted in their imprisonment. Despite incarceration, sickness, and death, the missionaries—and their replacements—persisted, and their work in the West Indies was extended to Saint Croix and then to Jamaica and Antigua (Fries 1962, 25–27). A year later, the Herrnhut Moravians sent two more missionaries to Greenland. Matthew Stach and Frederick Bohnisch, gravediggers by profession, suffered from disease, the cold, and starvation. Finally, after twenty-seven years, they witnessed their first Inuit converts, Kajarak and his family (see Gallagher 2008b, 240–43).

Firstfruits

Zinzendorf believed that the Holy Spirit is the only true missionary. The Spirit prepares the hearts of people to hear and receive the message of Jesus Christ. He calls individuals from among the people to be converted. The Spirit of God then leads the missionaries to these people. Zinzendorf encouraged the missionaries not to fear failure. Conversion did not rest on the ability of the missionary to preach and convince the people. In a lecture titled "Concerning the Proper Purpose of the Preaching of the Gospel," the count stated, "One is never converted by a preacher, never leaves a sermon in a blessed state if one did not come into the church already awakened" (Zinzendorf [1746] 1973a, 28). He continued, "There is no ground to debate whether God performs the work of conversion in a soul himself or whether he makes use of men to this end. Certainly he is in need of no one, for he himself can draw . . . through his Spirit all the souls whom he wants to give to his Son" (Zinzendorf [1746] 1973a, 32). The Holy Spirit prepares people so that when the missionary shares the gospel, "the work falls into prepared soil, into a cultivated field, and is nothing other than the explanation of the truth, which already lies in the heart" (Zinzendorf [1746] 1973c, 51).

Zinzendorf encouraged missionaries to pray that the Holy Spirit would lead them to these truth-seekers so that they could tell them about Jesus.

They should not be concerned about converting everyone because mission is done "not out of fear for the fate of the unconverted but because one wishes to follow Christ" (Schattschneider 1975, 72). The Moravian leader did not encourage mass conversions since he believed that this would not occur before the conversion of the Jewish people. Until then a few converts, "firstfruits" (Rev. 14:4), receive salvation.

At the Moravian mission in the Shekomeko village in Dutchess County, New York (1740–1744), Gottlob Buttner observed how the indigenous people were already "bent" toward the gospel (Westmeier 1994, 85). The believers were the "firstfruit," and the baptized received training for leading the local churches. Not only did the Spirit prepare the hearts of those who would hear but he would also care for those he called. If the Spirit cared for the new believers, then the missionary was not to be permanent (Schattschneider 1984, 66).

The count believed that the record of the conversion of the Ethiopian eunuch (Acts 8) and Cornelius (Acts 10) shows various aspects of mission to the firstfruits. First, the Holy Spirit prepares and initiates contact. "When the Holy Spirit comes into the heart, he melts the heart . . . this happened to Cornelius; this happened to Queen Candace's treasurer. They felt this joy, and they tasted this blessedness; but they did not know what name to give it" (Zinzendorf [1746] 1973c, 53). Second, the Spirit guides the missionary to those who need to hear the message, just as he did for Philip and Peter. Third, the missionary should "work directly on no heathen in whom one does not find a happy disposition to a righteous nature because it is just they, e.g., Cornelius, the Ethiopian eunuch etc., to whom Christ sent his messengers" (Schattschneider 1975, 77). The missionary should begin not "with public preaching but with a conversation with individual souls who deserve it, who indicate the Savior to you, and you will perceive it" (Schattschneider 1975, 77). Fourth, the few firstfruits should be water baptized as soon as possible, but only these chosen ones. In Acts the baptism of Cornelius and the Ethiopian "did not take several weeks of preparation first; there was no need to memorize a book; there was no need for answering twenty-four or thirty questions" (Schattschneider 1975, 53).

Ecumenical Movement

The early Moravians emphasized the unity of all Christians in love to Christ, believing that "the real church . . . is not confined to one place but is scattered over the whole world" (Spangenberg 1838, 20). Their focus was on Christ and his salvation because for them, true fellowship was through Calvary. The simplicity of their message of Christ left little room for denominational divisions. The count desired that Christians unite in Christ Jesus, asserting, "Jesus is the Universal Restorer of all mankind; and the propitiation, not for ours only, but for the sins of the whole world" (Wesley 1744, 7). This conviction of one gathered church of believers allowed the Moravians to work with many different religious groups. They were supportive of the Lutheran and the Anglican Churches as well as the Society for the Propagation of the Faith in Foreign Parts and the London Missionary Society. People remained within their churches, and proselytization was banned (Schattschneider 1984, 66).

In sending missionaries to foreign lands with the good news, Zinzendorf hoped for a cessation of the divisions of the Western church. He wrote in his letter to a missionary of the English society, "It pains me very much that I must see that the heathen become sectarians, again that people polish up their churches and ask them of what Christian religion they are" (Schattschneider 1984, 67). Zinzendorf never wanted the Moravians to become another denomination. His hope was to serve other churches throughout the world.

In his *Wanderjahr*, the year following university studies when most young noblemen traveled throughout Europe before taking on court responsibilities, Zinzendorf visited various religious leaders. At this time, he formed a friendship with the Catholic archbishop of Paris, Louis de Noailles. They discussed the differences between the Lutheran and the Catholic Churches, yet realized the commonalities they shared in their devotion to Christ. Both had a christocentric faith expressed in personal obedience to their Savior. They preserved their friendship through correspondence and occasional meetings.

In 1744 Zinzendorf told Spangenberg to call the movement in America the Evangelical Brethren rather than Moravian or Lutheran. He worked for an interdenominational fellowship to bring renewal and unity to churches and to take the message of Christ to those who had never heard (Van der Linde 1957, 420, 423). Yet in some places there were power struggles with other mission groups. When Christian David, a carpenter from the Herrnhut community, went to Greenland in May 1733, he was critical of the Norwegian Lutheran pastor Egede and his attempt to reach the Inuit people. David and his team of missionaries seemed to have little regard for the twelve missionary years endured by Egede and his family, viewing them as colonizers without any real understanding of the gospel message. The Moravians had to learn endurance and faithfulness before there was any fruit from their labor. As one of them recorded in 1740, there was also a need for flexibility in mission strategy:

> The method hitherto pursued by them consisted principally in speaking to the heathen of the existence, the attributes, and perfection of God, and enforcing obedience to the divine law. . . . Abstractly considered, this method appears the most rational; but when reduced to practice, it was found wholly ineffectual. . . . Now, therefore, they determined in the literal sense of the word to preach Christ and him crucified, without laying first "the foundation of repentance from dead works, and faith towards God." . . . This reached the hearts of the audience, and produced the most astonishing effects. . . . They remained no longer the stupid and brutish creatures that they had been. . . . A sure foundation being thus laid

in the knowledge of a crucified Redeemer, our missionaries soon found that this supplied the young converts with a powerful motive to the abhorrence of sin and the performance of every moral duty towards God and their neighbour. (Neill 1986, 202–3)

The Sifting Period

At the center of Moravian theology was the sacrifice of Christ. Sometimes called "blood and wounds" theology, the focus was on the suffering and death of Christ at his crucifixion. The mercy of God through Christ's suffering in our place atoned for the sins of the human race. Christ paid the price through his blood. The blood of Christ pardoned sins and made the human heart pure. The blood of the Savior was able to atone for the sinfulness of all human beings. Only the cross of the Savior could grant mercy and forgiveness to humanity, and to the Moravians it was through his blood.

Concerning Christ, Zinzendorf understood that "he, as a malefactor, hung upon the cross between two murderers, and was thus vilified, despised, torn and wounded, out of love for our souls" (Wesley 1744, 4). Christ's sacrificial love called forth a deep personal affection for the Savior and an appreciation of humanity's unworthiness. This brought forth humility in the missionaries as they prayed against "unhallowed ambition." The count claimed that Jesus "doth not hinder nor exempt his children from the cross and sufferings. He has suffer'd himself, and his kingdom in time present is and remains a kingdom of the cross" (Wesley 1744, 13).

During the "Sifting Period" (1743–1750), the count encouraged in his followers an extreme appreciation of the wounds and blood of Christ. Christ's suffering on the cross proclaimed the total sacrifice of God for humankind, and the Moravian congregation was to keep this awareness ever before them. This uniting with Christ in childlike faith would result in a joyful enthusiasm for life. Extreme practices arose during this time that centered on the wounds of Jesus. For instance, Christian Renatus, the son of Zinzendorf, built a hole in a sidewall of the church in Herrnhut to enable the congregation to imagine that it was the wound in Jesus's side. To experience the Savior's suffering the congregation would march through the "side wound."

The early Moravians viewed these mystical and sensual experiences as evidence of spirituality. They spoke of Christ as "Brother Lambkin" and of themselves as little wound-parsons, or worms in the wounds in his side, and little splinters of wood from the cross. A quote from Zinzendorf explains, "When he forgives our sins, we fall down at the footstool, and acknowledge, that it would be a Heaven Piercing sin, to with-hold the reward of his labour from him; as if the bloody sweat of Christ trickles down upon the ground in vain" (Wesley 1744, 57). The more the Moravians focused on identifying with Christ's suffering, the more they became introspective, which decreased their missionary and evangelistic zeal.

In the midst of the European Age of Reason, or Enlightenment, the Moravian church cultivated antirationalism, appealing to the sensual and emotional nature of their followers. Reason was unnecessary when as children in Christ's arms they could rest in his loving embrace. Their obsession with "blood theology" caused concern among orthodox Lutherans, who already were uneasy over the Moravians' unpopular stances on nonviolence, political

---

O God of all the world! Be pleased to let your grace and faithfulness, your omnipotence and sovereignty over all souls . . . be preached now to all creatures. Let all external circumstances also serve men to this end; bless them in their situation, and let everything that is a hindrance to others be for them an occasion to know themselves and thereby to come to the sense of a misery from which no one but you can deliver them.

A prayer by Zinzendorf ([1946] 1973b, 23)

---

involvement, and church and state relations. Zinzendorf eventually realized the excesses, confessed his error, and realigned the movement with the Augsburg Confession of the Lutheran Church.

Yet even in the early nineteenth century, the excesses of the "sifting period" were apparent among Moravian missionaries. John and Anna Rosina Gambold, both descendants from the Bethlehem community in Pennsylvania, ministered among the Cherokees in Springplace, Georgia. Their diaries (a handwritten manuscript recorded in an archaic writing convention called German script) focus on the blood and wounds of Jesus, especially the hole in the Savior's side. Their evangelistic work concentrated on the blood of Christ and being thankful for his bloody sacrifice. The Gambolds used pictures and tableaus of the agonies and suffering of Jesus in worship services and paintings of the crucifixion on the walls of the missionary houses and mission school to impart the message. Again, the side hole was the centerpiece of their Christianity.

It seems that the Cherokees had little interest in the Christianity of the Gambolds. For these Native Americans, the European treatment of killing their God was shocking and blasphemous. In addition, the Moravians ate the flesh and drank the blood of their God, which the Cherokees viewed as a cultural taboo and an abomination. Yet with all these fundamental differences between their beliefs, the Moravian missionaries showed respect to the Cherokees by extending hospitality, educating their children, and providing for various social needs. Though the Cherokees received a European worldview that was largely intolerant of cultural diversity, demonstrated in racial prejudice, dispossession of Native Americans, and false treaties, the Gambolds showed a humility and simplicity, which allowed peaceful and respectful interaction between two dissimilar worlds (McClinton 2002, 5–6).

Mission Methods

The Moravians began missions in 1732 with the journey of Dober and Nitschmann to Saint Thomas to minister to the slaves in the sugarcane fields. Many wondered whether these early missionaries would be successful since they were uneducated laborers and artisans. Zinzendorf had studied cases of

> **[Johann Leonhard Dober] was sent off with no particular instructions other than to let himself be led in all things by the Spirit of Jesus Christ.**
>
> C. G. A. Oldendorp (Oldendorp et al. 1987, 275)

pioneer missionaries such as Egede in Greenland and had formed ideas about missionary methods and motivations. The early Moravians had a simple reliance on the Holy Spirit and an intense devotion to preach and live for Christ. Zinzendorf wrote in a letter to an English friend:

> You are not to aim at the conversion of whole nations; you must simply look for seekers after the truth who, like the Ethiopian eunuch, seem ready to welcome the Gospel. Second, you must go straight to the point and tell them about the life and death of Christ. Third, you must not stand aloof from the heathen, but humble yourself, mix with them, treat them as Brethren, and pray with them and for them. (Hutton 1922, 20)

This quote shows the three basic characteristics of Moravian mission: the Holy Spirit guides both the seeker for truth and the missionary, preaching Christ is the central task of the missionary, and the missionary imitates Christ's example of humility.

Preached Christ

What did the convert need to believe to be water baptized? For Zinzendorf the key event in Jesus's life was his death. His death took the sin of the world, and his blood freed the believer from guilt and judgment: "The ordinary of our Saviour is not to prescribe souls a long preparation and form of repentance:

it costs him oftentimes but one word, and grace is present, and takes away all sins. It is highly exquisite to meditate furiously upon this matter; so that we may, by our own experience, be enabled to say, he can save, he can deliver all that come to him" (Wesley 1744, 11). To preach the gospel is to preach Christ. "Paul did not make anything known among the heathen except Jesus, and, indeed, hanged and crucified" (Schattschneider 1975, 90).

In Zinzendorf's view, non-Christians already know that God exists. What they need to realize is that "Christ came into the world to save sinners; and therefore, the missionary must always begin with the Gospel message. Moreover, how is it that missionaries have failed in the past? They have failed because, instead of preaching Christ, they have given lectures on theology" (Hutton 1922, 21). If the missionary begins by teaching the doctrine of creation, the fall, and humanity's sin, the people will stop listening before they hear about Christ. Christians need to speak of Jesus first, and then this will naturally lead to discussion about God and the rest of the biblical message.

The early Moravian missionaries in Greenland struggled to witness any response from the native people to the Christian message. Then Andrew Grassman visited Herrnhut and brought back this renewed emphasis on the wounds and death of Christ. The missionaries abandoned their preaching of systematic theological doctrine and focused on narrative theology, especially the passion of Christ. Following this redirection, many Inuits converted to Christ and received baptism. In a letter to Zinzendorf, John Beck claimed: "Henceforth we shall preach nothing but the love of the slaughtered Lamb" (Hutton 1922, 78).

The missionaries preached Christ and his salvation through the Holy Spirit before they spoke of creation, the history of the Jewish people, and the work of the early church. They centered on Christ, his person, and his work of salvation. Zinzendorf wrote to George Schmidt, a South African missionary, "You must tell the Hottentots [as the Khoikhoi were then called], especially their children, the story of the Son of God. If they feel something, pray with them, if not, pray for them. If feeling persists, baptize them" (R. Tucker 1983, 81). Zinzendorf gave the missionaries such a vision of God's love through Christ that for this love there was no challenge too great or difficult.

Culturally Sensitive

Zinzendorf was not interested in planting replicas of Herrnhut around the world. "Do not measure souls by the Herrnhut yardstick," he states in his "Instructions for Missionaries to the East" (Schattschneider 1984, 66). To preach Christ was to show love and humility, not to impose societal changes, even if they were for the good. For instance, in the West Indies, the missionaries did not attempt to win freedom for the slaves. This may appear to be a neglected moral obligation. Until the 1780s, however, there was no systematic attempt to convert

211

the slaves in the Caribbean except by the Moravians. In 1792 they had 137 men and women missionaries working in this region (Frey and Wood 1998, 129).

The early Moravians allowed but did not encourage the practice of polygamy in Africa since Zinzendorf believed that the people would see the problem with polygamy as they grew in their understanding of the gospel. The missionaries did not dismiss polygamous marriages to bring about conversion and baptism or force people to wear European clothing. For example, in the Caribbean Islands, compared to other Protestant missionaries, the Moravians were tolerant toward prior marriage arrangements and separations caused by slave owners. They believed in the sanctity of marriage but also viewed previous marital connections as God-ordained. For them it was inappropriate to "compel a man, who had, before his conversion, taken more than one wife, to put away one or more of them, without her or their consent." The hope was that the matter would be resolved through one of the partners agreeing to what would be a divorce. If this did not eventuate, then the man would remain in the congregation yet not have the opportunity to assume leadership responsibilities. For those cases where the slave masters forced the marriage partners to separate, "the Brethren [could] not advise, yet they [could] not hinder a regular marriage with another person" since "a family of young children, or other circumstances [might] make a help-meet necessary" (Buchner 1854, 44–45).

The missionaries learned the language and culture of the people. They desired to share Christ with minimal cultural interference. Among Native Americans, the Moravians related the gospel, emphasizing the mystical aspects of Christianity that closely related to the native people's religious worldview. God was the Great Spirit, and Christ the Prince of Peace, which correlated to the peace tradition of the Indian culture (Westmeier 1997, 173–74). Arcowee of Chota, a former war chief in the Upper Towns in the Cherokee Nation who had helped to sign peace treaties with President Washington in 1792, said to the Moravians on November 8, 1799, "I believe that you have been inspired by the Great Spirit to be willing to come to us and to teach us" (McLoughlin 1984, 35).

On visiting the Native American mission at the Shekomeko village in 1742, Zinzendorf said, "Apart from this, they shall remain Indians" (Westmeier 1994, 425), meaning that the Moravian mission had no intention of changing the Native American culture. This ideal did not always work out in practice. For example, David Zeisberger spent sixty-three years conducting missionary activities mostly among the Delaware Native Americans, establishing six missions in Tuscarawas County, Ohio. In the Christian villages that Zeisberger founded, he tried to find a common ground for the two cultures to live in harmony. Even though the European rules governing the villages were strict, he made provisions for compromise and forgiveness. In order to live in the Christian villages at Languntoutenunk (Friedensstadt) and Welhik-Tuppeek (Schoenbrunn), in August 1772 the Native Americans had to agree to nineteen statutes, which included the following:

IV. No person will get leave to dwell with us until our teachers have given their consent, and the helpers (native assistants) have examined him.

V. We will have nothing to do with thieves, murderers, whoremongers, adulterers, or drunkards.

VI. We will not take part in dances, sacrifices, heathenish festivals, or games.

VII. We will use no *tshapiet*, or witchcraft, when hunting.

VIII. We renounce and abhor all tricks, lies, and deceits of Satan. (Olmstead 1991, 246–47)

The Moravians had a unique missionary approach compared to previous Protestant efforts, which often measured success by the number of converts. The count developed a simple three-point approach:

First, silently observe to see if any of the heathen were prepared, by the grace of God, to receive and believe the word of life. Second, if even ONE were found, preach the gospel to HIM because God must give the heathens ears and heart to receive the gospel, otherwise all of his labors would be in vain. Third, preach chiefly to such heathens, who never heard the gospel. We were not to build on a foundation laid by others nor to disturb their work, but to seek the outcast and forsaken. (Loskiel 1794, 2:7)

The love of God and his redemption made available through Christ warranted a simple retelling of the salvation story everywhere. God in his way and time would then change the hearts of the people hearing the story of the Lamb of God. Sheer numbers of conversions of the nationals were not the prime motivation of the Moravians. David McClure, who visited the Moravian mission of Friedensstadt (south of present New Castle, Lawrence County, Pennsylvania) in 1770, two years after its founding by Zeisberger, wrote in his diary:

The Moravians appear to have adopted the best mode of Christianizing the Indians. They go among them without noise or parade, & by their friendly behaviour conciliate their good will. They join them in the chace, & freely distribute to the helpless & gradually instil into the minds of individuals, the principles of religions. They then invite those who are disposed to harken to them, to retire to some convenient place, at a distance from the wild Indians, & assist them to build a village, & teach them to plant & sow, & to carry on some coarse manufactures. (McClure 1899, 51)

Zeisberger's unique approach to the conversion of the Seneca Native Americans originated from his awareness of the cultural stress these people endured when they left their tribe and joined the mission community—a village that had elements of both cultures.

Translation Work

Moravians shared about Christ using the people's language. They translated the Scriptures into the indigenous language. For instance, Zeisberger translated the Bible into the Delaware and Mohican languages during the early days of the American colonies. Christian David served in Greenland using the Inuit dialect of the people and saw his first convert after five years. The reading of Jesus's agony in Gethsemane moved the leader Kayarnak, and "he became the first fruit of a glorious harvest" (Hassé 1913, 123–24). The missionaries also translated into the indigenous language other Christian literature such as hymns, litanies, and the catechism. Not every cross-cultural minister was successful in his or her attempts to learn and use the vernacular. For instance, no Moravian ever learned to speak Cherokee even though some of them had lived among the people for twenty-five years. The missionaries concluded, "Their language cannot be attained by Adults and when attained is incapable of conveying any Idea beyond the sphere of the senses; there seems to be no other way left by which the Spiritual or Temporal Good of these People can be promoted than by teaching them in our Language" (McLoughlin 1984, 64).

Tentmakers

The Moravian missionaries received only enough money to journey to their mission field. Upon arrival, they used their trade to support themselves. They believed that every Christian was a missionary and should be a witness in his or her daily work. This process, Zinzendorf believed, would teach the natives dignity of labor. This was an extension of what was common policy at home. For example, in 1747 there were no less than twenty-four shoemakers, one for every thirty-five people in the Herrnhut community.

In South Africa, Schmidt worked as a day laborer for the Khoikhoi farmers, pruning, threshing, butchering, and tanning. Eventually he obtained his own farm. In Labrador the missionaries owned trading posts and cargo ships. These enterprises supported their ministry and provided assistance to the poor and financial incentives for the people. In the American colonies, the agricultural and artisan efforts of the Moravians assisted in the success of European colonization. In Suriname the missionaries exerted economic influence as they founded tailoring, baking, and watchmaking businesses (Costas 2009, 35–37).

Social Welfare

Moravian communities provided social programs to help the people. Their members cared for widows and orphans, the sick, and the poor. Through these services, all who participated were missionaries. Virtually every Moravian community started a school. After their arrival on Saint Thomas, the missionaries offered to teach the slaves how to read, an incentive they hoped would lead them to desire religious instruction. The field-workers supported the program so well that by 1741 tutoring in reading was restricted to those who were "intent on their own conversion." Perhaps this development was an attempt by the Moravian Brethren to make the slave society culturally submissive in order to appease the disapproval of such instruction by the slave holders. Certainly, the burning of religious literature at this time by the slave masters on Saint Thomas was a symbolic act asserting control over the lives of the African Caribbeans (Frey and Wood 1998, 86).

The Moravians, who in 1801 had begun their work among the Cherokees who lived in Georgia, built a school at one of their two mission stations, which had forty-five students in 1830. This mission station was located near a major transport route, which meant that the Cherokees who lived there were more prosperous than others because they interacted with the European communities in obtaining supplies and had an opportunity to learn English. The location of the mission was a result of a calculated strategy by the Moravians to work among the more influential Cherokees, believing that through their impact they in turn would influence the more traditional members of the nation (McLoughlin 1990, 23, 93).

Colonel David Henley, the superintendent of Indian affairs in Knoxville, explained the Moravian purpose to the Cherokee chiefs at a council in 1800. The missionaries were

> good men who wish to know if the Cherokees would receive one or more of them favorably in the Nation to teach the young people to read and write, to be industrious in farming, etc., and above all, to teach both young and old to know the goodness of the Great Spirit and what He can do for them if they will follow the straight path which He will tell His servants to point out to them all. (Schwarze 1923, 50)

Friendship Evangelism

The Moravians lived and served beside the people and looked for the image of Christ in everyone who crossed their path. Motivated by the concept of Jesus as the servant leader, they stressed service to others from John 13:1–15; Mark 10:45; and Philippians 2:5–11. They wanted to go and serve others and, in loving persuasion, share Christ with the world.

In 1742 Christian Heinrich Rauch became the first Moravian missionary among the Mohicans at Shekomeko in central New York. Two years later Zinzendorf visited the mission and found the missionaries living in wigwams and the chapel operating in a birchbark structure. The Europeans worked alongside the nationals, plowing the fields and harvesting the corn.

215

As the Moravians lived and worked with the people, they built trust and respect. This earned them the opportunity to witness through word in addition to deed. Here was mission by loving persuasion rather than by force. They approached an indigenous culture and language with respect and in gentle evangelism. They offered a quiet invitation for those who were ready to embrace Christ by faith. Zinzendorf himself set forth this philosophy: "In order to preach aright, take three looks before every sermon: one at the depth of thy wretchedness, another at the depth of human wretchedness around thee, and a third at the love of God in Jesus; so that, empty of self, and full of compassion towards thy fellow men, thou mayst be able to administer God's comfort to souls" (A. Thompson 1885, 54).

Although Moravians accepted slavery as a part of God's social order in the world, at the same time they welcomed slaves into their multiracial Caribbean communities. They visited slaves in their cabins, sitting and talking with them "as if they were . . . equals," shared food and clothing, and greeted them by the shaking of hands "in the manner of good friends." These early missionaries even went as far as approving an interracial marriage between Matthaus Freundlich and Rebekka, a mulatto woman, to advance "God's work among the Negroes" on Saint Thomas (Bossard 1987, 280, 338–39, 351). This message of Christian fellowship did much to communicate racial equality, a notion that the slave owners tried to suppress in every way.

From the first contacts with the Moravians in the West Indies, the African slaves were involved with the sharing of the gospel news. Because they were unable to speak Creole, the language of most of the Africans, on February 5, 1738, the Moravians employed four men and a woman to give religious instruction to small groups of five to ten persons. Early success in this venture led the missionaries to commission the church's elders and preachers from the slave converts—both women and men. One such example was Abraham, who had "extraordinary gifts as a preacher" and whose sermons made "a ready access to the hearts of his listeners" (Bossard 1987, 360–61). His knowledge of Creole and the customs of his coworkers provided assistance to the missionary effort. In adopting these practices, the Moravians promoted a contextualized biblical message and reinforced the value of the shared language and culture.

Controversy and Persecution

The early Moravians accepted controversy and persecution. Even Zinzendorf, who had "many thousand friends, who loved him tenderly, and to whom he was indeed invaluable," at the same time had "a host of enemies, who painted him in vile colours, and persecuted him with more untiring ardour, than if he had been the worst of heretics" (Spangenberg 1838, iv). In 1741 at Gray's Inn Walks in London, for instance, Zinzendorf and John Wesley debated (in Latin) the contrary points of view between Moravians and Methodists concerning the saving work of Christ for the world. Wesley claimed that the Moravians overly emphasized Luther's justification by faith and neglected real holiness, not teaching correctly the goal of the Christian life, which was "Christian perfection." Zinzendorf disagreed: "I know of no such thing as inherent perfection in this life. This is the error of errors. I pursue it everywhere with fire and sword! I stamp it under foot! I give it over to destruction! Christ is our only perfection. Whoever affirms inherent perfection denies Christ." In reply to Wesley's argument that it was "Christ's own Spirit that works in true Christians to achieve their perfection," the count replied, "By no means! All Christian perfection is simply faith in Christ's blood. Christian perfection is entirely imputed, not inherent. We are perfect in Christ; never in ourselves" (Outler 1964, 367–72). For Zinzendorf, Wesley's message combined the law with the gospel.

The early Moravians not only stirred controversy but also were persecuted. In 1732, when Ulrich pleaded with the Herrnhut community to go to his people in the West Indies, he warned them that they would have to become slaves themselves to have any contact with the workers. Dober endured much hardship and the resentment of the European colonialists as he preached to the slaves. After Dober returned to Herrnhut to become an elder, in 1736 Frederick Martin arrived to continue Dober's work. Within a few months of arriving on Saint Thomas, he had won over two hundred converts to Christ. Martin had already been imprisoned for his faith in Moravia, and in the midst of witnessing to the slaves, he suffered imprisonment at the hands of the European colonists. The slaves, nonetheless, gathered outside his prison cell to hear him preach.

In 1738 Zinzendorf himself journeyed to the Caribbean with five missionary recruits to help those Moravians on Saint Thomas. Upon his arrival, he found Martin imprisoned and used his authority to have him released, after which Martin was able to minister on Saint Thomas for another fourteen years. While there, the count conducted daily services for the slaves and reorganized the mission to be more efficient.

From 1740 to 1745, John Cennick, a Moravian evangelist in Britain, was involved in an open-air evangelistic campaign in Gloucestershire and Wiltshire that drew large crowds and often a hostile reaction from some of the people. As he rode from village to village and from town to town, angry mobs constantly attacked him, objecting to his message and method. At Upton-Cheyny, some of the villagers tried to drown out his preaching by hitting pans together, and when this failed, they attacked him with the same pans. At Swindon, some rascals fired muskets over Cennick, and when this did not achieve the desired effect, they brought the local fire engine and drenched the Moravian with dirty water from the ditches. In 1741 Cennick stated in his journal:

> After I preached at Brinkworth about fifty persons on horses, and as many on foot, followed me to Stratton, where we had appointed a meeting. On the way

I opened my New Testament on these words, "We are persecuted but not forsaken," which served to hint to me what would happen. However, we had many hearers and a lovely meeting. But before I had said much the mob came again from Swindon, with swords, staves and poles, and without respect to age or sex they knocked down all that stood in their way. Some had the blood streaming down their faces, and others were almost beaten or trampled to death. . . . We escaped into a Baptist meeting-house just by, where I addressed the people with much affection. (Hassé 1913, 82–83)

Not all Moravian missions were successful. For example, in 1777 minister Karl Schmidt and doctor Johannes Grassman traveled to Serampon, India. In the midst of learning the language and culture so that they could translate the Bible, they received opposition from both Catholic and Protestant churches, as well as from higher-caste Indians. After they had labored for fifteen years, there was still no indication of a "pre-awakening" of the Holy Spirit in the people, and they finally left (Schattschneider 1998, 65, 84).

Missions to the Marginalized

Moravians seemed to choose the most neglected and oppressed places of the world to share Jesus. From the frozen deserts of Greenland to the scorching wastelands of Ethiopia, pioneering mission to the people of the Middle East and the Gold Coast of West Africa, Moravians worked and lived among the poor and oppressed.

George Schmidt, the first Moravian missionary to southern Africa (1737), ministered among the Khoikhoi, a people often hunted by other tribes and shipped to India as slaves. The Dutch colonists opposed Schmidt's work and eventually deported him to Holland to face charges of improper ordination in administering the sacraments. When he left, he had established a church of fifty Khoikhoi as well as some forty European converts (Hassé 1913, 125–26). Moravians also ministered among the slaves of the West Indies and Suriname and among the Native North Americans and African American slaves.

This mission focus on the oppressed may have been due to the Moravians' own history of persecution, and Zinzendorf's vow to minister among people whom no one else desired to serve, a vow made earlier with the friends of the "Society of the Mustard Seed" at Halle University (Westmeier 1997, 173). Before the count sent the missionaries, he challenged them: "Show forth a happy and joyous spirit. And they should not (even in the most insignificant external matters) rule over the heathen. Rather, they would receive their authority through the power of the Holy Spirit. And they should humble themselves below the people they minister to" (Westmeier 1994, 425).

Zinzendorf led by example. In 1741 he resigned from his responsibilities as a bishop of the Moravian Church to be free to serve the church in America.

Then, a year later, he renounced the title "Count" and the privilege of nobility to be more effective in his ministry in the colonies. The Moravian communities were now to call him "brother" (Weinlick 1956, 155).

Moral Disciplinarians

There was a strong system of moral discipline among the Moravian missions. The leadership interviewed each person regarding his or her spiritual condition to fulfill the covenant objective of walking in newness of life. In the West Indies, this led to the Moravian slaves being loyal, law abiding, and not involved with slave revolts. The early Moravians worked hard to avoid nominal conversions, but in doing so they neglected national issues of social justice that included slavery and the genocide of native people. Their ecumenical spirit extended to the political arena, however, and they made every attempt to convince the ruling order that mission activities brought peace, and not rebellion, to the Caribbean. For example, during the Napoleonic Wars, Moravian missionaries in Antigua rallied their membership to join the local black militia (Frey and Wood 1998, 138).

In the West Indies, the Moravian missionaries walked a moral tightrope in their work with the African slaves. Based on plantations, the mission stations were mainly dependent on the estate owners and their own labor for survival. This dependency meant that they needed to nurture cooperation with the colonialists. The slave owners used the Brethren in Jamaica, conversely, as "spiritual police" to rebuke troublesome slaves. The missionaries enforced plantation policy partly through dependency and partly through religious conviction that slaves should submit to their masters. In tension with this scenario were the actions of the missionaries "to challenge the very system that provided them with the means of subsistence by introducing radical social values into the existing social order" (Frey and Wood 1998, 86). Hence, the Christian message of racial equality attracted the slaves, and the Christian message of racial submission appeased the slave masters.

Disciplined Communities

The early Moravians had a highly organized communal system so that the adults could focus on missions and artisan crafts. They divided a congregation into ten "choirs": marrieds, widowers, widows, single men, single women, teenage boys, teenage girls, younger boys, younger girls, and infants.

This highly organized Bohemian structure extended to the mission field. In Bethlehem, Pennsylvania, Moravians developed a training school for missionaries to the Indians (Kane 1971, 96). The expectation was that the mission stations would become involved in mission sending, and nationals would be trained to become elders and teachers. Although David Allen Schattschneider

(1984, 66) states that the goal of the Moravian missions was to give the churches completely into the hands of the local leadership, the European organizational model stifled indigenous expressions of faith and training of leadership. This led to a lack of independence among the national Christians.

Moravian Influence

Zinzendorf's greatest contribution was to awaken Protestantism to its responsibilities for cross-cultural mission. In 1790, while still in England, William Carey had read the Moravian journal *Periodical Accounts relating to the Moravian Missions*. Addressing the Baptist Brethren at Kettering, he said, "See what the Moravians have done! Cannot we follow their example, and in obedience to our Heavenly Master go out into the world, and preach the Gospel to the heathen?" (Hutton 1909, 251–52). Two years later, the Baptist Missionary Society and the London Missionary Society had formed under Moravian inspiration.

The count brought understanding to the Protestant church that it was not only responsible for mission but also that missionary preaching should be about the atoning death of Christ, and that the renewal and unity of the worldwide church was important. Schattschneider summarizes Zinzendorf's mission theology: "He took as his model the work of the apostle Paul. Because of his acquaintance with the work of the Holy Spirit and his firm relationship to Christ, Zinzendorf was able to keep other aspects of the mission program in their proper perspective" (1984, 66).

Moravians proclaimed the doctrine of redemption by the blood of Christ and for the atonement to be the basis of all other Christian truth. They believed that they were to leave the work of winning souls to the Holy Spirit while the missionary followed the Spirit's guidance in speaking and living out the love of Christ. Laypeople trained as cross-cultural evangelists supported their witness by working alongside the people they sought to reach. Desiring to identify with their prospective converts as equals, and not as superiors, their goal was to proclaim Christ and the love of the Lamb.

Other Protestant groups, especially the Methodists, the Baptists, and the Anglicans, copied the missionary organization and discipline that the Moravian Brethren used in evangelizing the Caribbean Islands. The pioneering Moravians were highly successful, particularly in their slave missions in Antigua. In 1791 this station reported a membership of 7,400 slaves, free blacks, and people of color (Goveia 1965, 280–81). Apart from the religious conviction that Christians had a responsibility to convert slaves, the Moravian experience had convinced European missionaries that a religiously trained black membership could be effectively used in bringing moral discipline and submission to the larger black slave populations of the West Indies (Frey and Wood 1998, 132).

In other words, missionaries saw the christianization of slaves as a means to bring about behavioral change that would suppress any thought of rebellion and protect the outnumbered white population from spiritual and physical danger. The intention of Moravian missions was not to further the oppression of the slaves, but their beliefs were often twisted to further European slave owners' own ends.

As with the evangelization of slaves, the count's evangelistic zeal for humanity went far beyond those of his rank and station. As the leader of the Moravians, Zinzendorf often traveled in Europe, England, the West Indies, and the American colonies, overseeing the development of their unique cross-cultural witness.

Conclusion

At the time of Zinzendorf's death in 1760, Moravian mission stations existed in Danish Saint Thomas in the West Indies (1732); Greenland (1733); Georgia, North America (1734); Lapland (1735); Suriname, or Dutch Guiana, on the north coast of South America (1735); Cape Town, South Africa (1737); Elmina, the Dutch headquarters on the Gold Coast (1737); Demarara, now known as Guyana, South America (1738); and the British colonial islands of Jamaica (1754) and Antigua (1756). That same year, there were forty-nine men and seventeen women serving in thirteen stations around the world, ministering to over six thousand people. Further missions would be established in northern India (1764), Barbados (1765), Labrador (1771), Nicaragua (1849), Palestine (1867), Alaska (1885), and Tanzania (1891) (Hutton 1922, 55, 58; Latourette 1975, 893, 897, 951, 956; Neill 1986, 201–2; R. Tucker 2004, 99–105).

Not all native people quickly acculturated to this new religious system of Moravian Christianity, nor did the religious leadership pass easily and entirely to the new followers of Christ. In accepting the gospel, they drew on their national religious traditions, which often led to an indigenous syncretism. Furthermore, the structure of Moravian Protestantism perpetuated traditional Eurocentric leadership styles and roles.

In some cases, Christianity merely touched lives in a superficial manner, with acceptance being a matter of expediency. In other situations, however, many people found in Christianity an authentic Christian experience and belief. The Moravian focus on Christ's death, cultural sensitivity, the call of the Holy Spirit, and long-term discipleship brought a unique and often effective approach to missionary work worldwide.

Eternal Depth of Love Divine

CASE STUDY

Zinzendorf wrote his first hymn at twelve and throughout his life composed 2,196 sacred lyrics. Here are two samples for personal reflection. Zinzendorf wrote the song "Immanuel, God with Us" for the birthday of his friend Count Henkel of Oderberg on September 21, 1726. The song was later translated into English by John Wesley in *Hymns and Sacred Poems* in 1739. The second hymn, "Flock of Jesus, Be United," sung often in Moravian churches, continues to inspire its members to seek unity and reconciliation.

"Immanuel, God with Us"

Eternal depth of love divine,
In Jesus, God with us,
   displayed;
How bright thy beaming glories
   shine!
How wide thy healing streams
   are spread!
With whom doest thou delight
   to dwell?
Sinners, a vile and thankless
   race:
O God, what tongue aright
   can tell
How vast thy love, how great
   thy grace!
The dictates of thy sovereign
   will
With joy our grateful hearts
   receive:
All thy delight in us fulfills;
Lo! All we are to thee we give.
To thy sure love, thy tender
   care,
Our flesh, soul, spirit, we
   resign:

Oh, fix thy sacred presence
   there,
And seal the abode forever
   thine.
O King of glory, thy rich grace
Our feeble thought surpasses
   far;
Yea, even our crimes, though
   numberless,
Less numerous than thy mercies are.
Still, Lord, thy saving health
   display,
And arm our souls with heavenly zeal;
So fearless shall we urge our
   way
Through all the powers of earth
   and hell.

(Erb 1983, 289)

"Flock of Jesus, Be United"

Christian hearts, in love united,
Seek alone in Jesus rest;
Has he not your love excited?
Then let love inspire each
   breast;
Members—on our Head
   depending,
Light—reflecting him our Sun,
Brethren—his commands
   attending,
We in him, our Lord, are one.
Come then, come, O flock of
   Jesus,
Covenant with him anew;
Unto him, who conquered for
   us,
Pledge we love and service true;
And should our love's union
   holy
Firmly linked no more remain,
Wait ye at his footstool lowly,

Till he draws it close again.
Grant, Lord, that with thy
    direction,
"Love each other," we comply,
Aiming with unfeigned affection
Thy love to exemplify;
Let our mutual love be glowing;
Thus will all men plainly see,
That we, as on one stem
    growing,
Living branches are in thee.
O that such may be our union,
As thine with the Father is,
And not one of our communion
E'er forsake the path of bliss;
May our light 'fore men with
    brightness,

From thy light reflected, shine;
Thus the world will bear us
    witness,
That we, Lord, are truly thine.

(Hassé 1913, 512)

Reflection and Discussion

1. What does the language in these hymns teach us about Zinzendorf's theology?
2. What role does worship have in shaping and teaching theology in your own faith background?

11

Encountering
Methodist Missions

During his lifespan of fifty-two years (1739–1791), an English minister traveled over 250,000 miles, a distance equivalent to ten times around the world, mostly on horseback. Throughout his travels, this founder of English Methodism, John Wesley, preached over forty thousand sermons. He wrote 233 books on all sorts of subjects, including one on medical remedies that was in use for nearly two hundred years and one of the earliest texts on electricity that advocated using the effects of electric shock to treat nervous disorders, a practice he administered to thousands. His interests were wide and varied, ranging from publishing a fifty-volume collection of devotional enrichments for his disciples called *A Christian Library* (between 1749 and 1755) to writing a complete commentary on the whole Bible and composing hymns that we still sing today, as well as producing some five thousand sermons, tracts, and pamphlets.

Wesley rose daily at four in the morning and started preaching by five so that working men and women could attend services. He earned a reputation for being somewhat controlling by constantly formulating directions for his ministers on how to preach and live the Christian life. They were to get up early in the morning, not drink alcohol, read constantly for sermon preparation, and in their preaching not shout, scream, or preach too long. He proclaimed the gospel for over sixty-five years and left behind 750 preachers in England and 350 in America, 76,968 followers in England and 57,621 in America. The world was his parish.

This chapter will examine the early Methodist movement that John Wesley founded with a particular focus on its evangelism and mission strategy. After regarding the foundational lessons of the Holy Club, mission work in Georgia, and the influence of German Moravianism, the chapter considers the Methodists' mode of preaching, organizational structure, leadership selection and training, and hymnody. This background to English Methodism will enable us to appreciate the spread of the movement to America with ensuing adaptations to meet the pioneering environment, all the while reflecting on examples for contemporary missions. Before we begin, it would be helpful to understand the social and ideological context of eighteenth-century English Protestantism, from which this group emerged.

Enlightenment and Enthusiasm

Before John Wesley's evangelism, European deism had greatly influenced the eighteenth-century church in Great Britain. The Church of England, affected by the reasonableness of the European Enlightenment, demanded formalism and structure and ridiculed the unmanageable experience of the heart. A number of English scholars affirmed this ideology. In 1695 Oxford scholar John Locke anonymously wrote a book, *The Reasonableness of Christianity*, in opposition to religious enthusiasm, which many believed had caused the European wars of the previous century. Cambridge professor of mathematics Isaac Newton "proved" the belief that God ran the universe along rationalistic lines when he showed that the motion of objects on earth and of celestial bodies was governed by the same set of natural laws. In 1686 Newton wrote the *Philosophiae Naturalis Principia Mathematica*, in which he described universal gravitation and the three laws of motion, laying the groundwork for classical mechanics.

Anglican priest William Paley also supported deism when he wrote the influential book *Natural Theology; or, Evidences of the Existence and Attributes of the Deity, Collected from the Appearances of Nature*, first published in 1802. In this book, Paley understands the nature of God by reference to his creation, the natural world. He introduces one of the most famous metaphors in the philosophy of science, the image of the watchmaker. Paley argues that living organisms are even more complicated than watches, and only an intelligent Designer could have created them, just as only an intelligent watchmaker can make a watch: "Upon the whole, after all the struggles of a reluctant philosophy, the necessary resort is to a Deity. The marks of design are too strong to be got over. Design must have had a designer; that designer must have been a person; that person is God" (1803). Thus, Paley describes the God of the universe as a watchmaker who designed the universe, gave it the laws of nature, and now was in his heaven and all was right with the world. God had created the universe and upon setting his creation in motion had stepped back to allow humanity control of its own destiny by reason. There was no place for any witness of the Holy Spirit within the life of the individual or Christian community.

The sixteen volumes of Parson James Woodforde of Somerset and Norfolk, *A Country Parson: James Woodforde's Diary 1759–1802*, demonstrate a unique insight into the lifestyle of an Anglican vicar in rural eighteenth-century England affected by these ideas. For nearly forty-five years, this son and grandson of Anglican rectors kept a diary with almost daily entries. Woodforde was more a country gentleman than a minister of the gospel, and his droll and often whimsical comments provide a description of the manners and habits of rural clergy, as the following example illustrates.

> I read Prayers this morning again at C. Cary Church—I prayed for poor James Burge this morning, out of my own head, hearing he was just gone of almost in a Consumption. It occasioned a great tremulation in my voice at the time—I went after Prayers and saw him, & he was but just alive—He was a very good sort of young man & much respected—It was the Evil which was stopped & then fell upon his Lungs—Grant O Almighty God, that he may be eternally happy hereafter—I dined, supped and spent the Evening at Parsonage. (April 14, 1767, in Winstanley 1996)

The church was asleep to the needs of the English people. In large part due to the formalism of the church, Great Britain's society was suffering from moral decay, with unemployment, poverty, involvement in the slave trade, and crime commonplace. The Methodist revival was a heart response to the weaknesses of the cognitive approach to Christianity and the corrosion of British society. Geoffrey Best describes the evangelical revival in eighteenth-century England as "a reaction against certain features of the orthodox theology and religious outlook of the early Enlightenment" (1970, 38). Writing in 1781, Hull evangelical Joseph Milner criticized Edward Gibbon, author of the 1776 twelve-volume *The History of the Decline and Fall of the Roman Empire*, by stating, "Reason has impertinently meddled with the Gospel" (quoted in Stromberg 1954, 168). Against this backdrop of liberalizing, enlightened thought was the confirmed Reformation biblical teaching of John Wesley and other evangelicals.

The English evangelical revival was composed of four major strands: the Calvinistic Methodists of George Whitefield, the band of gospel clergymen in the Church of England, the inheritors of the Puritan traditions of the seventeenth century, and the Methodists (Bebbington 1993, 18–20). Thomas Haweis, writing in 1800, estimated that in that year these four strands of the evangelical movement had two thousand gospel preachers and some six hundred thousand adherents (331). This chapter will highlight the Methodist leadership of John and Charles Wesley, who provided some of the loudest voices that awakened the British church. We will now explore the instructional persuasions of Methodism that helped guide its development: the Holy Club, mission to the American colonies, and German Moravianism.

Early Mission Lessons

The Holy Club

John Wesley, raised in the Puritan-influenced Epworth home of an Anglican priest, entered Christ Church College at Oxford University at seventeen. At twenty-two years of age, following his schooling, he became an Anglican priest and missionary. When his younger brother, Charles, began his studies at Oxford in 1726, the university had the reputation of being a place of student drunkenness and gambling. Charles formed a small society of students to study the classics and the Greek New Testament. In addition to study, worship, receiving communion once each week, and fasting until three in the afternoon on Wednesdays and Fridays, the group served the poor, the sick, and the imprisoned and set up a small school. They attracted both admiration and scorn from their fellow students, who gave them names such as "the Holy Club" and "the Methodists" because of their methodical approach to a holy life.

John Wesley returned to Lincoln College at Oxford as a teaching fellow, joined his brother's group, and oversaw the group's spiritual growth. He served primarily to encourage the members to discuss the Scriptures with an emphasis on practical performance. John invited George Whitefield to join the group, which was an affront to the upper classes since he was an innkeeper's son. Though the number of members in the Holy Club never exceeded twenty-five, many became prominent Christian leaders. In addition to John and Charles Wesley, John Gambold became a Moravian bishop, John Clayton became a distinguished Anglican clergyman, James Hervey was an accomplished religious writer, Benjamin Ignham was a Yorkshire evangelist, Thomas Brougham became the secretary of the Society for Promoting Christian Knowledge, and

SIDEBAR 11.1

Are You a Child of God?

On February 8, 1736, James Oglethorpe introduced John Wesley to August Spangenberg, the Moravian pastor of the church at Herrnhut in Saxony, who raised questions concerning Wesley's salvation:

I asked Mr. Spangenberg's advice with regard to my own conduct. He said, "My brother, I must first ask you one or two questions. Have you the witness within yourself? Does the spirit of God bear witness with your spirit that you are a child of God?" I was surprised and knew not what to answer. He observed it, and asked, "Do you know Jesus Christ?" I paused and said, "I know he is the Sav-

iour of the world." "True," replied he, "but do you know he has saved you?" I answered, "I hope he has died to save me." He only added, "Do you know yourself?" I said, "I do." But I fear they were vain words.

John Wesley (1940, 31)

Reflection and Discussion

1. What role does the Holy Spirit play in the salvation of souls?
2. Is it enough to simply "believe and be saved" in order to know Jesus Christ? How would you respond to Spangenberg's questions?

George Whitefield was associated with the Great Awakening in America and the evangelical revival in England.

Missionaries to Georgia

John Wesley was an evangelist, administrator, and theologian, and Charles a hymn writer, yet both began their careers as missionaries. In October 1735 the two brothers, with the sponsorship of the Anglican Society for Promoting Christian Knowledge, sailed with Governor James Oglethorpe on his second expedition to the colony of Georgia. The British government had appointed John as chaplain to the English colonialists at Savannah, and Charles as chaplain and secretary to Oglethorpe.

Although John was still unsure of his own salvation, in part out of a desire to find God he yearned to share what he did know with the Native Americans of Savannah. Yet during the two years Wesley was in Savannah he never ministered to the Native Americans. He preached widely, yet a complicated legal battle over dashed romantic intentions marred his ministry. Eighteen-year-old Sophy Hopkey, with her new husband, William Williamson, filed a lawsuit against Wesley for defamation of her character. This legal action dragged on for six months and climaxed in a formal grand jury indictment on ten separate counts. After this fiasco so drastically damaged his personal and ministerial reputation, John hastily left America for home. He felt himself a failure as a pastor and a missionary. On the voyage home to England, Wesley's "mind was now full of thought" concerning his lack of Christian experience:

> I went to America to convert the Indians; but oh! Who shall convert me! Who, what is he that will deliver me from this evil heart of unbelief? . . . It is now two years and almost four months since I left my native country, in order to teach the Georgian Indians the nature of Christianity; but what have I learnt myself in the mean time? Why (what I least of all suspected), that I who went to America to convert others, was never myself converted to God. I am not mad, though I thus speak; but I speak the words of truth and soberness; if haply some of those who still dream may wake and see that as I am so are they. (Tuesday, January 24, and Wednesday, February 1, 1738, in Wesley 1940, 54–55)

Sway of the Moravians

Upon returning to England, both John and Charles spent time with Moravian missionary Peter Böhler, who explained salvation through faith in Christ's atoning work and the inner witness of the Holy Spirit. Böhler played a critical role in aiding the Wesleys in reassessing their Christian commitment and the meaning of faith. John Wesley studied the Moravian beliefs and discovered the idea of justification by faith. Salvation did not depend on works but was a gift of God through the work of Christ on the cross. This theological recognition culminated in John's conversion when, on the evening of May 24, 1738, he experienced God's salvation while attending a Moravian meeting in Aldersgate Street, London. He described the experience in his journal:

> In the evening, I went very unwillingly to a society [meeting] in Aldersgate Street, where one was reading Luther's preface to the *Epistle of the Romans*. About a quarter before nine, while he was describing the change which God works in the heart through faith in Christ, I felt my heart strangely warmed. I felt I did trust in Christ, Christ alone, for salvation; and an assurance was given me, that he had taken away *my* sins, even *mine*, and saved *me* from the law of sin and death. (1938, 1:475–76)

Swayed by these early Moravian missionaries, John Wesley toured Germany from early June to the end of August 1738 and met the movement's founder, Count Nikolaus Ludwig von Zinzendorf, at Marienborn; visited the Pietist center of August Herman Francke at Halle University; and spent time at Herrnhut with the missionaries Christian David and Martin Dober. Of this time he noted, "I would gladly have spent my life here; but my Master calling me to labour in another part of his vineyard, I was constrained to take my leave of this happy place" (Wesley 1940, 80). The next section of this chapter will focus on Wesley's labors in the British vineyard "to declare in my own country the glad tidings of salvation" by modifying the approach to evangelism of the Herrnhut community. Specifically, we will look at new methods of preaching: to save souls, for discipleship, outside the church, and to the poor and marginalized; new organizational structures: societies, classes, and bands; new ways of leadership selection and training, especially the role of women; and finally, new songs to sing. Hymnal theology is then discussed in more depth before considering the spread of Methodism in America.

Ministry in Britain

New Methods of Preaching

George Whitefield, Wesley's friend and a member of the Holy Club at Oxford University, began open-air preaching in 1739. After he was denied access to the Anglican pulpits, Whitefield began preaching to some one hundred coal miners at Kingswood near Bristol, reintroducing the subject of hell with marked success. After a week of continuous preaching, he had attracted an audience of over ten thousand. As Whitefield was leaving for Savannah, Georgia, to encourage the religious enthusiasm that had broken out there, he invited John Wesley to take his place in open-air evangelism on Hannam Mount in Bristol.

Into the growing industrial port-city of Bristol, with its squalid and spiritually neglected poor, came this Oxford-trained and politically conservative Anglican rector, who challenged the strict religious conventions by preaching

---

The congregations are very large and serious, and I have scarce preached this time amongst them without seeing a stirring amongst the dry bones.

George Whitefield (1978, 428)

---

not on a Sunday and not in a church. What Wesley did was revolutionary, yet not without inner turmoil. Writing in his journal of Saturday, March 31, 1739, he mused:

> In the evening, I reached Bristol, and met Mr. Whitefield there. I could scarcely reconcile myself at first to this strange way of preaching in the fields, of which he set me an example on Sunday; having been all my life (till very lately) so tenacious of every point relating to decency and order, that I should have thought the saving of souls almost a sin, if it had not been done in a church. (1938, 2:171)

Wesley saw God's blessing in awakening people through this new method. He reluctantly accepted the invitation since many more people came to hear him preach outside than attended in any church building. He continued in his journal of Monday, April 2, 1739:

> At four in the afternoon, I submitted to be more vile, and proclaimed in the highways the glad tidings of salvation, speaking from a little eminence in a ground adjoining to the city, to about three thousand people. The scripture on which I spoke was this (is it possible any one should be ignorant that it is fulfilled in every true minister of Christ?), "The Spirit of the Lord is upon Me, because He hath anointed Me to preach the gospel to the poor. He hath sent Me to heal the broken-hearted; to preach deliverance to the captives, and recovery of sight to the blind; to set at liberty them that are bruised, to proclaim the acceptable year of the Lord." (1938, 2:172–73)

At this stage, Wesley saw himself not as a dissenter but as one with the established church: "We look upon ourselves, not as the authors or ringleaders of a particular sect or party—it is the farthest thing from our thoughts—but as messengers of God, to those who are Christians in name but heathens in heart and life, to call them back to that from which they are fallen, to real, genuine Christianity" (Shelley 1982, 359).

At Bristol, Thomas Maxwell, an untrained layperson, preached in a meeting when the ordained Anglican preacher failed to come. This event challenged

Wesley's concept of ordination. The declaration of his mother, Susanna, that lay preachers were God's design moved her son to establish his own preachers. After John heard Maxwell, he became Wesley's first lay preacher in England and consequently was imprisoned and persecuted many times for his witness. Thirty-three years later, John still struggled with these innovations. He wrote in his journal, "To this day field preaching is a cross to me. But I know my commission and see no other way of 'preaching the gospel to every creature'" (September 6, 1772, in Doughty 1955, 51). Wesley never intended to form a church separate from the Church of England, but the Anglican Church excommunicated him because he ordained preachers of his own volition.

PREACHING TO SAVE SOULS

For Wesley, the paramount work of God was the conversion of the lost from sin to holiness. From the very beginning, he "had no view but to convince those who would hear what true Christianity was and to persuade them to embrace it" (Wesley 1831b, 104). This was a practical religion that "increased the life of God in the souls of men" (1831b, 179). As late as 1772 he wrote to his brother Charles, "Your business, as well as mine, is to save souls. . . . I think every day lost, which is not (mainly at least) employed in this thing" (1831b, 674). Moreover, to his preachers he gave the following instructions: "You have nothing to do but to save souls. Therefore, spend and be spent in this work. . . . It is not your business to preach so many times, and to take care of this or that society; but to save as many souls as you can; to bring as many sinners as you possibly can to repentance, and with all your power to build them up in that holiness without which they cannot see the Lord" (1831b, 219).

PREACHING FOR DISCIPLESHIP

In Wesley's preaching, he proclaimed a personal assurance of salvation and sanctification and an experience of the atoning work of Christ available to everyone who believed (Baker 1941, 29). Regarding the Christian walk, Wesley stated, "Whatever good he hath done from that hour when he first believes in God through Christ, faith does not find but bring. This is the fruit of faith. First the tree is good and then the fruit is good also" (Outler 1964, 205). The Methodists acknowledged the work of the Holy Spirit in the lives of the new converts, keenly observing whether an outward behavioral change was a genuine proof of an inward transformation. These questions of conversion became more important as the movement began to shift from the societies to the streets and fields.

Wesley believed in both numerical growth and depth of discipleship. He contended that the latter resulted in a growth of numbers since followers of

Christ would become growing members of a class and society. He believed that the test of a church's effectiveness in the gospel is the number of sinners who convert to Christ and continue in the faith, living changed lives. Wesley saw his mission holistically: a passion to win souls for Christ, coupled with a burning desire to see the converts grow in maturity.

The early Methodist mission consisted of awakening to God those outside the church, mostly by field preaching. Within the small groups of the church ("classes"), the ministers taught the new converts about Christ's justification and exhorted them to live in good works. The Methodist experience was that if the leaders did not place the believers in such classes, they "fell asleep" again, and their hearts became hardened to the gospel. In these accountability groups, the Christian faith had a better opportunity to grow and develop. The guiding principle was "preach in as many places as you can. Start as many classes as you can. Do not preach without starting new classes" (Hunter 1987, 119).

This tactic helps to explain why there is no record that Wesley ever invited people to accept Jesus Christ as their Savior in his field preaching. He would often engage in conversation after the preaching and invite people to join a class that would meet that evening. In these classes people mainly experienced the grace of God and discovered the gift of faith to follow Christ. Encouraging searching souls to attend a class was an essential evangelism strategy. Instead of the evangelist determining the occasion and time that a person received salvation, early Methodism stressed the need for people to join a small group in the church where, in God's timing, they were discipled in the Lord Jesus.

Preaching outside the Church

The early Methodists witnessed in the fields and streets and often in marketplaces and graveyards. Graveyards were acoustically ideal for open-air evangelism; Wesley could use the tombstones as a podium and the church building as a background amplifier. On June 6, 1742, he went to his hometown of Epworth to preach. The local curate did not allow him to speak in the church, so, Wesley explained, "According at six I came, and found such a congregation as I believe Epworth never saw before. I stood near the east end of the church, upon my father's tombstone and cried, 'The kingdom of heaven is not meat and drink; but righteousness, and peace, and joy in the Holy Ghost'" (Idle 1986, 154).

Market squares surrounded by buildings served as even better pulpits, with their center stages from which the preacher could speak. Wesley wrote in his journal on April 27, 1761: "I preached at eight in the marketplace. . . . The congregation, when I began, consisted of one woman, two boys, and three or four girls, but in a quarter-of-an-hour we had most of the town" (Idle 1986, 154).

Preaching to the Poor and Marginalized

The strategy of the Methodist preachers was to preach anywhere and everywhere and to help everyone regardless of class. The Methodist ministers not only preached the gospel but also served the poor, prisoners, widows, orphans, and slaves. At Bristol, for example, they established their first schools for orphans and children of the poor. Wesley recorded in his journal on September 18, 1738: "On Monday I rejoiced to meet with our little Society, which now consisted of thirty-two persons. The next day I went to the condemned felons in Newgate, and offered them free salvation" (Wesley 1940, 81). On December 24, 1760, twenty-two years later, Wesley commented: "I visited the sick. How much better is it to carry the relief to the poor, than to send it! And that both for our own sake and theirs. For theirs, as it is so much more comfortable to them, and as we may assist them in spirituals as well as temporals; and for our own as it is far more apt to soften our heart, and to make us naturally care for each other" (Idle 1986, 208).

Kenneth Carder has summarized Wesley's effectiveness with the powerless: "The poor and marginalized heard his sermon gladly. Those who responded were gathered into class meetings where they were nurtured, admonished, and held accountable" (1992, 105).

New Organizational Structures

Wesley was not convinced that preaching alone was sufficient for Christian growth. For those won to Christ through preaching, he believed that it was necessary to provide nurturing structures. In a time of field preaching and revival, he felt responsible to bring the new convert to Christian maturity within a community. "Through the proclamation of God's grace and . . . the nurture by communities of grace, people experienced forgiveness, dignity, self-worth, reconciliation, and transformation. Wesley's message, plus the nurture experienced in small groups were more important than the style of his preaching" (Heitzenrater 1995, 94).

In 1738 Wesley visited Zinzendorf and the Moravian settlements in Saxony, where he witnessed the Pietistic communities divided into small groups called bands. He observed the gathering of believers into small voluntary societies for mutual discipline, and saw that fellowship was essential to the continuing growth of the believer. Upon returning to London, he quickly adapted the Moravian structural model within his own Christian community (Henderson 1997, 52; Snyder 1980, 119). In a letter to the Herrnhut community, John Wesley wrote:

> Glory be to God . . . for His unspeakable gift for giving me to be an eyewitness of your faith. . . . We are endeavoring here also, by the grace, which is given

233

us, to be followers of you, as ye are of Christ. Fourteen were added to us since our return, so that we have now eight bands of men, consisting of fifty-six persons. . . . But there are many others who only wait till we have leisure to instruct them how they may most effectually build up one another in the faith and love of Him who gave Himself for them. (Jay 1987, 38)

The Methodist leader understood three principles regarding the relationship between Christian life and church structure. First, Christian growth is difficult without proper structures that provide discipleship. Second, for growth to take place the nurture structures need to address not only the cognitive aspects of the Christian life but also the behavioral ones. Third, the church needs to provide a variety of nurture structures depending on the maturity of the believer.

SOCIETIES, CLASSES, AND BANDS

Members of early Methodist congregations who submitted to the General Rules formed societies. Composed by Wesley in 1784, the rules were a requirement of continuation in societies and shaped the philosophy of Methodist life. The societies then divided into classes for encouragement, guidance, and accountability aimed at reforming past detrimental lifestyle patterns. The only requirement for admittance into a class meeting was the desire to "flee from the wrath to come and to be saved from sin" (Broholm 1977, 353). Class meetings considered three categories of behavior: prohibitions, exhortations or positive behaviors, and the maintenance of helpful practices. After six years of this Methodist habit, the results were visible, since before the formation of classes, the converts showed little sense of community, love, or Christian piety. Wesley commented on this change:

> Many now happily experienced that Christian fellowship of which they had not so much as an idea before. They began to "bear one another's burdens," and naturally to "care for each other." As they had daily a more intimate acquaintance with, so they had more endeared affection for, each other. And "speaking the truth in love, they grew up into Him in all things who is the Head, even Christ." (Wesley [1748] 1996, 254)

Further division of classes formed bands to provide opportunity for not only life transformation but also heart change. The band was for those who desired to share their struggles more intimately, especially regarding temptations and sins. Members divided into small groups of five or six—organized by gender, age, and marital status—to foster openness. In such an intimate setting, the members sought to unfold their attitudes, intentions, and affections before Christ. "Advice or reproof was given as need required, quarrels made up, misunderstandings removed: And after an hour or two spent in this labour of love, they concluded with prayer and thanksgiving" (Wesley [1748] 1996, 253–54). Wesley's use of bands shows a holistic understanding of Christian growth that involved right theology, transformed behavior, and inner purity.

An additional development of the movement's structure was the placement of people according to their readiness. The leadership, for instance, consigned people who were simply curious about religious matters into a trial band. If they experienced justifying grace through conversion to Christ, they progressed to the band meetings. Here the believers learned to grow as disciples. Next came the select band, where the believer sincerely desired sanctification to reach "spiritual adulthood." These men and women were the models of holiness in the community and became the pool for leadership selection and training for the classes. In turn, the leaders of the classes became the spiritual overseers of the society (Albin 2003, 42).

These multileveled nurture structures provided different avenues for growth, which matched the spiritual state and commitment of the person. The structures also provided a challenge for people to grow to the next level and continue in their spiritual walk. D. L. Moody acknowledged that "Methodist class-meetings are the best institutions for training converts the world ever saw" (Henderson 1997, 93). These novel ecclesiastical structures provided flexibility for new ways of leadership selection and training.

New Ways of Leadership Selection and Training

Wesley used lay preachers to spread the gospel in England, Scotland, Wales, and Ireland. Preachers were usually without any ministerial training and with little or no formal education. They sensed the call of God to proclaim Christ's love, and training occurred within the movement. Instructions for ministers included "reading constantly, some part of every day: regularly, all the Bible in order; carefully, with Mr. Wesley's notes; seriously, prayer before and after; fruitfully, immediately practicing what you learned there" (Coke 1784, 16).

Wesley's prime intention for his ministers was that they would glorify God and save souls from eternal death. These two objectives were to replace in his workers the pursuit of any love of the world, money, pleasure, or ambition. This criterion guided the movement into the future and also paved the way for effective leadership selection and training.

ROLE OF WOMEN

In the early Methodist movement, women also preached the gospel, which led to the conversion of many of their gender. In 1763 Sarah Crosby, Sarah Ryan, and Mary Bosanquet established a school and orphanage at Leytonstone, Essex, and used their home for Methodist activities. At one of these gatherings Crosby preached to over two hundred people when the male preacher

An Imagined Dialogue by a Methodist Itinerant Preacher in 1808

Q. Who is that up to his arms in snow?

A. A Methodist preacher.

Q. Who is that in a snug study by his warm fire?

A. The honorable settled preacher.

Q. What is the Methodist preacher doing?

A. Making his way to his appointment, where he hopes to call sinners to repentance.

Q. What is the settled minister doing?

A. Hunting his library over, selecting portions and adding, perhaps, some of his own thoughts, and writing out a sermon to read over to the people next Sabbath.

Q. Which of them looks most like a lazy man; and which gets the most money—the most reproaches, or follows the example of Christ and the Apostles nearest in traveling, suffering, preaching, self-denyings, watchings, fastings, and winning souls to Christ?

George Claude Baker (1941, 12)

Reflection and Discussion

1. Do you consider the Methodist minister's appraisal a fair one? Why or why not?

2. Can Christians be too comfortable in their approach to ministry? How do you determine this?

failed to show. Afterward she said, "I do not think it wrong for women to speak in public provided they speak by the Spirit of God" (Shiman 1992, 22). Wesley responded to Crosby's initiative in a letter: "Pray in private or public as much as you can. Even in public, you may properly enough intermix short exhortations with prayer. But keep as far from what is called preaching as you can. Therefore, never take a text; never speak in a continued discourse without some break, about four or five minutes. Tell the people, 'We shall have another prayer meeting at such a time and place'" (Heitzenrater 1995, 236).

In 1771 one of the Methodist preachers objected to Bosanquet and Crosby preaching. Bosanquet wrote a letter to Wesley outlining the objections and the answer to each one. In doing so, she illustrated her ability in biblical interpretation and asked for an equal opportunity with men. She wrote, "I do not believe every woman is called to speak publicly, no more than every man to be a Methodist preacher, yet some have an extraordinary call to it, and woe be to them if they obey it not" (Heitzenrater 1995, 247).

In the midst of eighteenth-century prejudices against women, Wesley accepted the argument of "extraordinary call" and privately gave permission to certain women preachers. Diana Thomas of Kingston, for example, was an early Methodist preacher who joined a society and actively contributed to its membership and influence. Her diary shows a woman regularly traveling to preach at various Sunday appointments (Redwood 1998, 126–27). Although Wesley recognized the necessity of education for women and gave them leadership roles, he never publicly recognized their position as preachers.

New Songs to Sing

New methods of preaching, new organizational structures, and new ways of leadership selection and training, coupled with new spiritual dynamics, allowed the gospel to penetrate British society as never before. The first Methodist gathering was in a meeting room at Bristol in 1739, where as a part of the service the attendees sang a hymn. This was revolutionary, since in the Anglican churches people only ever sang metrical versions of the psalms. The

---

The greatest monument to evangelical taste is the hymnody of John Wesley's brother Charles. Disciplined emotion, didactic purpose, clarity, and succinctness are qualities for which he is preeminent among hymn writers. A single line can exhibit all his traits: "Impassive he suffers, immortal he dies." Charles Wesley turned contemporary literary idiom into a powerful vehicle for revival.

David W. Bebbington (1993, 27)

---

congregations usually did not have individual hymnals, and the leader would sing aloud a line or two for the people to repeat.

Charles Wesley preached through his hymns and attempted to reform the contemporary psalm-singing practices. He believed that hymns could provide congregations with theological teaching that was both biblical and inspirational, enriching people's personal faith as they sang. Over a period of fifty-seven years, he composed an average of three hymns per week, and of his 8,989 religious poems, some 6,500 were hymns. Among the favorites of Methodists were "And Can It Be?" and "O, for a Thousand Tongues to Sing!" Because of its popularity and easy access, the hymnody provided a vehicle of transmission for the Wesleyan message to other cultures and settings in such diverse social milieus as New England camp meetings and British industrial cities (Hempton 2005, 50–68, 78–82).

Hymnal Theology

Though Charles wrote his poetry on many different theological topics, he kept returning to God's free grace and boundless atonement. The most prominent theological view at the time was Calvinistic, as expressed in the hymns of Isaac Watts. He could thank God for his own salvation yet offered none for others. The Wesleys, on the other hand, believed in the view of sixteenth-century Dutch theologian Jacobus Arminius that a person could choose whether to receive God's free grace offered to all humanity. Thus the believer was responsible to proclaim the good news for people to accept this salvation. This emphasis on God's love and favor was a positive message, bringing complete forgiveness and unlimited love to a generation bound by guilt and condemnation. Charles, along with his brother John, therefore, was a theological polemicist who wrote his polemics into his songs. In 1741 he poignantly wrote a fifteen-stanza hymn titled "The Horrible Decree" in opposition to the Calvinist doctrine of limited atonement. The first stanza reads:

> Ah! gentle, gracious Dove;
> And art Thou grieved in me,
> That sinners should restrain Thy love,
> And say, "It is not free:
> It is not free for *all*;
> The *most* Thou *passest by*,
> And mockest with a fruitless call
> Whom Thou hast doom'd to die."
> Defend Thy mercy's cause,
> Lift up the standard of Thy cross,
> Draw all men unto Thee. (Tyson 1989, 304–5)

In summation, Mark Noll affirms, Charles Wesley became "the greatest hymn-writer in the history of the [English] language . . . who made the hymn into the most powerful engine of Britain's eighteenth-century evangelical awakening" (1997, 221).

Spread of Methodism in America

The evangelical awakening of Methodism grew so rapidly that by 1790 there were some 71,568 members in Great Britain, many more "adherents," and thousands who had died and were therefore no longer included in the statistics. By the same year, American Methodism had grown to similar numbers, and within decades the movement had spread to over ninety countries, with millions of members. In the midst of this expansion, Wesley was a cautious advocate of cross-cultural mission. He believed that true revival began in the hearts of people and would naturally flow out to touch the world. A genuine heart change would result in behavioral transformation, which in turn would affect society. The need was first a reviving of the church in England that would then spread across Europe and the world (Campbell 1992, 46, 56).

When John Wesley sent his first missionaries to North America in 1769, there were only a few scattered classes of Methodists and their preachers. Four years later, the first American Methodist conference in Philadelphia registered 1,160 members in society, and by the time of its official formation at Baltimore in 1784, the Methodist Episcopal Church had 14,988 members in society, 84 itinerant preachers, and hundreds of local preachers. Within six years, those numbers had more than quadrupled to 57,631 members in society and 227 preachers. The influence of Methodism in America was even greater than these figures would indicate since they counted only those adherents who strictly followed the disciplines as members of a society. At its formation, the movement had nearly 200,000 followers (Boswell 1903, 22).

In the same year as Methodism's official formation in America, Wesley co-appointed Thomas Coke and Francis Asbury as the first superintendents of the Methodist Episcopal Church. In 1792 Coke began to send missionaries financed from his own funds to the West Indies, Sierra Leone, Nova Scotia, Ireland, and France. During the Napoleonic Wars, he organized Methodist missionaries to work among the seventy thousand French prisoners in England. On the other hand, Asbury duplicated Wesley's leadership model in America. Reminiscent of the founder, he wrote, "My horse trots stiff, and no wonder, as I have ridden him, upon an average, five thousand miles a year for the last five years successively" (A. Stevens 1867, 341).

Frontier Leadership Styles and Organizational Patterns

During the late eighteenth century, the vast majority of the American population lived in rural areas. Only 3 percent of the people lived in cities of eight thousand or more. After the Revolutionary War, there was migration to the North and the South, and especially the West, with the population increasing every decade by over 30 percent. Together with this population growth and dispersion, the demands and stresses of the war left a spiritual vacuum in the country (Barclay 1949, 102–3).

The depressed religious state of the country inspired the Methodists to proclaim Christ's good news of salvation and sanctification. Yet, with the growing population so dispersed throughout the vast territory of the American colonies, it was a formidable missional challenge. Methodism's structure of accountability, with its itinerant preachers and lay ministries, however, met the needs of this difficult American environment. These new models of itinerant ministry were a continuation of what the British Great Awakening introduced, with its elastic parish and congregational boundaries.

Methodism spread rapidly so that the societies were multiplying at a faster rate than the availability of preachers. To remedy this situation, societies within a region formed circuits whereby preachers began to travel around a set geographical area ministering at various locations. In this way, Methodism was

"And Can It Be?"

And can it be that I should gain
An int'rest in the Savior's blood?
Died He for me, who caused His
pain?
For me, who Him to death
pursued?
Amazing love! how can it be
That Thou, my God, should die
for me?

Refrain:
Amazing love! how can it be
That Thou, my God, should die
for me!

'Tis mystery all! Th' Immortal
dies!
Who can explore His strange
design?
In vain the firstborn seraph tries
To sound the depths of love
divine!
'Tis mercy all! let earth adore,
Let angel minds inquire no more.
(Refrain)

He left His Father's throne above,
So free, so infinite His grace;
Emptied Himself of all but love,
And bled for Adam's helpless
race;
'Tis mercy all, immense and free;
For, O my God, it found out me.
(Refrain)

Long my imprisoned spirit lay
Fast bound in sin and nature's
night;
Thine eye diffused a quick'ning
ray,
I woke, the dungeon flamed with
light;
My chains fell off, my heart was
free;
I rose, went forth and followed
Thee. (Refrain)

No condemnation now I dread;
Jesus, and all in Him is mine!
Alive in Him, my living Head,
And clothed in righteousness
divine,
Bold I approach th'eternal
throne,
And claim the crown, through
Christ my own. (Refrain)

Charles Wesley (in McGrath 1999, 166)

Reflection and Discussion

1. Identify the theological progression of the hymn as it moves verse by verse.
2. Recognize the likely biblical allusions that informed Charles Wesley's words and concepts in this hymn.
3. What does Wesley want us to believe because of singing the hymn?
4. Having sung the hymn, what does Wesley want us to do?

able to meet the pastoral needs of the scattered communities. Some circuits were as long as six hundred miles, with preachers using canoes to navigate the miles of rivers and either walking or riding on horseback to travel the lonely countryside. Circuit riders were promoted through the ranks of the organization from class member to class leader, to local preacher and circuit rider on trial, and then to a fully recognized circuit rider with "full connection."

The district superintendent, or presiding elder, was responsible for training the circuit preacher while they traveled, since these itinerant exhorters often had little or no education, and training was on the job. This informal mode of training had Wesley's model of self-education as its goal. The circuit preacher would spend several hours each day in the study of theology, church history, and biblical languages. This method proved successful as it allowed for training the leadership without taking them away from the growing demands of the people (Norwood 1974, 341–50).

Numbers of circuits then grouped to form a district. The Methodist structure was one of tight accountability, with bishops traveling the country, district superintendents covering the districts, preachers traveling the circuits, local pastors over congregations and societies, and class leaders meeting weekly with their flock. This method provided individual pastoral care for a dispersed and growing frontier population with a sense of belonging to something bigger than their families and church congregation. In 1820, for example, the population of Kentucky was 563,317, with 47,730 church members. Of that number, there were 21,000 Methodists, 21,000 Baptists, 2,700 Presbyterians, and 1,000 Cumberland Presbyterians.

Conclusion

Methodism started as a holiness movement within British Anglicanism, and in its growth adapted ideas from the Moravians to meet the discovered needs of the new English industrialism. The Methodists used the gospel in a way that quickly gave up inherited traditions of the church and experimented with new methods that working-class people could embrace. They had the ability to combine the traditional Protestant message with a willingness to be fashioned by the changing sociopolitical-cultural settings of their generation. In simpler terms, Methodism's mobility and adaptability in using societies and class meetings with street preaching and its army of traveling preachers allowed the movement to reach people whom the established church had neglected.

These practices, along with the reinforcement of traditional Reformation theology, have continued to influence Protestant life. In a century of great financial, political, and ideological flux, the Wesleys held firm to the belief that the gracious salvation of God proclaimed through the divine Scriptures is through faith in Christ Jesus alone. God's free grace saves sinners. In addition, through John Wesley's enlarged spiritual horizon, he provided a vehicle of opportunity for the adherents of Methodism to share their message from the British Isles to the far corners of the world, such as Antigua, Newfoundland, the West Indies, and America.

The Influence of Wesleyan Hymnody

Charles, the younger Wesley, influenced the musical and literary styles of hymnody. Contemporary songs commonly used three patterns of syllables per line (or meters), and Charles expanded the metric patterns to include over thirty varieties. Unlike Isaac Watts, who contended that a hymn was not a poem, Charles believed that the hymn should be poetic and raise the people to a new understanding, with a balance of theology and personal experience encouraging the singer to embrace the words. John, his older brother, said of his hymn writing, "In these hymns there is no doggerel; no botches; nothing put in to patch up the rhyme; no feeble expletives. There is nothing turgid or bombast, on the one hand, or low and creeping, on the other. Here are no words without meaning. Here are the purity, the strength, and the elegance of the English language; and, at the same time, the utmost simplicity, and plainness suited to every capacity" (Wesley 1831a, 325).

Both John and Charles used various sources for their musical inspiration—such as classical and popular melodies, the German chorale, and folk tunes. The purpose of the tune was to highlight the words and to encourage full participation of the congregation with reverence. While Charles focused on composing hymns, John became the main editor and publisher; he was especially vigilant in maintaining theological accuracy. In the preface to their 1780 hymnal, he wrote, "In what other publication of this time have you so full and distinct an account of scriptural Christianity? Such a declaration of the heights and depths of religion, speculative and practical? So strong cautions against the most plausible errors? And so clear directions for making our calling and election sure; for perfecting holiness in the fear of God?" (1876, 529–30).

From 1741 to 1791, John Wesley published a series of thirty thematic hymn tracts, which were eventually collected and organized along theological lines in 1780 and called *A Collection of Hymns for the Use of the People Called Methodists*. The first joint hymnal by the Wesley brothers, *Hymns and Sacred Poems*, published in 1739, omitted "Jesus, Lover of My Soul," since John was disturbed by the intimate language, though it did appear in the next hymnal a year later. Over the next forty-seven years, the Wesleys produced some sixty-four hymnals, with thirty-six having only hymns composed by the brothers.

Reflection and Discussion

1. How did Charles Wesley influence the musical and literary styles of hymnody?
2. How did John and Charles Wesley shape the direction of the Wesleyan faith through their hymns?

12

The Great Century
of Protestant Missions,
Part I

Missions historian Kenneth Scott Latourette coined the term "the Great Century" in his magisterial work, *A History of the Expansion of Christianity*. He dated the "Great Century" from 1800 to 1914. In this volume we are dating the Great Century from 1792 until 1910. Thus the Great Century began with William Carey's famous sermon in England and ended at the World Missionary Conference in Edinburgh, Scotland, in 1910.

Truly, this proved to be a great period of progress for Protestant missions. When the century began, there were only a few Moravian missionaries serving in a few countries. By the end of the period, thousands of missionaries were proclaiming the gospel all over the world, and two hundred thousand people attended the Ecumenical Missionary Conference in New York City.

The nineteenth century was great for several reasons. First, it was great because of *great missionaries*. Our hearts thrill to read the stories of great missionary pioneers such as William Carey and Adoniram Judson. Second, the sacrifices and service of these great pioneers inspired *great enthusiasm*. In this chapter, we will consider how missionary societies came into being and how the great missions conferences came to be held. Third, the century witnessed *great progress* in missions, both in the number of missionaries and in the number of fields served. Finally, *great movements* marked this century. During the nineteenth century, indigenous missions, "faith" missions, female missions, and the Student Volunteer Movement all developed. These movements have affected how we do missions today. The nineteenth century signaled the beginning of the modern missions movement.

General Factors Affecting Modern Missions

No historical movement originates in a vacuum. Certainly, that was true of the modern missions movement as well. Several general factors affected the development of missions in the nineteenth century. The first was *world exploration*. The Age of Exploration saw European explorers sail all over the earth. The accounts of their voyages excited the imagination of the reading public. Beyond that, their discoveries enlarged the geographical understanding of Europeans, informing them of the existence of peoples and places previously unknown. William Carey read Captain Cook's narrative of his voyages, and that reading piqued his interest in foreign lands. It also deepened his concern for the spiritual condition of the peoples who inhabited those lands.

World trade affected the development of the modern missions movement. Traders and merchants followed the explorers all over the world. As they established trading posts and communities, the merchants asked for chaplains and pastors to attend to their spiritual needs. Many of these chaplains developed an interest in the indigenous people and made efforts to communicate the gospel to them. Beyond this, as international trade developed, more merchant ships plied the oceans. These ships provided missionaries with a means of transportation that did not exist previously.

Improved education played a part in the progress of missions. Protestantism emphasized both Bible study and the priesthood of the believer. Pastors encouraged their congregations to read the Bible. This prompted the development of schools that taught children to read. As literacy flourished, so did publishing. Europeans demonstrated a keen interest in world exploration and geography, so publishers produced books on brave explorers and exotic lands. This excited the interest of Christians, who eventually became concerned about the spiritual condition of the peoples who inhabited those strange new lands.

The development of *humanitarianism* affected missions significantly. Most Europeans believed that God had blessed them with an advanced civilization. They felt a responsibility to share the blessings of this civilization with all the peoples of the earth.

Thus, the missionaries of the Great Century often embarked for the mission field committed to communicating the gospel of Christ and civilizing the "natives" to whom they ministered. This attitude of cultural superiority seems inappropriate today, but two hundred years ago it seemed right. The missionaries did not think of themselves as imposing an alien culture on reluctant recipients; they saw themselves as sharing the blessings of Western civilization with people who needed them desperately. These blessings included education, medicine, and sanitation.

A theological movement called *modified Calvinism* paved the way for modern missions. Before the time of William Carey, many Protestants embraced a form of Calvinism that emphasized the sovereignty of God so strongly that they rejected any human effort in evangelism. This view is sometimes called hyper-Calvinism. Andrew Fuller, a Baptist pastor in England, rejected this view and introduced a theology that called on Christians to work to bring people to Christ. Fuller was William Carey's mentor, and he taught this theology to Carey. For his part, William Carey applied the theology to missions and worked out its implications for world evangelization.

The Evangelical Revival in England (called the First Great Awakening in North America) prepared the way spiritually for the modern missions movement. As we saw in the previous chapter, in 1738 John Wesley was born again in a small Moravian chapel in Aldersgate, London. In 1739 he began an itinerant preaching ministry that led to a great revival in the British Isles. His work along with that of his brother Charles and the "Great Itinerant," George Whitefield, raised the spiritual temperature of both England and North America.

Colonialism affected modern missions in several positive ways. The movement of the European colonizers into new lands encouraged missionaries to follow them. Beyond that, colonial authorities provided protection for missionaries to work in lands where they could not previously. Third, colonial officials often expedited the work of missionaries, especially later in the Great Century. This symbiotic relationship is seen in the career of David Livingstone, who began his career as a missionary and ended it as a British consul in Africa. Negatively, in many countries the church became identified with the colonial power. When the colony achieved independence, the new government began to restrict the churches and the activities of missionaries.

As you can see, just as Jesus was born "when the set time had fully come" (Gal. 4:4), in the same way many factors made the nineteenth century ripe for the development of Protestant missions. Great missionaries, moved by the Holy Spirit, seized the opportunity to carry the gospel throughout the world.

The Birth of Modern Missions

The modern missions movement began with William Carey, who is rightly called *the father of modern missions*. William Carey was not the first Protestant missionary, but his example and writings inspired Christians of Great Britain and North America to engage in missions.

William Carey's Life

William Carey (1761–1834) was born and raised in England. Christened into the Anglican Church, he became a Baptist through the influence of Andrew Fuller. Carey received only a few years of formal education, but he possessed

Portrait of David Brainerd (1718–1747)

David Brainerd, a native of Connecticut, enrolled at Yale College to prepare for the ministry. He responded enthusiastically to the preachers of the First Great Awakening: George Whitefield, Gilbert Tennent, and James Davenport. His enthusiasm for the Awakening led to his expulsion from Yale. He then gave himself to itinerant preaching. Eventually, he became a missionary to the Native Americans, and he served in that capacity from 1743 to 1747. During those years, he kept a diary, in which he recorded his experiences and feelings. He suffered from tuberculosis throughout his adult life, and in 1747 he went to the home of Jonathan Edwards, his mentor and the father of his fiancée. Despite the tender care of his beloved Jerusha, David died in 1747.

Jonathan Edwards edited Brainerd's diary and published it as *An Account of the Life of the Late Reverend Mr. David Brainerd.* This book soon became a devotional classic. Both William Carey and Henry Martyn read it and made Brainerd's passion for Christ and missions their own.

a keen and inquiring mind. He taught himself to read Latin, Greek, Hebrew, French, and Dutch. He worked as a cobbler and as a teacher to support his family. He also served as the pastor of a small Baptist church. He read voraciously, and Captain Cook's *Voyages around the World* and Jonathan Edwards's *Life and Diary of David Brainerd* impressed the world's spiritual needs on him.

In 1792 Carey published his famous pamphlet *An Enquiry into the Obligation of Christians to Use Means for the Conversion of the Heathen.* The pamphlet enjoyed wide circulation, even though the author was unknown. Later the same year, Carey preached at a meeting of the Northampton Baptist Association. He based his sermon on Isaiah 54:2–3 and challenged the

---

After hearing an account of the spiritual needs of India, the secretary of the meeting remarked: "There is a gold mine in India, but it seems almost as deep as the center of the earth. Who will venture to explore it?"

"I will venture to go down," said [William] Carey, "but remember that you must hold the ropes."

www.wholesomewords.org/missions/msquotes.html

---

congregation to "expect great things from God; attempt great things for God." Carey's sermon moved the Baptist ministers at the meeting, and in October

Bible Translation

Bible translation has been a notable characteristic of Protestant missions from its inception until the present. In this era, Roman Catholic missionaries felt no compulsion to translate the Bible because they used the Latin Vulgate all over the world. Protestant missionaries took an entirely different approach due to their belief in the priesthood of the believer. The doctrine of the priesthood of the believer emphasizes the ability and responsibility of believers to read and interpret the Bible for themselves under the guidance of the Holy Spirit. Protestant missionaries, therefore, emphasized personal Bible study as a basic devotional discipline for all Christians. This study required two things: literacy and a Bible to read. Thus Protestant missionaries, from the time of the Moravians, have emphasized translating the Bible into the language of the people. William Carey, Adoniram Judson, Robert Morrison, and many others gave years of their lives to translating the Bible into the vernaculars of their peoples. William Carey translated the Bible, or part of it, into thirty-five different languages. No one has ever equaled his output, but thousands of missionaries today follow his example and labor to translate the Bible into the languages of the world.

Reflection and Discussion

1. Today, about two thousand language groups still do not have the Bible in their language. One question that faces Bible translators is whether to translate the Bible into the languages of people groups with limited populations. Will those languages survive, or will the language disappear as the people abandon the language for the regional language? What would you need to know before choosing to translate a Bible into an "endangered" language?

1792 they organized the Particular Baptist Society for Propagating the Gospel among the Heathen (later known as the Baptist Missionary Society).

The new missionary society chose John Thomas and William Carey as their first missionaries and raised money to send them to India. In 1793 Carey and his family sailed for India. There they faced many hardships: financial problems, illness, and opposition by the British East India Company, which controlled much of India. Carey had a gift for languages, and he soon learned to preach in the Bengali language, but he saw little response to his preaching. He worked in India for seven years before he made his first convert. Carey also struggled with family problems. His young son Peter died of fever, and his wife, Dorothy, became insane. Eventually, Dorothy had to be kept in a locked room, lest she injure herself or William.

Carey encouraged the missionary society to send reinforcements, and in 1799 Joshua and Hannah Marshman and William Ward arrived to help him. They moved to the Danish-controlled city of Serampore and established a mission station there. The Danish governor favored the missionaries and aided their work. Thus the famous Serampore Trio began their ministry. Hannah Marshman provided much-needed motherly guidance for Carey's sons. William Ward was a trained printer, so William Carey purchased a printing press and began to devote his time to Bible translation. Before he died, Carey had translated all or part of the Bible into thirty-five different languages. The trio planted several churches and established several schools. In 1819 they founded Serampore College to train Indian pastors.

SIDEBAR 12.3

The Serampore Trio

Many casual students of missions history know about William Carey. In contrast, few could identify William Ward and Joshua Marshman, yet they were key persons in William Carey's success. Before they arrived to help him in 1799, Carey struggled. Their assistance and wise counsel enabled Carey to achieve great things. If he were alive today, he would give God the glory and share the credit with his valued coworkers.

Ward was a printer, and he printed the Bible translations, grammars, and gospel literature that Carey wrote. Marshman was a teacher, and he led in the founding of schools. His wife, Hannah, took Carey's unruly children in hand and provided a stable home life for them. They lived together communally in a compound in Serampore, pooling their resources and making decisions as a team.

In 1804 they drew up the Serampore Covenant, which laid out the core values that would guide their team.

- to set an infinite value on the souls of humanity
- to acquaint themselves with the snares that hold the minds of the people
- to abstain from whatever deepens India's prejudice against the gospel

- to watch for every chance of doing the people good
- to preach "Christ crucified" as the grand means of salvation
- to esteem and treat Indians always as their equals
- to guard and build up the "hosts that may be gathered"
- to cultivate the Indians' spiritual gifts, ever pressing on them their missionary obligation, since only Indians can win India to Christ
- to labor unceasingly in biblical translation
- to be instant in the nurture of personal religion
- to give themselves without reserve to the cause, not counting even the clothes they wear as their own

Reflection and Discussion

1. Team ministry is a popular approach to missionary staffing today. What would happen if all modern missionary teams modeled themselves after the Serampore Trio?
2. In what ways are the principles of the covenant relevant to missions today?
3. In what ways are the principles of the covenant no longer relevant to missions?

William Carey's strategy was remarkably advanced for his time, especially as he had few examples to emulate. He believed that missionaries should

- carefully study the local language and culture;
- engage in widespread preaching;
- translate the Bible into the languages of the people;
- establish local churches as quickly as possible; and
- train national pastors and turn the churches over to them.

His strategy became a model for the Protestant missionaries who followed in his footsteps.

Historians have noted several keys to William Carey's success. First, he demonstrated an appreciation for his predecessors. He often mentioned the example of the Moravians and the dedication of David Brainerd. Second, he maintained a global view of missions. He encouraged Adoniram Judson to go to Burma so that the Burmese could hear the gospel. Third, he held a high view of Scripture and gave himself to translating it and distributing it to the people. Fourth, he respected Indian cultures. The Indians came to respect Carey because of his knowledge of their languages and their cultures. Fifth, he was committed to planting churches. Sixth, he served harmoniously with his missionary team. Seventh, he set a high priority on training Indian pastors. Eighth, his correspondence inspired many Christians in Europe and North America to become involved in missions. And, ninth, he displayed remarkable perseverance. Despite great difficulties, including the death of a child, he refused to give up.

William Carey's Impact

In addition to establishing a groundbreaking ministry in India, Carey also inspired believers in Great Britain and North America to do missions. In Great Britain several missionary societies were established, including the London Missionary Society (1795) and the Church Missionary Society (1799). Further, home missions societies were organized to do missions work in Great Britain. New churches were planted, and many existing churches increased in size.

In North America, Carey's letters inspired the organization of several local missions societies, which studied, prayed, and supported missions financially. Carey's example prompted the organization of the first American mission board in 1812, the American Board of Commissioners for Foreign Missions.

The Development of Missions Interest in North America

In 1806 Samuel Mills led a group of students at Williams College to form what they called the Society of the Brethren. This group, which included Luther

Rice, met frequently in the woods near the campus to discuss and pray for missions. One day a thunderstorm disrupted their meeting, and they took shelter under a haystack. They continued their prayer meeting under the hay, and when they finished, they vowed, "We can do it if we will." This "Haystack Group" signed a pledge to serve as missionaries.

After their graduation from college, several of the group enrolled in Andover Seminary. They were joined there by Adoniram Judson, Samuel Newell, and Samuel Nott Jr. At Andover they organized the Society of Inquiry on the Subject of Missions. In 1810 Judson, Mills, Nott, and Newell walked to Bradford, Massachusetts, to present themselves as missionary candidates to the General Association of the Congregational Ministers of Massachusetts. After the young men recounted how God had called them to foreign missions, the ministers of the Congregational Church voted to establish the American Board of Commissioners for Foreign Missions, the first American mission board.

The board of commissioners expressed some confusion and concern about how they should go about supporting and deploying missionaries. At one point they sent Adoniram Judson to consult with the London Missionary Society (LMS). On their behalf Judson asked whether the LMS would undertake the support and supervision of the new missionaries. The directors of the LMS declined to do so, recommending instead that the American board raise its own funds and supervise its own missionaries. The American board accepted their recommendation and appointed Judson, Nott, Newell, and Gordon Hall as their first missionaries. Luther Rice hesitated to join them, but at the last hour he decided to go to India with them. The board agreed to approve him as a missionary if he could raise his own support. The five men were ordained in Salem, Massachusetts, on February 6, 1812. They departed soon after for India. The American board subsequently opened new mission fields in Ceylon (1816), the Middle East (1820), and China (1830).

Rice and Judson embarked for India on different ships. They planned to visit William Carey in Serampore to seek his advice on where and how to begin their missionary work. Anticipating that meeting, both Rice and Judson studied the New Testament in order to be able to refute the Baptist position on baptism (that only believers should be baptized by immersion). Their church, the Congregational Church, practiced the christening of infants. As he studied his New Testament, Judson became convinced that the Baptist position was correct. When he arrived in Serampore, he and Ann, his wife, were baptized by William Ward. Later, Rice arrived in Serampore, and he too was baptized.

Their affiliation with the Baptist church presented the young missionaries with an ethical dilemma. After some deliberation, they decided that Rice should return to the United States to make their resignations to the American board and to seek financial support among the Baptist churches. Rice made the long journey and began a whirlwind tour of the East Coast. Everywhere he went he encouraged churches to join together to support missions. In May 1814 the General Missionary Convention of the Baptist Denomination in the United States for Foreign Missions was organized in Philadelphia. The new missions society was commonly called the Triennial Convention because it met every three years. The convention appointed Luther Rice, Adoniram Judson, and Ann Judson as its first missionaries. The Judsons had been forced to leave India for Burma, so Burma became the first mission field of the Triennial Convention. The convention asked Luther Rice to remain in the United States to raise support for foreign missions. The Triennial Convention divided in 1845 and became the American Baptist Foreign Mission Society and the Foreign Mission Board of the Southern Baptist Convention.

Soon afterward, other denominations joined the modern missions movement. The Methodist Episcopal Church organized its mission board in 1819, followed by the Presbyterian Church in 1831 and the Evangelical Lutheran Church in 1837.

Great Missionaries

William Carey was the first of many great missionaries who served during the nineteenth century. The stories of these missionary pioneers are filled with trauma and tragedy, but they left behind them a legacy of sacrifice that

SIDEBAR 12.4

Portrait of Ann Hasseltine Judson (1789–1826)

Ann Hasseltine met Adoniram Judson in her father's home, and she eventually agreed to become his wife. They arrived in Burma in 1814, and she gave herself unreservedly to the work. Her experience as a schoolteacher served her well in their ministry. She learned to speak the difficult Burmese language and used that skill in evangelism and educating Burmese children. She translated the Gospel of Matthew into the Thai language in 1819, and she assisted her husband with his translation of the Bible into Burmese, translating the books of Daniel and Jonah. She also wrote a catechism in Burmese.

Ill health forced her to return to the United States in 1822. During her furlough, she rallied Baptists in America to support their missionary work and to send more missionaries. She wrote *A Particular Relation of the American Baptist Mission to the Burman Empire* in 1823.

She returned to Burma not long before war between Great Britain and Burma began in 1824. The Burmese imprisoned her husband, suspecting him of being a British spy. Ann worked heroically to preserve her husband's life, appealing to government officials and bringing him food in prison. Not long after her husband's release, she died, and her little child died soon afterward. She remains an example of exemplary missionary service and the representative of many missionary women who have labored ceaselessly to advance the cause of Christ.

Portrait of Ko Tha Byu (1778–1840)

Ko Tha Byu was the great evangelist among the Karen people in Burma. A self-confessed murderer, he came to know Christ through the ministry of Adoniram Judson. Soon after George and Sarah Boardman arrived in Burma to work with Judson, they moved to Tavoy to do pioneer work among the Karen people. Ko Tha Byu accompanied them. As a Karen he gained instant credibility among his people. His amazing testimony, vibrant faith, and passionate preaching resulted in many professions of faith among the Karens. Though George Boardman worked with the Karens for only five years before he died, Ko Tha Byu served for many years, going from village to village to preach the gospel even in the face of fierce opposition. In 1833 the Karens began reaching out to other tribes, both in Burma and Thailand. This missionary endeavor led to the formation of the Bassein Home Mission Society in 1850 (R. Tucker 2004, 140; Pate 1989, 156).

matches the martyrs of the early church. They buried wives and children in lands far from home, but they also built the kingdom of God around the world.

Adoniram Judson (1788–1850)

Persecuted by the East India Company, Adoniram and Ann Judson fled India and traveled to Burma in 1813. There they endured great suffering and hardships. Judson worked hard at learning the difficult Burmese language and translating the Bible. He preached for seven years to the Burmese with no result, not one convert. Greatly frustrated, he decided to observe Buddhist teachers. He noticed that they often sat and taught in *zayats*, small, open-air pavilions. So Judson built a *zayat* and began to engage visitors in conversation. In 1820 Maung Nau became the first to profess Christ.

In 1824 war broke out between Great Britain and Burma. The Burmese government arrested Judson as a British spy. He suffered greatly in prison, but his faithful Ann finally secured his release. Later he served as the interpreter for the peace negotiations between the British and the Burmese. During the peace negotiations, Ann died. Adoniram fell into a deep depression that lasted for months. Through the care and prayers of the other missionaries, he finally recovered and resumed his work. In 1840 he published his Burmese Bible, a monumental achievement. When Judson died in 1850, the church in Burma had seven thousand members, and he supervised the fieldwork of 163 missionaries.

Soon after Ann Judson died, George and Sarah Boardman arrived in Burma to work with Judson. They agreed to work with a mountain tribe called the Karens. Wisely, they asked Ko Tha Byu, a Karen convert, to accompany them. The Karen people had a long-standing belief that a white man would one day bring them the "book of life." When George Boardman began to preach to them from his Bible with gold-trimmed pages, the Karens were mightily impressed and came to Christ in large numbers. Though Boardman lived to preach to the Karens only a few years, Ko Tha Byu carried on and expanded the work until a majority of the Karens accepted Christ (R. Tucker 2004, 139–41).

Robert Morrison (1782–1834)

Robert Morrison was the first Protestant missionary to serve in China. He worked under the London Missionary Society. The British East India Company refused to transport a missionary to China, so he had to travel by way of America. An American shipowner asked him, "So then, Mr. Morrison, you really expect to make an impression on the idolatry of the great Chinese Empire?" to which Morrison replied, "No, sir, but I expect God will" (R. Tucker 2004, 178).

Morrison had to study the Chinese language secretly because the emperor of China had forbidden his people to teach the "foreign devils" to speak Chinese. Morrison's fluency in Chinese enabled him to support himself by working as a translator for the East India Company. In 1823 he published his translation of the Chinese Bible. His Chinese dictionary proved invaluable for the many missionaries who followed him to China. He, too, preached for seven years before winning his first convert, and he baptized only twelve converts in all. Morrison said, "By the Chinese Bible, when dead, I shall yet speak" (Glover 1960, 148).

Robert Moffat (1795–1883)

Robert Moffat pioneered missionary work in South Africa. Appointed by the London Missionary Society, Moffat arrived in South Africa in 1817. He became known as the "Apostle to Bechuanaland." He established a model

---

While the Moffats were on their first furlough in England, David Livingstone asked Mr. Moffat whether he thought that he, perhaps, might also be used in the missionary work in Africa. Mr. Moffat replied, "Yes, particularly if you will not go to an old station but will push on into unoccupied fields." And then he added, "In the north I have seen in the morning sun, the smoke of a thousand villages where no missionary has ever been."

www.wholesomewords.org;missions/msquotes.html

---

mission station in Kuruman, where he served for fifty years. His mission station included a church, a school, a printing press, a medical clinic, a demonstration farm, plus housing for the missionaries and local workers. Moffat translated the Bible into the Sechuana language in 1857 and printed it on his own press. He and his wife had ten children, but only seven survived to adulthood. Their daughter Mary married David Livingstone. The Moffats served in South Africa for fifty-three years before retiring.

David Livingstone (1813–1873)

David Livingstone, a native of Scotland, trained as a physician. In 1841 the London Missionary Society appointed him and assigned him to work with Robert Moffat in South Africa. He married the Moffats' daughter Mary, and they had several children. Livingstone was a restless person, and he was not content to settle down and establish a mission station, as the Moffats had done. From 1852 to 1856 he traveled all the way across Africa with only a small party of African companions. He stated that he made the trip to discover suitable sites for mission stations.

When Livingstone returned to Great Britain, Christians and the general public hailed him as a missionary hero. He spoke to large crowds throughout the British Isles. He returned to Africa as a consul for the British government and devoted his remaining years to exploring Africa, especially in an attempt to find the source of the Nile River.

When he died in 1873 his faithful African companions buried his heart in East Africa. They carried his body to the coast, and the British government interred his remains in Westminster Abbey along with other great personages of British history.

Historians and missiologists have often debated whether David Livingstone was a missionary or an explorer. As a missionary, he left no mission station like Robert Moffat, nor a Bible like Robert Morrison. Still, he did much to popularize missions in the nineteenth century. He also did much to stop slave trading in East Africa.

John Geddie (1815–1872)

John Geddie, a Canadian, served in the New Hebrides Islands in the South Pacific (now called Vanuatu). In constant danger from the local people, who were cannibals, he learned the language well and translated the New Testament. He planted churches and established schools. His converts traveled to other islands to spread the good news. When he died, a plaque was erected with this inscription: "When he landed in 1848, there were no Christians; when he left in 1872, there were no heathen."

Henry Martyn (1781–1812)

A native of England, Henry Martyn studied at Cambridge University, where he won acclaim for his achievements in mathematics. Inspired by the story of David Brainerd and the example of William Carey, he sought ordination as an Anglican priest. He went to India to serve as a chaplain for the East India Company and met William Carey. Carey urged him to use his education and intelligence in the work of Bible translation. Martyn translated the New Testament into Arabic, Persian, and Urdu, significant languages for missionary work among Muslims.

Despite failing health, he traveled to Iran to improve and expand his Persian translation of the Bible. In Iran he became ill and set out for England. He died in Turkey while en route, but his diary inspired many students to follow his example and become missionaries.

Charlotte Diggs (Lottie) Moon (1840–1912)

Lottie Moon and her sister, Edmonia, were appointed as the first single women missionaries to China by the Foreign Mission Board of the Southern Baptist Convention in 1873. During her early years in China, Lottie Moon taught in a girls school in Tengzhou, but later, despite the concerns of male missionaries, she began a ministry of village evangelism and church planting in the Pingtu area that produced thirty churches. In 1888 she suggested that the Woman's Missionary Union collect a Christmas offering for foreign missions. The first year $3,400 was collected in Southern Baptist churches. In 2004 the figure reached $136 million. During a famine in 1912 Lottie Moon gave her own food to the starving Chinese. Too late her fellow missionaries discovered that she was suffering from malnutrition. The missionaries sent her home, but she died onboard a ship in Kobe, Japan. After her death, the annual Christmas offering was named for her.

Missionary Obstacles

The early missionaries encountered many obstacles as they carried the gospel around the world. They experienced indifference on the part of their audiences, and they often faced official opposition. The East India Company did all it could to prevent missionaries from serving in areas under its control. The officers of the company believed that missionary activity would agitate the people and adversely affect the company's profits. We have already seen how Adoniram Judson was imprisoned by the Burmese government. Sometimes the missionaries experienced violent attacks. In 1900 no fewer than 189 missionaries died during the Boxer Rebellion in China. Many of them were

Portrait of Samuel (Adjayi) Crowther (1807–1891)

Those who read this history book might get the impression that European missionaries did all the work. That would be an unfortunate misimpression. Though European missionaries pioneered the work in many lands, most of the work was done by national Christians. Samuel Crowther is an outstanding example of this.

Samuel Crowther was born in what is now Nigeria in 1807. His true name was Adjayi. Fulani raiders captured him at age thirteen and sold him as a slave. A British Navy ship intercepted the slave ship, and Samuel ended up in Sierra Leone. There he heard the gospel story. When he was baptized, he adopted the name of a famous cleric in England. He attended Anglican schools in Sierra Leone and proved to be an outstanding student. His intelligence won him a scholarship at the Church Missionary Society (CMS) college

in London. The Anglican Church ordained him in 1843, the first African to be ordained as a priest. He soon returned to Africa to begin CMS work among the Yoruba people of southern Nigeria.

Crowther did outstanding work in Yorubaland, evangelizing the lost and establishing new churches. He translated the Bible into Yoruba, producing an excellent translation. In 1857 Henry Venn, the CMS leader, sent Crowther to open and supervise a new mission along the Niger River. This work prospered, and in 1864 Crowther was appointed bishop of "the countries of West Africa." This appointment reflected Henry Venn's commitment to indigenous missions and the appointment of Africans to leadership positions. Samuel Crowther is revered today by the church in Nigeria as one of its heroes.

missionaries serving with the China Inland Mission. During the nineteenth and early twentieth centuries, civil wars and fighting between warlords disrupted missions work in China.

The missionaries also suffered greatly due to tropical diseases. In West Africa, many missionaries succumbed to yellow fever, not to mention typhoid fever, typhus, dengue fever, malaria, and dysentery. In the nineteenth century the average life expectancy of a new missionary in West Africa was three years. Ralph Winter has called these intrepid missionaries "a suicidal stream" (Winter 1981, 14). If you travel through Nigeria, you will find missionary cemeteries in all the major towns in the southern part of the country. Truly, their gravestones proved to be the foundation stones of the church.

All missionaries experience the pain of separation from their families and friends. The early missionaries also experienced grief as they buried spouses and children. William Carey buried two wives and a child. Adoniram Judson did the same. Many wives buried husbands. Their determination to carry on despite opposition, indifference, illness, and grief should inspire modern-day missionaries to greater faithfulness and fortitude.

Other Great Missionaries

The scope of this book does not permit even a cursory discussion of the many faithful missionaries who opened work in many lands. Karl Gutzlaff followed Morrison to China and did outstanding work. James Hepburn, Guido Verbeck, and Samuel Brown served in Japan and established the first Protestant churches in that resistant nation. Horace Underwood, a Presbyterian, and Henry Appenzeller, a Methodist, entered Korea in 1885 and established strong churches that bear much wonderful fruit today.

In West Africa, Melville Cox began Methodist work in Liberia in 1833, but he lived only three months afterward. Thomas Jefferson Bowen initiated Baptist work in Nigeria in 1850. Other African pioneers include Dan Crawford, James Stewart, Donald Fraser, and Alexander McKay.

The Indian subcontinent witnessed the arrival and success of many outstanding missionaries, including Alexander Duff, Reginald Heber, John Scudder, James Thoburn, William Miller, and Christian Schwartz. Much of the work in India revolved around schools. The Hindu majority in India proved resistant to the gospel, but they did embrace mission schools. Therefore, the missionaries established many schools in hopes of winning the students to Christ. In the Middle East, Muslims, too, came to Christ in small numbers, but they responded enthusiastically to Protestant universities. Cyrus Hamlin established Robert College in Istanbul. Daniel Bliss founded the Syrian Protestant College, which eventually became the famous American University of Beirut. Eli Smith and C. V. Van Dyck labored for years to translate the Bible into the difficult Arabic language.

Conclusion

In this chapter we have presented accounts of great pioneer missionaries. They endured daunting hardships to bring the gospel to the world. Most of these missionaries never studied missiology. They certainly had no training in linguistics; yet they translated the Bible, evangelized their peoples, and planted churches. In a sense, they were the first generation of modern missionaries (Moravians notwithstanding). In the next chapter we will study the second generation of modern missionaries. They learned from the successes and struggles of the first generation, and they developed more effective strategies and organizations.

13

The Great Century, Part II

In the previous chapter we examined the beginning of the modern missionary movement and the significant missionaries who made the nineteenth century a great one for Protestant missions. We will now turn to great movements that affected missions both then and now.

Indigenous Missions

The term *indigenous* comes from biology and indicates a plant or animal native to an area. In missions circles, indigenous refers to churches that reflect the cultural distinctives of their ethnolinguistic group. The missionary effort to establish indigenous churches is an effort to plant churches that fit naturally into their environment and to avoid planting churches that duplicate Western patterns.

Indigenous missions seeks to duplicate the missionary principles and pattern of the apostle Paul. Paul functioned as an itinerant missionary, never staying more than three years in any city. Paul's approach to evangelizing regions was to plant churches in cities, from which the gospel would penetrate the surrounding area. He never appealed to the churches in Jerusalem or Antioch for funds to support the new churches. Rather, he expected the new churches to support themselves from the beginning. Paul appointed and trained elders to lead all the churches he planted. He gave the churches over to their leadership and the guidance of the Holy Spirit, but he also visited them and wrote to them periodically.

Henry Venn (1796–1873) and Rufus Anderson (1796–1880)

Henry Venn served as the director of the Church Missionary Society in Great Britain, and Rufus Anderson led the American Board of Commissioners

258

for Foreign Missions in the United States. They first used the term *indigenous* in the mid-nineteenth century. They came to their convictions about missions principles independently, but they eventually corresponded with each other and harmonized their thinking. They both wrote about the necessity of planting "three-self" churches—churches that would be self-supporting, self-governing, and self-propagating (at first Venn called them self-extending). They exhorted their missionaries to establish churches that could support themselves, govern themselves, and carry out a program of evangelism and missions. They both cautioned missionaries about becoming absorbed in pastoring and maintaining existing churches, insisting that the missionaries focus on church planting as their primary task. Venn and Anderson desired churches that would be "self-reliant" and "purely native." They instructed their missionaries to train national pastors and hand over to them at the earliest opportunity the care of the churches.

Venn coupled the concept of indigenous churches with *euthanasia in missions*. By euthanasia he meant that missionaries should plant churches, train leaders, and then move on to new, unevangelized regions. He believed that missionaries should always be temporary workers, not permanent fixtures. He wanted the mission to die as the national church arose.

The missionaries in both of their agencies followed their principles while Venn and Anderson held office, but after they retired, the missionaries abandoned indigenous principles and began subsidizing the national churches and dominating them. They refused to relinquish control to national leaders, and this caused much resentment over time.

John L. Nevius (1829–1893)

John Nevius was a Presbyterian missionary who served for many years in northern China. Nevius reacted strongly against what he called the "Old China Method," which was characterized by

missionary control of the churches and their finances
establishment of missionary compounds
heavy foreign financial subsidies
founding many expensive institutions
extraction of converts from their homes and neighborhoods

In developing his own system, Nevius built on the foundation laid by Venn and Anderson. His convictions about effective missionary work are expressed in his classic book, *Planting and Development of Missionary Churches*. Nevius's principles came to be called the Nevius Plan. He held that (1) Christians should continue to live in their neighborhoods and pursue their occupations, being self-supporting and witnessing to their families, coworkers, and neighbors. (2) Missionaries should only develop programs and institutions that the national church desired and could support. (3) The national churches should call out and support their own pastors. (4) Churches should be built in the native style, with money and materials given by the church members. (5) Intensive biblical and doctrinal instruction should be provided for church leaders every year. His principles found little acceptance by missionaries in China, but they influenced mission work in Korea in a great way.

Horace Underwood, a missionary with the Northern Presbyterians, and Methodist missionary H. G. Appenzeller pioneered the work in Korea after arriving in 1885. They felt inadequate to the task of evangelizing that Buddhist nation, so in 1890 they invited John Nevius to visit and advise them. After hearing Nevius explain his methods, they adopted his approach. The Presbyterian missionaries, in particular, implemented Nevius's principles, and now there are more Presbyterians in Korea than in any other nation. Beyond that, the Presbyterian churches in Korea are marked by a great passion for missions and evangelism (Neill 1986, 290).

Roland Allen (1868–1947)

Roland Allen was an Anglican priest who served as a missionary in China with the Society for the Propagation of the Gospel in Foreign Parts from 1892 until 1904. Like Nevius, he reacted negatively to the missionary methods employed by most missions in China. He wrote several books and many articles, but he expressed his key ideas in *Missionary Methods: St. Paul's or*

SIDEBAR 13.1

Portrait of Roland Allen (1868–1947)

Roland Allen, born and educated in England, served as a missionary in China and East Africa, but he is primarily remembered as a missions theorist. He reacted sharply against the foreign control and institutionalism he encountered in China. He embraced the indigenous approach of Henry Venn and Rufus Anderson and expanded it. Though he was a "high church" Anglican, he emphasized the role of the Holy Spirit in missions. He wrote the following in *Missionary Methods: St. Paul's or Ours?*

There is no stage in which converts cannot do anything for themselves. There is no stage in which it is necessary that they should be slaves of a foreign system. The moment they are baptized they are the Temple of the Holy Ghost, and the Holy Ghost is power. They are not so incapable as we suppose.

Roland Allen (1912, 146)

Ours? (1912) and *The Spontaneous Expansion of the Church* (1927). Allen consistently emphasized the role of the Holy Spirit in missions and encouraged missionaries to work primarily in itinerant church planting, trusting the Holy Spirit to develop the churches.

Allen's main principles are these: (1) All permanent teaching must be intelligible and so easily understood that those who receive it can retain it, use it, and pass it on to others. (2) All organizations should be set up in a way that allows national Christians to maintain them. (3) Church finances should be provided and controlled by the local church members. (4) Christians should be taught to provide pastoral care for one another. (5) Missionaries should give national believers the authority to exercise spiritual gifts freely and at once. Allen's ideas exerted little influence during his lifetime; however, he affected the thinking of Donald McGavran, who commended Allen's writings to later generations.

Melvin Hodges (1909–1986)

Melvin Hodges served as an Assemblies of God missionary in Latin America and later as a mission administrator. He updated the indigenous method in his book *The Indigenous Church* (1953). This book presented the ideas of Venn, Anderson, Nevius, and Allen in a contemporary, popular format. Hodges provided many examples from his extensive field experience. He acknowledged the difficulty in changing a field from a subsidy approach to an indigenous approach and provided advice for making the change. He also emphasized training national workers and giving them responsibility for the care of the churches, freeing the missionaries to focus on planting new churches.

Alan Tippett (1911–1988)

Alan Tippett, an Australian, served as a Methodist missionary in the South Pacific. Later Tippett allied himself with Donald McGavran and became one of the founding faculty members of the School of World Mission at Fuller Theological Seminary. His writings, along with those of McGavran, Ralph Winter, and Peter Wagner, show that the church growth movement accepted and built on the work of earlier proponents of indigenous missions.

In his book *Verdict Theology in Missionary Theory*, Tippett proposed a sixfold description of an indigenous church: (1) Self-image—The church sees itself as being independent from the mission that birthed it. (2) Self-functioning—The national church is able to carry on all the normal functions of a church—worship, discipling, evangelizing, fellowship, and pastoral care—without the help of missionaries. (3) Self-determining—The church can and does make its own decisions. (4) Self-supporting—The church provides for its own financial needs through tithes and offerings. (5) Self-propagation—The national church sees itself as responsible to carry out the Great Commission, giving itself to evangelism and missions. (6) Self-giving—The church ministers to the needs of its members and the community.

In recent years some missiologists have suggested adding a seventh mark to Tippett's list: self-theologizing. They believe that a truly indigenous church will develop its own theology, expressed in culturally appropriate ways. These theologies would affirm the central doctrines of the Christian faith, but they would express those doctrines using metaphors and concepts that reflect their own unique cultures.

The indigenous missions movement still influences missions. David Garrison, who has written on fostering church-planting movements, emphasizes the importance of planting indigenous churches that will multiply themselves (2004). Henry Venn and Rufus Anderson lived, wrote, and worked more than 140 years ago, but their influence continues today.

In contemporary missions indigenization is still mentioned, but missiologists use the term *contextualization* more commonly. Indigenization focuses primarily on the church that results from missionary activity. Contextualization is broader and refers to the whole process of communicating the gospel and establishing churches that reflect the cultural context of the people.

The Faith Missions Movement

Definition

During the nineteenth century four basic types of missions developed: denominational missions, interdenominational missions, faith missions, and specialized missions. Faith missions are nondenominational or interdenominational missions that require their missionaries to raise their own financial support. In most (but not all) denominational missions, the missionaries receive a salary from the denominational mission board. They have responsibility to promote missions in the denomination's churches, but they are not required to raise personal support. In a faith mission the missionaries do deputation to raise the amount of monthly or yearly financial support required by their missions agency.

Reasons for Development

There were three primary reasons for the development of faith missions. First, the founders of these missions were convinced that the denominational agencies were not reaching the unevangelized areas of the world, especially the inland or interior areas. The words *inland* or *interior* in their names indicate this emphasis. Second, the missions' founders were concerned that

SIDEBAR 13.2

Portrait of Hudson Taylor (1832–1905)

What made Hudson Taylor so effective? One could describe him as a missions maverick, a person who thought outside the box. Many in his day considered him a "radical" missionary leader (Wigram 2005):

- He had a radical vision to evangelize all of China, not just the coastal area.
- He established a radical organization that relied on God to supply funds and workers.
- He called for radical prayer support, calling for prayer for missionaries in

every stage of their lives as well as for Chinese Christians.

- He had radical ideas about mission administration, placing the China Inland Mission's headquarters in China.
- He displayed radical ideas about missionary personnel, fielding single female missionaries all over China, even in troubled areas.
- He showed radical ideas about communication, using maps, charts, and magazines to communicate with CIM supporters.

denominational missions agencies had been negatively affected by theological liberalism. And, third, the founders observed that denominational agencies often lacked sufficient funds to send out missionaries, at least in adequate numbers. To address this dearth of missionaries, the faith missions asked their missionary candidates to raise their own support.

History of the Movement

The first and prototype faith mission was the China Inland Mission (CIM). Hudson Taylor founded the China Inland Mission in Great Britain in 1865. He had previously served for several years in China with the China Evangelization Society. Frustration with that society's administrative problems prompted Taylor to establish his own missions agency. He called it the China *Inland* Mission because he was dismayed at the failure of most missions agencies to penetrate the vast interior of China. Most of the missionaries lived in the international settlements in the five treaty ports on the east coast of China. They seldom ventured inland. Taylor found this unacceptable, and he vowed to place missionaries in every province in China.

Taylor organized his new mission board according to an innovative set of core values:

1. No appeals for funds would be made. The missionaries could describe their work and the needs in China, but no direct appeals would be made. Taylor said they should pray and trust God to move the hearts of donors.

Map 13.1 Missions to China by 1920

2. He made no requirements concerning educational attainment. He did not require his missionaries to have graduated from a university or Bible school. He only required that they be able to read and write.

3. He stated that the mission's purpose was to go inland and evangelize every province of China.

4. The mission would be interdenominational. Taylor said he would accept candidates from any Christian denomination or candidates with no denominational affiliation.

5. He welcomed single women to serve as missionaries. This was quite unusual, especially in Victorian England.

6. He insisted that the administration of the mission would be in China. He wanted to keep the administration of the mission as close to the field as possible.

7. He required his missionaries to learn to speak Chinese fluently and to identify with the Chinese people as closely as possible.

Taylor's emphasis on cultural identification was an extraordinary innovation, and many missionaries in China criticized him for it. The China Inland Mission grew rapidly. This was due in part to Taylor's vision and able ad-

> Let us see that we keep God before our eyes; that we walk in His ways and seek to please and glorify Him in everything, great and small. Depend upon it, God's work, done in God's way, will never lack God's supplies.
>
> Hudson Taylor (www.wholesomewords .org/missions/msquotes.html)

ministration, but it was also a result of his unusual ability to enlist new missionary candidates. By 1882 the CIM had fulfilled Taylor's goal and placed a missionary in every province in China. By 1895 the CIM had 641 missionaries in China, 50 percent of the total missionary force. By 1929 the CIM had 1,300 missionaries under appointment, by far the largest Protestant missions organization in the world.

The China Inland Mission inspired the establishment of many other faith missions. A. B. Simpson founded the Christian and Missionary Alliance in 1887. The Evangelical Alliance Mission (TEAM) followed in 1890. Roland Bingham established the Sudan Interior Mission in 1893, and the African Inland Mission began in 1895. All of them shared common characteristics with the CIM.

The Women's Movement in Mission

Motivation

In the early years of Protestant missions, the women who served as missionaries were the wives or sisters of missionaries. Gradually, single women became accepted as proper candidates for missionary service. What prompted these women, raised in the protective Victorian age, to travel to faraway places in order to advance the cause of Christ? One factor that motivated them was the opportunity to engage in ministry. Churches and denominations in North America and Europe afforded women few opportunities to exercise their spiritual gifts in the local church. Women had much greater liberty to minister on the mission field. Second, missions offered women the chance to experience the adventure and excitement of foreign travel. This was no small thing for women reared in a culture that restricted their activities outside the home. Third, poor women of lower social classes

Portrait of A. B. Simpson (1844–1919)

A. B. Simpson holds a unique place in church history. He established a mission board that became a denomination. Simpson gave up a lucrative pastorate in a Presbyterian church in Louisville, Kentucky, to go to New York City. Eventually, he planted an independent church. In 1887 he founded the Christian Alliance to do domestic missions and the Missionary Alliance to do foreign missions. In 1897 the two agencies merged to form the Christian and Missionary Alliance. This mission board gave birth to the denomination of the same name. Simpson's missiology was christocentric: he emphasized preaching Christ both in North America and overseas. He taught what he called the Fourfold Gospel: Christ as savior, sanctifier, healer, and coming king. Christian and Missionary Alliance churches have always demonstrated a commitment to missions praying, giving, and going that other denominations have not matched.

could raise their social status by becoming missionaries. The fourth factor was feminism. R. Pierce Beaver believes that the women's missionary movement was the "first feminist movement in North America" (quoted in R. Tucker 1983, 233). Ruth Tucker posits that missions provided women of North America and Europe a channel through which they could express their feminist sentiments (1983, 232–33).

Pioneers of Women's Missions

A number of women bravely pioneered in missions, opening the way for many others to follow. Betsy Stockton, an African American, went to Hawaii in 1823 and served under the American Board of Commissioners for Foreign Missions. Cynthia Farrar traveled to Bombay, India, and served there for thirty-four years under the Marathi Mission. In 1839 Eliza Agnew sailed to Ceylon. Lottie Moon departed for China in 1873 and achieved success as both an educator and an evangelist.

One of the great female missionaries was Mary Slessor of Nigeria. Born into a poor family in Scotland in 1848, at age eleven Slessor had to go to work in a textile mill to help support her family. Active in the local Presbyterian church, she eventually became involved in inner-city missions with the Queen Street Mission. She had always been interested in foreign missions, and in 1875 she applied for appointment with the Calabar Mission, which worked in southeastern Nigeria.

At first she served as a schoolteacher, but like Lottie Moon, she became dissatisfied with that role. Eventually, her mission allowed her to engage in village evangelism, and she walked from village to village, telling the gospel story. In the villages she encountered the pagan custom of twin murder. The local people believed that one twin was born possessed by an evil spirit. Because they could not tell which one was demonized, they killed both and ostracized the mother. Slessor rescued the babies and cared for their mothers. She adopted and raised seven African children.

In 1888 Slessor went to live and work among the Okoyong tribe. They had proved fiercely resistant to the gospel, and at first she saw few among them come to Christ. Nevertheless, she earned their respect by establishing

---

Prayer is the greatest power God has put into our hands for service—praying is harder than doing, at least I find it so, but the dynamic lies that way to advance the Kingdom.

Mary Slessor (www.wholesomewords
.org/missions/msquotes.html)

---

schools and providing medical care. She learned to be a mediator of disputes and a peacemaker. These skills earned her an appointment as a vice-consul for the British government. In that role she acted as the judge for the people in her district.

She adopted a simple lifestyle, wearing simple cotton dresses and living in a mud hut. She died in Nigeria in 1915, nearly forty years after she first arrived in Africa. Her example, the stories about her, and the talks she gave while on furlough inspired many young women to give their lives to missionary service.

Women's Missionary Organizations

The Protestant women of the nineteenth century demonstrated great concern for missionary support. They organized local and national missions societies to learn about missions, pray for missionaries, and raise money for mission. The first women's missions society was the Women's Union Missionary Society, founded by Sarah Doremus in 1861. Annie Armstrong led in the organization of the Woman's Missionary Union of the Southern Baptist Convention in 1888. By 1910 there were forty-four national women's missions societies with a total membership of more than two million. These societies raised more than four million dollars for missions in 1910 (R. Tucker 2004, 232).

Contributions

The number of single women missionaries increased over the course of the nineteenth century. By 1909 there were 4,710 single missionaries serving overseas. In some fields the number of female missionaries grew to the point that married and single women outnumbered the men two to one. Why and how did this remarkable increase happen? The factors that motivated the women have been discussed earlier. Surely, the strongest motivation was simply the opportunity to serve the Lord with less restriction. Beyond that, the women of Europe and North America displayed great compassion for the physical and spiritual needs of the world and a sensitivity to God's call to service that men did not match.

The female missionaries served especially effectively in work with women and children. The male missionaries and mission administrators gradually came to understand that in some cultures only women could reach women. The women also served with distinction in medical work. Schools played a key role in Protestant mission work, and those schools could hardly have functioned without the service of thousands of women. In more recent years women have proven their ability in Bible translation. It would be unfair to slight the work of the married women. Ann Hasseltine Judson and others proved their worth beyond a doubt. Still, these single women served effectively in part because they were not distracted by the responsibility of caring for husbands and children. That freedom prompted H. A. Tupper, director of the Foreign Mission Board, to write in 1879: "I estimate a single woman in China is worth two married men" (R. Tucker 2004, 294). In summary, the second half of the Great Century was different from the first in that women played a more prominent role during that time. Truly, without their involvement and passion for missions, the century would not have been great.

SIDEBAR 13.4

Portrait of Dwight L. Moody (1837–1899)

Dwight L. Moody was the greatest American evangelist of the nineteenth century. Raised in Massachusetts, Moody moved to Chicago in 1856 and soon established himself as a successful businessman. In 1860 he gave up business and served full time with the Young Men's Christian Association (YMCA). In 1871 he became an itinerant evangelist. He held successful evangelistic meetings throughout North America and Great Britain. His simple sermons on the love of God for sinners found great response among the working classes. His great contributions to missions were sponsoring the student conference that gave birth to the Student Volunteer Movement and founding Moody Bible Institute, which has been a premier missionary training institution, especially for faith missions. Moody made saving souls his highest priority. He said, "I look upon this world as a wrecked vessel. God has given me a lifeboat and said to me, 'Moody, save all you can'" (Beougher 2000, 657).

The Bible College Movement

The Bible college movement contributed much to evangelical missions, especially to faith missions. Bible colleges and Bible institutes were founded in reaction to theological liberalism and biblical higher criticism, both of which infiltrated universities and seminaries during the last thirty years of the Great Century. The founders of the Bible colleges desired to train effective Christian workers, untainted by heretical ideas. The founders had a great passion for evangelism and missions, and the Bible colleges they developed emphasized training missionaries for overseas service. Most of these served with faith missions.

The first school established was Nyack Missionary College, affiliated with the Christian and Missionary Alliance, in 1882. Dwight L. Moody, the famous evangelist, founded Moody Bible Institute in 1886. More than six thousand Moody graduates have served as foreign missionaries. The Toronto Bible College was founded in 1894, and the Bible Institute of Los Angeles (now Biola University) began operation in 1908.

The Student Volunteer Movement (SVM)

Background

Historians usually date the beginning of the SVM to 1886, when a significant student conference was held at D. L. Moody's retreat center in Northfield, Massachusetts. However, several things prepared the way for this missions awakening. The first was the Society of Brethren (who had the Haystack Prayer Meeting), which began at Williams College and eventually expanded to forty-nine campuses. The second factor was the ministry of the YMCA, which then exhibited a strong emphasis on missions and evangelism. The third factor was the Princeton Foreign Missionary Society at Princeton University and Seminary, which had an influence beyond its campus. The Princeton group was led by Robert Wilder, the son of missionaries.

Beginning

Moody and Pastor A. T. Pierson spoke to 251 college students at the Northfield conference. The conference emphasized missions, and while Robert Wilder attended the conference, his sister, Grace, prayed that one hundred students would dedicate themselves to missionary service. At the final service one hundred students pledged themselves to serve as missionaries. The students also agreed to establish an organization to promote missions on college campuses. They chose Robert Wilder and John Forman to serve as representatives who

269

would visit university campuses. During the following year they spoke on 162 campuses and found much enthusiasm.

As a result of this groundswell, the SVM was established in 1888, sponsored by the YMCA. John R. Mott was elected chairman of the SVM and began a distinguished career as a missions mobilizer. The students adopted this motto: "The evangelization of the world in this generation." Though the SVM originated in North America, it soon spread to Great Britain, the Netherlands, Germany, Switzerland, Scandinavia, New Zealand, Australia, Japan, India, and China. The movement grew rapidly, and more than six hundred missions volunteers from 159 institutions attended the 1891 convention. Each volunteer made this pledge: "It is my purpose, if God permits, to become a foreign missionary." The SVM mobilized the students for missions, and they went on to serve with many different missions agencies, mainly denominational mission boards.

History of the Movement

The SVM reached its zenith at its 1920 convention. That meeting registered 6,890 students from 949 institutions. At its peak more than 40,000 students participated in local SVM chapters. Unfortunately, after 1920 the SVM began a steady decline, mainly due to theological liberalism but also because the leaders who replaced John Mott were less capable.

Contributions

What contributions did the SVM make to missions? First, by 1940 more than twenty thousand missionaries recruited by the SVM had sailed from North America and Europe to serve around the world. Second, the SVM marked a shift in the base of missions sending. In the second half of the book of Acts, the focus shifts from the Jerusalem church to the church at Antioch. In a similar way, before the SVM the majority of missionaries came from Europe, while after the SVM most missionaries were sent from North America. For example, the number of missionaries from North America increased from 350 in 1890 to 4,000 in 1915. Third, the SVM not only recruited missionaries but also did important work in educating college students about missions. Fourth, the SVM laid the groundwork for the World Missionary Conference, which met in Edinburgh, Scotland, in 1910. Through this conference the SVM prepared the way for the ecumenical movement in the second half of the century (P. Pierson 2000b, 914).

Missions Conference Movement

Another characteristic of the Great Century was the development of missions conferences. These served to excite the interest of laypersons to give to and pray for missions while also inspiring young people to offer themselves for missionary service.

Early Conferences

One of the first missions conferences met in New York City in 1854. Alexander Duff, the famous missionary to India, served as the keynote speaker. The conferees adopted several resolutions, endorsing formal courses on missions in colleges and seminaries as well as comity agreements between mission boards. The concept was "derived from the general principle that mission groups ought not to compete with one another. The method used to promote this concept was to make one agency responsible for evangelism in a particular territory or among a particular people. Double occupancy of a region, with the exception of big cities, was to be avoided" (Corwin 2000, 212).

The Liverpool Missionary Conference convened in 1860 in Liverpool, England. It was a conference for both missions leaders and church laypersons. The London Secretaries Association sponsored the event, and 126 missionaries and missions administrators met during the day. At night public meetings were held, and large crowds gathered to hear missionary messages. The missions leaders agreed that a missions journal should be established and that more capable missionaries should be recruited and deployed.

Ecumenical Missionary Conference

The Ecumenical Missionary Conference was held in New York City in 1900. The conference lasted for ten days, and more than two hundred thousand people attended its many sessions in Carnegie Hall. Delegations from 162 mission boards attended. Prominent speakers included Hudson Taylor, John Mott, Governor Theodore Roosevelt, and William McKinley, who was the president of the United States as well as an active Methodist layperson.

The organizers used the term *ecumenical* to indicate a worldwide survey of missions rather than representation of all Christian entities. The conference aimed to inspire support for missions, and its broad program included sessions on medical missions, education, evangelism, and world religions. The conference also highlighted the role of women in missions. The conference called for a permanent committee to coordinate missions, but nothing was actually done (Askew 2000).

World Missionary Conference

The World Missionary Conference met in Edinburgh, Scotland, in 1910. It was a pivotal meeting, primarily attended by leaders in Protestant missions. Its organizers meant to celebrate a century of progress in Protestant missions, to assess the state of Christianity throughout the world, and to coordinate the work of Protestant missionary agencies in the future. The conference planners designed it to be a working meeting for agency administrators rather than an inspirational meeting for the public. Four great forces merged at Edinburgh and contributed to its triumphalistic tone: Pietism, revivalism, volunteerism, and optimism. Certainly, the conference reflected the optimism that characterized the turn of the century. Those attending the conference had no inkling that the inevitable progress they envisioned would be derailed by World War I, just four years later.

Edinburgh presaged later missions conferences by inviting national church leaders from the majority world. Seventeen attended, and they played an important part in the proceedings. The conference also pointed toward the future in that the participants voted to establish a continuation committee, which became the International Missionary Council. Many historians view the Edinburgh conference as the beginning of the ecumenical movement. It also signaled the transition of John R. Mott from a leader in "student missions" to the leadership of the Protestant missions movement (Anderson 2000, 1029).

Great Progress

When the Great Century began, William Carey and a few Moravian missionaries made up the entire body of Protestant foreign missionaries. By 1910 there were more than fifteen thousand Protestant missionaries serving around the world. Stephen Neill has listed a dozen reasons why the conferees at Edinburgh had reason for optimism:

1. Missionaries had penetrated every continent and almost every nation in the world.
2. The heavy work of pioneer missions had been done; the major cultures of the world had the Bible in their language.
3. Tropical medicine had alleviated many problems with disease and had made it possible for Westerners to live for extended periods in tropical climates.
4. Missionaries had won some converts from every religion in the world.
5. Every race of people in the world had responded to the gospel, though some more readily than others.
6. A rapidly increasing force of national workers stood ready to assist the missionaries in their work.
7. The younger churches in missionary lands were producing capable leaders with promise for the future.

8. The churches on the home front were supporting missions as never before.
9. Financial support had kept pace with missionary expansion.
10. The universities of North America and Europe were producing volunteers who evidenced great potential for effective missionary service.
11. The influence of the gospel of Christ was spreading beyond the numbers of people who had accepted it.
12. Opposition to the gospel seemed to have broken down in most lands. (Neill 1986, 333)

Yes, the delegates at the Edinburgh conference had good reason for optimism. The major non-Christian religions of the world seemed to be in decline, while Christianity appeared to be ascending and moving from triumph to triumph. No other religion had ever expanded as rapidly as had Protestant Christianity in the nineteenth century. It was with good reason that Latourette called it "the Great Century."

On the negative side, the Edinburgh conference failed to address the rising problem of liberal theology. Further, the conferees ignored the problems of Western colonialism and paternalism. Paternalism is sometimes referred to as the "White Man's Burden." This phrase refers to the belief that God had blessed Europe and North America with Western civilization. Thus blessed by God, Westerners had a responsibility to share that civilization with the rest of the world. Believing this, some missionaries went to the field with the idea that they needed to "civilize" the people in order to evangelize them. Of course, no one asked the local people whether they wanted to become "civilized." A fuller evaluation of this issue is included in chapter 15.

When a Woman Should Be a Man

Frances F. Hiebert

*Adapted from Hiebert and
Hiebert (1987, 205–8)*

Karen White stared out the window of the bedroom-cum-office in her home. Snow had fallen softly during the night and settled on the pine branches that framed the window. Now the sun was shining brightly, and the day glistened with all the promise of a winter reprieve. But Karen was only half aware of the winter wonderland outside. She was, in fact, quite deeply troubled about the future of her mission organization.

It was her organization. She had begun it and for several years had been its director. The purpose of the organization was to provide interim medical personnel for mission hospitals and clinics. Doctors and nurses from the United States took their vacation time, sometimes extended, to serve in place of missionaries who had gone on furlough. Karen's organization recruited the temporary workers and put them in touch with missions that needed them.

Karen worked with a volunteer committee of Christian doctors in the Boston area. At their last meeting, one of them, Dr. Brown, threw a bombshell into the discussion—at least from Karen's perspective. He raised the issue of having men under the authority of women, citing a well-known blogger he had read that day. He asked whether, now that the mission was well established, they should not consider recruiting a man to be in charge. Karen, he said, could certainly remain as assistant director and would be invaluable in training the new male director.

But with a man in charge, the mission would be in line with their evangelical constituency and with Scripture.

The rationale given for this proposed change of administration had caused turmoil in Karen's mind all week. Her background, training, and present commitment were to the full authority of the Bible. It had never occurred to her that she was doing anything "wrong" when she answered God's call to missions and administered the agency that she was sure God had called into being. The discussion in the meeting had left her thoroughly confused. She was a single woman. Did the instructions to wives in the New Testament mean that all women were subject to all men? Were they universal, for all time and every place? Or were the injunctions about women addressed to a particular situation for a particular reason?

Dr. Fleming, another member of the committee, at the same meeting had voiced concern about changing to a male administrator. With things going so well, he asked, why should they risk the slippage that is an inevitable part of change? He admitted that he didn't know quite what to think about the biblical issues and the church interpretations, but he did know about a real situation very much like this one that had failed after changing the leadership from a woman to a man.

As he shared the story, his discussion of women in leadership had made Dr. Brown bristle, and Karen herself flinched, because she always tried to avoid that discussion. She wanted to get on with the work of evangelism and avoid being embroiled in hassles over who should be in charge.

"And yet," Karen thought, as she reached for her coat and scarf, "I am in the middle of it just because I am a woman—whether I like it or not." When she opened the door, a fluff of snow landed on her head. She thought of 1 Corinthians 11:10 and smiled in spite of herself. Was the snow a sign that her authority was on her own head? No, she would need more concrete guidance than that.

Her heart lifted as she took in the grandeur of the day. But the weight of the decision she must make was still on her. Should she resign and be submissive in the way that she, like many other evangelical women, had been conditioned? Or should she follow the new urging that she had been convinced was a call from God and continue the work that God had begun in her?

As she walked away from the house, leaving a trail of footsteps in the soft snow, Karen realized that her decision, like the woman's decision in the story that Dr. Fleming had told, would be a precedent for many other women who were struggling to live out their calls to mission and ministry, in spite of misunderstandings and traditions in some sectors of the contemporary evangelical church. As she looked at the brilliant sky and the snow-crowned earth around her, Karen suddenly remembered the words of the psalmist: "I will trust and not be afraid."

Reflection and Discussion

1. What should Karen do? Should she accept Dr. Brown's request?
2. If she chooses to continue in leadership, how should she communicate that to Dr. Brown?

14

The Twentieth Century

If the nineteenth century was the Great Century for Protestant missions, the twentieth century could be called the tumultuous century. Missions agencies and missionaries faced many challenges and trials during this eventful period. Thankfully, many factors aided missionaries as well.

Hindrances to Missions in the Twentieth Century

World Wars

Only four years after the excitement and enthusiasm of the Edinburgh conference, World War I broke out in Europe. Eventually, the fighting spilled over into the Middle East and East Africa. The war lasted from 1914 until 1918. It affected missions in three primary ways. First, the war cost the lives of a generation of young men in Europe. The loss of life in the war was appalling, and many young men who might have become missionaries died in the battles. Second, the war burst the bubble of optimism that characterized Europe and North America at the turn of the century. The belief in the inevitability of human progress went down in flames like one of the new fighter planes on the western front. And, third, the war distracted the church from fulfilling its missions mandate.

World War II began in Asia in 1936, when Japan invaded China, and in Europe in 1939, when Germany invaded Poland. Historians often write that this war was really a continuation of the first, and that is true. The peace settlement negotiated at Versailles in 1918 sowed the seeds for the larger war that followed twenty years later.

World War II proved to be a truly global conflict. The navies of the Axis and the Allied nations fought on every ocean. Armies battled in China, the

South Pacific, the Philippines, Southeast Asia, Burma, North Africa, Russia, and both eastern and western Europe. The war had both negative and positive effects on missions. Negatively, the war disrupted missionary work. Missionaries could not travel to many nations. Second, many young men who might have gone as missionaries served in the military. Third, many missionaries became caught up in the conflict and found themselves captives, interned in concentration camps for years. This was true of many of the missionaries in China, the Philippines, and Southeast Asia. Some of them spent four long years in Japanese prison camps. Fourth, many churches and institutions were destroyed or damaged in the fighting, not to mention the congregations that were scattered.

World War II also affected missions in positive ways. Soldiers, sailors, marines, and air force personnel traveled all over the world to serve their countries. As these young men and women visited faraway places, they saw the spiritual and physical needs of the people. The Lord laid these needs on the hearts of many, and they vowed to return to preach the gospel and heal the sick. Second, the war disrupted the status quo in many cultures, providing missionaries with an opportunity to present the gospel to people who wondered whether their old ways and old gods were still valid.

The Great Depression

The Great Depression was an economic disaster that affected the whole world from 1929 to 1941. The New York stock market crashed in October 1929, banks failed, companies declared bankruptcy, and millions of workers lost their jobs. Severe droughts plagued the midwestern region of the United States, compounding the financial miseries of millions of people. The Great Depression deprived mission boards and missionaries of the funds they needed badly. For example, the Foreign Mission Board of the Southern Baptist Convention set its budget for 1930 at $1,390,000. By 1932 the board reported receipts of only $691,302. All the mission boards suffered the same kind of decline in income. Many missions agencies went into debt in order to keep their missionaries on the field. When those efforts failed, many missionaries were called home because the mission boards could not afford to remit their salaries. Some missionaries stayed on the field and functioned as tentmakers, living as best they could. The number of new missionaries being appointed dwindled to only a few. Faith missionaries often sought in vain for supporters to help them meet their required support level. Beyond these problems, there was no money for capital projects such as buildings or equipment. President Franklin Roosevelt tried to alleviate the effects of the Great Depression with the social programs of his New Deal, but the United States did not pull out of the Depression until 1941, when American industry geared up for war production.

Communism

The Bolshevik Revolution occurred in Russia in 1917. By the time the civil war in Russia ended, the Communists had seized control of the government. Under the cruel rule of Vladimir Lenin and Joseph Stalin, the church in Russia was severely persecuted and restricted. The Communist government desired to make the Soviet Union an atheistic state. The Soviet victory in World War II brought the Iron Curtain down on eastern and southern Europe. The Christians there suffered the same fate as those in Russia. Missionary activity basically ended, as well as the publishing and distribution of Bibles and Christian literature. The Communist governments imprisoned many pastors, outlawed evangelism, and oppressed Christians in many ways. For example, the Communist governments refused to grant Christian young people admission to universities.

When the Chinese Communists won the civil war in China in 1949 the Communist Party became the dominant force in that country. The new government expelled the missionaries and closed most of the churches, permitting only a few to remain open in large cities. Many Chinese pastors suffered greatly in "reeducation camps." The government closed Christian institutions or converted them to state institutions. Some churches remained open, but under Mao Tse-tung the churches were highly regulated and restricted. The government consolidated all the churches into one organization they called "The Three-Self Patriotic Church." The Communists chose that name to emphasize that the churches in China were no longer under the control of Western missions.

Because they could no longer worship in church, Chinese Christians met in home fellowships away from government oversight. These house churches grew and multiplied, especially during the disastrous Cultural Revolution of the 1960s. Eventually, networks of house churches developed, and the number of Christians grew rapidly after 1980. The number of Christians in China today is difficult to ascertain, but some estimate the number in 2005 at one hundred million. The deinstitutionalizing of the Chinese church may well have been an Acts 8 experience. Saul meant to destroy the church, but he actually caused the church to spread and grow. Similarly, the Communists meant to destroy the church in China, but they actually caused it to prosper. By closing institutions and churches, they forced the Chinese church to adopt a New Testament pattern of operation.

Theological Issues

Theological issues, particularly *universalism* and *pluralism*, affected missions negatively, especially in the Western mainline Protestant churches. *Universalism* is the belief that ultimately everyone will be saved. It takes several forms, but the most common is based on a view of God's love: God is viewed as too loving to send anyone to hell. As more denominations and seminaries embraced universalism, the motivation to do and support missions declined precipitously. For example, the number of missionaries deployed by the two denominations that became the Presbyterian Church-USA declined from 1,713 in 1961 to 463 in 2003. In the United Methodist Church, the numbers were similar. During the same period the number of missionaries deployed by the theologically conservative Assemblies of God increased from 812 in 1961 to 1,880 in 2001.

Pluralism is the concept that all religions are equally valid ways to God. This idea became very popular after 1960. It expressed acceptance of other cultures and "toleration," the dominant social value of the age. The question of how these different religions with their competing truth claims could all be true seemed not to trouble those who believed this idea.

The denominations whose leaders accepted these doctrines gradually reduced their missionary forces. The missionaries who remained on the field shifted their attention from evangelism and church planting to humanitarian activities. Beyond this change, these doctrines seemed to sap the mainline denominations' enthusiasm for evangelism and church growth. Mainline Protestant churches in the United States have experienced steady declines in membership since 1960.

Nationalism

Nationalism is the feeling of love and devotion people have for their nation. If a nation's population has too little loyalty, it is difficult for the nation to function. If a nation has too much, it can degenerate into a situation like that of Nazi Germany during the time of Adolf Hitler. So, nationalism is essential in moderation and dangerous in excess.

After World War II a number of nations gained their freedom from colonial powers. The Philippines gained its independence in 1946. India and Burma followed in 1947. In 1957 Ghana became the first country in sub-Saharan Africa to achieve independence. Nigeria, the most populous country in Africa, was granted self-rule in 1960. The period from 1945 to 1965 saw many nations establish new national governments. The impact of nationalism on missions varied widely. In the Philippines and Nigeria, missionaries continued to function as they had under the colonial powers. In other countries, though, major changes took place. Burma (now called Myanmar) expelled all foreign missionaries in 1966. India gradually placed more restrictions on missionaries, basically eliminating missionary visas. Many newly independent nations viewed Christianity as a Western religion closely identified with colonialism. Therefore, when they escaped the control of colonialism, they sought to limit the influence of Christianity as well.

Colonialism

Colonialism refers to the establishment of colonies in the majority world by Western nations between AD 1492 and 1950. Western powers established colonies in order to exploit weaker nations economically and establish worldwide political empires. Maxims such as "The sun never sets on the British Empire" demonstrate this mentality. A significant factor in colonialism was the belief that Western civilization was superior to all other cultures and that the Western nations had a responsibility to share the benefits of their advanced culture with the rest of the world.

For missionaries colonialism was both a blessing and a burden. It is true that Christianity often rode on the coattails of the conquering colonizers. This was true of Roman Catholic missions in Latin America and Protestant missions in the Philippines, for example. The colonial administrators usually protected and aided the missionaries, though this was not always the case. The East India Company actively discouraged and hindered missionaries from serving in India and China. In some places missionaries, such as Bartolomé de Las Casas, found themselves at odds with colonial administrators over the mistreatment of the native people.

Ultimately, colonialism proved to be a burden because Christianity came to be identified with Western civilization and colonial governments. Thus many cultures viewed Christianity as a "foreign" religion and a threat to cultural unity and societal harmony.

Any interpretation that sees colonialism as all good or all bad is too simplistic. It is best to take the view of Stephen Neill, who wrote that the missionaries were willing to "make the best of a situation they would not have freely chosen. Others, seeing some good in occupation by a western power, were prepared to accept it for the sake of the good, but sometimes to turn all too blind an eye to the evil" (1966, 413).

Reflection and Discussion

1. In Acts 5:29 Peter declares to the Sanhedrin, "We must obey God rather than human beings," but in Romans 13 Paul instructs the believers to obey the government. How can missionaries achieve a balance between obeying the law and obeying God?

Resurgent Islam

At the time of the Edinburgh conference in 1910, Islam seemed to be in a slow decline. Since 1950, however, Islam has made a remarkable comeback. There are three primary reasons for this. First, many Muslim nations gained their independence after 1950. This freedom allowed them to limit or eradicate the influence of Christianity in their lands. Many mission schools, hospitals, orphanages, and so on were closed or converted to government or Islamic institutions. The new governments expelled the missionaries who had entered these countries under colonial administrations. Second, the development of oil fields in many Muslim nations provided ample money for Muslim schools and missionaries. Many Muslim missionaries have been trained, especially in Saudi Arabia, and dispatched around the world to teach Islam to unbelievers and to inspire greater piety among Islamic populations. In addition, governments in the Middle East have built schools and provided free or inexpensive education for poor children in many underdeveloped countries, particularly in Africa. They have also provided funds for the construction of mosques and Islamic education centers at universities. Many bright students from Africa and Asia have received scholarships to study in the universities of the Middle East. Third, the twentieth century witnessed a revival or renewal within Islam. This has expressed itself most dramatically in the rise of Muslim fundamentalism. Muslim fundamentalists resent the encroachment of Western culture and values into their societies. They desire to purge their societies of these Western influences and to return to the pure Islam taught and practiced by Muhammad. This could be called a Muslim restorationist movement.

Materialism

Materialism is the worship of or devotion to material things. It is often said that materialism has more adherents than any world religion. Materialism distracts Christians from doing God's will and obeying his word. It causes people to be indifferent to the gospel of Christ. Materialism affects giving to missions in that Christians are more concerned about taking a vacation cruise than funding a new missionary or more interested in acquiring a new sports car than contributing to the purchase of a new vehicle for a church planter. As American Christians have become more materialistic, per capita giving to missions has decreased. James Engel has documented this in his disturbing study titled *A Clouded Future? Advancing North American World Missions* (1996).

Localism

Localism is an excessive concern for local people and activities. The motto of localists is "Charity begins at home." Often localists have little knowledge or concern for the world. They focus their attention on their church and their local community. This trend has affected missions dramatically. Churches in North America are keeping more of the funds they receive, and they are sending less to missions. For example, Southern Baptist churches give to missions weekly through the Cooperative Program, a kind of united fund for the denomination. Thirty years ago the average church gave 12 percent of its undesignated gifts to the Cooperative Program. Today the average church gives 6 percent. This trend has been seen in other denominations and independent churches as well. More and more churches have focused on local concerns, and the needs of missions and missionaries have gone unmet.

Helps for Missions

Though we listed hindrances to missions first, many factors have served to help or advance the cause of missions in the twentieth century. These include the following.

Improved Transportation

When William Carey and his family traveled to India in 1793, the voyage by sailing ship took about six months. By 1900 missionaries traveled by steamship, and the voyage took two or three weeks, depending on the number of stops along the way. By 2000 missionaries traveled by jet airplanes and complained if their journey lasted more than thirty hours. The dramatic improvements in transportation have meant that missionaries could get to their fields of service much more quickly, surely a better stewardship of time. Beyond that, improved transportation has meant that missionaries can be more mobile, ministering in multiple locations. Many missionaries now carry on a mobile training ministry, teaching short-term classes in many locations in the course of a year. Such a ministry would have been impossible a century earlier. Improved mobility has made it possible for mission administrators to visit the fields and their missionaries more often. This provides for better supervision and lower missionary attrition. The improvements have also made it possible for missionaries to return home for significant family events, such as weddings and graduations, as well as crises, such as the death of a family member.

Improved Medical Care

An earlier chapter mentioned the terrible loss of missionaries in West Africa between 1850 and 1910. The average duration of missionary service at that time was three years. The missionaries either died or returned home, too ill to continue in Africa. As tropical medicine improved, so did missionary longevity. Now, when missionaries go to West Africa, they receive a battery of vaccinations—nine or ten. Now a missionary's death due to tropical disease is unusual, even newsworthy. Much of this improvement in tropical medicine is due to the work of Dr. Walter Reed of the Army Medical Corps in Cuba during the Spanish–American War. He discovered that mosquitoes carry yellow fever. This breakthrough led to many other discoveries and to improved medical care.

Missionaries today not only have the advantage of vaccinations but they also receive improved medical care on their fields of service. Of course, this varies widely from place to place, but the medical care available now cannot be compared to the paucity of care available to missionaries in 1800.

Improved Communication

When the twentieth century began, missionaries communicated mainly by letters, sometimes by telegrams. As the years passed, more missionaries were able to use the telephone to stay in touch with one another, their supervisors, and their families. In the last years of the century, the internet and cellular telephones made communication much easier. Now, missionaries can stay in touch almost constantly with their colleagues and loved ones. This improvement in communication has affected missions in several ways. First, it has enabled missions agencies to modify their organizations. In many agencies several layers of administration have been removed because field supervisors can communicate more freely and quickly with missionaries. Second, improved communication has made the agencies more responsive. They can react to changing situations more rapidly. And, third, missionaries can monitor situations involving their children or aging parents more efficiently. Communication technology has changed so rapidly that it has jumped several technological generations. It is a strange experience to visit West Africa and observe a man talking on a cell phone in a village where there is no electricity. Typically, missionaries can purchase a cell phone, and the service begins immediately. Contrast that advantage with landline phone service. In some places missionaries had to wait for years for landline telephone service.

Specialized Missions

The twentieth century witnessed the establishment of many specialized missions agencies. During the nineteenth century, most missionaries concentrated on evangelism and church planting. The twentieth century saw the number of missions agencies increase dramatically. Many of these focused on a specialized aspect of missions. In fact, it could be said that specialized missions is an important characteristic of twentieth-century missions, and in chapter 16 we will explore these in greater detail.

The specialized missions undertook broadcasting, missionary aviation, disaster relief, tribal work, student work, and literature ministries. This is not to say that mission boards that maintain varied ministries disappeared. Still, the trend in missions after World War II was definitely toward specialized missions. This shift occurred in part because of the growing sophistication of technology. Another motivating factor was the conviction that some essential ministries had been neglected by broad-spectrum mission boards.

Some of the more prominent specialized missions agencies included the Wycliffe Bible Translators (1934), the New Tribes Mission (1942), the Missionary Aviation Fellowship (1945), and Campus Crusade for Christ (1951). These and many others sought to focus their efforts on one thing that they could do better.

Technological Advances

The twentieth century was in many ways the technology century. Early in the century radio was introduced. Missionaries soon grasped its potential for mass evangelism overseas. Missionaries began broadcasting the gospel from missionary radio station HCJB in Quito, Ecuador, in 1931. Other powerful radio stations followed. Missionaries also used motion pictures to capture audiences and communicate the gospel. Television is a costly medium to use, but missionaries used it extensively after 1950, especially in urban areas. Satellite television makes it possible to transmit a Billy Graham Crusade service all over the globe. Further, using satellite television, missionaries can beam gospel programs into countries closed to missionary presence and activity.

The invention of the audiocassette enabled missionaries to record music, stories, teaching, sermons, and Bible passages and to duplicate those cassettes for the masses. This enabled missionaries to communicate to many more individuals, families, or listening groups than they could personally. When videocassettes became available, missionaries used them to penetrate homes and nations that were inaccessible to ordinary missionary activity. The distribution of *The Jesus Film* and *The Passion of the Christ* on video and DVD has significantly affected evangelization in many countries, especially Muslim nations.

The invention of computers has also aided missions. Computers have made it possible to develop databases of information about ethnolinguistic groups, languages, and many other categories essential to missionary work. Beyond that, computers have cut in half the time required to complete the translation of the Bible into a given language. Of course, computers are essential to the internet and email. Through websites, much information on missions has been made available to students, supporters, and missionaries alike. Web posting is much cheaper than publishing books or journals. It also can be accomplished much more quickly. This interchange of information and resources helps missionaries work more quickly and effectively. There is less "reinventing the wheel." Computers have also made missionary mapping much more accurate. Combined with the use of Global Positioning System (GPS) devices, missionaries can produce more accurate maps, showing the locations of people groups.

Anthropology

Anthropology is the study of humans, especially human cultures. One of the social sciences, anthropology began to be taught late in the nineteenth century by E. B. Tylor and J. G. Fraser. Margaret Mead did much to enhance the acceptance of anthropology as an academic discipline.

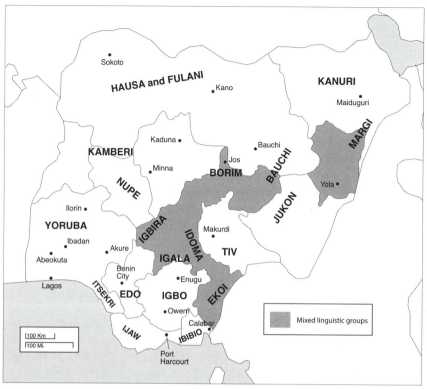

Map 14.1 People Groups in Nigeria

Eugene Nida of the American Bible Society began to lecture widely on linguistics and cultural anthropology and their application to missiology. His book *Customs and Cultures* was one of the first textbooks on missionary anthropology. William Smalley did much to advance missionary anthropology through his writings and *Practical Anthropology*, a journal that he edited. These two men slowly convinced evangelicals that missionaries needed to know more than Bible and theology in order to be effective field-workers. Donald A. McGavran emphasized the social sciences in his missions philosophy, the church growth movement. When he founded the School of World Mission at Fuller Seminary in Pasadena, California, he enlisted Allen Tippett to serve as professor of anthropology. More recently, Paul Hiebert and Charles H. Kraft have written helpful, popular books on missionary anthropology. Today anthropology is accepted as a required subject in missionary training. The result of anthropology's acceptance has been two generations of missionaries who were more cognizant of and sensitive to the cultures of the peoples they served. Anthropology has also enabled missionaries to present the gospel in more understandable and contextualized ways. Through anthropology, missionaries have been able to minimize the effects of culture shock, an occupational hazard for cross-cultural workers.

Improved Linguistics

Linguistics is the social science that studies languages. During the twentieth century this subcategory of anthropology made great strides. Through the efforts of gifted linguists such as Kenneth Pike, the application of linguistics to Bible translation both improved and sped up Bible translation work. As a result, missionary Bible translators produced better translations and completed them more quickly. Improved knowledge of linguistics also helped missionaries learn their adopted languages better and more quickly. Donald Larson and Thomas Brewster contributed much to this effort.

The Progress of Missions around the World

Missions to Muslims

Muslims represent the largest unreached population in the world. In 2004 demographers estimated their number to be 1.3 billion. Because Muslims maintain a high birthrate, this number seems likely to increase considerably in the twenty-first century. Missionary work among Muslims goes back to Ramon Llull in the thirteenth century. Henry Martyn and others did admirable work in the nineteenth century, but the twentieth century witnessed a great swell in missionary work among Muslims. This was especially true when the focus of missions shifted to the 10/40 Window.

Missions to Muslims represents a great challenge, not only because of their numbers but also because of their resistance to conversion. The obstacles to evangelization can be categorized as historical, theological, cultural, and political. *Historical obstacles* include the Crusades of the Middle Ages. Westerners may view the Crusades as ancient history, but Muslims do not. For Muslims the Crusades happened last year, and they engendered an antipathy that continues until today. The historical and continuing support of the American government for the state of Israel causes many Muslims to resent the United States. They identify Christianity with the United States, so they see Christian missionaries as agents of American imperialism. Finally, evangelical mission boards and missions agencies generally neglected the evangelization of Muslims throughout the nineteenth and twentieth centuries. Of course, some denominational and faith boards gave special attention to missions to Muslims, but the percentage of missionaries working among Muslims was low in proportion to their population.

Portrait of Samuel Zwemer (1867–1952)

Samuel Zwemer·is often called the "apostle to Islam." A native of the United States, he received ordination from the Reformed Church in America. In 1890 he founded the Arabian Mission, and he ministered in Iraq, Arabia, and Egypt. In 1929 he became a professor of missions at Princeton Seminary and served in that post until his retirement. For many years he edited an important journal, *Moslem World*. He also wrote many books on Muslim culture, Islamic religion, and missions to Muslims. Zwemer's approach is shown in this statement: "After forty years experience—sometimes heart-breaking experience of sowing on rocks and of watching birds pick away the seed to the last grain, I am convinced that the nearest way to the Moslem's heart is the way of God's love, the way of the cross" (Zwemer 1913, 225–26). Certainly, he was the leading figure in Muslim missions in the first half of the century and well deserves the title given him.

A whole book could be devoted to the *theological obstacles* to evangelizing Muslims. Muslims reject the incarnation, atonement, and resurrection of Jesus Christ. They believe that the Gospel accounts were corrupted and present a distorted picture of Jesus. The contention that God could have a son is a great blasphemy in the thinking of Muslims, and they categorically reject the doctrine of the Trinity. In fact, they contend that Christians are actually polytheists, while they are the true monotheists. Muslims believe in sin, but they reject the doctrine of original sin. Most Christians, especially Americans, value the concept of the separation of church and state, but Muslims, for the most part, desire complete integration of religion and government.

Cultural obstacles also make missionary work difficult. Western missionaries have typically emphasized individual salvation, while religion for Muslims is much more closely tied to family and community. It is quite difficult for a Muslim to make an individual decision apart from the approval of his or her family. Muslims who come to Christ face familial, social, economic, and government persecution. Further, identifying with Christianity is seen as identification with Western culture. In many Islamic nations to be a loyal citizen is to be a faithful Muslim.

Legal obstacles complicate mission work in several respects. In Islamic countries it is against the law for a Muslim to change religion. Such conversion is considered *apostasy*, and in some countries it is a capital crime. In other countries apostasy is punishable by imprisonment. Most Muslim countries refuse visas to missionaries, making it hard for missionaries to enter. In most Muslim countries it is illegal to witness to a Muslim, and these governments refuse Christians' requests to do mass evangelism or gospel broadcasts. In Saudi Arabia the only legal church is one for foreigners in an oil-company compound. In other countries, such as Egypt, churches are permitted, but their activities are restricted.

Through the years missionaries have employed many different models or approaches to the evangelization of Muslims. Many early missionaries used the *confrontational* approach to evangelism. These missionaries sought to win Muslims by public debate and disputation. They challenged the veracity of the Qur'an and questioned the prophethood of Muhammad. Ramon Llull, Henry Martyn, and Karl Pfander used this approach. They preached publicly in the bazaars. They produced apologetic and polemical literature in English

---

The spirit of Christ is the spirit of missions. The nearer we get to Him, the more intensely missionary we become.

Henry Martyn (https://home.snu.edu/~hculbert/slogans.htm)

---

and in the local languages. This approach never prompted much response. It garnered few converts and often increased antipathy toward Christianity. In the twentieth century it was used only in places where colonial governments could protect the missionaries from violent reprisals.

Samuel Zwemer, "the apostle to the Muslims," used an approach that might be called the *traditional evangelical* model. Through preaching, teaching, personal witnessing, and literature, Zwemer and others sought to communicate Jesus Christ to Muslims. They tried to win Muslims and gather the converts together into Western-style churches. Often, these missionaries practiced "extraction," removing converts from their homes, neighborhoods, and even countries in order to minimize the possibility that the convert would recant. This model was used throughout most of the twentieth century, but it, too, proved unsuccessful. The missionaries saw few conversions and few churches planted. The missionaries for their part acknowledge the meager results, but they insist that their method is biblically sound and should continue to be used, hoping and praying that obstacles will one day be removed.

The *institutional model* became popular early in the twentieth century. Presbyterians, Congregationalists, and Reformed churches gave special emphasis to Muslim missions, especially in the Middle East. They sought to win Muslims through hospitals, schools, and orphanages. These mission boards recognized that Muslims are suspicious of or even antagonistic toward Christianity; therefore, they sought to remove these prejudices by institutional demonstrations of love, compassion, and service. Indeed, in some countries institutions were the only way a mission board could establish and maintain a presence. In many places the institutions did make some converts, and in all cases they won the respect of the local people. Still, this model has been used less in recent years. The governments in many Islamic nations have assumed control of these mission-sponsored institutions. Also, economic inflation has made the funding of these institutions problematic, not to mention the difficulties involved in maintaining staff levels.

The *dialogical model* became popular in the early twentieth century. Temple Gairdner (1873–1928) pioneered this approach, and Kenneth Cragg developed it more fully. Dialogue has taken two forms, an ecumenical form and an evangelical form. The ecumenical form seeks dialogue that will result in mutual respect and theological compromise—a synthesis of concepts. The evangelical form seeks dialogue with Muslims based on mutual respect. The missionaries sincerely want to establish rapport, exchange views, and bring their Muslim friends to faith in Christ. The ecumenical approach had no impact on the evangelization of Muslims. The evangelical approach has proved helpful, and it is certainly culturally appropriate. Many Muslims enjoy discussing and debating religion, so this approach builds on that cultural trait.

Phil Parshall developed the *contextualized model* in his missionary work in Bangladesh. In this model the missionary seeks to become like the local people in order to present the gospel in culturally relevant forms. This approach is cognizant of the "offense of the gospel," but it does attempt to remove as many objectionable practices as possible. This model suggests changes in missionary lifestyle (dress modestly, do not eat pork), worship forms (meet on Fridays, leave shoes at the door), theological terms (refer to Jesus as Isa), and missionary strategy (wait to baptize until several converts are ready).

Parshall described his approach in his book *New Paths in Muslim Evangelism* (1980). In more recent years, other missionaries have adopted a more radical approach to contextualization that they call C-5 and C-6. Writing under pseudonyms in the *Evangelical Missions Quarterly* (Travis 1998, 404–17), these missionaries have advocated encouraging Muslims who accept Christ to remain in the mosque and in their communities, witnessing to their faith in Isa as they have opportunity. Parshall and others have expressed concerns about the more radical approach, fearing that syncretism will be the result.

Through the efforts of Zwemer and others, some Protestant churches were started in Muslim lands, but their numbers were scant. In fact, only a few Christians could be counted in most Islamic nations. Only three significant Muslim people movements to Christ can be cited in the twentieth century. In Indonesia, the nation with the largest Muslim population, the Communists attempted a coup in 1965. Their attempt failed, but during the harsh reprisals by the government, many Indonesians became Christians, especially on the island of Java. Some estimate that as many as one million became Christians. In North Africa a significant people movement developed among the Berber people between 1980 and 2000. In the last years of the century, a people movement began in south Asia that shows great potential, claiming five hundred thousand believers at the time of this writing.

Portrait of John Sung

John Sung (1901–1944) was the greatest Chinese evangelist of the twentieth century. Born into a pastor's home in southern China, he often traveled with his father and preached, even as a young boy. John received a scholarship to study in the United States. After he earned a PhD in chemistry at Ohio State University, many prestigious universities offered him positions. He rejected all those offers and went to Union Theological Seminary in New York. He experienced a crisis of faith while in seminary. When he experienced spiritual renewal, the seminary administrators believed him insane and had him hospitalized. While he was in the mental hospital, he read the entire Bible forty times.

Sung finally gained his release and returned to China in 1927. He served as an evangelist with the Bethel Mission, preaching 1,199 meetings to four hundred thousand hearers with eighteen thousand conversions. He also organized seven hundred evangelistic teams, called Bethel Bands. He left the Bethel Mission to become an itinerant evangelistic for the Methodist Church. In this capacity he preached in all of China's major cities as well as Taiwan, the Philippines, Singapore, Indonesia, and Thailand. Most of the Chinese people in those nations came from southern China, and they received Sung's preaching enthusiastically. Many of the Chinese churches in Southeast Asia were planted through Sung's ministry.

Western missionaries often opposed Sung's ministry because of his demonstrative preaching, emphasis on the ministry of the Holy Spirit, and outspoken criticism of Western missionaries. He often singled out missionaries in his meetings and called on them to repent. Sung led in the "Holy Ghost Revivals" of 1933–1936, which many believe prepared the Chinese church spiritually for World War II and the Chinese Civil War (R. Tucker 2004, 432–35; Ling 2000).

In the last two decades of the century, many more missionaries were appointed to Muslim people groups, especially in central Asia. Much of this effort was in response to the emphasis on the 10/40 Window. With this new emphasis and an increased missionary force, the twenty-first century may witness a great turning to Christ by Muslims. This hope is spurred by new missionary methods such as Chronological Bible Story Telling (see Tom Steffen's *Reconnecting God's Story to Ministry* [1996] for an introduction) and the Camel Method (Greeson 2004), which seem to hold promise for increased effectiveness in evangelism.

East Asia

East Asia includes China, Japan, Korea, Taiwan, and Mongolia. China has been the focus of missions praying and doing from the beginning of the modern missions movement. This is due to its vast population, 20 percent of the world's total, and its great influence throughout Asia. During the first fifty years of the twentieth century, missionaries in China experienced steady growth. There were local spiritual awakenings, but nothing on a national scale.

When the Communists gained control of the country in 1949, there were perhaps three million Christians in China, including Catholics and Protestants. The new government closed almost all the churches, which forced many faithful Christians to meet illegally in homes. Despite persecution, and perhaps in many ways because of it, these house churches prospered and multiplied.

Additionally, since the death of Mao Tse-tung, the Chinese government has allowed many former churches to reopen. Today the church in China consists of registered churches that operate openly under the auspices of the China Christian Council, unregistered underground house-church networks that operate illegally, and unregistered house churches that operate openly with the tacit permission of local authorities. The number of Christians is multiplying rapidly, especially in eastern China. Some speculate that the twenty-first century may be the century of the Chinese church (Phillips 2014).

Protestant missionaries entered Japan in 1859 and found some receptivity initially. The missionaries established Christian schools and colleges, and these proved effective in reaching Japanese youth. However, in 1890 the government severely restricted the religious education that mission schools could provide their students. Coupled with the declaration of Shinto as the state religion, this prohibition slowed the growth of Christianity considerably. World War II devastated Japan in several ways, and many Japanese turned to Christ during the period 1945–1955; however, after that time materialism and the influence of Confucianism and resurgent Buddhism seemed to negatively impact response to missionary activity. At the end of the twentieth century, less than 1 percent of the Japanese population was Christian despite more than a century of missionary activity.

The history of Christianity in Korea presents a very different picture indeed. Protestant churches in Korea grew steadily from their beginning in 1884. Presbyterians and Methodists gained the most converts in part because they entered Korea first, and also because they employed the Nevius method in their work. The indigenous approach proved effective among the industrious Koreans. More important than methodology, though, was the power of the Holy Spirit. The Korean church experienced a great spiritual awakening in 1905–1907. The revival in the churches of that era still reverberates today. One aspect of the revival was early morning prayer, which has become a hallmark of Korean Christianity. The close identification of the Protestant churches with the Korean independence movement gained the church social acceptance by the masses. Today, more than 25 percent of the population is Christian, and the church in South Korea is a leader in the sending of missionaries.

Southeast Asia

The situation in Southeast Asia varied greatly. Christianity first arrived in Southeast Asia when Magellan landed in the Philippines in 1521. The Roman Catholic Church established a strong presence throughout the islands, and the Spanish colonial government aggressively thwarted attempts by Protestant missionaries to enter. In 1898, after the Spanish-American War, the United States gained control of the Philippines. This opened the door for Protestant missionaries, and they flooded in. The growth of Protestant churches was slow and steady until World War II. After the war, the Philippines gained its independence, but the new constitution still provided for complete freedom of religion. Both nominal Catholics and tribal animists have readily accepted the invitation to come to new life in Christ. The postwar era saw a number of evangelical missions begin work in the islands. These included Southern Baptists, Conservative Baptists, New Tribes Mission, and the Overseas Missionary Fellowship. The Far Eastern Broadcasting Company set up transmitters that blanketed the islands as well as beamed programming all over Asia. Freedom of religion and the natural openness of the Filipino people have proven to be a beneficial combination for missionary efforts in the Philippines. Many Filipinos now serve as domestic and international missionaries, especially with the Summer Institute of Linguistics and Campus Crusade for Christ.

The situation in Indonesia varies from region to region. In formerly animistic areas, such as Irian Jaya, Christians are the majority, while in vast areas of Java and Sumatra, Islam holds sway. Some Islamic people groups contain only a few Christians. Christians of all types compose about 10 percent of the total population. In many areas Muslims have persecuted Christians, and this has been particularly acute in Ambon and northern Indonesia.

Missionary work in Vietnam, Cambodia, Laos, Thailand, and Myanmar (Burma) has been extensive but not very fruitful, at least among the majority populations. Generally, missionaries have experienced good responses among the animistic tribal people of the mountain areas, while the response of the lowland Buddhist majorities has been quite limited. Roman Catholics established a considerable presence in Vietnam because it was a French colony. The French government limited Protestant access for many years, but after 1920 the Christian and Missionary Alliance and Oriental Missions Society worked in Vietnam and Cambodia. Many missions agencies have worked in Thailand, which has been open to missionary presence, but, again, the response of the lowland Thai people has been quite limited. Response among the hill tribes has been much better.

In Myanmar, Christianity entered the country through the efforts of first the British and then the American Baptists. Adoniram Judson found limited response among the Buddhists, but his missionary associates found great response among the hill tribes. Today there are more than five hundred thousand Baptists among the Karen, the Kachin, and the Chin, among other hill tribes. Because these tribes have been fighting for independence from the central government, the government has oppressed the church in many ways. Response among the lowland Burmese Buddhists remains disappointing.

Singapore is a prosperous island nation. Christianity has made great gains among the Chinese population, especially the English-speaking Chinese. In Malaysia the Roman Catholic Church is the strongest church, although the Anglican Church and the Methodist Church also are strong. In recent years charismatic churches such as the Assemblies of God have seen much growth. Most of the Christians in western Malaysia are Chinese, while in eastern Malaysia tribal people are the majority among believers.

Africa

In 1900 Christians numbered roughly 7 million in Africa, while in 2000 the number had increased to almost 350 million. This dramatic growth represents one of the most interesting accounts in church history. In West Africa freed slaves who settled in Freetown, Sierra Leone, started churches up and down the coast and established a Christian training college, Fourah Bay College, in 1827. The Church Missionary Society established a strong base for the Anglican Church in Nigeria. Southern Baptists entered Nigeria in 1950 and planted many churches in southern Nigeria. The Sudan Interior Mission began work in Nigeria in 1893 and established the Evangelical Church in West Africa (ECWA). Presbyterians and Methodists planted many churches in Ghana, and that nation now boasts a Christian majority, though much nominalism is evident.

SIDEBAR 14.4

Portrait of Helen Roseveare (1925–2016)

Helen Roseveare, a native of England, trained to be a medical doctor at Cambridge University, an unusual step for a woman of her generation. She went to the Congo in 1953 to serve as a medical missionary under the Worldwide Evangelization Crusade. She established two hospitals and the Evangelical Medical Centre in Nyankunde, Zaire. She developed this center as a base for mobile clinics in rural areas. She also established training programs for rural health nurses, where they learned both the Bible and public health.

In 1964 the Simba uprising convulsed the Congo, and Dr. Roseveare suffered rape and a severe beating by the rebel soldiers. When she was rescued, she returned to England to recuperate. She returned to Africa and served until 1973. From that time until her death in 2016, she gave herself to speaking and writing on behalf of missions.

Portrait of Sundar Singh (1889–1929)

Sundar Singh was perhaps the most famous evangelist in Indian church history. He grew up in the Punjab region of northern India, practicing the Sikh religion. In 1904 he saw a vision of Christ and became his follower. When his parents cast him out, he became a traveling evangelist, though he never affiliated with any particular church. He often spoke to Hindus as well as Sikhs. After 1917 he spoke throughout Asia, Europe, and North America. In the 1920s he made evangelistic trips into Nepal and Tibet, which led to many health problems. Writers have described Singh as a Christian mystic, and it could be said that he contextualized Christianity in south Asia before it was fashionable to do so. He died in 1929 while on another mission trip into Tibet.

In East Africa the Anglicans also established many churches, particularly in Kenya and Uganda. The Africa Inland Mission began working in East Africa and established two well-known institutions, Scott Theological College, for the training of African workers, and Rift Valley Academy, for educating missionaries' children.

In South Africa the Boer settlers brought with them the Dutch Reformed Church, which remains quite strong. Evangelical groups such as the London Missionary Society worked among the indigenous tribes and saw good results. When British settlers entered South Africa in 1820, Anglicans, Methodists, Presbyterians, and Baptists also entered. Methodists accomplished much among the black population. In recent times churches have labored to erase the ill effects of apartheid and achieve Christian unity. The increased freedom under the new regime has made possible the development of many independent churches, especially of the charismatic type. In recent years the churches of South Africa have deployed a number of missionaries around the world.

In central Africa the Roman Catholic Church has dominated in nations that once were colonies of Portugal and Belgium, such as Angola, Congo, and Zaire. Civil war in these countries has disrupted missionary work and brought incredible suffering to the people.

Independent churches became a hallmark of African Christianity. Because missionaries tended to be reluctant to yield control of the churches and denominations, Africans started churches on their own, apart from the influence of missionaries. These churches are known as AICs. Over the course of time, the acronym has stood for "African Independent Churches," "African Indigenous Churches," "African Initiated Churches," and "African Instituted Churches." Regardless of the exact word used for the "I," AICs now number in the thousands and reflect a wide divergence in theology and practice. Some can scarcely be described as Christian, some are very evangelical, but the majority could be described as charismatic or Pentecostal.

SIDEBAR 14.6

Portrait of Amy Carmichael (1867–1951)

Amy Carmichael was a native of Northern Ireland. She served briefly in Japan before transferring to India in 1891. She never left India. In 1901 she established the Dohnavur Fellowship in Tinnevelly in order to rescue and care for young girls who had been forced into temple prostitution. Eventually, she began rescuing young boys as well, and the number of children living at Dohnavur swelled to over nine hundred. She administered the fellowship and raised all the financial support herself. She wrote many books and used the royalties to support the fellowship. She experienced a crippling fall in 1931, but she continued administering the fellowship from her bed. When she died, she was one of the best-known missionaries in the world.

India

Missionaries operated under the colonial protection of Great Britain during the first half of the twentieth century. After India gained its independence in 1947, the government gradually introduced more restrictions on foreign missionaries. This was partly due to nationalism and a natural reaction to colonialism. The restrictions also reflected the influence of Hindu nationalist politicians. According to the government, Christians comprise 3 percent of the population, though many Christian researchers believe the actual number is double that. Most of the Christians live in the southern states of India. The Indian church has shown great concern for evangelism and missions. A number of indigenous missions agencies have developed, such as the India Evangelical Mission, Gos-

> **God Hold us to that which drew us first, when the Cross was the attraction, and we wanted nothing else.**
>
> Amy Carmichael (www.goodreads
> .com/quotes/tag/missionary)

pel for Asia, the India Evangelical Team, and the famous Friends Missionary Prayer Band. These agencies and a host of others have deployed missionaries all over the subcontinent to evangelize and plant churches. Traditional mainline denominations have displayed a disappointing nominalism, much as in North America. Newer, charismatic churches have multiplied and grown considerably.

Europe

Western Europe was once the primary base for sending Christian missionaries. Sadly, that is no longer true. Ravaged by two destructive world wars

SIDEBAR 14.7

Portrait of Bruce Olson (1941–)

At age nineteen Bruce Olson left his home in Minnesota and traveled to South America with only a one-way plane ticket and seventy dollars in his pocket. Eventually he found himself lost in the jungles of Colombia, where he encountered the Motilone Indians, a fierce tribe that was feared by all the surrounding tribes. After wounding Olson with an arrow, the Indians brought him to their village as a captive. As he learned their language and culture, Olson was able to win the Motilones to Christ and to establish churches, medical clinics, and schools. In 1988 Communist guerrillas captured Olson and held him for nine months. When fifty Indian tribes threatened to attack the rebels, they released Olson. Now the Motilones are sending missionaries to the other tribes of the Catatumbo region of Colombia. Olson's amazing story is recounted in the popular missions book *Bruchko*.

and affected by secularism, Europe is now seen as the object of missionary endeavors. Though the state churches of Europe claim most of the population as members, only 3 percent of Europe's population attends worship services on a regular basis. This has led many to call for a re-evangelization of Europe.

Eastern Europe was closed to missionary work for much of the twentieth century due to the influence of the Communist governments. When the Iron Curtain came down in 1989, missionaries and Christian organizations poured into Russia and eastern Europe. This proved to be a mixed blessing. Many missionaries and groups brought badly needed personnel and resources. On the other hand, the indiscriminant use of money and influence fostered financial dependency that inhibited natural, healthy church growth. The initial response to the gospel after 1989 was quite positive, especially in the nations of the former Soviet Union. After several years, though, materialism and the resistance of the governments and the Russian Orthodox Church negatively affected church growth. Poland stands out as a Catholic nation, and Romania shows promise of becoming an evangelical lighthouse in eastern Europe.

Latin America

In Latin America the Roman Catholic Church is the dominant religious force. In fact, about 50 percent of all Catholics live in the region. Still, during the second half of the century evangelical churches saw significant growth in many countries, especially in Brazil, Chile, Guatemala, and El Salvador. Much of this growth came in the Pentecostal/charismatic wing of Protestantism. Today many Latinos are going as foreign missionaries to Spain, Portugal, and North Africa, where they are serving with distinction.

Summary

At the end of the twentieth century, missions leaders could reflect on a remarkable century of progress. Though they did not achieve their ambitious goal of evangelizing all the peoples of the world by the year 2000, much was accomplished. According to David Barrett's *World Christian Trends*, in 1900 there were 558 million people in the world who called themselves Christians, while in 2000 that number had increased to almost 2 billion. In 2000 Christianity was the largest religion in the world. Beyond that, the concerted efforts of evangelical missionaries brought the gospel to 58 percent of the world's people groups, especially the larger, more populous groups, according to the Joshua Project website. Gospel radio broadcasts blanketed the globe, and the Bible was available in languages understood by 80 percent of the world's population. In most nations the leadership of the church had passed to local leaders. Though much remained to be done, much had been accomplished. As Ruth Tucker has written, "The spread of Christianity into the non-Western world, principally as a missionary achievement, is one of the great success stories of all history" (2004, 480).

When Baptism Means Breaking the Law

S. J. Dhanabalan

Reprinted with permission from Hiebert and Hiebert (1987, 164–65)

Pastor Prabhudas was uncomfortably aware that Rukhmini's eyes often fastened on him as she sat quietly in the corner of the front pew, awaiting the outcome of the church-council meeting. Somehow he felt she would hold him most responsible for the decision. But he said very little, allowing the elders to carry on the discussion.

All she wanted was for the church to baptize her on the confession of her faith. How ironic it was, he thought to himself. The church prayed often and hard for Hindu converts, especially from among the castes that have been almost entirely resistant to Christianity. Now that they had an authentic convert from a high caste, the council was thoroughly perplexed about whether or not to baptize her. If, like the vast majority of Christians, she had come from the "untouchable" portion of society, now called "scheduled castes" in deference to the reforms of Gandhi, they probably would have baptized her immediately.

Pastor Prabhudas remembered his own joy when Rukhmini had come to his office to ask about baptism. He had heard something of her story from her college friends who were members of his church, but he listened gladly as she told him about her life and her conversion to Christ.

Rukhmini told the pastor that she was the eldest daughter of poor but high-caste parents who had sacrificed and struggled to send her to college so that her job and marriage prospects would be enhanced. They saw this, in the traditional cultural way, as a means to gain more income to support themselves and their younger children.

Once in college, Rukhmini became friends with some Christian students. They gladly drew her into their circle, although no one put any pressure on her to become a Christian. One reason for their "Christian presence" style of witness was that it is against the law in the state of Orissa to make converts from other religions. It is punishable by imprisonment.

Nevertheless, Rukhmini saw something in these Christians that was very attractive to her. She noted the joy and peace in their lives and wished it for herself. After a while, she asked to go to church with them. There she heard the story of Jesus and accepted him as her Savior. The experience transformed her life. She began to study the Bible with her college friends and grew in her faith.

For a while, Rukhmini remained a "secret believer," like other caste people, some of whom never take baptism because it would mean total ostracism from family and caste. In the case of a single woman like herself, it would mean that her parents could hardly find anyone to marry her, because there were so few Christian young men from the upper castes. No Hindu parents would give them a son, and for her parents to give her in marriage outside the caste would be unthinkable.

The time came, however, when Rukhmini decided that she could no longer hide her Christian faith. That was when she came to Pastor Prabhudas and asked for baptism. He had not tried to hide the consequences from her, and it became clear as they talked that she knew them only too well. Her parents would object strongly, and her disobedience to them would itself become a reason for criticism of Christianity. This would be seized upon by the local organization of the Hindu Samaj, who were fanatical in their opposition to Christians and used any breach of cultural norms to condemn them. And, of course, if it could be proven that the Christians had converted Rukhmini, the Samaj would bring a legal case against them. It was not unlikely that baptism of a high-caste woman would become an opportunity for persecution of the entire poor and largely powerless Christian community in that town.

Pastor Prabhudas had promised Rukhmini that she could put her request for baptism before the church's council of elders. Now they had spent almost two hours discussing the issues and seemed to be no closer to a decision. Some of them thought the whole church should be involved; others thought the decision should be made here and now by the council. The pastor finally let his eyes meet those of the young woman who sat patiently waiting for them to arrive at some conclusion. He knew it was time for him to enter the discussion. Choosing his words carefully, he began to speak. . . .

Reflection and Discussion

1. What would you advise Pastor Prabhudas to say?
2. What creative solutions might you consider?

15

Missionary Councils and Congresses

One approach to studying missions in the twentieth century is to examine the various missionary councils and congresses that were held. These meetings reflect both theological and missiological changes in Christianity, both Protestant and Roman Catholic. One can trace the theological arc of the mainline Protestant churches that negatively affected their level of missions activity. In regard to evangelical missions, the Lausanne congresses, especially, reveal how evangelical missions became more inclusive in regard to leaders from the majority world. For Roman Catholic missions, the Second Vatican Council marked significant changes that affected that church's ministry around the world.

Ecumenical Missions

The World Missionary Conference that met in Edinburgh, Scotland, in 1910 voted to organize a continuation committee. This continuation committee eventually became the International Missionary Council (IMC), in 1921. The council existed for forty years. During those years, the IMC sponsored a number of international missions conferences and published a noted missions journal, the *International Review of Missions* (since 1969 the *International Review of Mission*). Studying these conferences reveals much about the state of missions thinking and practice among Western—especially mainline—agencies during the first half of the twentieth century.

The Jerusalem Conference (1928)

The first IMC-sponsored missions conference, which was held in Jerusalem, attracted 231 delegates, including many national leaders from Africa, Asia, and Latin America. The conference attempted to relate the task of missions to a world that was changing rapidly, especially in regard to secularism and pluralism. The discussions centered on the social gospel and the relationship of Christianity to world religions. The conference divided itself into seven sections in order to expedite its work. They were focused on the following topics: (1) the Christian message in relation to non-Christian religions; (2) the relationship between the older churches and the emerging churches; (3) religious education; (4) Christian missions and racial reconciliation; (5) Christian missions and industrial difficulties; (6) Christian missions and rural issues; and (7) international missions cooperation (Briggs 2000a, 516).

Even a quick reading of the list shows that the IMC had a very different agenda from the Edinburgh conference. In Edinburgh the missions leaders did not debate their responsibility to convert adherents of other world religions; they assumed it. In Jerusalem this topic engendered considerable debate, revealing a major theological shift in Protestant missions since 1910. The Jerusalem conference emphasized Christian service, stressing social service more than evangelistic activity.

The Laymen's Foreign Missions Inquiry (1931–1932)

The Laymen's Inquiry was not an IMC project, but it certainly affected the IMC. In 1931 John D. Rockefeller, a wealthy American businessman, provided funding for a worldwide survey of Christian missions. Eight mission boards led in the effort, and they compiled seven volumes of reports. The reports prompted no controversy, but the summary volume, *Re-thinking Missions*, did. William Earnest Hocking, a professor of philosophy at Harvard University, edited the series and authored the summary (see sidebar 15.1).

The thinking advocated in his book provoked a vigorous response from many missionaries and theologians. They accused Hocking of espousing syncretism and pluralism. Perhaps the most significant response came from Hendrik Kraemer, a Dutch missionary and theologian. His book *The Christian Message in a Non-Christian World* presented a strong criticism of Hocking and a strong case for christocentric missions. In this he reflected the theology of Karl Barth, the most influential theologian of the era. Many readers concluded that Hocking's work undermined support for foreign missions.

The Tambaram Conference (1938)

During the ten years between the Jerusalem conference and the Tambaram conference, missiologists debated the relationship between Christianity and the world's religions. Some, such as Nicol Macnicol, saw the world religions as valid means by which other cultures seek God. Others, such as J. N. Farquhar, saw Christianity as the fulfillment of Hinduism in the same way that

William Ernest Hocking and *Re-thinking Missions*

William Ernest Hocking was a professor of philosophy at Harvard University. Well known for his books on the philosophy of religion, he became known in the field of missions when he chaired the Laymen's Foreign Missions Inquiry. In this capacity he traveled extensively in Asia in 1931–1932 to study Protestant mission work. He edited the findings of the Commission and authored the summary chapter in *Re-thinking Missions* (1932). His conclusions provoked much controversy because he wrote that all religions contain a germ of religious truth and that the world religions, including Christianity, should stimulate one another in religious growth. In light of that, he wrote that the primary purpose of missionaries is

1. to discover the best elements in other world religions;

2. to help adherents to those religions understand their religion better;
3. to help adherents of all religions to see the admirable elements in other religions; and
4. to help adherents of all religions to cooperate together in social reform.

He categorically rejected proselytism, the attempt to win converts from another religion. Rather, he projected a world in which the religions would all respect and admire one another and emulate the finer elements in one another (Neill 1986, 418).

Reflection and Discussion

1. Discuss your response to each of the points above.
2. In what ways is there validity to each point?
3. In what ways does each point go too far?

Christianity was the fulfillment of Judaism. William Ernest Hocking argued that missionaries should work to achieve "the creation of a common spiritual life among men" (Yates 1994, 73).

In rebuttal, Julius Richter, professor of missions at the University of Berlin, emphatically stated that Jesus Christ was the exclusive way to salvation. These competing views, often expressed in the pages of the *International Review of Missions*, pointed toward a theological confrontation at the next meeting of the IMC.

The IMC met in 1938 in Tambaram, India, near Madras. More than five hundred delegates attended, representing sixty-nine countries. This conference reflected the development of the church around the world, especially the growth of churches on "the mission field." The conference focused on the nature of the church, and the report of the conference was titled *The World Mission of the Church*. The building crisis in the world influenced the delegates. In fact, the conference planners meant to hold the meeting in China but had to move it due to Japan's invasion of that country. The conference pitted Hendrik Kraemer and his supporters against William Earnest Hocking and

Portrait of Hendrik Kraemer (1888–1965)

Hendrik Kraemer was a Dutch missionary and professor. Raised in an orphanage, Kraemer came to Christ through reading the Bible. He served as a missionary in Indonesia with the Dutch Bible Society. He taught missiology at the University of Leiden from 1937 to 1947. He later became the founding director of the Ecumenical Institute in Bossey, Switzerland. Karl Barth's theology influenced Kraemer, and he responded sharply to William Ernest Hocking's *Re-thinking Missions* by writing *The Christian Message in a Non-Christian World*. In this book he presented a strong case for salvation through Christ alone.

his admirers. In the end the delegates sided with Kraemer, concluding that "world peace will never be achieved without world evangelization" (Briggs 2000b, 929). Beyond that, the conference also emphasized the maturity of the national churches and their role in world evangelization. The conference report stated the aspiration that the national churches would be "the primary factor in accomplishing the task of evangelism" in their countries (Yates 1994, 121).

The Whitby Conference (1947)

The next IMC conference was held in Whitby, Canada, in 1947. It was attended by 112 delegates representing forty countries. The delegates devoted much of their time to surveying the status of missions around the world after the devastation of World War II. They warned of the danger of communism, recognizing it as a rival to Christianity. They also discussed the purpose of the IMC and how to partner together more effectively. The conferees agreed that worldwide evangelism is the main purpose of the church, but they weakened their position by broadening the definition of evangelism to include all phases of life. This conference acknowledged the maturation of the younger churches and assigned responsibility for evangelizing their countries to them, even though they were not ready or able to assume that responsibility. Thus the conference inadvertently "wrote off" large population groups. The decisions of this conference did much for global ecumenical feeling, but they led to diminished evangelistic activity (Mulholland 2000, 1014).

The Willigen Conference (1952)

At this meeting of the IMC, 190 delegates met in Willigen, Germany, to debate the missionary nature of the church. They agreed that the mission of the church originates in the triune nature of God, but they had trouble spelling out what the church should do. They finally declared that the church's missionary obligation is to preach the rule of Christ in every believer in every aspect of life. Just how this would be worked out in missions was left unspecified. This conference, like the one in Whitby, emphasized the unity of the worldwide church, and that unity seemed to take precedence over the expansion of God's kingdom on earth. They noted the loss of China to communists and the rise of nationalism. They also discussed their relationship with the newly organized World Council of Churches (WCC).

The Accra Conference (1958)

The IMC held its final plenary meeting in Accra, Ghana, in December 1957 and January 1958. The delegates voted to merge with the World Council of Churches, believing this action would make missions and evangelism central in the work of the WCC. The conference at Accra marks an important point in the history of the ecumenical movement. The merger of the IMC with the WCC brought many of the younger churches from the "mission fields" into the WCC. Also, at Accra the IMC voted to establish the Theological Education Fund to provide financial assistance for young majority-world scholars to receive theological education. John D. Rockefeller provided the seed money for this fund, which has produced many notable scholars who have an ongoing influence within WCC circles.

Summary

In 1961 the IMC formally merged with the WCC and became the Commission on World Mission and Evangelism within the WCC. Unfortunately, the definitions of evangelism and missions used by the WCC have undergone

---

If the Church is "in Christ," she is involved in mission. Her whole existence then has a missionary character. Her conduct as well as her words will convince the unbelievers and put their ignorance and stupidity to silence.

David Bosch (www.harvestministry.org/100-mission-mottos)

---

significant modification over the past forty years. The council has come to define salvation more in economic and political terms, and for the WCC ecumenism has become a greater goal than evangelizing the world.

What were the main accomplishments of the IMC in its forty-year history? It was the first international ecumenical organization, and it prepared the way for the establishment of the WCC. Further, it fostered deep theological discussion of significant issues faced in mission circles. Finally, it published a well-respected academic missions journal, the *International Review of Mission.*

What were the problems that plagued the IMC? As the years passed, the IMC seemed to lose its focus on missions. Instead, various constituents of the IMC embraced pluralism, universalism, and ecumenism.

Roman Catholic Conferences

The most significant Roman Catholic conference in the twentieth century was the Second Vatican Council, more commonly called Vatican II. Pope John XXIII surprised everyone by calling for the council in 1959. The council began in 1962 and met in four two-month sessions through 1965. More than 2,500 bishops from all over the world convened in Rome to discuss the church's present and future. The council also included Roman Catholic theologians and observers from Protestant bodies. The conference was general in nature rather than focused on missions. It aimed to modernize the church and make it relevant.

The participants at Vatican II produced sixteen lengthy documents, but in regard to missions the most significant was *Ad Gentes* (To the Nations). This document presented the conference's conclusions regarding the church's missionary activity. One of the most quoted statements from that document is "The pilgrim Church is missionary by her very nature." Several decisions by the council directly affected evangelical missions. The first was the decision to seek a degree of reconciliation with Protestants and the Orthodox Church. The council voted to describe non-Catholic Christians as "separated brethren," recognizing their baptism as valid. This led to a significant reduction in opposition to evangelical missionary work in predominantly Catholic countries such as those in Latin America.

Second, the council voted to cooperate with national Bible societies in the printing and distribution of Bibles. This meant that many Roman Catholics in the majority world had an opportunity to own their own Bible.

Third, the council encouraged Catholic laypersons to study the Bible. Before Vatican II the Roman Catholic Church advised laypersons not to read the Bible lest they become confused. This new ruling led to an explosion of interest in Bible study.

Fourth, the council required local parishes around the world to offer masses in the local language rather than in Latin. This helped laypeople understand their faith better.

In summary, though Vatican II was a Roman Catholic conference, its decisions affected evangelical missions, especially in Latin America and the Philippines, in a major way, making it much easier for missionaries to do evangelism (Nyquist 2000, 863–64).

Portrait of the IFMA

The IFMA stands for the Interdenominational Foreign Mission Association of North America. At the invitation of Paul Groef, a businessman and board member of the South Africa General Mission, several "faith" mission boards joined together to form the IFMA in 1917. These included the China Inland Mission, the Africa Inland Mission, and the Central American Mission.

The founders desired an organization that would provide missions leaders with opportunities for fellowship and exchange of information. All member agencies were required to be "faith" missions, be nondenominational, and have a noncharismatic stance. They consistently endeavored to counter theological liberalism. In 2005 the IFMA had eighty-five member agencies and maintained its headquarters in Wheaton, Illinois. In 2007 the IFMA changed its name to the Mission Exchange, and in 2012 it merged with CrossGlobal Link (formerly EFMA), becoming MissioNexus (http://missionexus.org).

Evangelical Conferences

For several decades evangelicals had grown increasingly frustrated with the direction of the IMC. Once the WCC was formed in 1948 and the IMC merged into it in 1961, they tried to work in and through the WCC, but they eventually became convinced that the WCC had turned irrevocably away from the traditional understanding of Christian mission. In reaction, as well as to demonstrate the strength of the worldwide evangelical movement, evangelicals sponsored a number of their own conferences that affected the progress of worldwide missions and demonstrated just how large the evangelical movement was. The first of these was held in Wheaton, Illinois, in 1966.

Congress on the Church's Worldwide Mission

This congress met in April 1966. This consultation, usually called the Wheaton congress, was sponsored by the Interdenominational Foreign Mission Association (IFMA) and the Evangelical Fellowship of Missions Agencies (EFMA). More than nine hundred delegates from seventy-one countries, representing 258 missions agencies, attended the congress. The sponsoring bodies intended for the congress to state evangelical convictions about salvation, evangelism, and missions in response to those of the WCC. At the conclusion of the congress, the delegates adopted the Wheaton Declaration, which stated in part: "We regard as crucial the 'evangelistic mandate.' The gospel must be preached in our generation to the peoples of every tribe, tongue, and nation. This is the supreme task of the Church" (Hedlund 1991, 172).

306

Portrait of the EFMA

The EFMA (Evangelical Fellowship of Missions Agencies) was organized in 1945 by the National Association of Evangelicals and counted fourteen missions agencies as charter members. The EFMA welcomed all evangelicals, including Pentecostals. The EFMA provided a forum for evangelical missions leaders to study and discuss common problems in missions strategy and administration. The EFMA maintained its headquarters in Washington, DC.

For a time the EFMA experienced some tension with the older IFMA, but those differences were resolved in the 1960s. In that decade the two bodies cooperated to found the Evangelical Missions Information Service (now the Evangelism and Missions Information Service), which has published *Evangelical Missions Quarterly* (*EMQ*) since 1964. The two organizations also cosponsored the Congress on the Church's Worldwide Mission, also known as "Wheaton '66." In addition, the EFMA supported the founding of the World Evangelical Fellowship (now World Evangelical Alliance). Along with the IFMA, the EFMA worked to promote and develop Theological Education by Extension, especially during the 1970s. In 2007 the EFMA changed its name to CrossGlobal Link, and in 2012 CrossGlobal Link and the Mission Exchange merged to form MissioNexus (http://missionexus.org).

World Congress on Evangelism

The World Congress on Evangelism was held in Berlin from October 26 to November 4, 1966. These dates coincided with Billy Graham's Berlin Crusade. Graham served as the honorary chairman of the congress, and the Billy Graham Evangelistic Association provided most of the funding for the event. *Christianity Today* magazine was the official sponsor of the congress. Carl F. H. Henry, editor of *Christianity Today*, chaired the steering committee, and his conservative theological convictions guided the planning and conduct of the congress.

More than twelve hundred delegates from one hundred countries met in Berlin to discuss world evangelization under the theme of the congress: "One Race, One Gospel, One Task." Billy Graham delivered the opening and closing addresses of the congress. In his opening address he laid out the seven purposes of the congress:

1. To define and clarify biblical evangelism for our day.
2. To establish beyond any doubt its relevance to the modern world.
3. To underline its urgency in the present situation.
4. To explore new forms of witness now in use throughout the world.
5. To deal frankly with problems of resistance to the Gospel.
6. To challenge the church to renew its own life through an intensified proclamation of historic faith.

Portrait of Billy Graham (1918–)

William Franklin Graham was born in North Carolina and raised on a dairy farm near Charlotte. He accepted Christ as a teenager at an evangelistic meeting conducted by Mordecai Ham. He studied at Florida Bible Institute and Wheaton College. After pastoring a church in the Chicago area, he joined Youth for Christ and became its traveling evangelist. Following the success of his Los Angeles crusade in 1949, he organized the Billy Graham Evangelistic Association (BGEA) in 1950. He traveled all over the globe, preaching in 185 countries to more than 200 million people. He understood the power of mass media and founded two magazines, *Decision* and *Christianity Today*, as well as producing evangelistic movies and television programs. He and the BGEA sponsored many conferences on missions and evangelism, most notably the Lausanne Congress on World Evangelization (1974). Certainly, Graham has been the primary leader in the evangelical movement.

7. To show the world in a fresh and dramatic way that God is in truth Lord of all, and that He saves men through His Son (Johnston 1978, 171).

The delegates heard a who's who of evangelical luminaries during the congress, including John R. W. Stott, Harold Ockenga, Richard Halverson, and Francis Schaeffer from the West as well as Andrew Ben Loo of Taiwan, Doan van Mieng of Vietnam, Takesaburo Uzaki of Japan, and Ruben Lores of Costa Rica from the majority world. At the end of the congress, the delegates voted to adopt a closing statement that harkened back to the SVM's motto: "As an evangelical ecumenical gathering of Christian disciples and workers, we cordially invite all believers in Christ to unite in the common task of bringing the word of salvation to mankind in spiritual revolt and moral chaos. Our goal is nothing short of the evangelization of the human race in this generation, by every means God has given to the mind and will of men" (Johnston 1978, 224).

Lausanne Congress on World Evangelization

The Lausanne Congress proved to be a pivotal conference for evangelical missions. Called for and sponsored by Billy Graham, the congress met for ten days in Lausanne, Switzerland, in July 1974. More than three thousand delegates and observers from 150 nations attended the congress. The largest delegation (five hundred) came from the United States, and that number did not include American missionaries who represented the countries where they served. The congress offered many discussion groups, organized under four broad categories: national strategy groups, evangelistic methods, specialized evangelistic strategies, and theology of evangelization. The four categories demonstrate the emphasis on the evangelization of the world. Nevertheless, the needs of the poor and the social implications of the gospel attracted much attention and comment at the congress.

The plenary program revolved around seven Biblical Foundation Papers and five Issue Strategy Papers. The roster of speakers included Billy Graham,

---

We must be global Christians with a global vision because our God is a global God.

John Stott (https://home.snu.edu/~hculbert/slogans.htm)

John Stott, Donald McGavran, René Padilla, Michael Green, George Peters, Samuel Escobar, Susumu Uda, and Ralph Winter. Winter's plenary address challenged the delegates to focus their efforts on evangelizing all the unreached people groups of the world. His address motivated missions strategists and administrators to do more ethnographic research in order to identify the people groups yet to be reached with the gospel.

At the close of the congress, the delegates were asked to sign the Lausanne Covenant, and more than 2,200 did so. The Lausanne Covenant stated an evangelical consensus on seven key issues:

1. The relationship of evangelism and social concern;
2. The unity, diversity, and cooperation among Christians;
3. The uniqueness of Christ;
4. The validity of missions;
5. The work of the Holy Spirit in evangelism;
6. Religious liberty and human rights; and
7. The relationship of the gospel to culture.

The delegates also voted to create a continuation committee, called the Lausanne Committee for World Evangelization (LCWE). This committee has coordinated what came to be called the Lausanne Movement.

The LCWE has sponsored a number of international, regional, and national meetings, including the Consultation on World Evangelization in Pattaya, Thailand, in 1980, out of which came more than two dozen Lausanne Occasional Papers; Lausanne II in Manila in 1989; and the 2004 World Forum for Evangelization, also in Pattaya, which produced another thirty occasional papers (www.lausanne.org).

In addition, the LCWE has sponsored many specialized consultations on evangelizing particular groups such as Muslims, Jews, and Chinese

Portrait of John R. W. Stott (1921–2011)

John Stott was an English pastor, scholar, author, and noted speaker. For twenty-five years he served as rector of All Souls Langham Place, an Anglican church in London. He often taught and evangelized on behalf of InterVarsity Christian Fellowship, both in Great Britain and North America. He took a leading role in the Lausanne Congress and edited the definitive work on that epic conference. His book *Christian Mission in the Modern World* demonstrates his concern for world missions. To encourage evangelical leaders around the world, he founded the Langham Trust and the Evangelical Literature Trust to provide scholarships and free books to theological students in the majority world.

peoples as well as consultations on critical topics such as the homogeneous unit principle (www.lausanne.org/Brix?pageID=14289) and the gospel and culture, which produced the Willowbank Report (www.lausanne.org/Brix?pageID=14321). The committee has encouraged regional and national committees, and it has sponsored periodicals such as *World Evangelization* (no longer in publication) and *Lausanne World Pulse* (www.lausanneworldpulse.com) as well as books such as *Making Christ Known: Historic Documents from the Lausanne Movement 1974–1989*, which was edited by John Stott. It would not be an exaggeration to say that the Lausanne Congress charted the course of evangelical missions for more than a generation (Reapsome 2000b, 562–63).

Lausanne II

The second Lausanne Congress met in Manila in 1989. Almost 3,600 participants from 190 countries gathered to discuss missions, hear inspiring addresses, and participate in 450 workshops. The participants at Lausanne II were generally younger than at the first congress, and 25 percent of them were women.

The issues discussed at Lausanne II were much the same as those at the first, though there was more emphasis on the internationalization of missions. The ethnicity of the participants reflected world politics. Seventy delegates from Russia attended Lausanne II, and three hundred from China planned to come, only to be blocked by their government at the last minute.

Lausanne II differed from the first in its emphasis on the twenty-first century. The leaders of the AD2000 & Beyond Movement called on the participants to complete the evangelization of the world by the year 2000. At the end of the congress, the participants adopted the Manila Manifesto, which reaffirmed the decisions of the first congress (Reapsome 2000b, 562).

International Conferences for Itinerant Evangelists

The Billy Graham Evangelistic Association sponsored conferences for itinerant evangelists in Amsterdam in 1983, 1986, and 2000. The first conference attracted 3,827 evangelists from 133 countries, with 70 percent coming from the majority world. Most of these participants required travel scholarships in order to attend, and more than half reported that they had no formal theological training. Billy Graham spoke at the opening session and challenged the evangelists to (1) maintain the purity of the gospel, (2) demonstrate morality in their personal life, family life, and finances, (3) cooperate with local churches, and (4) give effective public invitations to receive Christ.

Because many evangelists could not attend the first conference, a second conference was held in 1986. This conference drew more than ten thousand participants from 170 different countries. The organizers provided simultaneous translation of the speeches in twenty-five different languages. The second conference, like the first, aimed to "encourage, equip, and motivate" the world's evangelists. The conference certainly ministered to evangelists from around the world; 78 percent came from the majority world (Glasser 2000, 496–97).

The Billy Graham Evangelistic Association held the third conference in 2000. The attendees numbered more than 10,000. The United States sent 2,767 delegates, and the next five highest sending countries were India (495), Ghana (249), Kenya (204), and South Africa (184). John Stott declared, "There is great diversity here in Amsterdam, but the unity here is even more remarkable" (quoted in Olsen 2000). The conference stressed evangelizing the unreached people groups of the world. It also emphasized theological orthodoxy, especially in regard to salvation through Christ alone (exclusivity). Ajith Fernando of Sri Lanka preached on that theme. While acknowledging that some see this as arrogance, Fernando declared, "Real arrogance is to reject what the Lord of the universe says about himself" (2000).

Edinburgh 2010 Conference

As a centennial celebration of the 1910 Edinburgh conference, the World Council of Churches sponsored the 2010 conference, which met June 2–6, in Edinburgh. The 2010 conference differed from the 1910 in several ways. First, the earlier conference assumed a generic evangelical theology, while the 2010 conference reflected the ecumenical perspective of the World Council of Churches. Second, the 2010 conference differed in its participants. The participants in 1910 were all Western mission leaders, and they were all Protestant. In contrast, the three hundred participants who attended the 2010 conference represented Protestant, Roman Catholic, and Orthodox churches. Further, they came from nations all around the world.

311

Lausanne III (Cape Town 2010)

The Lausanne III Congress on World Evangelization was held in Cape Town, South Africa, in 2010. More than four thousand participants attended, coming from 198 different countries. The organizing committee deliberately limited the number of Western participants to ensure that most of the participants came from the majority world. The conferees approved the Cape Town Commitment, a statement of faith and intention that affirmed evangelical theology and the church's missionary purpose.

Summary

The changes in Protestant missions in the twentieth century reflect the developments in Protestant missions. As mainline Protestant denominations and their creation, the WCC, became more liberal, traditional missions became embarrassing to them. Rather, they embraced a theology and missions praxis that emphasized social, political, and economic liberation. In response, evangelicals withdrew and formed their own structures to encourage world evangelization in the traditional sense, though acknowledging the social implications of the gospel. At the end of the twentieth century, the membership, income, and influence of the WCC declined along with the precipitous declines in mainline Protestant denominations.

Mature National Church

Nathan Porter was enjoying a soda at the retreat center's snack shack when a young Filipino pastor approached him and said, "Tatay Nathan, the executive committee wants to speak with you."

Curious, Nathan readily followed the pastor. When they joined the committee, the members offered him another soda. After the obligatory small talk, the chairman came to the point. "You know that all these years the missionaries have set the strategy, and we have cooperated with them."

"That's true," replied Nathan. "We've worked together well and planted lots of churches."

The committee members nodded their agreement. The chairman continued, "Now, we want to make the strategy, and we want the missionaries to cooperate with us."

Nathan absorbed this and answered, "I agree. You all are seminary graduates and have lots of experience. There is no reason why you should not set the strategy."

At that, the committee members all smiled broadly and nodded again. The chairman said, "We're glad you agree; now we want you to tell the other missionaries."

Reflection and Discussion

1. What would you do in Nathan's place?
2. Identify criteria by which missionaries can determine when national church leaders are ready to move into positions of church leadership.

16

Specialized Missions

Previously we noted that specialized missions was a characteristic of twentieth-century missions. Why was that true? In earlier times missionaries tended to be generalists; they preached, taught new converts, translated the Bible, distributed medicine, and did many other things as well. By the twentieth century, though, specialization affected all areas of life. In the nineteenth century a medical doctor performed all kinds of procedures, while in the twentieth century, especially after 1950, doctors tended to specialize. The same thing held true for Christian service. Bible colleges and seminaries began to offer many different courses of study, and students could major in pastoral studies, missions, church music, youth ministry, religious education, counseling, and church recreation. Of course, in doing this the seminaries were simply responding to the demands of the churches. This emphasis on specialization carried over into missions. After 1950 missionaries went out to serve as specialists in Bible translation, media, medicine, and so on.

Another factor that influenced the development of specialized missions was neglect. Often, visionary leaders established missions organizations because they believed some aspect of ministry had been neglected. They believed that God had led them to meet the need. Specialization is such an important trend in missions that we should understand how it developed in its various aspects.

Bible Translation

Bible translation by missionaries goes back to the time of Ulfilas (311–382). He worked among the Goths in what is now Romania. He always considered his Gothic Bible to be his greatest achievement. William Carey set the pattern for modern missions when he gave most of his attention and considerable talent to translating the Bible. During his forty-one years in India, Carey translated all or part of the Bible into thirty-five languages. Robert Morrison, the first Protestant missionary to China, spent sixteen years translating the Bible into Chinese. Of course, Adoniram Judson and

---

Oh for a fresh, clear, arresting vision of the whole world to break upon the Church of Christ, constraining all Christians to lift up their eyes and look out unselfishly beyond their own narrow boundaries and local interests, and share their Savior's burden of heart for the souls of all mankind!

Robert Hall Glover (http://missionaryquotes.com)

Robert Moffat did the same in Burma and South Africa, respectively. These early missionaries, though not trained in linguistics, labored long and hard to provide the Scriptures to their people. Notice, though, that they also worked at evangelism, leadership training, and church development. The speed and accuracy of Bible translation increased considerably through the work of specialized Bible translators.

The Wycliffe Bible Translators

Cameron Townsend led the way in Bible translation in the twentieth century. As a young missionary in Guatemala, he became frustrated that the Cakchiquel Indians with whom he worked could not understand the Spanish Bible. Without prior training in linguistics, he spent ten years translating the New Testament into the Cakchiquel language. When he finished, in 1929, Townsend wanted to translate the Bible into other Indian languages. His mission board, the Central American Mission, did not share his vision, so he resigned in 1934. In that year he and L. L. Legters organized Camp Wycliffe in the Ozark Mountains of Arkansas and offered their first Summer Institute of Linguistics (SIL). They established the SIL in order to train missionaries and missions volunteers in the science of Bible translation.

The first SIL attracted two students, and the second drew five. Four of the students in the second session accompanied Townsend and his wife to Mexico, where they began translation work among Indian groups. Kenneth L. Pike participated in the second SIL and went to Mexico with the Townsends. He worked on the Mixtec language in a remote area of Oaxaca, Mexico. This work inspired him to do formal study in linguistics, and he eventually earned a PhD at the University of Michigan. He became director of the SIL and served in that capacity until 1979. He also served as a professor of linguistics

Portrait of Cameron Townsend (1896–1982)

Cameron Townsend founded the Summer Institute of Linguistics (1936), the Wycliffe Bible Translators (1942), and the Jungle Aviation and Radio Service (1948). When he established these organizations, he insisted that he serve under the authority of an executive committee. During his tenure he espoused several causes that were not popular with his constituency. In one instance he recommended that a Roman Catholic be appointed as a Bible translator. This recommendation was rejected. On another occasion he recommended the appointment of a couple with a Pentecostal background. In this case Townsend prevailed. He also argued for the appointment of single women to serve in pairs in remote locations. Many considered this too dangerous, but again "Uncle Cam" persuaded the majority, and the single women soon proved their capability. Throughout his career Townsend championed the cause of Bible translation. He often said, "The greatest missionary is the Bible in the mother tongue. It never needs a furlough and is never considered a foreigner" (R. Tucker 2004, 379).

at the University of Michigan. His studies in linguistics did much to assist missionary translators in their work.

The SIL grew to the point that the camp in Arkansas could no long accommodate all who wished to study. The University of Oklahoma invited the SIL to meet at its campus, and they held their sessions there until 1987. Today the SIL offers summer programs at the University of Texas at Arlington, the University of Oregon, and the University of North Dakota. In addition, the SIL holds sessions in Canada and Australia.

Gradually, the SIL expanded its program beyond training to include field translation projects. Using the name "Summer Institute of Linguistics" afforded translators access to some countries where the Wycliffe Bible Translators (discussed below) would not have been allowed access. Their approach to translation work was similar to Wycliffe's: live among the people, learn to speak the local language, understand the culture, study phonological and grammatical structures, develop an alphabet, prepare a dictionary, and translate helpful materials, including the Bible. Their products, especially grammars and dictionaries, were provided to government agencies, educational institutions, and missionaries. Their work began in the Americas, but it expanded into Asia in 1953, to Africa in 1962, and to Europe in 1974. At present, the SIL is working in fifty different countries. The SIL publishes many different aids for translators as well as the *Ethnologue*, the primary reference work on the world's languages. The latest edition lists more than 6,800 languages.

As the number of trained translators increased, Cameron Townsend saw the need to establish a missions agency dedicated to Bible translation work.

Portrait of Eugene Nida (1914–2011)

Eugene Nida was a pioneer in missionary anthropology and Bible translation. When he graduated from UCLA, he met Cameron Townsend and attended the Summer Institute of Linguistics. He participated in the SIL from 1937 until 1953 as both a student and an instructor. After he completed his PhD in 1943, Nida joined the staff of the American Bible Society. He eventually became the executive secretary for translations. As a linguist he published many reference books for Bible translators. As a missionary anthropologist he published one of the first books on cultural anthropology for missionaries: *Customs and Cultures*. He also wrote an influential book on missionary communication: *Message and Mission*. One of Nida's most significant contributions to Bible translation work is his concept of dynamic equivalence. This approach to translation allows the translator to express the meaning of the original text of Scripture without being bound to a literal translation of its linguistic structure (Hoke 2000, 690).

Thus in 1942 he founded the Wycliffe Bible Translators. The Wycliffe Bible Translators (in 2015) have completed translation of the entire Bible into five hundred languages, and they have eighteen hundred translation projects under way.

The nature of the translators' work has changed over the years. For most of its history Wycliffe missionaries focused on specific Bible translation projects. Missionaries went to live in remote places and continued there for ten to twenty years, working to finish their projects. In recent years, though, Wycliffe has redirected its focus somewhat. Now the missionaries come from sixty different countries, and they give themselves primarily to serving as consultants and trainers for local translators who are native speakers. Thus, while Wycliffe continues to work toward Bible translation, it accomplishes this indirectly, by being a catalyst in the translation process.

Bible Societies

Bible societies are organizations that work to translate, publish, and distribute the Scriptures. The first Bible society was the Canstein Bible Institute in Halle, Germany. This Pietist institution supplied the poor people in Germany with Bibles or Scripture portions. The British and Foreign Bible Society was founded in 1804 to serve Great Britain, Europe, and all the British colonies. The society initiated work in India in 1811. The American Bible Society began its ministry in 1816, providing the Scriptures to the United States and other countries where American missionaries served.

A number of Bible societies joined together in 1946 to form the United Bible Societies (UBS). This organization serves as an umbrella organization that coordinates the activities of its 135 member societies. The UBS provides trained translation consultants, especially for societies in less developed nations.

For most of their history Bible societies received support primarily from Protestant denominations and churches. However, after the Second Vatican Council the Roman Catholic Church began to cooperate with Bible societies in many countries. Bible societies have also enjoyed improved relations with the Orthodox Church in many places. Evangelical Christians have established and supported the work of the International Bible Society, which has published and distributed the New International Version of the Bible (Søgaard 2000, 123).

The Wycliffe Bible Translators (including the SIL) and the United Bible Societies have accomplished most of the translation work. However, it is important to acknowledge the efforts of the Lutheran Bible Translators (founded 1964) and the New Tribes Mission (founded 1942). The Lutheran Bible Translators (as of 2015) are working with fifty different language groups around the world. New Tribes Mission emphasizes the evangelization of unreached tribes. Often these tribes do not have a written language, so the pioneer missionary develops an alphabet, dictionary, and grammar in order to translate the Bible into the tribal language.

Evangelization of Students

The Young Men's Christian Association

George Williams founded the Young Men's Christian Association (YMCA) in London in 1844. He wanted to evangelize and minister to young men in the cities. The YMCA promoted evangelism, prayer, and Bible study. The YMCA movement spread to the United States and Canada in 1851. In the same year the Young Women's Christian Association was founded in England. It shared similar aims with the men's organization. In 1855 several national YMCAs joined together to form the World Alliance of YMCAs.

The YMCA in the United States received a blessing when Luther Wishard was named as its first national secretary. Wishard worked tirelessly to unite the scattered chapters. John R. Mott succeeded Wishard in 1888. Both Wishard and Mott shared a concern to see college students saved and to lead them to lives of Christian service. Mott added world missions to the normal emphases on evangelism and discipleship. In the twentieth century, the YMCA continued its work with college students but also reached out to military personnel, refugees, young professionals, and children. In more recent years, the YMCA, especially in the United States, has discontinued its evangelistic efforts and become more of a health and recreational center for families.

Inter-Varsity Christian Fellowship

Like the YMCA, the Inter-Varsity Christian Fellowship (IVCF) began in England in 1877 at Cambridge University. Soon groups began on other campuses in Great Britain, and these groups formed the British Inter-Varsity Christian Fellowship. These students had a burning desire to carry the gospel all over the world. Pleas from Canada prompted Inter-Varsity to send Howard Guiness to Canada in 1928. Inter-Varsity began its ministry in the United States in 1938 at the University of Michigan. Led by C. Stacy Woods, this organization functioned on college campuses and focused its efforts on evangelism, discipleship, and missions. By 1950 there were 499 college and university chapters in the United States alone. Today there are 750 chapters on campuses in the United States.

In 1946 IVCF sponsored a student missions conference in Toronto, Canada. In 1948 the conference transferred to the campus of the University of Illinois at Urbana. Since then, thousands of college students have gathered at Urbana every three years to study the biblical basis for missions and to learn about opportunities for missionary service. In 2006 the Urbana Conference moved to St. Louis to gain space for more delegates, and over 22,250 registered in that year, a record. The 2012 Urbana Conference saw 16,000 participate. In addition, IVCF has missionaries working with students in 12 different countries, and they relate to student ministries in 143 countries as part of the International Fellowship of Evangelical Students.

Cru (formerly Campus Crusade for Christ)

North American college enrollment increased rapidly after World War II. The demobilization of the armed forces and the new GI Bill, a government scholarship program for military veterans, made it possible for many to enroll in college. A perceived need to reach these students prompted Bill Bright to found Campus Crusade for Christ in 1951. Bright testified, "God commanded me to invest my life in helping to fulfill the Great Commission in this generation, specifically through winning and discipling the students of the world for Christ" (Quebedeaux 1979, 16–18).

Called in a vision by God that would guide him the rest of his life, Bright sold his successful business and withdrew from Fuller Theological Seminary, even though he was close to graduation. He rented a house near the UCLA campus and began ministering to students. He recruited an outstanding board of directors that included Billy Graham, Henrietta Mears, Dawson Trotman, and J. Edwin Orr. Within a few months, more than 250 students, including the student body president and Olympic champion Rafer Johnson, had made professions of faith.

Within one year Campus Crusade expanded its ministry to other campuses on the West Coast. By 1960 Campus Crusade had a staff of 109 ministering

Portrait of Bill Bright (1921–2005)

William (Bill) Bright was the founder of Campus Crusade for Christ. Born in Coweta, Oklahoma, after graduating from college he moved to California to engage in business. There he came under the influence of Henrietta Mears at First Presbyterian Church in Hollywood. He enrolled in Fuller Seminary, but after being called by God in a vision, he gave up his studies and started Campus Crusade at UCLA in 1951. His simple evangelistic booklet, "Have You Heard of the Four Spiritual Laws?," proved to be an effective evangelistic tool for campus evangelism.

After seeing rapid progress in North America, Bright extended the ministry of Campus Crusade to South Korea in 1958. Eventually, Campus Crusade's overseas work grew to more than six thousand full-time workers in 152 countries. In his last years Bright emphasized the role of the Holy Spirit in evangelism and missions and the importance of prayer and fasting in the Christian life. When he died in 2005 he was honored as one of the giants among evangelicals (Reapsome 2000a, 147).

on forty campuses in fifteen states as well as in South Korea and Pakistan. In that same year Campus Crusade acquired a defunct resort hotel in California called Arrowhead Springs. This facility provided space for a great headquarters and training center.

From the beginning Campus Crusade demonstrated a commitment to aggressive evangelism. As Bill Bright stated, "Aggressive evangelism is simply taking the initiative to share Christ in the power of the Holy Spirit and leaving the results to God. We make it a special point that aggressive evangelism does not mean being offensive; it does mean taking the offensive. Everywhere we go we tell everyone who will listen about Christ" (Quebedeaux 1979, 91).

Throughout its history, Cru has maintained this approach. Cru staff members engage in aggressive (though not rude), confrontational evangelism, using a booklet Bright wrote, "Have You Heard of the Four Spiritual Laws?" Bright believed that evangelism should be *physical* because it involves going to people; *verbal* because the message of salvation is presented verbally; and *volitional* in that the witness seeks a voluntary, willful response from the hearer. In 2011 Cru reported twenty-five thousand staff members serving in 191 countries. Of course, most of these were national Christians who serve with Cru.

Cru has demonstrated great creativity and variety in its methods. Its basic approach to evangelizing students has been one-on-one evangelism, utilizing the Four Spiritual Laws. It also employs small group meetings in dormitories and sponsors public programs. It supplements these basic approaches with other approaches, such as Athletes in Action. Athletes in Action fields sports teams that tour campuses, competing with collegiate teams and sharing their testimonies at halftime. These teams regularly tour North America and also travel overseas. Campus Crusade has also sponsored major events such as Explo '72 in Dallas, Texas, and Explo '74 in Seoul, Korea, which attracted three hundred thousand participants. Cru also sponsored EXPLO 85, a televised conference to train evangelists around the world. The first satellite-based conference held in multiple worldwide locations, EXPLO 85 featured four days of training sessions, which equipped hundreds of thousands of evangelism workers, who viewed the sessions at ninety sites in more than fifty countries by means of closed-circuit transmissions from seventeen communications satellites.

The Navigators

Dawson Trotman (1906–1956) founded the Navigators in 1933. At first it was a ministry directed toward military personnel, but later the organization broadened its ministry to include college and local church ministries. The Navigators emphasize personal evangelism, follow-up, and Bible memorization. In 2005 the Navigators reported thirty-eight hundred staff members from sixty-two different nations working in more than one hundred countries.

Youth for Christ International

In 1944 Torrey Johnson, a pastor in Chicago, founded the Chicagoland Youth for Christ. Its success in reaching youth in the Chicago area led to the founding of Youth for Christ International in 1945. Torrey Johnson stated that the fourfold purpose of Youth for Christ was (1) to reach every town in North America with the good news of Jesus Christ, (2) to conduct citywide revival meetings, (3) to help people see the lost condition of the world, and (4) to reach the whole world in one generation. Billy Graham served as the traveling evangelist and promoter for Youth for Christ. His dynamic preaching and personal charisma contributed to the organization's rapid growth. In the 1950s Youth for Christ began to organize high school Bible clubs, called Campus Life. By 1951 Youth for Christ had held rallies in fifty-nine countries. Today Youth for Christ International ministers in more than one hundred countries.

Gospel Broadcasting

Radio broadcasting began in North America in the 1920s. Calvary Episcopal Church of Pittsburgh, Pennsylvania, broadcast the first church service on January 2, 1921. In 1922 the mayor of Chicago, "Big Bill" Thompson, built a radio tower on the roof of city hall and invited the public to provide programs. Paul Rader, a local pastor and evangelist, produced an evangelistic program, which may have been the first evangelistic broadcast (Terry 1994,

199). Missionaries soon realized the potential that radio held and began establishing radio ministries.

Radio HCJB

Clarence Jones studied at Moody Bible Institute and worked with Paul Rader's radio program while he was in school. Later he served as program director for the broadcast. In 1928 he made a trip to South America to explore opportunities for a missionary radio station. He visited Venezuela, Colombia, Panama, and Cuba, but every country rejected his overtures. Very discouraged, he returned to Chicago and contemplated leaving the ministry altogether.

In 1930 Reuben and Grace Larson, veteran Christian and Missionary Alliance missionaries to Ecuador, spoke at the Chicago Gospel Tabernacle. When they heard Jones's story, they encouraged him to pursue his dream. Back in Ecuador, Reuben Larson petitioned the government for permission to establish a radio station. On August 15, 1930, he cabled Jones to say that they had been granted a twenty-five-year contract. Despite many obstacles and setbacks, Radio Station HCJB broadcast its first program on Christmas Day 1931. The ministry endured great financial hardships during the economic depression of the 1930s, but Jones's commitment and vision never failed. Gradually, HCJB expanded its studios and increased its power. Eventually, listeners all over the world could pick up the broadcasts of La Voz de los Andes (the voice of the Andes), not only in Spanish but also in fifteen other languages. HCJB added transmitters in Panama and Texas and founded two hospitals, mobile medical clinics, a printing press, and even television programming (R. Tucker 2004, 382–83).

Far Eastern Broadcasting Company (FEBC)

The ministry of FEBC began in the hearts of John Broger and Robert Bowman, two soldiers in the U.S. Army Signal Corps during World War II. During their military duty in Asia, these men felt God's call to broadcast the gospel to Asia. When they mustered out of the Army, they returned to the United States and established their mission. Using Army surplus equipment, they set up their first transmitter in Shanghai, China. They made their first broadcast in 1945, but the civil war in China made continuing there difficult. In 1948 they moved their station to Manila, Philippines, and on June 4, 1948, they broadcast their first program, beginning with a hymn: "All Hail the Power of Jesus' Name."

The next year they resumed broadcasting into China, and soon they developed programming in other languages. Today FEBC operates forty-one radio stations and maintains major transmitters in Manila and Saipan. The ministry produces programs in 154 languages, broadcasting 627 hours of programming each day. FEBC has done great service for the persecuted church in China. Not only does it broadcast evangelistic programs; it also beams Bible teaching programs, including a seminary of the air to assist the house churches (www.febc.org/about/history).

Trans World Radio

Paul E. Freed had a burden for the lost in Spain. He felt so strongly that he sold his house and car to start the ministry. Forbidden to set up a station in Spain, he established a radio station in Tangier, Morocco. The "Voice of Tangier" aired its first broadcast in 1954. The ministry expanded quickly, and by 1956 programs were broadcast in twenty languages into forty countries. When the Moroccan government nationalized all the radio stations, Trans World Radio moved to Monte Carlo, on the coast of France. Today Trans World Radio maintains more transmitters than any other ministry, principally in Monaco, Bonaire, and Guam (www.gospelcom.net.twr).

The World by 2000

In 1985 the presidents of the principal radio missions covenanted together to make the gospel available via radio to all the major language groups of the world (languages spoken by at least one million people). As they analyzed what they were already doing, they discovered 128 people groups without gospel broadcasts. Additional research caused that number to increase to 200. The nations with the largest numbers of groups were India, China, Indonesia, and Pakistan. By 2005 the researchers had listed a total of 372 megalanguages. Since the initiative began in 1985, the ministries have added 111 new language services, with only 78 languages still lacking the gospel. This is an excellent example of networking in missions (Gray 2000).

Missionary Aviation

Missionary aviation has been a terrific help to missionaries, especially those serving in remote places. Before the advent of missionary aviation, missionaries often spent days or even weeks trekking or paddling into isolated villages. This isolation made resupply difficult and medical evacuation almost impossible. Missionary aviation expanded the territory accessible to missionaries.

Most missionary planes are small, single-engine craft that can land on short airstrips hacked out of the jungle. In recent years some helicopters have been deployed as well as large cargo planes, which are mainly used for disaster relief operations.

SIDEBAR 16.4

Portrait of Betty Greene (1921–1997)

Elizabeth (Betty) Greene was a pioneer in missionary aviation. She learned to fly at age sixteen; then, during World War II, she served as a pilot in the Women's Airforce Service. Along with Jim Truxton, she founded the Christian Airmen's Missionary Fellowship in Los Angeles (later the Missionary Aviation Fellowship) in 1944. She became the orga-nization's first field pilot in Mexico in 1946. Eventually, she flew all over the world for MAF, including tours of service in Nigeria, Sudan, Kenya, Uganda, Ethiopia, Zaire, and Irian Jaya. For many years she edited MAF's prayer letter, "Wings of Praise and Prayer" (Lamb 2000, 415).

Missionary aviation has always been a hazardous operation. Flying small planes over rugged terrain is inherently dangerous. More than twenty missionary pilots have died in crashes.

Missionary aviation began in 1943, when several American military pilots met together and discussed the need for aviators to assist missionaries. As a result,

---

There are only three kinds of Christians when it comes to world missions: zealous goers, zealous senders, and disobedient.

John Piper (http://missionaryquotes.com)

Jim Truxton founded the Christian Airmen's Missionary Fellowship in 1945. In 1946 he gave the mission a new name, Mission Aviation Fellowship (MAF), and purchased the first aircraft. Betty Greene, a World War II test pilot, became the organization's first full-time missionary, flying for Wycliffe missionaries in Mexico. In the 1950s the MAF added shortwave radio service to its ministry. These radios enabled missionaries in remote places to keep in touch with their headquarters and supply bases. The MAF first served in Central and South America, but in 1954 it began flying in New Guinea. Today MAF serves 160 different missions agencies (www.maf.org/about/history; Bennett 2000, 101).

Jungle Aviation and Radio Service (JAARS)

After a near-fatal plane crash in Mexico in 1947, Cameron Townsend, the founder of the Wycliffe Bible Translators, decided to organize an aviation division for Wycliffe. Despite the misgivings of his board, he persisted, and in 1948 JAARS was begun. JAARS has its headquarters in Waxhaw, North Carolina, near Charlotte. JAARS serves the transportation and logistical needs of SIL and Wycliffe missionaries all over the world. Cameron Townsend once said, "Airplanes and radios don't make Bible translation easier, they make it possible" (www.jaars.org/history).

Great Commandment Agencies

Sometimes missiologists divide missions agencies into two broad categories: Great Commission agencies and Great Commandment agencies (http://www .sidneyherald.com/community/religion/great-commission-great-command ment-work-together/article_00df2e8f-d34d-5117-bbe6-7919c673979d.html). Great Commission agencies are those that primarily focus on making disciples of all nations (Matt. 28:19). Great Commandment agencies seek to fulfill the commandment Jesus Christ gave in Matthew 22:39—"Love your neighbor as yourself." These agencies emphasize human-needs ministries such as disaster relief and community development. The distinction is somewhat artificial because Great Commission agencies often minister to human needs, and Great Commandment agencies certainly desire to see people come to Christ. Still, the emphases are somewhat different, thus the distinction.

World Vision

The oldest, largest, and best known of the Great Commandment agencies is World Vision. It was founded by Bob Pierce. Pierce, an evangelist and writer for Youth for Christ, traveled through Asia after World War II. His heart broke as he saw the devastation and needs brought on by the war. "Dr. Bob," as he was known to many, had a heart full of compassion for those in need. He wrote in the flyleaf of his Bible, "Let my heart be broken with the things that break the heart of God."

Pierce was especially touched by the desperate needs of children orphaned during the Korean War (1950–1952). He traveled thousands of miles throughout the United States and raised funds to establish orphanages and hospitals in Korea. In 1953 he introduced the first child-sponsorship program to provide for orphaned and needy children. The program began in Korea, but it eventually expanded to Africa and Latin America.

In the 1960s World Vision began providing relief for victims of natural disasters. This involved shipping and delivering food, clothing, and medical supplies. To expedite these efforts World Vision founded a nonsectarian organization, World Vision Relief Organization, that could receive grants, commodities, and shipping assistance from the U.S. government. Eventually, the organization began soliciting and receiving donations of clothing, food, and other merchandise from corporations. In the 1970s World Vision broadened its ministries to include community development, which included sanitation, agriculture, leadership development, vocational training, well drilling, irrigation, and health care.

Portrait of Bob Pierce (1914–1978)

Bob Pierce is remembered as the founder of both World Vision and Samaritan's Purse. His life is a lesson that God can use a person with personality flaws. While conducting evangelistic meetings in China after World War II, Bob Pierce was struck by the great physical needs in east Asia, especially on the part of children. When he returned to the United States, he worked to alleviate their suffering, founding World Vision in 1951. He had a special concern to care for Korean war orphans. "Dr. Bob" traveled ten months of every year, visiting Asia and traveling in North America to raise funds. As a result, his family life suffered. Eventually his daughter, Sharon, committed suicide, and he left his wife, Lorraine. When he died in 1978, he was remembered as a big man with an even bigger heart. His life serves to teach two important lessons: Christian compassion should move believers to meet both the physical and spiritual needs of the world, and wise missionaries give appropriate time and attention to their own families (R. Tucker 2004, 460).

Although World Vision had begun as a North American ministry, it gradually drew support and interest from around the world. Thus in 1980 World Vision International was established. The name reflected the ministry's efforts in 103 countries. World Vision truly gained notice in the 1980s, when a terrible famine occurred in Ethiopia. World Vision's graphic television spots gripped millions, prompting viewers to contribute millions of dollars for the famine victims.

Today World Vision continues to minister to those affected by disasters, but it also continues its community development efforts. A good example of the latter is the Ghana Rural Water Project. Begun in 1986, this project is a massive effort to provide safe water for rural Ghana. Since its inception more than 1,100 wells have been dug, saving the villages served from the ravages of guinea worm disease and dysentery. In 2005 World Vision reported work in ninety-nine nations and income of $1.5 billion. The agency remains "child focused," and it provides support for 2.4 million children.

Samaritan's Purse

Bob Pierce broke with World Vision's board of directors in 1967. In 1970, with World Vision's blessing, he founded Samaritan's Purse. After Pierce died in 1978, Franklin Graham, son of Billy Graham, became the president of the agency. This organization has demonstrated remarkable creativity and innovation. Its ministries include Operation Christmas Child, World Medical Mission, HIV/AIDS ministry in Africa, emergency relief, community development, evangelism, children's programs, pastoral training, and church rebuilding. The last two ministries have been carried out in southern Sudan, where Muslim forces have burned many churches and Christian institutions. Franklin Graham has made many trips to Sudan to intercede for the Christian population there.

Compassion International

In 1952 Everett Swanson, an American evangelist, traveled to Korea to preach to the troops of the Republic of Korea during the Korean War. While he toured South Korea, he encountered many Korean orphans. A missionary friend challenged him: "You have seen the tremendous needs and unparalleled opportunities of this land. What do you intend to do about it?" Swanson returned home and immediately received two unsolicited financial gifts for Korean orphans. He saw this as a confirmation of God's leading, so he founded Compassion International to minister to the orphans' needs. He began to establish orphanages in Korea, and by 1961 his organization operated 108 orphanages. In 1954 he introduced a child-sponsorship program like that of World Vision. His many evangelistic meetings in the United States provided him with opportunities to raise money for the orphanages.

In the 1960s Compassion International began to expand into other countries, a strategic move as the economy of Korea improved and needs declined there. In 1970 Compassion began establishing Special Care Centers that provided for special educational and medical needs. In 1990 Compassion launched its Bibles for All Kids program, which provided a Bible for every sponsored child. Indeed, Compassion insists that all the children sponsored by its agency receive biblical teaching. In 1991 Compassion introduced a scholarship program to assist its children in furthering their education. In 2005 Compassion ministered to seven hundred thousand children in twenty countries.

Mass Media

Print Media

Missionaries have always sought ways to get the gospel to as many people as possible as quickly as possible. The invention of the printing press was a big step forward toward this goal. William Carey's ministry was much enhanced when William Ward arrived and set up his printing press. The press in Serampore produced the Bibles that Carey translated, but it also produced evangelistic tracts and discipleship materials. Robert Morrison and his colleagues published the Bible in Chinese as well as a number of Christian pamphlets. By 1921 there were 160 missionary presses operating around the globe. Most denominational mission boards established printing houses that published all manner of Christian literature in hundreds of languages. One example of a denominational printing ministry is Casa Bautista (the Baptist Spanish publishing center), which is now located in El Paso, Texas. In 2005 it celebrated its 150th anniversary.

Some missions agencies have specialized in literature ministry. These include Christian Literature Crusade, which publishes Christian books and operates bookstores in many cities. In Asia the Overseas Missionary Fellowship has a rich history of publishing materials, especially in Chinese. Every Home for Christ and Operation Mobilization have done great service in distributing evangelistic tracts all over the world. In recent years, missiologists have become more aware that 60 percent of the world's population is illiterate or functionally illiterate. These oral learners cannot access information through reading. This presents a challenge to mission strategists in that most evangelistic methods have been based on literacy.

The Jesus Film

The Jesus Film has proven to be one of the most remarkable stories in the history of missions. *The Jesus Film* was envisioned by Bill Bright and produced in 1978 by John Heyman as part of the Genesis Project. The film's dialogue comes from the Gospel of Luke. In the United States, Warner Brothers distributed the film, and it was shown in two thousand movie theaters. Later it was sold to television networks around the world for public viewing.

Beginning in 1979, Campus Crusade began dubbing *The Jesus Film* into the world's languages. Soon missionaries all over the world began to request that the film be dubbed into their ministry languages. Beyond that, Campus Crusade organized Jesus Film Project teams to show the film in towns, villages, and neighborhoods all over the world. Notice the amazing statistics reported by the Jesus Film Project as of April 2015: *The Jesus Film* is available in 1,311 languages; the film has been shown in 228 countries; more than 60 million copies of the film and its audio track have been distributed; crews showing *The Jesus Film* are active in 120 nations; people in 220 countries can view *The Jesus Film* online; and as a result more than 200 million have professed faith in Christ (www.jesusfilm.org). Missionaries have been discussing and doing mass media for many years, but there has never been an impact like this in the history of missions.

Gospel Recordings

The ministry of Gospel Recordings, now the Gospel Recordings Network, began in 1939. Joy Ridderhof, a missionary to Honduras, became ill and had to return to the United States. In her tiny apartment in Los Angeles, Joy prayed for the people she had to leave behind in Honduras. As she prayed, God reminded her of the gramophone records that were so popular in the villages of Central America. She decided to make a record with Christian songs and a gospel message in Spanish. She made the record and sent it to Honduras. The mountain people responded enthusiastically to the gospel record, and soon requests for the record came from many Spanish-speaking countries.

Joy Ridderhof's ministry grew in an unplanned way when a missionary to the Navajo tribe in the southwestern United States asked for a recording in the Navajo language. He promised to send a bilingual Navajo to Los Angeles if Joy was willing to make the recording. As Joy prayed about the opportunity, she became convinced that God wanted her to make the message of salvation available in all the languages of the world. She vowed, "Lord, I'll make recordings in as many languages as you want me to." By 2005, 4,662 language groups around the world had heard the gospel through Gospel Recordings. Surely, God used a sick missionary in a remarkable way.

Today Gospel Recordings has more than two hundred staff members working out of thirty centers around the world. This agency gives priority to people groups who have no access to the gospel. Gospel Recordings began with vinyl records, but now they primarily use audiocassettes. In remote areas these are played on wind-up cassette players that operate without batteries.

The ministry faces several barriers in its quest to bring the gospel to the eight thousand language groups that still have no gospel recording. The *illiteracy barrier* represents more than two billion people who cannot read and write. Of course, *The Jesus Film* and radio broadcasts can also meet this need, but gospel recordings are much less costly. The eight thousand languages and dialects that still lack gospel recordings comprise the *language barrier*. The *geographical barrier* is the obstacle missionaries face in making and distributing gospel recordings to people groups in remote places. *Political barriers* are erected by governments that are hostile to Christianity. They may keep missionaries out, but they can hardly keep audiocassettes out. Gospel recordings can help to overcome the *prejudice barrier*. In places where missionaries are not welcome, the gospel can come in, carried by migrant workers. Gospel recordings also help missionaries overcome the *manpower barrier*. One missionary can visit only so many homes or villages to tell the gospel story, but by distributing gospel cassettes, the missionary can multiply her ministry many times over.

Many missionaries have noted that when they distribute the cassettes, the recipients listen to the tapes over and over. This saturation with the gospel is a strong positive and makes gospel recordings a valuable tool in evangelism (R. Wood 1996).

Satellite Television

One of the most recent efforts in missionary mass media is SAT-7. SAT-7 is a missionary satellite that beams Christian television programming into

329

North Africa and the Middle East, a region of 500 million people. Satellite television receivers are quite popular in this region, and their use increases daily. Though most of the governments in this region do not allow missionaries to work openly, the gospel can penetrate by means of the satellite broadcasts. Each week SAT-7 broadcasts eighty-four hours of gospel programs in Arabic and Farsi (Persian), reaching an estimated six million viewers each day. The impact of the satellite is revealed by this fact: every day Iraqi Christians record programs from SAT-7 and sell the DVDs on the streets of Baghdad.

Missions Research

A new type of missions agency developed in the last two decades of the twentieth century: missions research. Of course, some research had been done previously. Most large mission boards and missions agencies had a research department; however, in the late twentieth century several missions organizations specializing in research were founded. David Barrett was a pioneer in such research. His seminal research on African Indigenous Churches opened the eyes of many to the multiplication and growth of these movements. Later he helped the International Mission Board of the Southern Baptist Convention set up its research department. His own research, published in *The World Christian Encyclopedia* and *World Christian Trends*, has provided much-needed information on the status of Christianity around the world.

At the Lausanne conference in 1974, Ralph Winter challenged evangelicals to identify and evangelize the unreached people groups (UPGs) of the world. The delegates at Lausanne II in Manila in 1989 and at the Global Consultation on World Evangelization in Seoul in 1995 discussed this need and called for more research. As a result, Luis Bush founded the AD2000 & Beyond organization to focus attention on UPGs and to coordinate efforts to fulfill the Great Commission by the year 2000.

Joshua Project

The need for more complete and accurate research prompted the AD2000 & Beyond organization to establish the Joshua Project in 1995. The Joshua Project maintains a list of UPGs and supports a database that provides information about the UPGs and missionary efforts to reach them (www.joshuaproject.org).

Operation World

Patrick Johnstone and his team have done a great service for world missions. Their publication, *Operation World*, provides a thorough guide to the progress of the gospel in all the nations of the world. *Operation World* also serves as a prayer guide, and it has prompted many believers to pray more intensely and with more knowledge for the needs of the world.

Global Mapping International

Bob Waymire founded the Global Mapping Project at the U.S. Center for World Missions in Pasadena, California, in 1983. He had previously worked in the research department of Overseas Crusades (now OC International). He envisioned an organization that would provide accurate maps and an up-to-date database of missions information. In 1991 the organization moved to Colorado Springs. The purpose of the organization has remained the same, and Global Mapping International has assisted with the publication of *Operation World*, *Peoples of the Buddhist World*, and *The Future of the Global Church*.

Frontier Ventures

In 1976 Ralph Winter, a professor in the School of World Mission at Fuller Theological Seminary, purchased the campus of a defunct college in Pasadena, California. On that campus he founded the U.S. Center for World Mission (now Frontier Ventures). He envisioned a facility that would promote missions research, education, training, and publication. By God's grace, his vision was fulfilled. In 1977 the center began publishing *Missions Frontiers*, a missions magazine that became influential. The next year Winter founded William Carey University to train missionaries. In later years the center established the *International Journal for Frontier Missiology* (www.ijfm.org) and the *Global Prayer Digest*. The center also houses the William Carey Library, a company that publishes books on missions. Through the center Winter promoted his Perspectives on the World Christian Movement course, a study program on international missions. This study program has been offered at thousands of churches in North America.

Other Specialized Missions

Space limitations do not permit a full discussion of all the specialized missions agencies at work today. There are medical missions of many types, ethnic missions (such as Jews for Jesus and Arab World Ministries), tribal missions (such as New Tribes Mission and Regions beyond Missionary Union), schools for missionary children (such as Faith Academy in Manila), member care organizations, technical support, and organizations that provide missionary training.

Christian Witness in Vietnam

Paul G. Hiebert

Reprinted with permission from Hiebert and Hiebert (1987, 212–14)

Harry Miller looked beyond the rice paddies bordered by the tropical jungle to the distant columns of smoke rising from the villages controlled by the Viet Cong as he listened to the deep rumble of the bombs dropped by giant B-52s invisible in the cloudy sky. The destruction only heightened the unease that had come over him as he prepared his message for tomorrow's meeting of the Joint Council of the South Vietnam Mission and the South Vietnam Evangelical Church. His earlier confidence that the mission had chosen the best of strategies had been shaken. Had they indeed presented the whole of the gospel and presented it in the right ways? What would he recommend to the missionaries and national leaders now, when it seemed likely that the North Vietnamese might win the war? And how would he have done it differently if he could do his missionary service over again?

Harry had come to Vietnam twenty years earlier, confident that God was using America to establish the Pax Americana and had set before her an open door to evangelize the world. Even after the war arrived, he had seen the church grow and was certain that American armed forces were necessary to keep the doors open for evangelism and protect the young Vietnamese church from persecution.

However, as hostilities continued, he became increasingly troubled. Harry's relationships and those of his fellow missionaries with other expatriates in Vietnam, including the U.S. military officers who occasionally helped in the mission's programs, helped determine their identity within the country. The common people in Vietnam identified Catholic Christianity with France and evangelical Protestant Christianity with the United States. As the war progressed, evangelicals became increasingly identified with violence and militarism.

Moreover, the close alliance between the United States and the Thieu regime identified evangelical missions with the Saigon government. Although Harry knew that preaching the gospel sometimes meant potential conflict with the political ideology of a country, he decided to boldly declare his Christian convictions despite opposition. In the early years the missionaries took strong stands in challenging their converts to obey their Christian convictions. But, as Vietnam became more politicized and the government's propaganda barrage increased along with the war, the missionaries became less aggressive. They justified their "neutral" stance by pointing out that they would be expelled from the country if they took too bold a position and that it was more important for the church that they stay.

When American policies concentrated on the pacification of the people through the WHAM program ("Win the Hearts and Minds"), the missionaries did not want the gospel to be confused with American propaganda. Their policy was to help all Vietnamese alike on the basis of need. But, because security and logistics made it impossible to help both sides equally, the benefits were reaped largely by the Saigon government. Some critics even charged them with prolonging the war and increasing the pain. By supplying the people's necessities, the missionaries freed the government to use more of its funds for destruction. The tension in Harry became particularly sharp when he realized that while the missionaries saw themselves as giving bread in the name of Christ, the Vietnamese saw them as Americans with Saigon government permits, handing out U.S. surplus goods for the interests of both those governments. All of their work as missionaries had political import. Even evangelism was seen by many as supporting the cause of South Vietnam.

For a moment Harry's thoughts turned to the young South Vietnam Evangelical Church. What would happen to the Christians if the war was lost and the American presence removed? Had the missionaries done all they could to help prepare the Vietnamese church to live under a radically different political system? The Catholic Church had experienced alternating periods of persecution and toleration from the state. The Protestant churches had generally seen themselves existing alongside the state, showing little interest in the government and giving it no official support. Individual Christians could involve themselves in the affairs of state, and members were encouraged to fulfill the "duties of a citizen," but

these were usually defined by the state. Nevertheless, there was an implicit assumption, brought largely by the missionaries, that the church could thrive only in the context of political freedom and governmental goodwill.

But now the Thieu government had canceled military deferments for religious studies. The Catholics and Buddhists protested in public, but the president of a leading Protestant denomination urged the students at the Bible institutes to follow government orders and join the army.

Harry wondered what he should say to the Joint Council. What was the most effective missionary witness in such a context? Was it to adjust to political realities or was it to take a bold stance in opposition to the governments and their questionable practices? How could missionaries avoid being identified with the war, and what would be best for the Vietnamese church? He thought long and hard, and then he began to write his message for the council. . . .

Reflection and Discussion

1. What should Harry communicate to the council?
2. While this case is set during the Vietnam War, which circumstances parallel those of more recent wars? In what ways are they different?

17

The Church
Growth Movement

The church growth movement significantly affected evangelical missions between 1955 and the end of the century. The movement has been defined by Peter Wagner this way:

> Church growth is that discipline which seeks to understand through biblical, sociological, historical, and behavioral study, why churches grow or decline. True church growth takes place when "Great Commission" disciples are added and are evidenced by responsible church membership. The discipline began with the functional work of Donald McGavran. The church growth movement includes all the resources of people, institutions, and publications dedicated to expounding the concepts and practicing the principles of church growth. (1976, 114)

The church growth movement changed the way missionaries and mission administrators thought about missions and measured missions progress. This movement reflected a new philosophy of missions, one that emphasized evangelism and church planting.

The foundations for the church growth movement were laid in 1955 with the publication of Donald McGavran's book *The Bridges of God*. This book, though obscure at first, soon became a topic of discussion all over the world. Eventually, a whole school of thought developed, and McGavran's ideas began to influence the way missionaries went about their work.

Before 1955 many missions agencies had become content to establish and maintain permanent mission stations. These mission stations involved much property and many buildings, and they required a lot of maintenance and attention from their missionary residents. Missionaries often spent their entire careers at one station, and missionaries who did so were held up for praise. In many lands missionaries served mostly in and through institutions such as hospitals, schools, orphanages, seminaries, agricultural stations, and leprosariums. All these institutions required lots of missionary personnel and funds. Yet, understandably, the missions agencies were reluctant to abandon these costly institutions because much money had been spent to establish and maintain them. As a result, field evangelists and church planters were routinely called in from their fieldwork to supervise these institutions. Beyond this, many "field" missionaries continued to serve unproductively for years on end. Though others in similar circumstances baptized many and established multiple churches, they rationalized their lack of success by offering platitudes like, "I may not be fruitful, but I am being faithful."

Theologically, shifts occurred in the WCC that eroded the motivation to do missions on the part of the member churches. The World Council gradually came to describe missions as social ministry and economic and political activism rather than as evangelism and church planting. The rise of modernism among mainline Protestant denominations in the United States in the first half of the twentieth century led to a dramatic decline in their missionary forces in the second half of the century. This depressing situation called for a prophetic word, and God raised up Donald Anderson McGavran to call the church back to its central purpose.

Donald Anderson McGavran: The Founder

It is hard to imagine someone better qualified to expound on the practice of missions than Donald McGavran. He was born in India in 1897, the son and grandson of missionaries. He grew up in India and then returned to the United States for his higher education. He earned his BA at Butler University, his BD at Yale Divinity School, and an MA at the College of Missions in Indianapolis. Later, he earned a PhD in education from Columbia University. As a student he participated in the Student Volunteer Movement and offered to serve in India as a missionary.

In 1923 McGavran returned to India, serving under the United Christian Missionary Society (Disciples of Christ). During his missionary career, which lasted thirty-four years, he served in many different capacities: school superintendent, hospital administrator, rural evangelist, and Bible translator. Through these varied positions, he saw missionary service from every possible angle.

After several years of service, McGavran became aware of the efforts by J. Waskom Pickett and others to survey the progress of Christian missions in India. Bishop Pickett had a special interest in what he called "mass movements." By mass movements he meant occasions when large numbers of people became Christians within a short period of time. Pickett's survey was published in 1933 under the title *Christian Mass Movements in India*. Pickett asked Donald McGavran to continue the survey by studying the status of Christianity in central India. McGavran agreed to do so, and his life was changed. He recounted that he became fascinated by church growth. Why was the church growing in

SIDEBAR 17.1

Influences on McGavran

The first great influence on McGavran was India, where he was born and raised. He lived there most of his life, and India, with its many languages, cultures, castes, and religions, cast a long shadow over his life. It is often said that one cannot understand McGavran unless one understands India.

The second influence on McGavran was Bishop J. Waskom Pickett. Pickett enlisted McGavran to assist in the survey of Christianity's progress in India. The two men then were colleagues for many years. McGavran gained two convictions from Pickett: the importance of statistical research and fierce pragmatism. Pickett had no patience for vague reports; he wanted hard statistical data. Beyond that, Pickett challenged the missionaries to evaluate their work honestly and make needed changes. He could not understand missionaries who pursued ineffective methods year after year.

The third influence on McGavran was Roland Allen. McGavran often spoke of his debt to Allen, and he encouraged his students to read Allen's books. From Allen came the concepts of planting indigenous churches, working in reproducible ways, and the spontaneous expansion of the church.

Reflection and Discussion

1. Is it possible for people to come to salvation in groups?
2. How does McGavran's approach to missions differ from Roland Allen's?

one district, while in an adjacent district the church was not growing at all? He said that he dedicated the rest of his life to answering the question, Why do churches grow? McGavran published his research and conclusions in his first book, *Christian Mission in Mid-India* (1936). The book was published later under the title *Church Growth and Group Conversion* (1956).

In 1953 McGavran rented an isolated cabin in rural India and devoted himself to writing his philosophy of missions. The result was his book *The Bridges of God*, which was published in 1955. In this book McGavran challenges the mission-station approach to missions and lays out his ideas for a better alternative. Reaction was swift, both positive and negative. Kenneth Scott Latourette, the eminent missions historian, wrote in the foreword to the book, "To the thoughtful reader this book will come like a breath of fresh air, stimulating him to challenge inherited programmes and to venture forth courageously on untried paths. It is one of the most important books on missionary methods that has appeared in many years" (McGavran 1955, xiv). Georg Vicedom also praised the book: "This is in many respects a revolutionary book and the author is to be congratulated on his courage in writing it. Nobody can read it without being stimulated to re-think missionary policy in many lands" (Vicedom 1965, 331).

Truly, McGavran's ideas were revolutionary. He challenged conventional missionary wisdom and practice at every turn. Theologically, he emphasized making disciples, not just converts. He also insisted that the missionary's primary task is helping lost people become Christians. Ethically, he insisted that administrators must hold missionaries accountable for their work by demanding and analyzing statistics from every field. Missiologically, McGavran called for fierce pragmatism in evaluating missionary methods. He rejected winning people one by one and called on missionaries to use the new converts' networks of social relationships as bridges that would lead to "people movements." McGavran desired to see people come to Christ in masses, and his research convinced him that this was possible. He criticized missionaries for leaving the work of "discipling" (evangelizing) in order to "perfect" (teach) a handful of new converts.

After the publication of *The Bridges of God*, McGavran's life changed considerably. He was invited to lecture at a number of seminaries, and his own mission board began to send him on research and consultation trips around the world, most notably the Philippines. In 1957 he and his wife retired from active missionary service and returned to the United States. During the next four years McGavran traveled widely, doing field research and writing *How Churches Grow* (1959). In this book he explained his philosophy of missions more fully and answered his many critics.

In 1961 he established the Institute of Church Growth in Eugene, Oregon, on the campus of Northwest Christian College. He meant for this institute to be a think tank for church growth research and seminars. He invited Alan Tippett, an Australian missiologist, to join him at the institute. During these years, Cal Guy of Southwestern Baptist Seminary and Eugene Nida of the American Bible Society visited the Eugene campus and presented lectures. Additionally, during this period McGavran began to publish the *Church Growth Bulletin*. This was a simple newsletter on church growth, but at the zenith of its popularity it boasted ten thousand subscribers.

In 1965 Fuller Theological Seminary invited McGavran to come to Pasadena to become the founding dean of its new School of World Missions. The move to Fuller Seminary provided McGavran with the platform he needed to propagate his philosophy. He soon assembled an outstanding faculty that included Arthur Glasser, Ralph Winter, Alan Tippett, Peter Wagner, and Charles Kraft. Students flocked to Fuller to enroll in the School of World Missions. Missionaries and national leaders alike profited from the instruction and interaction. Their master's theses and doctoral dissertations quickly built a formidable body of church growth literature.

McGavran served as dean of the School of World Mission from 1965 until 1971. He continued to teach as an emeritus professor for years after his retirement. During his years as dean, McGavran found time to publish his magnum opus, *Understanding Church Growth*, which summed up his views on church growth as it applied to international missions. He continued to write and lecture until his death in 1991. Thankfully, his mind remained clear until the end, and he contributed to missions in many ways, even in his last years.

Development of the Movement

The church growth movement was initiated with the publication of *The Bridges of God* in 1955. McGavran did not mean to start a movement, and he did not consciously name it the "church growth movement." His main concern was fostering people movements. In fact, in later years McGavran said that if he had it to do over, he would have called his movement "effective evangelism." In writing of "church growth," McGavran sought to use a term that did not carry the negative baggage that the liberal church had piled on the traditional terms *missions* and *evangelism*. They had redefined missions as social ministry and evangelism as "dialogue" with adherents of other religions. McGavran sought to return missions to making disciples and planting churches.

From 1955 until 1972, McGavran and his colleagues concentrated their research, teaching, and writing on international missions. After 1972 the church growth movement exhibited a clear North American emphasis, which came about through the courses McGavran taught at Fuller Seminary. Many of his seminary students took the missions courses even though they did not intend to serve as missionaries. As they graduated and began to work in churches,

---

Planting new churches is the most effective evangelistic methodology known under heaven.

C. Peter Wagner (http://www.acts29
.com/why-church-planting)

---

they observed that McGavran's principles could be applied in North America as well. When Fuller Seminary began offering a doctor of ministry in church growth in 1975, hundreds of North American pastors responded and received a graduate-level education in church growth theory and practice.

In 1972 McGavran and Peter Wagner team-taught a course on North American church growth at Fuller Seminary. Among the students in that class were Win Arn and John Wimber. Soon afterward, Arn founded the Institute of American Church Growth, and Wimber was named the first director of the Department of Church Growth at the Fuller Evangelistic Association, later known as the Charles E. Fuller Institute of Evangelism and Church Growth. Both organizations provided seminars, materials, and church growth consultation.

The 1970s proved to be a period of rapid growth for the movement. In 1972 Paul Benjamin published *The Growing Congregation* and established the National Church Growth Research Center. Kent Hunter founded the Church Growth Center in Indiana, and Elmer Towns introduced church growth to the fundamentalist churches of North America. Towns demonstrated that the

McGavran's Jargon

Donald McGavran loved to coin words and phrases. This penchant for making up words sometimes proved confusing. For example, he coined the term *Africasia*, meaning Africa and Asia. *Eurica* refers to Europe and America. *Latfricasia* is meant to communicate Latin America, Africa, and Asia. Rather than use the familiar term *evangelism*, McGavran preferred to use *discipling*. This terminology is confusing to students today who think of discipling as helping new Christians grow in their faith. McGavran described that ministry of nurture by using the word *perfecting*. All this requires explanation for modern students, especially those who have not read McGavran's books.

Reflection and Discussion

1. Do you find McGavran's coined words helpful or confusing? Why?

church growth movement was compatible with the Sunday school movement. Southern Baptists soon joined the movement after Charles Chaney and Ron Lewis wrote and published *Design for Church Growth* (1977), which "baptized" church growth and showed its relevance to Baptist churches. Donald McGavran and Win Arn coauthored *How to Grow a Church* (1973), and Peter Wagner followed with *Your Church Can Grow* in 1976. These and a host of similar books introduced church growth concepts to a generation of pastors and church leaders in North America. Naturally, the publication of these books led to numerous church growth seminars, conferences, and institutes.

Delos Miles identified seven factors that affected this surge in the church growth movement (1981, 14–26). The first factor was evangelical cooperation. The International Congress on World Evangelization, held in Lausanne, Switzerland, in 1974, manifested this new level of cooperation. This congress provided an international forum for the discussion of church growth, and Ralph Winter delivered one of the plenary addresses. Coming out of this meeting, the Lausanne Covenant reflected considerable influence from proponents of church growth, and these proponents continued to influence evangelicals worldwide through continuing meetings of the Lausanne Committee for World Evangelization.

The second factor was the megachurches. As church growth theory began to be applied to local church growth, there developed a fascination with large churches. These megachurches became prime examples of church growth, and they began to hold their own church growth conferences. For example, thousands of pastors have attended seminars at Willow Creek Church in Chicago and Saddleback Church in Southern California.

Third, the surge of the church growth movement paralleled that of the lay witness movement. During the 1970s the lay witness movement empowered the laity in the churches to take a greater role in witnessing, testifying, and sharing in their own churches and in others. Lay Witness Weekends became popular and encouraged laypeople to visit other churches to encourage the members there. Many organizations developed to promote and coordinate these efforts: Faith at Work, Laity Lodge, the Yokefellows, and the Institute for Church Renewal. One could add to these departments in almost every Protestant denomination.

Fourth, many parachurch organizations and denominations developed programs to train laypersons to share their faith. The most prominent of these in the United States was Evangelism Explosion, but it was just one of many.

Fifth, the church growth movement benefited from the neo-Pentecostal (or charismatic) movement. The neo-Pentecostal movement (sometimes called the second wave) began in the 1960s, but it reached its full force in the 1970s. This movement operated mainly within traditional Christian denominations. It aided the church growth movement by emphasizing the need for evangelism.

Sixth, most of the proponents of the Sunday school movement gladly joined the church growth movement. This was true of Baptists, who had used Sunday school as their main growth engine for fifty years, and it was especially true of Elmer Towns. He authored one book after another, documenting how churches were growing by means of Sunday school outreach programs.

Seventh, Miles mentions the Keswick movement. The Keswick movement began in Great Britain in the 1870s, but it became a popular movement in the United States as well. Though the Keswick movement emphasized the Christian's inner life, the movement's approval of evangelism contributed to an atmosphere favorable to church growth.

Another factor, not mentioned by Miles, was the general interest in the rise and decline of denominations. In 1977 Dean Kelley, an official with the National Council of Churches, published his surprising book *Why Conservative Churches Are Growing*. Kelley was no great friend of conservative churches or their leaders, but he documented the troubling membership declines in several mainline Protestant churches. This prompted significant study of denominational growth and decline by evangelicals and liberals alike.

In the 1980s the church growth movement divided into several streams, much like the Nile River does as it nears the Mediterranean Sea. The first stream was the megachurch movement. This movement focused on the development of megachurches—that is, churches with more than two thousand in weekly attendance. John Vaughn wrote *The World's Twenty Largest Churches* (1984) and *The Large Church* (1985) to educate pastors about the characteristics of megachurches.

Another stream from church growth was the cell church movement. Led by Paul Yonggi Cho and Ralph Neighbour Jr., this movement highlighted the virtues of cell churches. Of course, the primary example was the Yoido Full Gospel Church in Seoul, Korea. Its attendance grew to over eight hundred thousand in the 1990s. Carl George of the Fuller Institute of Church Growth advocated a similar model of church, what he called "meta-church" in his book *Prepare Your Church for the Future* (1991).

As McGavran aged, Peter Wagner seemed to be his anointed successor as leader of the movement. Wagner appeared to relish the role and gradually became the primary spokesman and advocate for church growth. However, in 1988 Wagner published *How to Have a Healing Ministry without Making Your Church Sick*. This book revealed Wagner's fascination and identification with the signs and wonders movement (sometimes called the third wave of Pentecostalism). Previously, Wagner had held the cessationist view, believing that spiritual gifts such as healing and speaking in tongues ceased at the end of the first century. Eventually, however, through the influence of John Wimber, he became an advocate of signs and wonders as an aid to church growth.

In fact, he and Wimber began offering a course, "Signs, Wonders, and Church Growth," at Fuller Seminary. At the end of each class period, the students were invited to stay for a period of ministry that included prayers for healing. As news of the course spread, many of the seminary's supporters—as well as some of the theology faculty—expressed concern about the theological direction of the course, and eventually the course was withdrawn and recast. Still, Wagner's identification with the signs and wonders movement negatively affected his standing in the eyes of many proponents of church growth (Rainer 1993, 62–63).

A fourth stream again reflects the interests of Peter Wagner. Perhaps as a result of his excursion into signs and wonders, in the mid-1980s Wagner and others began to teach the importance of spiritual warfare and strategic mapping. Wagner came to believe that a host of demonic spirits opposes the expansion of God's kingdom. Proponents of this approach believe these spirits can be identified and their power over a location or people broken through what is called "strategic-level warfare prayer," which is an attack on the most powerful spirit(s) discovered through the process. Wagner articulated his views on this subject through such books as *Warfare Prayer* (1992), *Confronting the Powers* (1996), and *Confronting the Queen of Heaven* (1998); he also organized "Celebrate Ephesus," which was a conference held in Turkey in 1997 as an attempt to break the power of the spirit named Artemis, whom Wagner believed to be the most powerful spirit hindering evangelism around the world.

A fifth stream focused on church health. Two names stand out in this stream: Rick Warren and Christian Swarz. In 1981 Rick Warren and his wife moved to Orange County in Southern California with the goal of planting a church. They succeeded in planting one that became the Saddleback Community Church, which now reports a weekly attendance of more than sixteen thousand. Warren's book *The Purpose Driven Church* (1995) became a best seller in Christian bookstores, and his *The Purpose Driven Life* (2002) became a best seller in all bookstores. Warren's approach reflects the church growth principles that he learned from Cal Guy, a professor of missions at Southwestern Baptist Seminary in Fort Worth, Texas. Warren teaches that the main thing is not church growth but church health. He believes healthy churches will naturally grow. Christian Swarz has promoted a similar concept through his book *Natural Church Development* (1996) and a seminar of the same name.

The sixth stream stemming from the church growth movement is the unreached peoples movement. This movement grew from a seed planted by Donald McGavran. Beginning in 1955, McGavran wrote and taught that missionaries should not view nations as cultural monoliths but rather should see them as cultural mosaics. Most missiologists agreed with McGavran's point, but little was done about it. In 1974, speaking at the Lausanne Congress, Ralph Winter called on the participants to identify and evangelize every ethnolinguistic group (people group) in the world. Winter's address inspired the creation

---

The Bible is not the basis of missions; missions is the basis of the Bible.

Ralph Winter (https://home.snu .edu/~hculbert/slogans.htm)

---

of several different organizations that gave themselves to identifying these unreached peoples and arranging for their adoption by missions agencies. These organizations include AD2000 & Beyond, the Caleb Project, and the Peoples Information Network.

A last stream is what are now called "church-planting movements" (CPMs). David Garrison (2004) and others have taught that missionaries should be planting churches that multiply rapidly and exponentially. This idea seems to be an extension of McGavran's concept of people movements, which was itself derived from Roland Allen's writing on the spontaneous expansion of the church. Regardless of derivation, this result is highly desirable and one that McGavran would applaud heartily.

Listing all these streams raises a pertinent question: Where is the church growth movement going? Surely, it has gone to places that Donald McGavran never imagined or intended! Still, church growth as he meant it to be is still practiced overseas, often by missionaries who today would not recognize the name Donald McGavran nor understand the contribution he made to the missions strategy they are implementing.

Principles of Church Growth

McGavran and the church growth movement developed a set of principles that greatly influenced missionary theory and practice after 1955. The following are a distillation of their philosophy of missions.

Emphasize Evangelism

McGavran said and wrote over and over again: God wants his lost sheep found. McGavran believed that evangelism and church planting should always be missionary priorities. He did not reject social ministries completely, but he believed they often distracted missions and missionaries from their primary task.

Disciple All People Groups

McGavran shared a great insight when he wrote that missionaries should see each nation-state as a cultural mosaic. In this age of "Adopt-a-People Group," his point may not seem original or striking, but it was in 1955. McGavran, and later Ralph Winter, raised the banner of concern for people groups. For McGavran this inclination is easy to understand. His background in India, with its hundreds of languages, castes, and ethnic groups, helped him understand that all Indians are not alike. Instead, missionary strategists need to identify all the people groups and systematically evangelize them, using contextualized methods.

Sociology and Anthropology Can Be Helpful

McGavran's PhD was in education, not theology or missions. In his studies at Columbia University, his professors exposed him to the latest sociological theories. As he understood their value in the field of education, he began to see how these social sciences could help missionaries as well. When McGavran and his colleagues accepted the responsibility of developing a seminary curriculum in missions, they included a significant emphasis on cultural anthropology.

Anthropology is now accepted as a standard element in missionary training, but it was not always so. Modern missionaries who depart for the field with an understanding of cultural anthropology can thank Donald McGavran and his friend Eugene Nida, who promoted the study of cultural anthropology by missionaries.

Emphasize Discipling (Evangelism) Rather than Perfecting

McGavran observed many missionaries in India who would win a few converts to Christ and then drop their evangelistic efforts in order to "perfect" (teach) the new converts. McGavran believed this practice stifled any possibility of a people movement. He believed that the Holy Spirit ripens people groups at different times. Therefore, when a people group is ripe for the gospel, the missionary must not stop harvesting (evangelizing) until all the ripened souls have been gathered. This concept has prompted some to say that McGavran rejected nurturing new believers, but that does not reflect McGavran's view. He insisted that those won to Christ as part of a people movement need instruction; he just rejected the idea of stopping evangelistic efforts in order to do the teaching/nurturing.

SIDEBAR 17.3

Concepts of Evangelism

McGavran taught that evangelism varies according to the person being evangelized. He explained his system of variations this way.

- E-0 evangelism aims to bring existing church members to a personal commitment to Christ.
- E-1 is near-neighbor evangelism of a non-Christian whose language and customs are those of the Christian who is witnessing.

- E-2 is evangelism across a small ethnic, cultural, or linguistic gap.
- E-3 is evangelism across a large linguistic, cultural, or ethnic chasm.

Donald McGavran (1990, 27)

Reflection and Discussion

1. Should churches engage in all types of evangelism or emphasize just one?

MISSIONARIES SHOULD IDENTIFY AND AVOID HINDRANCES TO CHURCH GROWTH

In *Understanding Church Growth* (1990), McGavran discusses many hindrances to avoid. These include the following:

1. *Statistical causes*. McGavran laments the fact that few missions agencies keep careful records of the number of churches, newly baptized members, new churches, newly established preaching points, and so on. He insists that these records are like a medical patient's vital statistics—an indication of health or illness, progress or regress.

2. *Poor mission administration*. McGavran notes that missions administrators often foster mediocrity by not rewarding productivity. Generally, all the missionaries are treated alike, regardless of their success or failure. He believes strongly that administrators should pour money and personnel into situations where the church is growing.

3. *Cultural overhang*. In many cases, missionaries have assumed what worked back home in North America would work just as well overseas. This problem, McGavran says, is particularly acute for denominational missionaries, who feel obligated to promote denominational structures and programs. But regardless of affiliation, missionaries are prone to take effective North American programs and to try to make them work abroad. Sometimes this works, but often it does not due to cultural differences and church differences.

4. *Semantic causes*. McGavran expresses much frustration with the fuzzy language used by missionaries. For example, a missionary might report that he has opened a "work" in Santa Cruz. What does that mean? It might mean that he has planted a church, or preached a sermon, or

distributed gospel tracts, or visited a family there. *Witness* is another ambiguous term. A report might say, "We have a witness in seven villages in Padagor province." Of course, this leaves the reader wondering whether the "witness" was seven churches planted or seven preaching points opened or simply seven villages visited by the missionary.

5. *Psychological causes.* Typically, missionaries or missions administrators with few results to report seek to rationalize their failures. They say, "We may not be fruitful, but we have been faithful." Or they say, "We are not infected with *numberitis*; we are concerned with nurturing and developing true disciples, though they be few in number." Usually, their reports and promotional literature abound with high-sounding phrases but little hard data. McGavran argues that every statistic represents another person added to the kingdom of God. He makes no apology for seeking to win as many to Christ as possible.

6. *Promotional causes.* Missionaries and administrators must raise the money necessary for missionary work. This work is expensive and requires lots of promotion. Promotional efforts tend to be general and optimistic. They seek to touch the emotions of the givers by dwelling on stories of human interest. The recounting of one extraordinary response to the gospel may give the listeners or readers the impression that this response is typical. All of this is natural, but McGavran observes that it obscures the reality of church growth and makes it difficult for supporters to understand exactly what they are funding.

7. *Theological causes.* McGavran notes that several theological issues might hinder church growth. One such issue is a nonconversionist theology. Many today would espouse universalism and contend that ultimately all persons will be saved. Universalism necessarily discourages evangelism and missions. After all, what is the point of expending time and money and effort if all will be saved anyway? A second theological issue is akin to the first: pluralism. Pluralists believe that all the world's religions are equally valid or efficacious; therefore, missionaries should refrain from proselytizing their adherents. The third issue is humanitarianism. Those who advocate "presence evangelism" believe that missionaries should give their attention to ministering to the physical needs of the world's people, letting their presence and Christlike attitudes influence people. McGavran understands these positions, but he rejects them.

Toward the end of his life McGavran wrote:

I rejected the moral theory of the atonement, which had been taught at Yale Divinity School. I accepted the substitutionary view of the atonement, which the Bible so clearly expresses. My renewed conviction concerning biblical authority also motivated my concepts concerning missionary labors of all kinds. I saw clearly that unless the Bible was accepted as God's authoritative, infallible revelation, there was no reason at all for missionary labors. Instead, let the people of each great religion move forward at their own pace, reforming their own religion, and gradually growing into a unified world society. I came to see that any real missionary movement must depend upon an authoritative Word of God made known in the Bible and manifested by our Lord and Savior Jesus Christ. This is the only theological position that makes the communication of the gospel, the discipling of *panta ta ethne*, the multiplication of congregations in every segment of all societies, essential. This is the theological conviction underlying the church growth movement. (1988, 57)

RESOURCES SHOULD BE CONCENTRATED IN RESPONSIVE AREAS

This is sometimes called the "Harvest Principle." McGavran and his disciples taught that spiritual harvests, like grain harvests, have a limited life. That is, church growth teaches that missionaries must reap the harvest of souls while a people group is ripe for the gospel. One common example is the response of the Japanese after World War II. From 1945 to 1955, the Japanese were responsive to the gospel, but after 1955 the response slowed dramatically. The same could be said of Russia. After the Soviet Union collapsed in 1989, the Russian people readily responded to evangelistic efforts; however, within ten years the response slowed markedly. McGavran contended that missions agencies need to consider this phenomenon and pour money and resources into situations where there is a good response to the gospel.

MISSIONARIES SHOULD MAKE CULTURAL ADAPTATIONS

The church growth movement has taught that missionaries should make every effort to achieve fluency in the appropriate language and learn to function in their host culture. McGavran believed that people need to hear the gospel in their heart language. He noted that many missionaries preferred to work in English or in the regional trade language. He insisted that missionaries should make the effort to learn to communicate in the local language. He also taught that missionaries should adjust their lifestyle in order to win more to Christ.

MISSIONARIES SHOULD USE REPRODUCIBLE METHODS

Church growth proponents hold that missionaries should take care to do everything in ways that can be duplicated by local Christians. In this they follow the teaching of Roland Allen, who taught that missionaries should strive to communicate in ways easily intelligible to the local people and easily passed on by them to others. McGavran taught his students to be careful to use methods of church planting that the local people could duplicate. On the

SIDEBAR 17.4

Five Kinds of Leaders

Donald McGavran taught that the developing church on the mission field needs five kinds of leaders.

- Class One leaders are the volunteers who serve in the church week by week. They include Bible teachers, ushers, choir members, and so on. The church needs more of this type than any other.
- Class Two leaders are volunteers who have been trained in outreach and evangelism. They can visit, witness, and lead home Bible studies.
- Class Three leaders are pastors of small congregations. These will be volunteer or bi-vocational pastors.
- Class Four leaders are the full-time pastors of churches.
- Class Five leaders are well-educated leaders who can train others and exercise a widespread ministry.

Reflection and Discussion

1. Historically, missions agencies have focused on training Class Four and Class Five leaders. What might contemporary missionaries do to achieve more balanced training?

one hand, a missionary who uses a video projector and portable generator to show evangelistic films may be unconsciously teaching his disciples that they cannot plant churches unless they possess that expensive equipment. On the other hand, a missionary who plants churches by organizing evangelistic home Bible studies is demonstrating a method that the local people can imitate because no special resources are required.

THE CHURCH MULTIPLIES FASTEST BY PLANTING NEW CHURCHES

The church growth movement has always contended that church planting is the key to fulfilling the Great Commission (Matt. 28:18–20). This is the example of the New Testament church in Acts. These believers obeyed Jesus's command by planting churches all over the Roman Empire. In modern times church growth research has demonstrated that new churches are more evangelistic than older churches. Further, new churches are more active in church planting. In other words, new units multiply more rapidly than older units. Therefore, the church growth movement has consistently advocated aggressive church planting.

HOMOGENEOUS UNITS GROW FASTER

Undoubtedly, this has been the most controversial principle advanced by Donald McGavran. Some speakers and writers have even accused him and the church growth movement of racism. Actually, McGavran was simply making a sociological observation. He noted that people like to worship with people like themselves, and they are more likely to come to Christ if they can do so without crossing language, racial, or cultural barriers. He meant that missionaries would see more church growth if they planted churches that focus on one caste or language.

McGavran was not a racist; he lived most of his life in India. When he returned to the United States to live, he wrote several articles suggesting how the United States might resolve its racial problems. In church growth the homogeneous factor could be almost anything—language, job, caste, age group, or worship style—that people have in common. McGavran's point is simply that people cannot demonstrate a kingdom ethic until they come into God's kingdom. He believed that homogeneous churches would bring more people into God's kingdom.

Though McGavran and his disciples made their case for the homogeneous unit principle, René Padilla and others raised strong objections to this principle. While conceding that the church should use the insights of anthropology and sociology to enhance its evangelistic work, Padilla states, "The real issue is whether church planting should be carried out so as to enable people to become Christians without crossing barriers." Padilla goes on to write, "It is quite evident that the use of the homogeneous unit principle for church growth has no biblical foundation. Its advocates have taken as their starting point a sociological observation and developed a missionary strategy; only then, *a posteriori*, have they made the attempt to find biblical support. As a result the Bible has not been allowed to speak" (1983, 300–301).

SIDEBAR 17.5

Persuasion Evangelism

The church growth movement speaks of persuasion evangelism. It distinguishes this from presence evangelism and proclamation evangelism.

Presence evangelism is often advocated by the WCC. It involves maintaining a winsome, Christlike presence in non-Christian cultures. The idea is that the nonbelievers will be drawn to Christ by the missionary's life, though a verbal witness may not be shared.

Proclamation evangelism teaches that Christians have a responsibility to clearly communicate the gospel to unbelievers. Once that has been done, the Christian's responsibility has been fulfilled.

Persuasion evangelism holds that Christians should persist in their evangelistic efforts, employing various means to persuade people to become believers in Jesus Christ.

Church growth proponents appreciate the value of presence and proclamation evangelism, but they insist that evangelism must not stop there but must include fervent persuasion.

Reflection and Discussion

1. Is it possible for people to come to faith in Christ without hearing a verbal explanation of the gospel? Explain your answer.

EVALUATE METHODS REGULARLY AND HONESTLY

McGavran and Wagner both took pride in being fiercely pragmatic. They insisted that missionaries assess their results on a regular basis in order to evaluate their methods. They believed the task of world evangelization was so important that missionaries could not waste time and money on ineffective methods. McGavran taught his followers the value of statistical research in making these evaluations. To the critics who sneered at their pragmatism, church growth proponents asked whether their critics advocated using impractical methods. The point of this is simple: missionaries should regularly analyze their approach to see where improvement can be made.

The Impact of the Church Growth Movement

A retrospective look at the church growth movement reveals several significant accomplishments. First, the movement helped the Protestant missions movement, or at least the evangelical wing, rediscover its traditional emphasis on evangelism and church planting. The movement prioritized the lost and the unchurched.

Second, the church growth movement's emphasis on homogeneous units prompted missions leaders in North America to plant ethnic churches. Today, many denominations report that their most dynamic growth is in their ethnic congregations. In practice the homogeneous unit principle is usually applied in language congregations. That is, church planters start churches to reach particular ethnic/language communities, such as Hispanics or Koreans. Thus, one sees new Spanish-speaking churches or churches that worship in Korean or Chinese and in ways that are culturally appropriate.

Third, the movement challenged the theology of the WCC. As the theology that characterized WCC publications and thinking became increasingly liberal, Donald McGavran and his associates challenged all Christians not to abandon the unreached billions in Africa, Asia, and Latin America.

Fourth, the church growth movement affected North American seminaries and Bible colleges. Today most evangelical seminaries and Bible colleges offer courses on church growth. If church growth is not mentioned in the course title, it is certain to be found in the syllabus. Missionaries, pastors, and agency leaders have written hundreds of dissertations, theses, and reports on church growth topics. The Great Commission Research Network (formerly the American Society of Church Growth) convenes annually to hear scholarly papers on topics pertaining to church growth.

Fifth, the church growth movement has affected the local church. Every year dozens of church growth seminars and conferences are offered for the benefit of local church practitioners. Church growth consultants cross North America, assisting churches in evaluating their programs and facilities. A number of

The Church Growth Movement's Influence in the Lausanne Covenant

The influence of the church growth movement is evident in the Lausanne Covenant. Adopted at the Lausanne Congress on World Evangelization, this covenant sets out what evangelicals believe about evangelism and missions. Notice the influence of church growth thinkers in article 4, "The Nature of Evangelism," in the Lausanne Covenant.

> To evangelize is to spread the good news that Jesus Christ died for our sins and was raised from the dead according to the Scriptures, and that as the reigning Lord he now offers the forgiveness of sins and the liberating gifts of the Spirit to all who repent and believe. Our Christian presence in the world is indispensable to evangelism and so is that kind of dialogue whose purpose is to listen sensitively in order to understand. But evangelism itself is the proclamation of the historical, biblical Christ as Saviour and Lord, with a view to persuading people to come to him personally and so be reconciled to God. In issuing the gospel invitation we have no liberty to conceal the cost of discipleship. Jesus still calls all who would follow him to deny themselves, take up their cross, and identify themselves with his new community. The results of evangelism include obedience to Christ, incorporation into his Church and responsible service in the world.

The phrase "with a view to persuading" shows that the influence of the church growth proponents was decisive. The same could be said of the phrase "incorporation into his Church." The church growth movement has always placed great emphasis on responsible church membership.

Reflection and Discussion

1. McGavran did not like to count professions of faith. He insisted it was better to count baptisms. Why do you think he took that position? What is the difference?

periodicals have appeared, including *Growing Churches* and the *Church Growth Bulletin*, which has been published under several titles over the years. These are primarily popular journals, intended to help missionaries and pastors.

Sixth, the church growth movement aided field missionaries in several ways. The research emphasis of church growth helped missionaries and field administrators learn how to assess the potential for church growth in unreached areas and evaluate progress in existing fields. The movement also promoted the study of anthropology, which equipped new generations of missions to acculturate more quickly and minister more effectively. The innovations that church growth introduced in leadership training, such as Theological Education by Extension (TEE), made possible the rapid multiplication of churches.

Finally, the movement taught missionaries *how* to plant churches. Missionaries knew they should plant churches, but many did not know how. They had been trained, by and large, to be pastors, not church planters. The church growth movement changed that and began equipping missionaries specifically for church planting. Indeed, the title for missionary service changed from "field evangelist" to "church planter."

Needed Improvements in Church Growth

Ebbie Smith, a longtime missions professor and disciple of McGavran, has listed some corrections that the church growth movement needs to make today.

- The church growth movement needs to return to its roots. Most church growth literature today pertains to the growth of individual North American congregations, not the multiplication of churches in the 10/40 Window.
- Most of the church growth literature today focuses on the growth of middle-class churches that appeal to baby boomers and baby busters.

SIDEBAR 17.7

Theological Education by Extension

The Presbyterian Theological Seminary in Guatemala pioneered the leadership training model called Theological Education by Extension (TEE). In 1962 Ralph Winter and his fellow professors realized that most of the pastors who needed training could not come to the seminary campus in the capital to receive it. They resolved to take the education to the students. As a result, they developed a system of training that involved self-study materials and weekly visits by a professor. The students gathered at churches, and a professor from the seminary visited them to teach, encourage, and help them with the application of the lessons to their ministries.

Winter and his colleagues identified five advantages of TEE:

1. This system opened the door of theological education to those who had no access to it before. These included mature, married men with large families who could not leave their farms or jobs to become full-time students at the residential seminary.
2. The church leaders could learn in the midst of their own culture without having to relocate to the city.
3. The system provided for students to begin their theological education without risking loss of face through failure at the residential seminary.
4. The TEE system helped the students develop the habit of studying daily at home, a desirable discipline for bi-vocational pastors.
5. Finally, TEE proved to be an economical way to deliver theological education.

Justice C. Anderson (2000, 944)

Reflection and Discussion

1. Do you believe McGavran and his associates would approve of the contemporary emphasis on online theological education?

McGavran would call the movement back to consider the needs of the poor and oppressed.

- The church growth movement should avoid overemphasizing the role and importance of megachurches. Certainly, they are an interesting phenomenon, but most churches are small. That fact will not change. Smaller churches need affirmation and attention from the movement.
- The church growth movement needs to reaffirm its emphasis on reproducibility. Western fascination with technology and media is understandable, but the methods employed in premodern societies should be technologically appropriate for those environments.
- The church growth movement has accomplished much in evaluating quantitative growth. The movement should now turn to research into qualitative growth. How can the churches grow better, as well as bigger?
- The church growth movement should resist the temptation to teach that a set of missionary methods will work in every circumstance. All aspects of the missionary task must be contextualized, including the methods. (1995, 18)

The church growth movement never developed a thorough theological foundation. Peter Wagner wrote *Church Growth and the Whole Gospel* (1981), and Alan Tippett wrote *Church Growth and the Word of God*. Both books were meant to lay out a biblical basis for the church growth movement, but the movement never produced a substantial book that explained the biblical basis and theology of church growth. Howard Snyder, in his book *The Problem of Wineskins*, observes: "While in essential agreement with the emphasis—which argues forcefully that Christian churches are divinely intended to grow significantly in number—I feel it also needs the corrective of other biblical emphases to keep it from turning into a mere 'spiritual technology.' Starting as it did from a pragmatic and sociological point of view, church growth has needed to put down deeper theological and biblical roots" (1975, 17).

McGavran was a missionary practitioner, not a theologian. He assumed a generic evangelical theology and worked from there. The church growth movement's antagonism toward institutions on the mission field is understandable but overly broad. The movement needs to revisit this issue. One student of church growth noted that McGavran never met an institution that he liked. His successors need to develop a more nuanced approach to institutions overseas.

Conclusion

In 1973 Peter Wagner wrote an article on church growth for *Christianity Today*. He concluded the article with these words:

Three moods characterize all church-growth advocates, I have found, and these can therefore be said to be moods of the movement in general:

- *Obedience.* Full obedience to the Word of God and the will of God is essential. No apologies at all are made for whatever unswerving obedience might involve.
- *Pragmatism.* Church-growth people do not hesitate to use whatever means God provides to do the best possible job in reaching the goals. They are not very much interested in what *should* bring unbelievers to Christ, but they are acutely interested in what does, in fact, bring unbelievers to Christ.
- *Optimism.* Christ said, "I will build my church and the gates of hell shall not prevail against it." There is no warrant to be gloomy in Christian work. We are ultimately on the winning side. If God be for us, who can be against us? (1973, 14)

What Language Should We Use?

In an Introduction to Missions class, the teacher was explaining various missions strategies. In the discussion on the church growth strategy, she listed the principles of church growth, including the homogeneous unit principle. One student raised his hand. When recognized, he declared, "I don't like the homogeneous unit principle; it's racist." Several other students murmured their agreement.

The professor responded, "I can understand why you say that, but let me ask you a question. Would you say that all people should worship in the same church? Should all ethnicities join together to worship?"

Several students said, "Yes, everyone should be welcome in the church."

The professor replied, "I agree that everyone should be welcome to worship in the church. But what happens when the people attending the same church speak different heart languages? What language should a church use when these people attend?"

This question surprised the outspoken student. He thought for a moment and said, "I guess they should use the language spoken by the majority, or a trade language which they all speak."

"Fine," said the professor. Then she continued, "What about people in the community who do not speak that trade language? Or do not know it well enough to speak to issues of the heart? What shall we do for them?"

Again, the student thought for a moment. "Well, I suppose we'll need to start churches that worship in the language they know best."

The professor nodded and said, "Welcome to the homogeneous unit principle. Often it simply means planting a church for each language group."

Reflection and Discussion

1. What language should a church use when multiple languages are spoken by the congregation?
2. What are some implications of your answer?

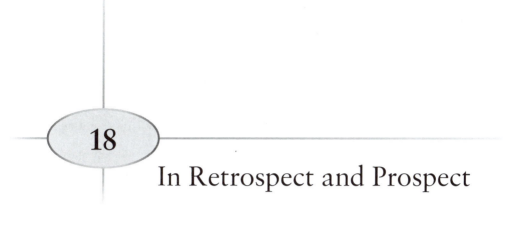

18

In Retrospect and Prospect

In this final chapter we shall look back at two thousand years of missionary endeavor and try to evaluate missionaries' ministry. What did they do right, and what did they do wrong? Then we shall look ahead to what remains to be done in missions. Finally, we shall discuss how missions might be done in the future. By listing and discussing trends in missions, perhaps we can understand how missions will develop.

A Retrospective Evaluation

The late J. Herbert Kane served as a professor of missions at Trinity Evangelical Divinity School near Chicago. He wrote many books, among them an introduction to missions called *Understanding Christian Missions*. In that book he included a section in which he evaluated missionaries' performance over the centuries. His evaluation is still helpful today (1978, 278–95).

What Missionaries Did Wrong

1. *Missionaries displayed a superiority complex.* For the most part, missionaries went overseas believing that Western civilization was superior. They also believed that they were doing the local people a favor by introducing Western civilization. Some believed they had to "civilize in order to Christianize." While this attitude grates on modern readers, one should evaluate missionaries in light of their own times. In expressing these views, they reflected the prevailing attitudes of their home cultures.

2. *Missionaries demonstrated negative attitudes toward "pagan" religions.* Of course, one would expect missionaries to believe that Christianity is the only true faith. Unfortunately, many early missionaries criticized the religions

of their host cultures in derogatory ways. Rather than present a positive message about Jesus, they attacked the predominant religions in ways that greatly offended their listeners. In many cases, missionaries could utter these religious diatribes only because they enjoyed the protection of colonial police forces. Eventually, missionaries abandoned such negativism, finding this approach was counterproductive. Still, the damage had been done, and resentment lingers yet.

Why did they engage in such a negative approach? First, the pioneer missionaries often understood very little about the religions they attacked. Their religious texts had not yet been translated. Second, they reacted against the idolatry and immorality they saw. And, third, they judged the religions by the lives of their adherents, comparing the worst Muslims or Hindus or Buddhists to the most pious Christians.

3. *Missionaries failed to distinguish between Christianity and Western culture.* Missionaries carried lots of cultural baggage with them, and they tried (with some notable exceptions) to make the national believers into proper Westerners, introducing Western dress, political forms, and social customs (such as afternoon tea). As a result, Africans saw Christianity as the "white man's religion," and Asians viewed Christianity as a "foreign" religion. Perhaps this synthesis of Christianity and Western civilization was inevitable, given the influence of Christianity on Europe's history and culture. Even modern missionaries, thoroughly trained in anthropology and contextualization, struggle to communicate the gospel to other people groups without attaching Western customs to it.

4. *Missionaries exported denominationalism along with the gospel.* Early missionaries did not want this to happen, but the denominational divisions of Protestant Christianity in the West were replicated around the world. This is really not too surprising. Missionaries had, in the main, grown up and been trained in denominational churches and schools. Beyond that, most of them received their support from the churches of their denominations, and those churches wanted reassurance that the missionaries were planting the "right kind" of churches. The folks back home did not understand that a convert from Hinduism or Islam facing untold persecution might not appreciate the doctrinal distinctives of their particular denomination. One should not stress this point too much. Stephen Neill was surely right when he wrote, "In point of fact Christian divisions have wrought less harm than might have been expected. Both Hinduism and Islam are themselves religions of many sects" (1970, 25).

5. *Missionaries failed to encourage the indigenization of Christianity.* Missionaries failed to plant churches that looked and seemed like culturally appropriate churches. Instead, missionaries imported architecture, liturgy, literature, and even vestments from the West. Thus Korean believers were taught to sing Western hymns, and Western-style churches were built in India. The Roman Catholics insisted (until Vatican II) that the same Latin Mass be said

all over the world. Beyond that, the curriculum of the theological colleges and seminaries was imported wholesale from the West, often including textbooks. As a result, theological students in East Africa learned all about the Synod of Dort but not about the exorcism of demons and the veneration of ancestors.

6. *Missionaries were guilty of paternalism.* Naturally, missionaries took the lead in the work in the early years. However, even after capable national leaders emerged, missionaries clung to control of the churches, especially the institutions. Three concerns prompted this unwillingness to yield control. First, missionaries worried that if they yielded control, the new leaders might allow doctrinal error to creep into the churches. Second, missionaries expressed concern about the ability of national leaders to handle funds correctly. And, third, missionaries hesitated to surrender control for psychological reasons. It was hard for them to acknowledge that their "baby" had grown up. This reluctance to grant leadership caused hard feelings on many "fields" throughout the world.

7. *Missionaries were unwise in their use of Western funds.* Missionaries, with the best of intentions, used money in such a way that the national churches became dependent on Western money. The use of subsidy hindered the development of good financial stewardship in churches. People will not do for themselves what someone else is willing to do for them. Missionaries reacted to the grinding poverty they saw on most mission fields with Christian charity. This is certainly understandable, but the result was national churches and institutions still dependent on Western money long after they should have been self-supporting. Henry Venn and Rufus Anderson taught missionaries to establish indigenous churches, but missionaries, for the most part, did not follow their method. When the Communists expelled missionaries from China

SIDEBAR 18.1

Mission–National Church Relations

Historically, missionaries and national churches have gone through four stages of development:

Pioneer Stage—Missionaries are planting the first churches.

Parental Stage—Missionaries lead the church and train nationals for leadership.

Partnership Stage—Missionaries and nationals work side by side as equals.

Participation Stage—Missionaries serve under the direction of the national church.

W. Harold Fuller (1980, 272)

Reflection and Discussion

1. What do you see as the most challenging stage and why?

357

in 1950, most institutions and churches still depended on Western money after more than one hundred years of missionary work.

8. *Missionaries were too closely identified with the colonial system.* In general, missionaries came to be identified with the colonial governments. To be sure, there were exceptions to this—Korea, for example. In Korea missionaries supported the Koreans' aspirations for independence from Japan. Also, after the Boxer Rebellion the China Inland Mission refused the reparations called for by the Western powers. Still, in most colonies the missionaries came to be identified with the colonizers. When the former colonies gained their independence, they reacted negatively against the missionaries, and sometimes against Christianity.

What Missionaries Did Right

1. *Missionaries loved the people among whom they worked.* Missionaries labored ceaselessly under difficult conditions because they loved the Lord and they loved the people among whom they ministered. Why else would they suffer disease, loss of loved ones, misunderstanding, imprisonment, persecution, and even martyrdom? It is easy to look back on the pioneer missionaries and list their mistakes. Nevertheless, what they did, they did because of love and with sincere intentions.

2. *Missionaries developed a genuine appreciation for the indigenous cultures and languages.* Many secular anthropologists accuse missionaries of destroying cultures. History tells a different story. By and large, missionaries preserved cultures and preserved languages. William Carey promoted the use of the Bengali language, making reading and writing Bengali accessible to the common people. He even translated Hindu classics into English. Many of the early treatises and essays on culture were produced by missionaries, and the same was true of dictionaries and grammars. Today the work of the Summer Institute of Linguistics helps to prevent the demise of languages all around the world and helps prevent the assimilation of those tribes into larger people groups.

3. *Missionaries translated the Scriptures.* Bible translation work is a long and arduous task. Today, even with the advances in linguistics and the use of computers, it takes about ten years to translate the New Testament. In the pioneer days of missions, it took much longer. By 2004 missionary translators had completed 405 translations of the whole Bible, 1,034 New Testament translations, and portions of the Bible in 883 languages. Bible translation work is surely one of the great accomplishments of Protestant missions.

4. *Missionaries provided modern education for the peoples of the majority world.* In most of the majority world, missionaries established the first schools. Not only that, but in many nations missionaries pioneered in the education of

girls. Missionaries also founded colleges, universities, and technical schools around the world. Many of the great universities in the world began as missionary endeavors. These schools did much for national development throughout the world. Indeed, most of the leaders of Africa's newly independent nations received their education in mission schools.

5. *Missionaries opened hospitals, clinics, and medical schools.* Many complaints and criticisms of missionaries have been made over the years, but none have complained about the work of missionary doctors and nurses. All over the world, hospitals and clinics offered loving, Christian care to those ravaged by disease. In China missionaries founded 270 hospitals, and in 1930 more than 90 percent of the nurses in China were Christians. In India there are more than 400 Christian hospitals. Beyond that, missionaries taught public health and sanitation that saved millions of lives. In recent years mobile clinics have proven effective in reaching people in the rural areas. Missionaries also established medical schools and schools of nursing. Their graduates helped many countries initiate their health-care systems.

6. *Missionaries formed a bridge between East and West and helped to bring the two together.* Through their essays, reports, books, and furlough talks missionaries helped people in the West understand the peoples of the East. In the same way, missionaries helped the peoples of the majority world understand European civilization. For example, Professor E. A. Hootan of Harvard University writes, "As an anthropologist, I have completely reversed my opinion of missionaries. These men and women have contributed more to our knowledge of the peoples of the world than have the entire ruck of professional travelers and explorers. They may have done more than anthropologists themselves" (Hootan 1941, 96).

7. *Missionaries introduced social and political reforms.* Earlier chapters have mentioned social reforms introduced by missionaries. They lobbied to make widow burning illegal in India, agitated against foot-binding in China, opposed the killing of twins in Calabar, and fought against the slave trade in Africa. Besides these efforts, missionaries taught the ethical principles found in the Bible, both through instruction and through example. Missionaries in China influenced Sun Yat-sen, who led the revolution that overthrew the Manchu dynasty. Many leaders of the new Chinese republic were graduates of the Anglo-Chinese College in Tientsien.

8. *Missionaries planted the church in nearly every country in the world.* When Ziegenbalg and Plütschau traveled to India in 1705, Christianity was confined mainly to Europe and North and South America. Now, three hundred years later, the church of Jesus Christ is found in every nation of the world. More than two billion people claim to be Christians, and Christianity is by far the largest religion on earth. If missionaries made mistakes, they also achieved their goal of spreading the gospel around the globe. They made Isaac Watts's hymn a reality:

Jesus shall reign wher'er the sun
Does its successive journeys run
His kingdom spread from shore to shore
Till moons shall wax and wane no more.

What Remains to Be Done

It is an amazing thing to think about more than two billion Christians in the world. However, as the world's population now numbers more than seven billion people, the church still has much to do.

In the field of Bible translation, the Wycliffe Bible Translators estimate that three thousand people groups still lack the Scriptures in their heart language. In 2003 Bible translators completed forty-one New Testament translations and two complete Bibles. In 2004 missionaries began work on ninety-three translation projects. For example, Nigeria has 351 people groups with a combined population of fifteen million who do not have even a portion of the Bible in their heart language. So, much remains to be done in the field of Bible translation. In fact, there may be more demand for translations now than previously. As missionaries have penetrated the 10/40 Window, they have planted churches among previously unreached peoples. This has led to more calls for translation work. Many church-planting teams have requested a Bible translator to serve on their teams, but there are not enough trained translators to fulfill the many requests.

SIDEBAR 18.2

Missionaries in Retrospect

"The missionaries were the one group of foreigners whose major endeavor was to make the impact of the West upon the Middle Kingdom of benefit to the Chinese. Bigoted and narrow they frequently were, occasionally superstitious, and sometimes domineering and serenely convinced of the superiority of Western culture and of their own particular form of Christianity. When all that can be said in criticism of the missionaries has been said, however, and it is not a little, the fact remains that nearly always at considerable and very often at great sacrifice they came to China, and in unsanitary and uncongenial surroundings, usually with insufficient stipends, often at the cost of their own lives or the lives that were dearer to them than their own, labored indefatigably for an alien people who did not want them or their message. Whatever may be the final judgment on the major premises, the methods, and the results of the missionary enterprise, the fact cannot be gainsaid that for sheer altruism and heroic faith here is one of the bright pages in the history of the race."

Kenneth Scott Latourette (1929, 824–25)

The Joshua Project maintains a website that presents the research they and other missions organizations are doing on unreached peoples of the world. In July 2015 they reported these statistics:

16,163	People groups in the world
6,567	Unreached people groups
40.6 percent	People groups that are unreached
7.3 billion	People in the world
2.96 billion	People with little or no access to the gospel

While missions organizations can be justifiably proud of the progress made, these statistics remind us that much remains to be done. Many of the people groups listed by the Joshua Project are in inaccessible areas where political and religious gatekeepers do all they can to keep out missionaries and the gospel message.

The challenge to complete world evangelization is daunting when one reads the statistics. The task will require more than pioneer church planting and effective evangelism. Missionaries will be needed to disciple new believers and train pastors. Support personnel will be needed to administer funds

---

The unfinished task remains. Over 28% of the world has no access to the Gospel. Over 39% belong to an ethnic group without viable churches. There are over 4,000 "least evangelized" ethno-linguistic groups and over 6,700 "unreached" peoples. Nearly two billion need to hear the Good News for the first time.

Justin Long (2006, 8–9)

---

and arrange travel. Missionary broadcasters are still needed to air gospel broadcasts to the millions who are still waiting to hear. How will the task be completed? How will missionaries do their work in the future?

Conclusion

The history of missions is as inspiring as it is instructional. By studying the work of missionaries in the past, we can avoid mistakes in the future. Similarly, by studying their ministries, we are inspired to imitate their zeal and dedication in our circumstances. Through their sacrifice the kingdom of our Lord and Christ has spread throughout the world. They have labored faithfully to increase the throng mentioned by John in Revelation 7:9: "After this I looked, and there before me was a great multitude that no one could count, from every nation, tribe, people and language, standing before the throne and before the Lamb." Countless missionaries of the past were faithful, some faithful unto death. May we be equally faithful.

Reference List

Accardy, Chris. 2001. "Calvin's Ministry to the Waldensians." *Reformation & Revival* 10 (4): 45–58.

Adams, D. J. 1980. "Matteo Ricci and the New China." *Ching Feng* 23 (2): 93–101.

Albin, Tom. 2003. "Finding God in Small Groups." *Christianity Today* 47 (8): 42.

Allen, Roland. 1912. *Missionary Methods: St. Paul's or Ours?* London: Robert Scott.

Anderson, Justice C. 2000. "World Missionary Conference." In Moreau 2000, 1029.

Aprem, Mar. 1976. *Nestorian Missions*. Kerala, India: Mar Narsai Press.

Askew, Thomas A. 2000. "Ecumenical Missions Conference." In Moreau 2000, 300.

Atiya, Aziz S. 1968. *A History of Eastern Christianity*. London: Methuen.

Bainton, Roland H. 1950. *Here I Stand: A Life of Martin Luther*. Nashville: Abingdon-Cokesbury.

———. 1952. *The Reformation of the Sixteenth Century*. Boston: Beacon Press.

Baird, Henry M. 1896. *History of the Rise of the Huguenots of France*. Vol. 1. New York: Charles Scribner's Sons.

Baker, George Claude. 1941. *An Introduction to the History of Early New England Methodism 1789–1839*. Durham, NC: Duke University Press.

Bangert, William V. 1986. *A History of the Society of Jesus*. St. Louis: Institute of Jesuit Sources.

Barber, W. T. A. 1903. *Raymond Lull: The Illuminated Doctor*. London: Charles H. Kelly.

Barclay, Wade Crawford. 1949. *History of Methodist Missions*. Vol. 1. New York: Board of Missions and Church Extension, and the Methodist Church.

Barkey, Paul E. 1986. "The Russian Orthodox Church in Mission: A Comparative Study of Orthodox Missions in China, Alaska, Japan, and Korea." ThM thesis, Fuller Theological Seminary.

———. 1988. "The Russian Orthodox Church in Its Mission to the Aleuts." DMiss diss., Fuller Theological Seminary.

Bartholomew, John. 1987. "The Missionary Activity of St. Nicholas of Japan." PhD diss., St. Vladimir's Orthodox Theological Seminary.

Baskerville, Stephen. 2004. "Hussites, Puritans, and the Politics of Religious Revolutions." *Communio viatorum* 46 (2): 192–202.

Baum, Wilhelm. 2003. "The Age of the Arabs: 650–1258." In *The Church of the East: A Concise History*, edited by W. Baum and D. W. Winkler, 42–83. New York: Routledge Curzon.

Beach, Harlan. 1904. *India and Christian Opportunity*. New York: Student Volunteer Movement for Foreign Missions.

Beaver, R. Pierce. 1973. "The Genevan Mission to Brazil." In *The Heritage of John Calvin*, edited by J. H. Bratt, 55–73. Grand Rapids: Eerdmans.

Bebbington, David W. 1993. "Revival and Enlightenment in Eighteenth-Century England." In *Modern Christian Revivals*, edited by Edith L. Blumhofer and Randall Balmer, 17–41. Urbana: University of Illinois Press.

Benedetto, Robert. 2008. "Brethren of Common Life." In *The New Westminster Dictionary of Church History*, 1st ed., 1:104. Louisville: Westminster John Knox.

Bennett, Charles. 2000. "Aviation Mission Work." In Moreau 2000, 101.

Beougher, Timothy K. 2000. "Moody, Dwight Lyman." In Moreau 2000, 657.

Bergendoff, C. 1928. *Olavus and the Ecclesiastical Transformation in Sweden (1521–1552): A Study in the Swedish Reformation*. New York: Macmillan.

Bergsland, K., and J. Rischel, eds. 1986. *Pioneers of Eskimo Grammar: Hans Egede's and Albert Top's Early Manuscripts on Greenlandic*. Copenhagen: Linguistic Circle of Copenhagen.

Best, Geoffrey. 1970. "Evangelicalism and the Victorians." In *The Victorian Crisis of Faith*, edited by Anthony Symondson, 37–56. London: Society for Promoting Christian Knowledge.

Bettenson, Henry, ed. 1956. *The Early Christian Fathers*. New York: Oxford University Press.

Bieler, Ludwig, trans. 1953. *The Works of St. Patrick, St. Secundinus, Hymn on St. Patrick*. Ancient Christian Writers: The Works of the Fathers in Translation Series, edited by Johannes Quasten and Joseph C. Plumpe. Westminster, MD: Newman Press; London: Longmans, Green.

Biller, Peter. 2006. "Goodbye to Waldensianism?" *Past & Present* 192:18.

Blácam, Hugh De. 1942. *The Saints of Ireland: The Life Stories of SS. Brigid and Columcille*. Milwaukee: Bruce.

Bobé, Louis. 1952. *Hans Egede: Colonizer and Missionary of Greenland.* Copenhagen: Rosenkilde & Bagger.

Bolshakoff, Serge. 1943. *The Foreign Missions of the Russian Orthodox Church.* New York: Macmillan.

Bonaventure, Saint. 1983. "Major and Minor Life of St. Francis." In *St. Francis of Assisi: Writings and Early Biographies,* edited by Marion A. Habig, 4th ed., 627–831. English Omnibus of the Sources for the Life of St. Francis. Chicago: Franciscan Herald Press.

Bonner, Anthony. 1985. *Selected Works of Ramon Llull (1232–1316).* Vols. 1 and 2. Princeton: Princeton University Press.

Bosch, David, J. 1991. *Transforming Mission: Paradigm Shifts in Theology of Mission.* Maryknoll, NY: Orbis Books.

Bossard, Johann Jakob, ed. 1987. *C. G. A. Oldendorp's History of the Evangelical Brethren on the Caribbean Islands of St. Thomas, St. Croix, and St. John.* Ann Arbor, MI: Karoma.

Boswell, John. 1903. *A Short History of Methodism.* Nashville: Publishing House, Methodist Episcopal Church.

Boxer, C. R. 1978. *The Church Militant and Iberian Expansion, 1440–1770.* Baltimore: Johns Hopkins University Press.

———. 1991. "Jesuits at the Court of Peking." *History Today* 41 (5): 41–47.

Brading, D. 1997. "Prophet and Apostle: Bartolomé de Las Casas and the Spiritual Conquest of America." In *Christianity and Missions, 1450–1800,* edited by J. S. Cummins, 117–38. Brookfield, VT: Ashgate.

Briggs, John A. Y. 2000a. "Jerusalem Conference (1928)." In *Evangelical Dictionary of World Missions,* edited by A. Scott Moreau, 516. Grand Rapids: Baker.

Briggs, John A. Y. 2000b. "Tambaram Conference." In *Evangelical Dictionary of World Missions,* edited by A. Scott Moreau, 928–29. Grand Rapids: Baker.

Broholm, R. R. 1977. "The Evangelizing Community and Social Transformation." *Foundations* 20 (5): 352–61.

Brown, Abraham Rezeau. 1830. *Memoirs of Augustus Hermann Francke.* Philadelphia: American Sunday School Union.

Brown, Dale W. 1978. *Understanding Pietism.* Grand Rapids: Eerdmans.

Buchner, J. H. 1854. *The Moravians in Jamaica. History of the Mission of the United Brethren's Church to the Negroes in the Islands of Jamaica, from the Year 1754 to 1854.* London: Longman, Brown.

Bunkowske, Eugene W. 1985. "Was Luther a Missionary?" *Concordia Theological Quarterly* 49 (April–June): 161–79.

Bury, J. B. 1905. *The Life of St. Patrick and His Place in History.* London: Macmillan.

Butler, A. 1868. *The Lives of the Fathers, Martyrs, and Other Principal Saints.* Vol. 8. New York: D. & J. Sadlier.

Cahill, Thomas. 1995. *How the Irish Saved Civilization: The Untold Story of Ireland's Heroic Role from the Fall of Rome to the Rise of Medieval Europe*. New York: Doubleday.

Calvin, John. 1960. *Institutes of the Christian Religion*. Edited by John T. McNeill. Translated by Ford Lewis Battles. Vol. 2. Philadelphia: Westminster.

———. 1963. *Calvin: Commentaries*. Translated and edited by Joseph Haroutunian. Library of Christian Classics 23. Philadelphia: Westminster.

———. 1970. *Calvin's Commentaries: Ephesians–Jude*. Vol. 12. Wilmington, DE: Associated Publishers.

———. 1999. *Commentary on the Prophet Isaiah*. Translated by William Pringle. Vol. 1. Grand Rapids: Baker.

———. 2001. *John Calvin: Writings on Pastoral Piety*. Edited and translated by Elsie Anne McKee. Mahwah, NJ: Paulist Press.

Cameron, Euan. 2001. *The Waldenses: Rejections of Holy Church in Medieval Europe*. Oxford: Wiley-Blackwell.

Campbell, Ted A. 1992. "John Wesley on the Mission of the Church." In *The Mission of the Church in Methodist Perspective: The World Is My Parish*, edited by Alan Padgett, 45–62. Studies in the History of Missions 10. Lewiston, NY: Edwin Mellen.

Carder, Kenneth L. 1992. "Doctrinal/Theological Themes for Preaching: John Wesley and the Galatian and Colossian Letters." *Quarterly Review* 12 (Summer): 103–19.

Carey, John. 1996. "Saint Patrick, the Druids, and the End of the World." *History of Religions* 36 (August): 42–53.

Caroazza, P. 2003. "The Catholic Tradition and the Idea of Human Rights in Latin America." *Logos* 6 (4): 81–103.

Carver, W. O. 1932. *The Course of Christian Missions*. New York: Fleming H. Revell.

Cary, Otis. 1909. "Roman Catholic and Greek Orthodox Missions." *A History of Christianity in Japan*. Vol. 1. New York: Fleming H. Revell.

Cesareo, F. C. 1993. "Quest for Identity: The Ideals of Jesuit Education in the Sixteenth Century." In *The Jesuit Tradition in Education and Missions*, edited by C. Chapple, 17–33. Scranton, PA: University of Scranton Press.

Chaney, Charles. 1964. "The Missionary Dynamic in the Theology of John Calvin." *Reformed Review* 17 (3) (Summer): 24–38.

Charlesworth, J. H., ed. and trans. 1977. *The Odes of Solomon*. Chico, CA: Scholars Press.

Chasteen, John Charles. 2001. *Born in Blood and Fire: A Concise History of Latin America*. New York: W. W. Norton.

Church Missionary Gleaner, The. 1850. Vol. 1. London: Seeley, Jackson & Halliday.

Clark, J. M. 1926. *The Abbey of St. Gall as a Centre of Literature and Art*. Cambridge: Cambridge University Press.

Coates, Thomas. 1969. "Were the Reformers Mission-Minded?" *Concordia Theological Monthly* 40 (October): 600–611.

Coke, Thomas. 1784. *Form of Discipline for the Ministers, Preachers, and Members of the Methodist Episcopal Church in America.* Elizabeth-Town, PA: Shepard Kollock.

Conner, R. Dwayne. 1971. "The Hierarchy and the Church's Mission in the First Five Centuries." ThD diss., Southern Baptist Theological Seminary.

Corwin, Gary. 2000. "Comity Agreements." In Moreau 2000, 212.

Costas, Orlando E. 2009. "Captivity and Liberation in the Modern Missionary Movement." In *Landmark Essays in Mission and World Christianity*, edited by Robert L. Gallagher and Paul Hertig, 33–45. Maryknoll, NY: Orbis Books.

Couling, C. E. 1925. *The Luminous Religion: A Study of Nestorian Christianity in China, with a Translation of the Inscriptions upon the Nestorian Tablet.* London: Carey Press.

Covell, Ralph. 2004. *Confucius, the Buddha, and Christ: A History of the Gospel in Chinese.* Eugene, OR: Wipf & Stock.

Cowie, Leonard W. 1970. *The Reformation of the Sixteenth Century.* London: Wayland.

Crantz, David. 1767. *The History of Greenland.* London: Brethren's Society.

Cunningham, Mary. 2002. *Faith in the Byzantine World.* Downers Grove, IL: InterVarsity Press.

Curtayne, Alice. 1954. *St. Brigid of Ireland.* New York: Sheed & Ward.

Dalmases, Cándido de. 1985. *Ignatius of Loyola, Founder of the Jesuits: His Life and Work.* Translated by Jerome Aixala. St. Louis: Institute of Jesuit Sources.

Daniel-Rops, Henri. 1959. *The Heroes of God.* Garden City, NY: Echo Books.

Davies, J. G. 1967. *The Early Christian Church.* Garden City, NY: Anchor Books.

De Blois, Austen Kennedy. 1929. *Fighters for Freedom: Heroes of the Baptist Challenge.* Philadelphia: Judson Press.

De Félice, G. 1851. *History of the Protestants of France.* New York: Edward Walker.

De Jong, B. 1995. "Mission in Reformation Perspective—Part 2." *Missionary Monthly* 99 (3) (March): 8–10.

De Schweinitz, Edmund. 1885. *The History of the Church Known as the Unitas Fratrum, or the Unity of the Brethren.* Bethlehem, PA: Moravian Publication Office.

DiSalvo, Angelo J. 1993. "Spanish Dominicans: The Laws of the Indies and the Establishment of Human Rights." *Romance Quarterly* 40 (2) (Spring): 89–96.

Doughty, W. L. 1955. *John Wesley: Preacher.* London: Epworth Press.

Dowley, Tim, ed. 1987. *The Baker Atlas of Christian History.* Grand Rapids: Baker.

Dries, Angelyn. 1998. "Mission and Marginalization: The Franciscan Heritage." *Missiology: An International Review* 26 (1) (January): 3–13.

Drummond, Richard Henry. 1971. *A History of Christianity in Japan.* Grand Rapids: Eerdmans.

Dubois, Marguerite-Marie. 1963. "Saint Columbanus." In *Irish Monks in the Golden Age*, edited by John Ryan, 45–56. Dublin: Clonmore & Reynolds.

Dunkley, E. 1948. *The Reformation in Denmark*. London: SPCK.

Dunne, George H. 1962. *Generation of Giants: The Story of the Jesuits in China in the Last Decades of the Ming Dynasty*. London: Burns & Oates.

Dvornik, Francis. 1970. *Byzantine Missions among the Slavs: SS. Constantine-Cyril and Methodius*. New Brunswick, NJ: Rutgers University Press.

Egede, Hans. (1741) 1973. *A Description of Greenland*. Millwood, NY: Kraus.

Elert, Werner. 1962. *The Structure of Lutheranism*. Translated by W. A. Hansen. St. Louis: Concordia.

Ellens, J. Harold. 1975. "The Franciscans: A Study in Mission." *Missiology: An International Review* 3 (4) (October): 487–99.

Ellis, Peter Berrisford. 2003. *The Celts: A History*. Philadelphia: Running Press.

Elwood, Christopher. 2002. *Calvin for Armchair Theologians*. Louisville: Westminster John Knox.

Emhardt, W. C., and G. M. Lamsa. 1926. *The Oldest Christian People*. New York: Macmillan.

Engel, James. 1996. *A Clouded Future? Advancing North American World Missions*. Milwaukee: Christian Stewardship Association.

England, John C. 1996. *The Hidden History of Christianity in Asia: The Churches of the East before the Year 1500*. Delhi: Indian Society for Promoting Christian Knowledge.

———. 1997. "Early Asian Christian Writings, 5th–12th Century: An Appreciation." *Asian Journal of Theology* 11 (1) (January): 154–71.

Erb, Peter C., ed. 1983. *The Pietists: Selected Writings*. Classics of Western Spirituality. Mahwah, NJ: Paulist Press.

Estep, William R. 1986. *Renaissance and Reformation*. Grand Rapids: Eerdmans.

Eusebius Pamphilus. 1994. *Life of Constantine*. Translated by Ernest Cushing Richardson. In *Select Library of the Nicene and Post-Nicene Fathers*, 2nd series, 1:481–559. Peabody, MA: Hendrickson.

———. 1995. *Ecclesiastical History*. Translated by C. F. Cruse. Grand Rapids: Baker.

Farr, William E. 1974. *John Wycliffe as Legal Reformer*. Leiden: Brill.

Fedotov, G. P. 1966. *The Russian Religious Mind*. Vol. 2, *The Middle Ages*. Cambridge, MA: Harvard University Press.

Fell, M. 1999. *And Some Fell into Good Soil: A History of Christianity in Iceland*. New York: Peter Lang.

Fenger, J. Ferd. (1863) 1906. *History of the Tranquebar Mission*. Translated by Emil Francke. Madras, India: M. E. Press.

Fernando, Ajith. 2000. "Amsterdam 2000." http://www.christianitytoday.com/ct/2000/julyweb-only/32.0d.html.

Floristan, C. 1992. "Evangelization of the 'New World': An Old World Perspective." *Missiology: An International Review* 20 (2): 132–49.

Ford, Rosalie Judith. 1985. "Matteo Ricci, SJ, in China, 1583–1610: A Case Study of a Precursor in Educational Anthropology." PhD diss., University of Connecticut.

Francis of Assisi. 1982a. "The Earlier Rule (1221)." In *Francis and Clare: The Complete Works*, edited by Regis J. Armstrong and Ignatius C. Brady, 107–35. New York: Paulist Press.

———. 1982b. "The Later Rule (1223)." In *Francis and Clare: The Complete Works*, edited by Regis J. Armstrong and Ignatius C. Brady, 136–45. New York: Paulist Press.

Francke, August Hermann. 1705. *Pietas Hallensis: or, A Publick Demonstration of the Footsteps of a Diven Being yet in the World; In a Historical Narration of the Orphan House, and Other Charitable Institutions, at Glaucha near Hall in Saxony.* London: J. Downing.

———. 1770. *The Holy and Sure Way of Faith of an Evangelical Christian.* Philadelphia: Henry Miller.

———. 1774. "The Holy and Sure Way of Faith of an Evangelical Christian." In *A Choice Drop of Honey from the Rock of Christ, or a Word of Advice to All Saints and Sinners.* Translated by Thomas Wilcox. Philadelphia: Henry Miller.

Franke, Wolfgang. 1976. "Matteo Ricci." In *Dictionary of Ming Biography*, edited by L. Carrington Goodrich and Chaoying Fang, 2:1137–44. New York: Columbia University Press.

Frend, W. H. C., ed. 1976. "The Mission of the Early Church." In *Religion Popular and Unpopular in the Early Christian Centuries*, 9–10. London: Variorum Reprints.

———. 1982. *The Early Church.* Philadelphia: Fortress Press.

Frey, Silvia R., and Betty Wood. 1998. *Come Shouting to Zion: African American Protestantism in the American South and British Caribbean to 1830.* Chapel Hill: University of North Carolina Press.

Fries, Adelaide L. 1962. *Customs and Practices of the Moravian Church.* Winston-Salem, NC: Moravian Board of Christian Education and Evangelism.

Frisbee, Samuel. 1907. "Anima Christi." In *The Catholic Encyclopedia.* Vol. 1. New York: Robert Appleton. Available at http://www.newadvent.org/cathen/01515a.htm.

Fry, C. George. 1970. "John Calvin: Theologian and Evangelist." *Christianity Today* (October 28): 3–6.

Frykenberg, Robert Eric. 1999. "The Legacy of Christian Friedrich Schwartz." *International Bulletin of Missionary Research* (July): 130–32, 134–35.

Fudge, Thomas A. 1998. *The Magnificent Ride: The First Reformation in Hussite Bohemia.* Aldershot, UK: Ashgate.

———. 2011. "Jan Hus at Calvary: The Text of an Early Fifteenth-Century 'Passio.'" *Journal of Moravian History* 11:45–81.

Fuller, W. Harold. 1980. *Mission-Church Dynamics: How to Change Bicultural Tensions into Dynamic Missionary Outreach*. Pasadena, CA: William Carey Library.

Gallagher, Robert L. 2005a. "Present to Potential Prospect." In *Changing Worlds: Our Part in God's Plan*, edited by Nathan Bettcher, Robert L. Gallagher, and Bill Vasilakis, 129–42. Adelaide, South Australia: CRC Churches International.

———. 2005b. "Protestantism to the Present." In *Changing Worlds: Our Part in God's Plan*, edited by Nathan Bettcher, Robert L. Gallagher, and Bill Vasilakis, 107–27. Adelaide, South Australia: CRC Churches International.

———. 2005c. "Pentecost to Protestantism." In *Changing Worlds: Our Part in God's Plan*, edited by Nathan Bettcher, Robert L. Gallagher, and Bill Vasilakis, 87–106. Adelaide, South Australia: CRC Churches International.

———. 2008a. "The Integration of Mission Theology and Practice: Zinzendorf and the Early Moravians." *Mission Studies: Journal of the International Association for Mission Studies* 25 (2) (October): 185–210.

———. 2008b. "Zinzendorf and the Early Moravians: Pioneers in Leadership Selection and Training." *Missiology: An International Review* 36 (2) (April): 237–44.

———. 2012a. "Figourovsky, Innocent." In Kurian 2012, 2:938–39.

———. 2012b. "Gloukharev, Macarius." In Kurian 2012, 2:1040–41.

———. 2012c. "Herman of Alaska." In Kurian 2012, 2:1124–25.

———. 2012d. "Ilminski, Nicholas." In Kurian 2012, 2:1181–82.

———. 2012e. "Ivanovsky, Paul." In Kurian 2012, 2:1217–18.

———. 2012f. "Kassatkin, Nicholas." In Kurian 2012, 2:1267–68.

———. 2012g. "Stephen of Perm." In Kurian 2012, 4:2262–63.

———. 2012h. "Veniaminov, Innocent." In Kurian 2012, 4:2453–54.

Galli, Mark. 2002. *Francis of Assisi and His World*. Downers Grove, IL: InterVarsity Press.

Gallico, Paul. 1958. *The Steadfast Man: A Life of Saint Patrick*. London: Michael Joseph.

Garrison, V. David. 2004. *Church Planting Movements: How God Is Redeeming a Lost World*. Midlothian, VA: WIGTake Resources.

Genischen, Hans-Werner. 1957. "Imitating the Wisdom of the Almighty: Ziegenbalg's Program of Evangelism." *Concordia Theological Monthly* 28 (11): 835–43.

———. 1998. "Schwartz, Christian Friedrich." In *Biographical Dictionary of Christian Missions*, edited by Gerald H. Anderson, 606. New York: Macmillan Reference USA.

George, Carl. 1991. *Prepare Your Church for the Future*. Grand Rapids: Revell.

George, Charles H. 1971. *Revolution: European Radicals from Hus to Lenin*. Glen View, IL: Scott Foresman.

Ghezzi, Bert. 1996. *Miracles of the Saints: A Book of Reflections*. Grand Rapids: Zondervan.

Glasser, Arthur F. 2000. "International Conferences for Itinerant Evangelists." In Moreau 2000, 496–97.

Glover, Robert H. 1960. *The Progress of World-Wide Missions*. Revised by Herber Kane. New York: Harper & Row.

Gonzalez, Justo L. 1992. "Lights in the Darkness." *Christian History* 35:32–34.

Goveia, Elsa V. 1965. *Slave Society in the British Leeward Islands at the End of the Eighteenth Century*. New Haven: Yale University Press.

Gray, Frank. 2000. "The Unlikely Missionary." *Mission Frontiers* (December): 18–22.

Greek Orthodox Archdiocese of America. 2013. "Methodius & Cyril, Equal-to-the Apostles Illuminators of the Slavs." http://www.goarch.org/chapel/saints_view ?contentid=486.

Green, Michael. 1970. *Evangelism in the Early Church*. Grand Rapids: Eerdmans.

Greenway, George William. 1955. *Saint Boniface*. London: W. & J. Mackay.

Greenway, Roger S. 2000. "Calvinism." In Moreau 2000, 155–56.

Greeson, Kevin. 2004. *The Camel Training Manual*. Midlothian, VA: WIGTake Resources.

Grell, Ole Peter. 1992. "Scandinavia." In *The Early Reformation in Europe*, edited by Andrew Pettigree, 94–119. New York: Cambridge University Press.

———. 1995. *The Scandinavian Reformation*. New York: Cambridge University Press.

Grew, Eva Mary. 1938. "Martin Luther and Music." *Music and Letters* 19 (January): 67–78.

Grindel, Gracia. 2006. "The Rhetoric of Martin Luther's Hymns: Hymnody Then and Now." *Word & World* 26 (2): 179.

Gritsch, Eric W. 2002. *A History of Lutheranism*. Minneapolis: Augsburg Fortress.

Grousset, René. 1970. *The Empire of the Steppes*. Translated by Naomi Walford. New Brunswick, NJ: Rutgers University Press.

Guerike, Henry Earnest Ferdinand. 1837. *The Life of Augustus Herman Francke*. Translated by Samuel Jackson. London: R. B. Seeley & W. Burnside.

Guicharrousse, H. 1995. *Les Musiques de Luther*. Geneva: Labor et Fides.

Gutiérrez, Gustavo. 1993. *Las Casas: In Search of the Poor of Jesus Christ*. Translated by Robert R. Barr. Maryknoll, NY: Orbis Books.

Hale, Reginald B. 1976. *The Magnificent Gael*. Brandon, MB: World Media Productions.

Hames, Harvey J. 2000. *The Art of Conversion: Christianity and Kabbalah in the Thirteenth Century*. Leiden: Brill.

Hamilton, George Fredrick. 1932. *St. Patrick and His Age*. Dublin: Church of Ireland Printing and Publishing.

Hanke, Lewis. 1951. *Bartolomé de Las Casas: An Interpretation of His Life and Writings*. The Hague: Martinus Nijhoff.

Hanson, R. P. C. 1983. *The Life and Writings of the Historical Saint Patrick*. New York: Seabury Press.

Harkins, C. 1994. "Modern Medieval Man." *Christian History* 13 (2) (Spring): 40–42.

Harnack, Adolf von. 1908. *The Mission and Expansion of Christianity in the First Three Centuries.* Translated by James Moffatt. 2 vols. New York: G. P. Putnam's Sons.

Hassé, Evelyn R. 1913. *The Moravians.* London: National Council of Evangelical Free Churches.

Hatch, Janene Pinchot. 1980. *New Apostles of Christ.* Syosset, NY: Department of Religious Education of the Orthodox Church in America.

Haweis, Thomas. 1800. *An Impartial and Succinct History of the Rise, Declension and Revival of the Church of Christ.* Vol. 3. London: J. Mawson.

Haykin, Michael A. G. 2001. "John Calvin's Missionary Influence in France." *Reformation and Revival* 10 (4) (Fall): 35–44.

Hedlund, Roger E. 1991. *The Mission of the Church in the World.* Grand Rapids: Baker.

Heitzenrater, Richard P. 1995. *Wesley and the People Called Methodists.* Nashville: Abingdon.

Hempton, David. 2005. *Methodism: Empire of the Spirit.* New Haven: Yale University Press.

Henderson, D. M. 1997. *John Wesley's Class Meeting: A Model for Making Disciples.* Nappanee, IN: Evangel.

Heymann, Frederick G. 1955. *John Zizka and the Hussite Revolution.* Princeton: Princeton University Press.

Hieber, Eugene A. 1905. "Bicentennial of Protestant Foreign Missions." *Luther League Review* (November 29): 8–9.

Hiebert, Paul G., and Frances F. Hiebert. 1987. *Case Studies in Missions.* Grand Rapids: Baker.

Hillgarth, J. N., ed. (1969) 1986. "Pope Gregory II Commends Bishop Boniface to the Christians of Germany (December 1, 722)." In *Christianity and Paganism, 350–750: The Conversion of Western Europe*, 171–72. Philadelphia: University of Pennsylvania Press.

Hoke, Stephen. 2000. "Nida, Eugene A." In *Evangelical Dictionary of World Missions*, edited by A. Scott Moreau, 689–90. Grand Rapids: Baker.

Holcomb, Helen Harriet Howe. 1901. *Men of Might in Indian Missions: The Leaders and Their Epochs (1706–1899).* London: Oliphant, Anderson, & Ferrier.

Hootan, E. A. 1941. *Christian World Facts.* New York: Foreign Missions Conference of North America.

Huc, M. L. 1857. *Christianity in China, Tartary and Thibet in Two Volumes.* Vol. 1, *From the Apostleship of St. Thomas to the Discovery of the Cape of Good Hope.* New York: D. & J. Sadlier.

Hudson, Anne, ed. 1978. *Selections from English Wycliffite Writings.* Cambridge: Cambridge University Press.

———. 1985. *Lollards and Their Books.* London: Hambledon Press.

———. 1988. *The Premature Reformation: Wycliffite Texts and Lollard History*. New York: Clarendon Press and Oxford University Press.

Hughes, Kathleen, and Ann Hamlin. 1977. *The Modern Traveller to the Irish Church*. London: SPCK.

Hunter, George G., III. 1987. *To Spread the Power: Church Growth in the Wesleyan Spirit*. Nashville: Abingdon.

———. 2000. *The Celtic Way of Evangelism: How Christianity Can Reach the West . . . Again*. Nashville: Abingdon.

Hutton, Joseph Edmund. 1895. *A Short History of the Moravian Church*. London: Moravian Publication Office.

———. 1909. *A History of the Moravian Church*. London: Moravian Publication Office.

———. 1922. *A History of Moravian Missions*. London: Moravian Publication Office.

Hyde, Walter W. 1946. *Paganism to Christianity in the Roman Empire*. Philadelphia: University of Pennsylvania Press.

Idle, Christopher. 1986. *The Journal of John Wesley*. Tring, UK: Lion.

Ignatius of Loyola. 1970. *The Constitutions of the Society of Jesus*. Translation and Commentary by George E. Ganss. St. Louis: Institute of Jesuit Sources.

———. 1991. *Spiritual Exercises and Selected Works*. Translation by George E. Ganss. New York: Paulist Press.

Ingvarsson, B. 2004. "Saint Francis and the Sultan." *Swedish Missiological Themes* 92 (3) (Fall): 311–12.

Irvin, Dale T., and Scott W. Sunquist. 2001. *History of the World Christian Movement*. Vol. 1, *Earliest Christianity to 1453*. Maryknoll, NY: Orbis Books.

Jackson, Herbert C. 1964. "The Missionary Obligation of Theology." *Occasional Bulletin* 15 (1) (January): 1–6.

James, Frank A. 2001. "Calvin the Evangelist." *Reformed Quarterly* 19 (2–3) (Fall). http://rq.rts.edu/fall01/james.html.

Jay, Elizabeth, ed. 1987. *The Journal of John Wesley*. New York: Oxford University Press.

Jenkins, Philip. 2002. *The Next Christendom: The Coming of Global Christianity*. Oxford: Oxford University Press.

———. 2008. *The Lost History of Christianity: The Thousand-Year Golden Age of the Church in the Middle East, Africa, and Asia—and How It Died*. New York: HarperCollins.

Jennes, Joseph. 1973. *A History of the Catholic Church in Japan, from Its Beginnings to the Early Meiji Era (1549–1873): A Short Handbook*. Rev. ed. Tokyo: Oriens Institute for Religious Research.

Jesus Film Project. 2007. "Official Ministry Statistics—January 1, 2007." http://www.jesusfilm.org/progress/statistics.html.

Jiang, Wenhan. 1983. "The Present Situation of Christianity in China." *Missiology: An International Review* 11 (3): 259–65.

Johnston, Arthur. 1978. *The Battle for World Evangelism*. Wheaton: Tyndale House.

Johnstone, David M., M. Glukharev, N. I. W. Ilminskii, and R. O. E. Church. 2007. "Czarist Missionary Contact with Central Asia: Models of Contextualization?" *International Bulletin of Missionary Research* 31 (April): 66–72.

Johnstone, Patrick. 2011. *The Future of the Global Church: History, Trends and Possibilities*. Colorado Springs: Global Mapping International.

Jones, A. H. M. 1948. *Constantine and the Conversion of Europe*. London: Hodder & Stoughton.

Joyce, Timothy J. 1998. *Celtic Christianity: A Sacred Tradition, a Vision of Hope*. Maryknoll, NY: Orbis Books.

Kaminsky, Howard. 1967. *A History of the Hussite Revolution*. Los Angeles: University of California Press.

Kane, J. Herbert. 1971. *A Global View of Christian Missions from Pentecost to the Present*. Grand Rapids: Baker.

———. 1978. *Understanding Christian Missions*. Grand Rapids: Baker.

Kantor, Marvin, and Richard Stephen White, trans. 1976. *The Vita of Constantine and the Vita of Methodius*. Ann Arbor: Michigan Slavic Publications.

Keevak, M. 2008. *The Story of a Stele: China's Nestorian Monument and Its Reception in the West, 1625–1916*. Hong Kong: Hong Kong University Press.

Kelly, Matthew. 1857. *Calendar of Irish Saints*. Dublin: J. Mullany.

Kidd, B. J., ed. 1920. *Documents Illustrative of the History of the Church*. 3 vols. London: Society for Promoting Christian Knowledge.

Kittelson, James M. 1986. *Luther the Reformer: The Story of the Man and His Career*. Minneapolis: Augsburg.

Klijn, A. F. J. 1962. *The Acts of Thomas*. Supplements to *Novum Testamentum* 5. Leiden: Brill.

Koch, John T., ed. 2005. *Celtic Culture: A Historical Encyclopedia*. Santa Barbara, CA: ABC-CLO.

Komroff, Manuel, ed. 1930. *The Travels of Marco Polo, the Venetian*. Garden City, NY: Garden City Publishing.

Koschade, Alfred. 1965. "Luther on Missionary Motivation." *Lutheran Quarterly* 17 (August): 224–39.

Kuhns, Oscar. 1907. *John Huss: The Witness*. Cincinnati: Jennings & Graham.

Kuriakose, M. K., ed. 1982. *History of Christianity in India: Source Materials*. Madras, India: Christian Literature Society.

Kurian, George Thomas, ed. 2012. *The Encyclopedia of Christian Civilization*. Chichester, UK: Wiley-Blackwell.

Lacko, Michael. 1963. *Saints Cyril and Methodius*. Rome: Slovak Editions.

Laman, Gordon D. 1989. "The Origin of Protestant Missions." *Reformed Review* 43 (4) (Fall): 52–67.

Lamb, Gary. 2000. "Greene, Elizabeth 'Betty.'" In *Evangelical Dictionary of World Missions*, edited by A. Scott Moreau, 415. Grand Rapids: Baker.

Larsen, K. 1948. *A History of Norway*. Princeton: Princeton University Press.

Lasance, Francis Xavier. 1911. *With God: A Book of Prayers and Reflections*. Chicago: Benziger Brothers.

Las Casas, Bartolomé de. 1974. *The Devastation of the Indies: A Brief Account.* Translated by Herma Briffault. New York: Seabury Press.

———. 1992a. *The Only Way.* Edited by Helen Rand Parish. Translated by Francis Patrick Sullivan. Mahwah, NJ: Paulist Press.

———. 1992b. *Witness: Writings of Bartolomé de Las Casas.* Edited and translated by George Sanderlin. Maryknoll, NY: Orbis Books.

Latourette, Kenneth Scott. 1929. *A History of Christian Missions in China.* New York: Macmillan.

———. 1937. *A History of the Expansion of Christianity.* 7 vols. New York: Harper & Brothers.

———. 1953. *A History of Christianity.* New York: Harper & Row.

———. 1975. *A History of Christianity.* Vol. 2, *Reformation to the Present.* San Francisco: Harper & Row.

———. (1975) 2005. *A History of Christianity.* Vol. 1, *Beginnings to 1500.* Peabody, MA: Prince Press.

Léger, Jean. 1669. *General History of the Evangelical Churches of the Piedmontese or Vaudois Valleys.* Vols. 1 and 2. Leyden, France: Chez Jean le Carpentier.

Lehmann, E. Arno. 1956. *It Began at Tranquebar.* Translated by M. J. Lutz. Madras, India: Christian Literature Society.

Lenker, John Nicholas. 1896. *Lutherans in All Lands: The Wonderful Works of God.* 5th ed. Milwaukee: Lutherans in All Lands Company.

Lerner, R. 1986. "A Case of Religious Counter-Culture: The German Waldensians." *American Scholar* 55:234–47.

Lewis, Gillian. 1994. "The Geneva Academy." In *Calvinism in Europe, 1540–1620*, edited by Andrew Pettegree, Alastair Duke, and Gillian Lewis, 35–63. Cambridge: Cambridge University Press.

Lewis, James F. 2000. "Matteo Ricci." In Moreau 2000, 834.

Li, Dun J., ed. 1969. *China in Transition: 1517–1911.* New York: D. Van Nostrand.

Lindquist, C. R. 1990. "Remonking the Church." PhD diss., Fuller Theological Seminary.

Ling, Samuel. 2000. "Sung, John." In Moreau 2000, 918.

Llull, Ramon. 1985a. "Contemporary Life." In *Selected Works of Ramon Llull*, vol. 1, translated by Anthony Bonner, 3–70. Princeton: Princeton University Press.

———. 1985b. "Felix, or the Book of Wonders." In *Selected Works of Ramon Llull*, vol. 2, translated by Anthony Bonner, 659–1105. Princeton: Princeton University Press.

Loewe, Michael. 1988. "Imperial China's Reactions to the Catholic Missions." *Numen* 35 (2): 179–212.

Long, Justin. 2006. "Least-Reached Peoples." *Mission Frontiers* (May–June): 8–9.

Lorenz, Erika, ed. and trans. 1985. *Ramon Llull: Die Kunst, Sich in Gott zu Verlieben*. Freiburg im Breisgau: Herderbuecherei.

Loskiel, George Henry. 1794. *History of the Missions of the United Brethren among the Indians of North America*. Published as one volume in three parts. Translated by Christian Latrobe. London: Burlinghouse.

Luther, Martin. 1884. *The Table Talk of Martin Luther*. London: George Bell & Sons.

———. 1965. *Luther's Works*. Vol. 53, *Liturgy and Hymns*. Philadelphia: Fortress Press.

Lynch, Cyprian J. 1982. "The Bibliography of Franciscan Spirituality: A Poor Man's Legacy." *American Theological Library Association Summary of Proceedings* 36: 89–108.

MacCulloch, Diarmaid. 2009. *Christianity: The First Three Thousand Years*. New York: Penguin Group.

Mackensen, H. 1920. *Raymund Lull: A Missionary Pioneer in the Moslem Field*. Minneapolis: Lutheran Orient Mission.

Mackinnon, James. 1939. *The Origins of the Reformation*. London: Longmans, Green.

Mallard, William. 1961. "John Wyclif and the Tradition of Biblical Authority." *Church History* 30:50–60.

Marsden, Richard. 2011. "The Bible in English in the Middle Ages." In *The Practice of the Bible in the Middle Ages: Production, Reception, and Performance in Western Christianity*, edited by Susan Boynton and Diane J. Reilly, 272–95. New York: Columbia University Press.

Marshall, Henrietta Elizabeth. 2011. *The Country of Ours: The Story of the United States*. Radford, VA: Wilder.

Maust, John. 1992. "Champions for the Oppressed." *Christian History* 35:35–38.

McCarthy, Daryl. 2002. "Heart and Minds Aflame for Christ: Medieval Irish Monks— A Model for Dynamic Learning and Living." http://www.iics.com/irishmonks.html.

McClinton, Rowena. 2002. "Early 19th-Century Cherokee and Moravian Spirituality Converges at Springplace, Georgia." *Annotation* 30:1–6.

McClure, David. 1899. *Diary of David McClure, Doctor of Divinity, 1748–1820*. New York: Knickerbocker Press.

McGavran, Donald. 1955. *The Bridges of God: A Study in the Strategy of Missions*. New York: Friendship Press.

———. 1988. *Effective Evangelism*. Phillipsburg, NJ: P&R.

———. 1990. *Understanding Church Growth*. Grand Rapids: Eerdmans.

McGavran, Donald, and Win Arn. 1973. *How to Grow a Church*. Glendale, CA: Regal Books.

McGrath, Alister E. 1999. *Christian Spirituality: An Introduction*. Malden, MA: Blackwell.

McLoughlin, William Gerald. 1984. *Cherokees and Missionaries, 1789–1839*. New Haven: Yale University Press.

———. 1990. *Champions of the Cherokees: Evan and John B. Jones*. Princeton: Princeton University Press.

McMullen, Ramsay. 1984. *Christianizing the Roman Empire*. New Haven: Yale University Press.

McNaspy, C. J. 1993. "Conquest or Inculturation: Ways of Ministry in the Early Jesuit Missions." In *Critical Moments in Religious History*, edited by K. Keulman, 77–89. Macon, GA: Mercer University Press.

McNeil, William H., and Mitsuko Iriye, eds. 1971. *Modern Asia and Africa: Readings in World History*. Vol. 9. New York: Oxford University Press.

McNeill, John T. 1954. *The History and Character of Calvinism*. New York: Oxford University Press.

———. 1974. *The Celtic Churches: A History A.D. 200 to 1200*. Chicago: University of Chicago Press.

Meyendorff, John. 1962. *The Orthodox Church*. London: Darton, Longman, & Todd.

Miles, Delos. 1981. *Church Growth: A Mighty River*. Nashville: Broadman.

Mitchell, Alexander W. 1853. *The Waldenses: Sketches of the Evangelical Christians of the Valleys of Piedmont*. Philadelphia: Presbyterian Board of Publication.

Moffett, Samuel Hugh. 1975. "The Earliest Asian Christianity." *Missiology: An International Review* 3 (4) (October): 415–30.

———. 1982. "Mission in an East Asian Context: The Historical Context." *Princeton Seminary Bulletin* 3 (3) (July): 242–51.

———. 1987. "Early Asian Christian Approaches to Non-Christian Cultures." *Missiology: An International Review* 15 (4) (October): 473–86.

———. 1998. *A History of Christianity in Asia*. Vol. 1, *Beginnings to 1500*. Maryknoll, NY: Orbis Books.

Monter, William. 1967. *Calvin's Geneva*. New York: Wiley.

Moore, W. Carey, ed. 1982. "The Rich Young Ruler Who Said Yes." *Christian History* 1 (7–9): 31–35.

Moorman, John R. 1973. *A History of the Church of England*. 3rd ed. London: A&C Black.

Moreau, A. Scott, gen. ed. 2000. *Evangelical Dictionary of World Missions*. Grand Rapids: Baker.

Mould, Daphne D. C. Pochin. 1953. *Ireland of the Saints*. London: B. T. Batsford.

Mulhern, K. 2000. "The Festive Abbess." *Christian History* 60:30–31.

Mulholland, Ken. 2000. "Whitby Conference." In Moreau 2000, 1014.

Munro, Dana C. 1901. "Original Sources of European History: Urban and the Crusaders." 3rd ed. Vol. 1. New York: Longmans, Green.

Mussolini, Benito. 1929. *John Huss*. Translated by Clifford Parker. New York: Albert & Charles Boni.

Muston, A. 1875. *The Israel of the Alps: A Complete History of the Waldenses and Their Colonies*. Translated by J. Montgomery. London: Blackie & Son.

Muthuraj, Joseph Gnanaseelan. 2006. "Money, Chaplains, Missionaries and Bishops in the Protestant Mission in India." *Bangalore Theological Forum* 38 (1): 59–75.

Nassif, Bradley. 1997. "Kissers and Smashers." *Christian History and Biography* 54 (2): 22–24.

Neale, J. E. 1943. *The Age of Catherine de Medici*. London: Jonathan Cape.

Neill, Stephen. 1964. *A History of Christian Missions*. London: Penguin Books.

———. (1964) 1990. *A History of Christian Missions*. 2nd ed. New York: Penguin Books.

———. 1966. *Colonialism and Missions*. New York: McGraw-Hill.

———. 1970. *Call to Mission*. Philadelphia: Fortress.

———. 1986. *A History of Christian Missions*. 2nd ed. London: Penguin Books.

Noll, Mark A. 1997. *Turning Points: Decisive Moments in the History of Christianity*. Grand Rapids: Baker; Leicester, UK: Inter-Varsity Press.

Noll, Ray R., ed. 1992. *100 Roman Documents concerning the Chinese Rites Controversy (1645–1941)*. San Francisco: Ricci Institute for Chinese-Western Cultural History.

Norwood, Frederick A. 1974. *The Story of American Methodism: A History of the United Methodists and Their Relations*. Nashville: Abingdon.

Nyquist, John W. 2000. "Second Vatican Council." In Moreau 2000, 863–65.

Obolensky, Dmitri. 1963. "Sts. Cyril and Methodius, Apostles of the Slavs." *St. Vladimir's Theological Quarterly* 7 (1): 3–13.

———. 1971. *The Byzantine Commonwealth: Eastern Europe, 500–1453*. New York: Praeger.

———. 1986. "The Cyrillo-Methodian Mission: The Scriptural Foundations." *St. Vladimir's Theological Quarterly* 30 (2): 101–16.

O'Connor, J. 1913. "Saint Dominic." In *The Catholic Encyclopedia*, 15:234–37. New York: Robert Appleton.

Oldendorp, C. G. A., Johann Jakob Bossart, Arnold R. Highfield, and Vladimir Barac. 1987. *C.G.A. Oldendorp's History of the Mission of the Evangelical Brethren on the Caribbean Islands of St. Thomas, St. Croix, and St. John*. Ann Arbor, MI: Karoma.

Oleksa, Michael, ed. 1987. *Alaskan Missionary Spirituality*. Sources of American Spirituality. Mahwah, NJ: Paulist Press.

Olmstead, Earl P. 1991. *Blackcoats among the Delaware: David Zeisberger on the Ohio Frontier.* Kent, OH: Kent State University Press.

Olsen, Ted. 2000. "Amsterdam 2000 Called the Most Multinational Event Ever." *Christianity Today* (August 2). Available at http://www.christianitytoday.com/ct/2000/julyweb-only/32.0d.html (subscription required).

Olson, D. R., and N. Torrence. 2001. "Conceptualizing Literacy as a Personal Skill and as a Social Practice." In *The Making of Literate Societies*, edited by D. R. Olson and N. Torrence, 3–18. Malden, MA: Blackwell.

O'Malley, John W. 1993. *The First Jesuits.* Cambridge, MA: Harvard University Press.

O'Neal, Norman. 2000. *The Life of St. Ignatius of Loyola.* http://lemoyne.edu.

Outler, Albert C., ed. 1964. *John Wesley.* Oxford: Oxford University Press.

Padilla, René. 1983. "The Unity of the Church and the Homogeneous Unit Principle." In *Exploring Church Growth*, edited by Wilbur Shenk, 298–312. Grand Rapids: Eerdmans.

Paley, William. 1803. "Natural Theology: Review of Religious Publications." *Evangelical Magazine* 11:494.

Pate, Larry D. 1989. *From Every People: A Handbook of Two-thirds World Missions with Directory/Histories/Analysis.* Monrovia, CA: MARC.

Paulinus. 1952. *Life of St. Ambrose.* Translated by John Lacy. New York: Fathers of the Church.

Pearson, Hugh. 1835. *Memoirs of the Life and Correspondence of the Reverend Christian Frederick Schwartz.* Vol. 2. London: J. Hatchard & Son.

Peers, E. Allison. 1969. *Ramon Lull: A Biography.* New York: Burt Franklin.

Perrin, J. P. 1624. *Luther's Fore-runners: A Cloud of Witnesses Deposing for the Protestant Faith.* Translated by S. Lennard. London: Nathanael Newbery.

Peterson, Willard J. 1988. "Why Did They Become Christians? Yang T'ing-yün, Li Chih-tsao, and Hsü Kuang-ch'i." In *East Meets West: The Jesuits in China, 1582–1773*, edited by Charles E. Ronan and Bonnie B. C. Oh, 129–52. Chicago: Loyola University Press.

Phan, P. C. 2011. *Christianities in Asia.* Malden, MA: Wiley-Blackwell.

Philip, T. V. 1996. "The Missionary Impulse in the Early Asian Christian Traditions." *International Review of Mission* 85 (4) (November): 505–21.

———. 1998. *East of the Euphrates: Early Christianity in Asia.* India: CSS & ISPCK.

Phillips, Tom. 2014. "China on Course to Become World's Most Christian Nation within 15 Years." *Telegraph.* http://www.telegraph.co.uk/news/worldnews/asia/china/10776023/China-on-course-to-become-worlds-most-Christian-nation-within-15-years.html.

Pierson, Paul E. 2000a. "The Reformation and Mission." In Moreau 2000, 813–14.

———. 2000b. "The Student Volunteer Movement for Foreign Missions (SVM)." In Moreau 2000, 914–15.

Pierson, Steven J. 2000. "Ansgar (801–65)." In Moreau 2000, 65–66.

Polo, Marco. (1958) 1987. *The Travels of Marco Polo.* Translated by Ronald Latham. London: Penguin Books.

Porter, J. M. 1974. *Luther—Selected Political Writings.* Philadelphia: Fortress Press.

Powathil, Joseph. 2004. "Foreword." In *Patriarch Mar Dinkha IV: The Man and His Message,* edited by Mar Aprem, 8–10. Trichur, India: Mar Narsai Press.

Power, Rosemary. 2006. "A Place of Community: 'Celtic' Iona and Institutional Religion." *Folklore* 117:33–53.

"A Prophet without Honor: Waldo of Lyons." 1989. *Christian History* 8/2 (22): 6–7.

Quebedeaux, Richard. 1979. *I Found It! The Story of Bill Bright and Campus Crusade.* New York: Harper & Row.

Rahner, Karl, and Paul Imhof. 1979. *Ignatius of Loyola.* London: Collins.

Rainer, Thom S. 1993. *The Book of Church Growth.* Nashville: Broadman.

Reapsome, James. 2000a. "Bright, William." In Moreau 2000, 147.

———. 2000b. "Lausanne Congress II." In Moreau 2000, 562.

Redwood, Brian C. 1998. "Diana Thomas of Kingston: An Early Methodist Lay Preacher." *Proceedings of the Wesley Historical Society* 51 (February): 125–29.

Reid, W. Stanford. 1955. "Calvin and the Founding of the Academy of Geneva." *Westminster Theological Journal* 18 (November): 1–33.

Ricci, Matteo. 1953. *China in the Sixteenth Century: The Journals of Matteo Ricci (1583–1610).* Translated by Louis J. Gallagher. New York: Random House.

———. 1985. *The True Meaning of the Lord of Heaven.* Translated by Douglas Lancashire, Peter Hu Kuo-chen, and Edward Malatesta. St. Louis: Institute of Jesuit Sources.

Richstatter, Thomas. 2001. "Franciscan Spirituality." *Liturgical Ministry* 10 (Fall): 206–8.

Richter, Julius. 1908. *A History of Missions in India.* Translated by Sydney H. Moore. New York: Fleming H. Revell.

Rivera, Luis N. 1990. *A Violent Evangelism: The Political and Religious Conquest of the Americas.* Louisville: Westminster John Knox.

Roberts, Alexander, and James Donaldson, eds. 1951. *The Ante-Nicene Fathers.* Vols. 1–4. Grand Rapids: Eerdmans.

Ross, Andrew C. 1994. *A Vision Betrayed: The Jesuits in Japan and China, 1542–1742.* Maryknoll, NY: Orbis Books.

———. 1999. "Alessandro Valignano, SJ." *Missiology: An International Review* 27 (4): 503–13.

Rothrock, George A. 1979. *The Huguenots: A Biography of a Minority.* Chicago: Nelson Hall.

Rule, Paul A. 1968. "Jesuit and Confucian? Chinese Religion in the Journals of Matteo Ricci SJ 1583–1610." *Journal of Religious History* 5 (2): 105–24.

Runciman, Steven. (1951) 1999. *A History of the Crusades: The Kingdom of Acre and the Later Crusades*. Vol. 3. Cambridge: Cambridge University Press.

Rutherford, John. 1896. *Missionary Pioneers in India*. Edinburgh: Andrew Elliot.

Ryan, John. 1972. *Irish Monasticism: Origins and Early Development*. Ithaca, NY: Cornell University Press.

Sabiers, Karl G. 1944. *Little Biography of Great Missionaries*. Los Angeles: Robertson.

Saeki, P. Y. 1916. *The Nestorian Monument in China*. London: Society for the Propagation of the Gospel.

Sattler, Gary R., and August Hermann Francke. 1982. *God's Glory, Neighbor's Good*. Chicago: Covenant Press.

Saunders, J. J. 1965. *A History of Medieval Islam*. London: Routledge & Kegan Paul.

Schaff, David S. 1949. *History of the Christian Church*. Vol. 5. Edited by Philip Schaff. Grand Rapids: Eerdmans.

Schaff, Philip. 1910. "The German Reformation from the Diet of Worms to the Peasants' Wars, AD 1521–1525." In *History of the Christian Church*, vol. 4, *Mediaeval Christianity*, 191–205. New York: Charles Scribner's Sons.

———. 1919. "The Bohemian Brethren and the Waldenses." In *Creeds of Christendom*. Vol. 1, *The History of Creeds*, 6th ed., 565–76. New York: Harper & Brothers.

Schalk, C. 1983. "Martin Luther's Hymns Today." *Hymns* 34 (3): 130–33.

Schattschneider, David Allen. 1975. "Souls for the Lamb: A Theology for the Christian Mission." PhD diss., University of Chicago.

———. 1984. "Pioneers in Mission: Zinzendorf and the Moravians." *International Bulletin of Missionary Research* 8:63–67.

———. 1998. "William Carey, Modern Missions, and the Moravian Influence." *International Bulletin of Missionary Research* 22:8–10, 12.

Scherer, James A. 1982. *That the Gospel May Be Sincerely Preached throughout the World: A Lutheran Perspective on Mission and Evangelism in the 20th Century*. Geneva: Lutheran World Federation.

———. 1994. "Luther and Mission: A Rich but Untested Potential." *Missio Apostolica: Journal of the Lutheran Society for Missiology* 2 (May): 17–24.

———. 1999. "Bartholomew Ziegenbalg." *Missiology: An International Review* 27 (4): 487–94.

Schroeder, Roger P. 2000. "Women, Mission, and the Early Franciscan Movement." In *Missiology: An International Review* 28 (4) (October): 411–24.

Schwarze, Edmund. 1923. *History of the Moravian Missions among the Southern Indian Tribes of the United States*. Bethlehem, PA: Times Publishing.

Scott, D. 1985. "Christian Responses to Buddhism in Pre-Medieval Times." *Numen* 32 (1): 88–100.

Scott, Stevan. 1989. "The Collapse of the Moravian Mission of Saints Cyril and Methodius." PhD diss., University of California, Berkeley.

Seaver, Paul S. 1998. "Recent Studies of the English Reformation." *Religious Studies Review* 24 (January): 31–36.

Senn, Frank C. 1997. *Christian Liturgy: Catholic and Evangelical*. Minneapolis: Augsburg Fortress.

Shelley, Bruce L. 1982. *Church History in Plain Language*. Waco: Word Books.

———. 1995. *Church History in Plain Language*. 2nd ed. Dallas: Word.

Shiman, Lilian Lewis. 1992. *Women and Leadership in Nineteenth-Century England*. New York: Palgrave Macmillan.

Singh, Brijraj. 1999. *The First Protestant Missionary in India: Bartholomaeus Ziegenbalg*. New Delhi: Oxford University Press.

Skarsten, Trygve R. 1985. *The Scandinavian Reformation: A Bibliographical Guide*. St. Louis: Center for Reformation Research.

Skidmore, Thomas E., and Peter H. Smith. 2001. *Modern Latin America*. Oxford: Oxford University Press.

Sladden, John Cyril. 1980. *Boniface of Devon: Apostle of Germany*. Exeter, UK: Paternoster Press.

Smirnoff, Eugene. 1903. *A Short Account of the Historical Development and Present Position of Russian Orthodox Missions*. London: Rivingtons. Repr., Willits, CA: Eastern Orthodox Books, n.d.

Smith, Barbara S. 1980. *Orthodoxy and Native Americans: The Alaskan Mission*. Orthodox Church in America, Department of History and Archives, Historical Society, Occasional Papers, No. 1. Crestwood, NY: St. Vladimir's Seminary Press.

Smith, Ebbie. 1995. "What's Right With Church Growth?" Unpublished document in author's possession.

Smyth, Marina. 2008. "The Body, Death and Resurrection: Perspectives of an Early Irish Theologian." *Speculum* 83:531–71.

Snyder, Howard. 1975. *The Problem of Wineskins*. Downers Grove, IL: InterVarsity.

———. 1980. *The Radical Wesley and Patterns for Church Renewal*. Downers Grove, IL: InterVarsity.

———. 1989. *Signs of the Spirit: How God Reshapes the Church*. Grand Rapids: Zondervan.

Socrates Scholasticus. 1952. *Ecclesiastical History*. In *Socrates, Sozomenus: Church Histories*, translated by A. C. Zenos, *Select Library of Nicene and Post-Nicene Fathers*, 2nd series, 2:1–178. Grand Rapids: Eerdmans.

Søgaard, Viggo. 2000. "Bible Societies." In Moreau 2000, 123.

Sozomen. 1952. *Ecclesiastical History*. In *Socrates, Sozomenus: Church Histories*, translated by Chester Hantranft, *Select Library of Nicene and Post-Nicene Fathers*, 2nd series, 2:179–427. Grand Rapids: Eerdmans.

Spangenberg, August Gottlieb. 1838. *The Life of Nicholas Lewis Count Zinzendorf: Bishop and Ordinary of the Church of the United (or Moravian) Brethren*. Translated by Samuel Jackson. London: Samuel Holdsworth, Amen-Corner.

Spence, Jonathan D. 1984. *The Memory Palace of Matteo Ricci*. New York: Penguin Books.

Spener, Philipp Jakob. 1964. *Pia Desideria*. Translated by Theodore G. Tappert. Philadelphia: Fortress Press.

Spinka, Matthew. 1941. *John Hus and the Czech Reform*. Chicago: University of Chicago Press.

———. 1966. *John Hus' Concept of the Church*. Princeton: Princeton University Press.

———. 1968. *John Hus: A Biography*. Princeton: Princeton University Press.

———, trans. 1972. *The Letters of Jan Hus*. Manchester, UK: Manchester University Press.

Stacey, John. 1958. "The Theology of John Wyclif." *Expository Times* 69:356–59.

———. 1962. "The Piety of John Wyclif." *Expository Times* 73:327–29.

Stamoolis, James J. 1980. "An Examination of Contemporary Eastern Orthodox Missiology." PhD diss., Stellenbosch University.

———. 1986. *Eastern Orthodox Mission Theology Today*. American Society of Missiology Series 10. Maryknoll, NY: Orbis Books.

Starr, Frederick. 1987. *Russia's American Colony*. Durham, NC: Duke University Press.

Steffen, Tom A. 1996. *Reconnecting God's Story to Ministry*. La Habra, CA: Center for Organizational and Ministry Development.

Stephens, George. 1991. "Saint Stephan of Perm: In the Spirit of Pentecost." *Again* 14 (4): 8–10, 22.

Stevens, Abel. 1867. *A Compendious History of American Methodism*. New York: Carlton & Porter.

Stevens, Carl D. 1992. "Calvin's Corporate Idea of Mission." PhD diss., Westminster Theological Seminary.

Stewart, John. 1928. *Nestorian Missionary Enterprise: The Story of a Church on Fire*. Edinburgh: T&T Clark.

———. 1961. *Nestorian Missionary Enterprise: The Story of a Church on Fire*. Trichur, India: Mar Narsai Press.

Stoeffler, F. Ernest. 1973. *German Pietism during the Eighteenth Century*. Leiden: Brill.

———. 1976. *Continental Pietism and Early American Christianity*. Grand Rapids: Eerdmans.

Strickland, Debra Higgs. 2003. *Saracens, Demons, and Jews: Making Monsters in Medieval Art*. Princeton: Princeton University Press.

Stromberg, Roland N. 1954. *Religious Liberalism in Eighteenth-Century England*. Oxford: Oxford University Press.

Struve, Nikita. 1963. "Orthodox Missions, Past and Present." *St. Vladimir's Seminary Quarterly* 7:31–42.

Sunquist, Scott W., David Wu Chu Sing, and John Chew Hiang Chea, eds. 2001. *A Dictionary of Asian Christianity*. Grand Rapids: Eerdmans.

Swihart, Altman K. 1960. *Luther and the Lutheran Church (1483–1960)*. London: Peter Owen.

Takahashi, Matushka Naomi. n.d. "Enlightener of Japan Blessed Nicholas Kassatkin." *Orthodox America*. http://www.roca.org/OA/17/17e.htm.

Talbani, Aziz. 1996. "Pedagogy, Power, Discourse: Transformation of Islamic Education." *Comparative Education Review* 40 (1) (February): 66–82.

Talbot, C. H. 1954. *The Anglo-Saxon Missionaries in Germany*. London: Sheed & Ward.

Te Brake, Wayne. 1998. *Shaping History: Ordinary People in European Politics, 1500–1700*. Los Angeles: University of California Press.

Terry, John Mark. 1994. *Evangelism: A Concise History*. Nashville: Broadman.

Thekkedath, Joseph. 1988. *History of Christianity in India*. Vol. 2, *From the Middle of the Sixteenth Century to the End of the Seventeenth Century*. Bangalore: Christian History Association of India.

Theodoret. 1854. *Ecclesiastical History*. Translated by E. Walford. London: H. G. Bohn.

Thomas of Celano. 1983. "First and Second Life of St. Francis." In *St. Francis of Assisi: Writings and Early Biographies*, edited by Marion A. Habig, 4th ed., English Omnibus of the Sources for the Life of St. Francis, 225–355, 357–543. Chicago: Franciscan Herald Press.

———. 1999. "The Life of Saint Francis." In *Francis of Assisi: Early Documents*, edited by Regis J. Armstrong, J. A. Wayne Hellmann, and William J. Short, 363–422. Hyde Park, NY: New City Press.

Thompson, Augustus C. 1885. *Moravian Missions: Twelve Lectures*. New York: Schribner's Sons.

Thompson, E. A. 1963. "Christianity and the Northern Barbarians." In *The Conflict between Paganism and Christianity in the Fourth Century*, edited by Arnaldo Momigliano, 56–78. London: Oxford University Press.

Tinker, George E. 1993. *Missionary Conquest: The Gospel and Native American Cultural Genocide*. Minneapolis: Augsburg Fortress.

Tobin, Greg. 1999. *The Wisdom of St. Patrick: Inspirations from the Patron Saint of Ireland*. New York: Ballantine Books.

Tourn, Giorgio. 1980. *The Waldensians: The First 800 Years (1174–1974)*. Translated by C. P. Merlino. Vol. 1. Torino: Claudiana.

Travis, John [pseud.]. 1998. "The C1–C6 Spectrum." *Evangelical Missions Quarterly* 34 (4) (October): 407–8.

Tucker, Henry St. George. 1938. *The History of the Episcopal Church in Japan*. New York: Charles Scribner's Sons.

Tucker, Ruth A. 1983. *From Jerusalem to Irian Jaya: A Biographical History of Christian Missions*. Grand Rapids: Zondervan.

———. 2004. *From Jerusalem to Irian Jaya: A Biographical History of Christian Missions*. 2nd ed. Grand Rapids: Zondervan.

Tugwell, S. 1982. *Early Dominicans: Selected Writings.* Classics of Western Spirituality. New York: Paulist Press.

Tweedie, W. K. 1884. *Earnest Men: Their Life and Work.* London: Nelson & Sons.

Tyson, John R., ed. 1989. *Charles Wesley: A Reader.* New York: Oxford University Press.

Ugolino di Monte Santa Maria. 1998. *The Little Flowers of St. Francis of Assisi.* Translated by W. Heywood. New York: Vintage Books.

Van der Linde, J. M. 1957. "The Moravian Church in the World, 1457–1957." *International Review of Mission* 46 (October): 417–23.

Van Dyke, Paul. 1926. *Ignatius Loyola: The Founder of the Jesuits.* New York: Charles Scribner's Sons.

Veronis, Luke A. 1994. *Missionaries, Monks, and Martyrs: Making Disciples of All Nations.* Minneapolis: Light and Life.

———. 2000. "Herman of Alaska." In Moreau 2000, 430.

Vicedom, Georg F. 1965. *The Mission of God.* Translated by G. A. Thiele and D. Hilgendorf. St. Louis: Concordia.

Wagner, C. Peter. 1973. "'Church Growth': More than a Man, a Magazine, a School, a Book." *Christianity Today* (December): 11–14.

———. 1976. *Your Church Can Grow.* Glendale, CA: G/L Publications.

———. 1981. *Church Growth and the Whole Gospel: A Biblical Mandate.* San Francisco: Harper & Row.

Walker, Williston. 2005. *John Calvin: Revolutionary, Theologian, Pastor.* Ross-shire, UK: Christian Focus Publications.

Walsh, M. 1985. *Butler's Lives of the Saints.* Concise ed. New York: HarperCollins.

Wang, Zhicheng, Guicai Wang, and Purple Kwong. 1999. "Inculturation and Its Constraints: A Critique of Preaching Christ in Late Ming China; The Jesuits' Presentation of Christ from Matteo Ricci to Giulio by Gianni Criveller." *Tripod* 19 (111): 30–39.

Ware, Timothy. 1993. *The Orthodox Church.* New York: Penguin Books.

Weinlick, John R. 1956. *Count Zinzendorf.* Nashville: Abingdon.

Weinrich, William C. 1981. "Evangelism in the Early Church." *Concordia Theological Quarterly* 45 (January–April): 61–75.

Wesley, John. 1744. *Extract of Count Zinzendorf's Discourses of the Redemption of Man by the Death of Christ.* Newcastle, UK: John Gooding.

———. (1748) 1996. "A Plain Account of the People Called Methodists: In a Letter to the Reverend Mr. Perronet, Vicar of Shoreham, in Kent, Written in the Year 1748." In *The Works of John Wesley,* 8:248–68. Grand Rapids: Baker.

———. 1831a. *The Life of the Rev. John Wesley, A.M.* Edited by Richard Watson. London: John Mason.

———. 1831b. *The Works of the Reverend John Wesley, A.M.* Edited by John Emory. Vols. 6–7. New York: J. Emory & B. Waugh.

———. 1876. "The Preface of the 1780 Hymnal." *Wesleyan-Methodist Magazine.*

————. 1938. *The Journal of the Rev. John Wesley.* Edited by Nehemiah Curnock. 8 vols. London: Epworth Press.

————. 1940. *The Journal of John Wesley.* Edited by Nora Ratcliff. London: Thomas Nelson & Sons.

Westmeier, Karl-Wilhelm. 1994. "Zinzendorf at Esopus: The Apocalyptical Missiology of Count Nicolaus Ludwig von Zinzendorf—A Debut to America." *Missiology: An International Review* 22 (4): 419–36.

————. 1997. "Becoming All Things to All People: Early Moravian Missions to Native North Americans." *International Bulletin of Missionary Research* 21 (4): 172–75.

White, Newport J. D. 1918. *A Translation of the Latin Writings of St. Patrick.* London: SPCK.

Whitefield, George. 1978. *George Whitefield's Journals.* London: Banner of Truth Trust.

Whyte, Bob. 1988. *Unfinished Encounter: China and Christianity.* London: Font Paperbacks.

Wigram, Chris. 2005. "East Asia's Millions." *OMF International Newsletter* (August/September): 1–2.

Wilcox, Peter. 1993. "'*Églises plantées*' and '*églises dressées*' in the Historiography of Early French Protestantism." *Journal of Ecclesiastical History* 44 (4) (February): 689–95.

Williams, Gregory Neal. 1996. "A Study of Matteo Ricci's Method of Adaptation." PhD diss., Columbia International University.

Williams, J. E. Caerwyn. 1973. *Studia Celtica.* Oxford: Oxford University Press.

Wilson, T. 1903. *History of Church and State in Norway: From the Tenth to the Sixteenth Century.* Westminster, UK: Archibald Constable.

Winkler, Dietmar W. 2003. "The Age of the Sassanians: Until 651." In *The Church of the East: A Concise History,* edited by W. Baum and D. W. Winkler, 7–41. London: Routledge Curzon.

Winstanley, Roy L. 1996. *Parson Woodforde: The Life and Times of a Country Diarist.* Bungay, UK: Morrow.

Winter, Ralph. 1981. "Four Men, Three Eras." *Mission Frontiers* (February): 3–5.

————. 2000. "Willibrord (658–739)." In Moreau 2000, 1017.

Winters, Roy Lutz. 1938. *Francis Lambert of Avignon (1487–1530): A Study of Reformation Origins.* Philadelphia: United Lutheran Publication House.

Won Yong, Ji. 1996. "A Lutheran Understanding of Mission." *Concordia Journal* 22 (April): 141–53.

Wood, Douglas C. 1984. *The Evangelical Doctor: John Wycliffe and the Lollards.* Welwyn, UK: Evangelical Press.

Wood, Rick. 1996. "The History of Gospel Recordings and the AD2000 Audio Communications Network." http://www.ad2000.org/Tracks/gosprec.htm.

Woodward, R. 1910. *Piae Cantiones: A Collection of Church and School Song.* London: Chiswick Press.

Workman, Herbert B. 1904. *The Letters of John Hus.* London: Hodder & Stoughton.

Wu, David Chusing. 1983. "The Employment of Chinese Classical Thought in Matteo Ricci's Theological Contextualization in Sixteenth-Century China." ThD diss., University of California, Berkeley.

Wuorinen, J. 1965. *A History of Finland.* New York: Columbia University Press.

Yannoulatos, Anastasios. 1969. "Monks and Mission in the Eastern Church during the Fourth Century." *International Review of Missions* 58 (April): 208–26.

———. 1989. "Orthodox Mission: Past, Present, Future." In *Your Will Be Done: Orthodoxy in Mission; Commission on World Mission and Evangelism Consultation of Eastern Orthodox and Oriental Orthodox Churches*, edited by George Lemopoulos, 63–92. Geneva: WCC Publications.

Yates, Timothy. 1994. *Christian Missions in the Twentieth Century.* Cambridge: Cambridge University Press.

Young, John D. 1980. *East-West Synthesis: Matteo Ricci and Confucianism.* Hong Kong: University of Hong Kong.

Young, John M. L. 1984. *By Foot to China: Mission of the Church of the East to 1400.* Assyrian International News Agency Books Online. http://www.aina.org/books/ bftc/bftc.htm.

Zeman, Jarold K. 1976. "Restitution and Dissent in the Late Medieval Renewal Movements: The Waldensians, the Hussites and the Bohemian Brethren." *Journal of the American Academy of Religion* 44 (1) (March): 7–27.

Ziegenbalg, Bartholomaeus. (1713) 1869. *Genealogy of the Malabar (South-Indian) Gods: A Manual of the Mythology and Religion of the People of South India.* Edited by W. Germann. Translated by G. J. Metzger. Madras, India: Higginbotham.

Zimmer, H. 1969. *The Irish Element in Medieval Culture.* Translated and annotated by Jane Loring Edmands. First published in 1891 by Knickerbocker Press. New York: G. P. Putnam's Sons.

Zinzendorf, Nikolaus Ludwig von. (1746) 1973a. "Concerning the Proper Purpose of the Preaching of the Gospel." In *Nikolaus Ludwig von Zinzendorf: Nine Public Lectures on Important Subjects in Religion*, edited and translated by George W. Forell, 24–33. Iowa City: University of Iowa Press.

———. (1746) 1973b. "Concerning the Simple Meaning and the Great Idea of the Lord's Prayer." In *Nikolaus Ludwig von Zinzendorf: Nine Public Lectures on Important Subjects in Religion*, edited and translated by George W. Forell, 10–23. Iowa City: University of Iowa Press.

———. (1746) 1973c. "That Aspect of Faith Which Actually Makes One So Blessedly Happy." In *Nikolaus Ludwig von Zinzendorf: Nine Public Lectures on Important Subjects in Religion*, edited and translated by George W. Forell, 43–60. Iowa City: University of Iowa Press.

Zorn, H. M. 1933. "Bartholomaeus Ziegenbalg." In *Men and Missions*, edited by L. Fuerbringer, 10:1–50. St. Louis: Concordia.

Zwemer, Samuel M. 1902. *Raymund Lull: First Missionary to the Moslems*. New York: Funk & Wagnalls.

———. 1913. "Editorial." *Moslem World* 3 (3): 225–26.

Index